For all of those who have influenced the creation of
the Autism Partnership Method:

Ivar Lovaas, Tony Cuvo, James Sherman,
Beth Sulzer-Azaroff, Sandra Harris, Barbara Etzel
Don Baer, Mont Wolf, and Ted Ayllon

For All the Children and Families Who We Have the Honor of
Working with and Learning From Each and Every Day

For All Past and Current Employees of Autism Partnership and
Autism Partnership Foundation Who Have Dedicated a Portion
of Their Lives in Helping Individual's Diagnosed with Autism
Spectrum Disorder and Their Families.

The Autism Partnership Method: Social Skills Groups

Copyright © 2020 Autism Partnership Foundation

Published by: Different Roads to Learning, Inc.
12 W. 18th Street, Suite 3E
New York, NY 10011
Phone: 212-604-9637
Fax: 212-206-9329
www.differentroads.com

Book Design: Melissa DiPeri
Cover Photography: Alistair Berg Photographer, DigitalVision Collection, Getty Images.

ISBN: 978-0-9910403-6-0
Library of Congress Control Number: 2020912674

The Autism Partnership Method: Social Skills Groups

Justin B. Leaf[1,2]

Christine M. Milne[1,2] & Jeremy A. Leaf[3]

Jonathan Rafuse[3], Joseph H. Cihon[1,2] & Julia L. Ferguson[1]

Misty L. Oppenheim-Leaf[1]

Ronald Leaf[1], John McEachin[1] & Toby Mountjoy[3]

1 Autism Partnership Foundation

2 Endicott College

3 Autism Partnership

About the Authors

Justin B. Leaf, Ph.D., BCBA-D

Justin Leaf, Ph.D., is the Co-Director of Research and Director of Training for Autism Partnership Foundation. Justin is also a Professor at Endicott College. Justin received his doctorate degree in Behavioral Psychology from the Department of Applied Behavioral Science at the University of Kansas. Currently, Justin leads the research team at Autism Partnership Foundation, which conducts research nationally and internationally. His research interests include examining methods to improve social behaviors for children and adolescents with autism and developing friendships, comparing different teaching methodologies, evaluating parameters of reinforcement, and evaluating long term outcomes for individuals diagnosed with autism. Justin has over 90 publications in either peer reviewed journals, books, or book chapters and has presented at both national and international professional conferences and invited events.

Christine M. Milne, Ph.D., BCBA-D

Christine Milne is the Research Coordinator for Autism Partnership Foundation and a consultant for Autism Partnership. Christine received her bachelor's degree in cognitive sciences at the University of California, Irvine, her master's degree in applied behavior analysis from St. Cloud State University, and her doctoral degree from Endicott College under the mentorship of Dr. Justin Leaf. Christine has over 10 years of clinical experience working with children and adolescents diagnosed with autism spectrum disorder. This includes leading social skills groups for various ages, supervising client cases, training staff to implement intervention in both individual and group settings, and consulting in school districts and an international clinic. She believes individuals with ASD have the desire to interact socially, however they do not always have the skills to do so appropriately to meet their needs. In addition, there are several life skills that require social interaction; therefore, she considers providing effective interventions for social skills a priority, especially with peers in a group setting. Her research interests include interventions to improve social skills for individuals diagnosed with ASD, outcomes of behaviorally based social skills groups, and staff training. Christine has published several articles in peer reviewed journals, served as a reviewer for peer reviewed journals, and has presented at national and international conferences.

Jeremy A. Leaf., M.A., BCBA

Jeremy Leaf is a supervisor and curriculum developer for the Autism Partnership Foundation Academy. Jeremy received his master's degree in Special Education at Loyola Marymount University. Jeremy has over 10 years of experience working with children, adolescents, and adults diagnosed with autism spectrum disorder (ASD) and other developmental disabilities. Jeremy has worked extensively on creating social skills curriculum and being part of social skills groups; including participating and publishing research to show the effectiveness of social skills groups on increasing behavior and social skills. Additionally, Jeremy has published 16 peer reviewed publications while conducting research at Autism Partnership Foundation, and has presented his research at national and international conferences. In addition to his work in Seal Beach, California, Jeremy also works as a consultant both nationally and internationally, helping staff, children, and families reach their full potential.

Jonathan M. Rafuse, M.S., BCBA

Jon continues to build on over 30 years of clinical experience in the field of ABA. He works with children diagnosed with Autism Spectrum Disorder (ASD) and supervises therapy teams to better provide treatment to this highly individualized population. He graduated from UCLA in 1988 with a bachelor's degree in psychology and then, in 1991, earned his master's degree in clinical psychology from Antioch University. In 1992, he began work at the May Institute in Chatham, Massachusetts, eventually running one of the off-campus group homes serving students dramatically impacted with ASD. Jon joined Autism Partnership in 1995, where he is currently a Curriculum Developer. In addition to this role, he provides advanced training, mentoring, and supervision to ABA-service providers and teaching staff within school districts across the country. He has presented both nationally and internationally at conferences on Applied Behavior Analysis, and continues consulting and supervising families, program staff, and school district personnel throughout the United States, Australia and Asia. One of his pet passions is developing stronger social skills in children, adolescents and adults diagnosed with ASD through the use of the Autism Partnership Method (APM).

Joseph H. Cihon, Ph.D., BCBA-D

Dr. Joseph Cihon is the Co-Director of Research for Autism Partnership Foundation. Joe received his bachelor's degree in special education from Fontbonne University, master's degree in behavior analysis at the University of North Texas under the mentorship of Dr. Shahla Alai-Rosales, Dr. Jesus Rosales-Ruiz, and Dr. Manish Vaidya, and his doctoral degree at Endicott College under the mentorship of Dr. Mary Jane Weiss. Joe has over fifteen years of experience working with children, adolescents, and adults diagnosed with autism spectrum disorder and other developmental disabilities in home, school, and community settings. His research interests include evaluating approach based interventions, shaping, increasing favorable interactions among children, their families, and interventionists, developing contingencies to promote generalization and maintenance, social skills interventions, and improving mealtimes for selective eaters.

Joe has published and served as a reviewer for several prominent journals and presented research at national and international conferences.

Julia L. Ferguson, M.S., BCBA

Julia Ferguson is the Research and Assessment Coordinator for Autism Partnership Foundation. Julia received her bachelor's degree in applied behavior analysis and her master's degree in behavior analysis from the University of North Texas and is currently pursuing her doctoral degree in applied behavior analysis from Endicott College. Julia has over 8 years of experience working with children diagnosed with autism spectrum disorder (ASD) in home, school, community, and clinical settings. Her research interests include evaluating social skills interventions for individuals diagnosed with ASD, staff training to teach others to implement social skill interventions, and evaluating best practice interventions and comparing different teaching methodologies for individuals diagnosed with ASD. Julia has published several articles in peer reviewed journals on social skills interventions, authored book chapters pertaining to social skills interventions for individuals diagnosed with ASD, and has presented at national and international conferences on the subject matter.

Misty L. Oppenheim-Leaf, M.A., BCBA

Misty Oppenheim-Leaf has over 15 years of experience working with children diagnosed with autism spectrum disorders and other developmental disabilities. Misty received her master's degree in Applied Behavioral Science at the University of Kansas under the mentorship of Dr. James Sherman and Dr. Jan Sheldon. Currently, Misty helps on projects for Autism Partnership Foundation, is a Behavior Consultant and Behavior Therapy and Learning Center, and is the Director of Contemporary Behavior Consultants. Misty's primary interests are providing consultations services in-home behavior programs, teaching social behavior, and focusing on parent education and support.

Ronald Leaf, Ph.D.

Dr. Ronald Leaf is a licensed psychologist with over 45 years of experience in the field of autism. Dr. Leaf began his career working with Professor Ivar Lovaas, while receiving his undergraduate degree at University of California, Los Angeles (UCLA). Subsequently, he received his doctorate under the direction of Prof. Lovaas. During his years at UCLA, he served as Clinic Supervisor, Research Psychologist, Lecturer and Interim Director of the Young Autism Project. He was extensively involved in several research investigations, contributed to *The Me Book*, and is a co-author of *The Me Book Videotapes*, a series of instructional tapes for teaching autistic children. Dr. Leaf has consulted to families, schools, day programs and residential facilities on a national and international basis. He is the Co-founder and Director of Autism Partnership, which offers comprehensive services for families with children and adolescents diagnosed with Autism Spectrum Disorder (ASD). With offices in 10 countries, Ron and his team have developed the Autism Partnership Method, a progressive approach to implementing Applied Behavior Analysis (ABA) treatment. Dr. Leaf is also the Executive Director of Behavior Therapy and Learning Centre, a mental health agency that consults with parents, care-providers and school personnel. He is co-author of *A Work In Progress, Time for School, It Has to Be Said, Crafting Connections, A Work In Progress Companion Series,* and *Clinical Judgment.* He has co-authored over 65 articles in research journals and presented over 90 times at professional conferences. Last but not least, Dr. Leaf is the co-founder of the Autism Partnership Foundation, a non-profit dedicated to advancing professional standards and treatment of individuals with autism through research and training.

John McEachin, Ph.D., BCBA-D

John McEachin is a behavior analyst and licensed psychologist who has been providing intervention to children with autism as well as adolescents and adults with a wide range of developmental disabilities since 1977. He received his graduate training under Professor Ivar Lovaas at UCLA on the Young Autism Project. During his 11 years at UCLA, Dr. McEachin served in various roles including Clinic Supervisor, Research Assistant and Teaching Assistant. His research has included the long-term follow-up study of the participants in the Young Autism Project, which was published in 1993. In 1994 he joined with Ron Leaf in forming Autism Partnership, which they co-direct. In 1999 they published A Work in Progress, a widely used behavioral treatment manual and curriculum for children with autism. Dr. McEachin has lectured throughout the world and co-authored numerous books and research articles. He consults regularly to families, agencies, and school districts, assisting in the development of treatment programs and providing training to parents, therapists, and teachers.

Toby Mountjoy, M.S., BCBA

Mr. Toby Mountjoy is a Board Certified Behavior Analyst and holds a Master of Science in Applied Behavior Analysis. With over 23 years of experience working with individuals with ASD, he has been extensively trained by Dr. Ronald Leaf and Dr. John McEachin. Besides overseeing the Autism Partnership operation in Hong Kong, Korea, the Philippines, and Singapore with over 200 staff, including psychologists, consultants, and therapists, he has also provided consultations to school districts, agencies, and families worldwide. Mr. Mountjoy has also contributed chapters to publications such as "Sense & Nonsense" and "It's Time for School". In 2007, he founded the charitable Autism Partnership Foundation and Aoi Pui School to offer more services for children with Autism.

Table of Contents

Part One

Introductory Information

Chapter One
An Overview of Social Behavior and Autism Spectrum Disorder

I want you to think about some of the most memorable experiences in your lifetime. They could be during elementary school, high school, college, or even your professional life. When I do this, my favorite memories are often special because of the people I shared them with. I remember having *Rocky* movie marathons with my elementary school friends, attending middle school dances, hanging out with teammates after baseball games in high school, partying with friends in college, meeting my wife in graduate school, and now sharing experiences with my two amazing children.

Chances are, when you think about your experiences, you are not thinking about the classes you took in high school, the Individualized Education Plan (IEP) you had to write, or the presentation you had to give: you are remembering a time shared with a friend, significant other, or family member. Being social is such a big part of life and I would argue it may be the most important part of who we are as humans. From the time we are born until we die, most of us engage in social behaviors every day and look for positive human connections through friendship and companionship.

Unfortunately, individuals diagnosed with autism spectrum disorder (ASD) have qualitative impairments in social behavior (American Psychological Association, 2013). These impairments limit their access to appropriately initiating, engaging in, and responding to social behavior, which may limit their chances to form meaningful friendships and positive social relationships. This means it is often more difficult for individuals diagnosed with ASD to acquire the social skills necessary to engage in the prosocial behavior to have meaningful relationships with others.

Professionals who are committed to helping individuals diagnosed with ASD improve their social functioning face a major hurdle, as there is an extensive range of social deficits commonly observed in individuals diagnosed with ASD. As a spectrum disorder, there are vast differences across individuals in the specific skills they lack. Like snowflakes, there are commonalities, but each individual displays different patterns of strengths and weaknesses. Social deficits associated with a diagnosis of ASD can range from an individual unable to tolerate sitting next to another person to an individual possessing social desire but unable to use perspective-taking to resolve conflicts.

Within this wide range of potential social deficits, there are some common skill deficits across individuals diagnosed with ASD. One critical social skill that children begin to display as early as nine months is joint attention (White et al., 2011). Joint attention, sometimes referred to as shared attention, is when an environmental event occurs and one person lets another person know (usually by pointing, looking, or talking) that the event has occurred and seeks acknowledgment from that person.

For example, if a mother and son are walking down the street and a plane goes by, the child may look at the plane, look at his mother, and point to the plane so the mother and son can enjoy the plane passing by together. Another example would be if two kids (e.g., Kenny and Jeff) are playing in the classroom and a third child (e.g., Billy) comes in wearing a cool new baseball jersey, Kenny looks up at Billy, looks over at Jeff, and says, "Hey Jeff, look at Billy's cool new jersey!" as both look over at Billy. Joint attention has been associated with an increase in language development as well as overall social development. It is a common skill deficit observed with individuals diagnosed with ASD; researchers have reported that a deficit in joint attention may result in lower levels of language and can impact overall relationship development (Charman, 2003).

Observational learning is another critical skill that emerges early in typically developing young children. Observational learning occurs when a child watches another child engage in a behavior followed by a consequence, then the child either imitates or does not imitate that behavior based upon the consequences observed (Varni et al., 1979). For example, if a child within a group of peers tells a knock-knock joke and the joke is met with laughter, the other children in the group might be more likely to make a knock-knock joke after seeing their peers' reaction. In another example, if a younger sibling watches an older sibling steal a cookie, the younger sibling is more likely to also attempt to steal a cookie if they observe the older sibling enjoy the cookie without punishment. However, if the younger sibling watches the older sibling get scolded following the heist, the younger sibling is less likely to make the same attempt.

Observational learning is a critical skill because it can expedite the learning process in that learners can learn by observing free from direct consequences or instruction. Additionally, observational learning may lead to improvements in relationship development, as the learner might learn which behaviors to engage in or not engage in with certain peers. Observational learning is an important skill for all individuals; unfortunately, it is infrequently displayed by individuals diagnosed with ASD (Varni et al., 1979).

A more advanced skill that can enhance the development of friendships and meaningful social relationships is *theory of mind* (Baron-Cohen et al., 1985). Theory of mind is a complex set of social behaviors that arise from a child's understanding of the perspective and mental states of others (e.g., emotions, beliefs, imagination) and allows the child to adjust their behavior in a variety of social contexts. An everyday example of theory of mind would be telling someone a story. This requires theory of mind because in order to tell a story correctly, the storyteller must know what the other person already knows and what information they are missing, then fill in those blanks. Displaying the behaviors that emanate from theory of mind are very important in successfully relating to others. Once again, theory of mind is often cited as a deficit for individuals diagnosed with ASD (Baron-Cohen et al., 1985).

These represent just a small sample of social behaviors that are common deficits for individuals diagnosed with ASD. Other social deficits may include, but are not limited to, a lack of empathy, attending, eye contact, tolerating others, and sharing. It is important to know the common social deficits associated with individuals diagnosed with ASD so these deficits can be targeted proactively and prioritized accordingly through intensive intervention. Failing to design an intervention curriculum that targets these social deficits can lead to a lack of progress in these social behaviors and negative outcomes, such as the individual becoming a victim of bullying, loneliness, depression, and suicidal ideation and behavior (Mayes et al., 2013). Although the results vary across studies, overall they paint a grim picture of what can occur later in life for adults diagnosed with ASD. Researchers have shown that up to 35.3% of individuals diagnosed with ASD show signs of anxiety and 54% show signs of depression (Sturmey et al., 2017).

Researchers have also evaluated friendships of individuals diagnosed with ASD. One of the leaders in this area is Nirit Bauminger-Zviely, who has conducted many studies on friendship development (e.g., Bauminger & Kasari, 2000; Bauminger & Shuman, 2003; Bauminger et al., 2008). The research has shown that individuals diagnosed with ASD do report having friendships; however, these friendships usually last for shorter durations, have fewer interactions, and are of lower quality than friendships of same-age typically developing children. The research also indicates that these friendships are heavily facilitated by parents instead of being initiated by the children themselves, begging the question whether they are true and meaningful friendships or just prompted interactions.

Finally, one of the most important studies I have come across was conducted by Mayes and colleagues (2013). In this study, the authors evaluated parents' reports of suicidal thoughts or attempts for 791 individuals diagnosed with ASD, compared to 186 typically developing children. The data, as indicated by parents' reports, was startling: 14% of individuals diagnosed with ASD had thought about or attempted suicide "sometimes to very often." This is compared to only 0.5% of typically developing individuals whose parents reported their child sometimes to very often had thought about or attempted suicide.

When I read this study, I was devastated. It made me think, "What is the point of teaching academics if suicide is a possible terminal outcome?" It made me question programming priorities. It also confirmed my belief that it is of the utmost importance to teach social behaviors to all individuals diagnosed with ASD, research the best methods to teach those social behaviors, and disseminate this information to professionals working with these individuals.

We decided to write the first chapter of this book addressing the importance of social behaviors and some of the negative consequences that can occur if children do not develop these skills because so often I hear that teaching social behaviors is important, but they should not be the priority. I hear that we must concentrate on increasing language or academic skills. I am often told that social behaviors do not have a place in IEPs, but can perhaps be addressed at a later time. I see professionals endorsing and selling pseudoscientific and non-evidence-based procedures as a way to improve social behaviors without the data and evidence to support these assertions. The purpose of this chapter is to emphasize the importance of teaching social behaviors early for every professional working with individuals diagnosed with ASD.

We wrote this manual and curriculum to provide professionals and parents a guide for how to conduct behaviorally based social skills groups (referred to as "social skills groups" throughout the book), which has evidence supporting its effectiveness. In doing so, we will describe the Autism Partnership Method (AP Method) for running social skills groups for individuals diagnosed with ASD, including intervention strategies and a social curriculum that can be taught in the context of social skills groups. Consistent with the AP Method, the manual and curriculum should be taken as guidelines rather than strict protocols; readers should modify the material based upon the individual needs of their children, students, and clients.

References

American Psychiatric Association. (2013). *Diagnostic and statistical manual of mental disorders* (5th Ed.). Washington, DC: Author.

Baron-Cohen, S., Leslie, A. M., & Frith, U. (1985). Does the autistic child have a "theory of mind"? *Cognition, 21*(1), 37-46.

Bauminger, N., & Kasari, C. (2000). Loneliness and friendship in high‑functioning children with autism. *Child development, 71*(2), 447-456.

Bauminger, N., & Shulman, C. (2003). The development and maintenance of friendship in high-functioning children with autism: Maternal perceptions. *Autism, 7*(1), 81-97.

Bauminger, N., Solomon, M., Aviezer, A., Heung, K., Gazit, L., Brown, J., & Rogers, S. J. (2008). Children with autism and their friends: A multidimensional study of friendship in high-functioning autism spectrum disorder. *Journal of abnormal child psychology, 36*(2), 135-150.

Charman, T. (2003). Why is joint attention a pivotal skill in autism? *Philosophical transactions of the Royal Society of London. Series B, Biological sciences, 358*(1430), 315-24.

Chartoff, R., & Winkler, I. & Avildsen, JG (Director). (1976). *Rocky [Motion picture]*. United States: United Artists.

Mayes, S. D., Gorman, A. A., Hillwig-Garcia, J., & Syed, E. (2013). Suicide ideation and attempts in children with autism. *Research in Autism Spectrum Disorders, 7*, 109-119.

Sturmey, P. (2017). Have a happy, fun, assertive life! (Avoid depression, anxiety, loneliness, and suicide!) In J. B. Leaf (Eds). *Handbook of Social Skills and Autism Spectrum Disorder: Assessment, Curricula, and Intervention. Autism and Child Psychopathology Series.* Springer, Cham.

Varni, J. W., Lovaas, O. I., Koegel, R. L., & Everett, N. L. (1979). An analysis of observational learning in autistic and normal children. *Journal of Abnormal Child Psychology, 7*(1), 31-43.

White, P. J., O'Reilly, M., Streusand, W., Levine, A., Sigafoos, J., Lancioni, G., Fragale, C., Pierce, N., & Aguilar, J. (2011). Best practices for teaching joint attention: A systematic review of the intervention literature. *Research in Autism Spectrum Disorders, 5*, 1283-1295.

Chapter Two
Applied Behavior Analysis

Applied Behavior Analysis, the Science

Applied behavior analysis (ABA) is a science, one that looks at how the environment affects behavior for all individuals. Utilizing this science, behavior analysts determine ways to improve socially important behaviors for their clients.

As a science, behavior analysis has been around since the 1800s. The field started with the early basic scientific work of pioneers including Edward Thorndike, Ivan Pavlov, John Watson, and B.F. Skinner who evaluated how behavior is established and how it can be changed through the systematic manipulation of the environment. The next generation in the field moved to evaluating ways to improve socially important behaviors. The incredible work of Donald Baer, Montrose Wolf, Sandra Harris, Todd Risley, James Sherman, Ivar Lovaas, Sigrid Glenn, Teodoro Ayllon, Nathan Azrin, and Jack Michael showed us the applied power our science offers. Their work demonstrated that children who did not have any language could learn to speak; adults who had no adaptive skills could learn vocational and independent living skills, thereby becoming valuable members of their communities; and that through the use of behavior analytic principles, we could reduce life-threatening behaviors for our clients (Leaf et al., 2019).

One of these seminal studies was conducted by Wolf et al. (1963). In this study, a 3.5-year-old child diagnosed with autism spectrum disorder (ASD) named Dickey participated. Dickey had a long history of temper tantrums, self-injurious behavior, mealtime challenges, and vision problems requiring glasses that he refused to wear. The researchers demonstrated that shaping could be used to teach desired behaviors. Through this systematic shaping procedure, Dickey learned to wear, rather than throw, his glasses. In later sessions, the researchers continued to teach Dicky additional skills. Wolf et al. were the first to show the power that ABA could have for a child diagnosed with ASD. This study helped pave the way for the first comprehensive behavioral intervention study for individuals diagnosed with ASD.

Lovaas et al. (1973) evaluated the effects of a comprehensive behavioral intervention for 20 individuals diagnosed with ASD, whose ages ranged from 3–10 years. Within this study, participants received intervention for up to 14 months. Intervention consisted of (but was not limited to) developing reinforcers, discrete trial teaching, and shaping. The researchers demonstrated improvements in prosocial behaviors (e.g., play and appropriate speech) while decreasing inappropriate behaviors (e.g., self-stimulatory behaviors and echolalia).

After the study, participants were placed back in an institutional setting or returned home to live with their parents, who were trained in the principles of ABA. The participants who returned to an institutional residential setting regressed across all skills taught, whereas the participants who lived at home with their parents maintained or improved upon their newly acquired skills. These results demonstrated the effects and importance of trained caretakers—and, even further, that parents could be effectively involved in the learning process. This study also led to arguably the most famous and seminal work in behavioral treatment of ASD, the Young Autism Project (Lovaas, 1987).

Lovaas (1987) evaluated the effects of comprehensive behavioral intervention with young children diagnosed with ASD. The study consisted of three groups of participants. The first group was a treatment group of 19 children. These 19 children received only ABA-based intervention for an average of 40 hours per week, their parents were well-trained in the principles of ABA, punishment was used for aberrant behavior, and intervention lasted for two or more years. The second group was a comparison group of 19 children. These 19 children received an average of 10 hours of ABA-based intervention per week for two or more years, received therapies using other approaches, and punishment was not used for aberrant behavior. The third group was a comparison of 21 children who did not receive ABA-based intervention.

After treatment, the children were categorized into three outcome groups (i.e., normal functioning, aphasic, and autistic/retarded[1]). Participants were classified as normal functioning if they had an intelligence quotient (IQ) score in the normal range, had completed first grade in a general education classroom with other typically developing children, were advanced to second grade by their teacher, and no longer presented with the features of autism. Participants were classified as aphasic if they had an IQ score

---

1   This term is used in the work cited. It is, however, no longer an accepted or appropriate term.

falling within the mildly retarded range and passed first grade in an aphasia classroom (i.e., classroom for language delayed, language handicapped, or learning disabled). Participants were classified as autistic/retarded if their IQ score fell in the profoundly retarded range and were placed in a classroom for autistic/retarded children.

The results showed that comprehensive, quality intervention can lead to significant improvements in the lives of children diagnosed with ASD. Prior to intervention, approximately 10% of all participants across groups scored within the normal range of intellectual functioning (i.e., IQ score falling within in the normal range), approximately 37% fell within the moderate range (i.e., IQ score falling within the mildly retarded range), and approximately 53% of participants fell in the severely impacted range (i.e., IQ score falling within the severely retarded range). Following intervention for children in the intensive treatment group, 47% were classified as normal functioning, 42% were classified as aphasic, and 11% were classified as autistic/retarded. For children in the first control group, 0% were classified as normal functioning, 42% were classified as aphasic, and 58% were classified as autistic/retarded. For children in the second control group; 6% were classified as normal functioning, 47% were classified as aphasic, and 47% were classified as autistic/retarded. The results demonstrated how important quality, intensive early behavioral intervention is for the long-term success of individuals diagnosed with ASD.

These three studies as well as others (e.g., Foxx & Azrin, 1973; Koegel & Covert, 1972; Risley, 1968) paved the way for thousands of studies showing that a variety of procedures based on the principles of ABA are effective in developing prosocial behaviors and decreasing aberrant behaviors for individuals diagnosed with ASD. These include, but are not limited to, studies on discrete trial teaching (Lovaas, 1981), functional analysis (Iwata et al., 1994), group instruction (Leaf et al., 2017), video modeling (McCoy & Hermanen, 2007), and even social skills groups (Leaf et al., 2017). These studies, as well as others, have made behavioral interventions the most validated procedures for individuals diagnosed with ASD (Leaf, Leaf, et al., 2016) and have resulted in the proliferation of clinical interventions based upon the principles of ABA.

ABA Interventions for Social Skills

Today, interventions based upon the principles of ABA are widely used in everyday clinical practice. There are currently more clinics, home-based agencies, university programs, and community-based programs providing ABA-based intervention for individuals diagnosed with ASD than ever before. Additionally, I have witnessed an increase in the number of undergraduate and graduate programs for training professionals on the conceptual basis of ABA and how to implement ABA-based interventions for individuals diagnosed with ASD. This has resulted in more professionals in the field providing behavioral interventions for individuals diagnosed with ASD—which, in turn, has resulted in more individuals obtaining much needed services.

One intervention commonly implemented to improve social behavior is discrete trial teaching (Lovaas, 1981). Discrete trial teaching is a method consisting of three components: (1) an instruction is given to the learner, (2) the learner makes a response, (3) and feedback is provided based on the response. Typically, a learner is provided numerous trials to acquire a new behavior. Another commonly implemented intervention is video modeling (McCoy & Hermansen, 2007). Video modeling consists of the learner watching a video of another person engaging in the targeted social skill and then the learner practicing the skill. A third intervention based on the principles of ABA to target social skills is behavioral skills training (Seiverling et al., 2012). In behavioral skills training, the interventionist describes the skill, models the skill for the learner, the learner practices the skill, and the interventionist provides feedback throughout.

A fourth intervention that has been used to increase social behavior is the Cool versus Not Cool™ procedure (Leaf et al., 2012; Leaf, Mitchell, et al., 2016). Within this procedure, the interventionist models the appropriate version and inappropriate version of the target behavior, the learner discriminates between the cool (appropriate) and not cool (inappropriate) versions, and then the learner practices the target behavior the cool way.

Another intervention that has been used to target social behaviors is the teaching interaction procedure (Leaf et al., 2017). The teaching interaction procedure consists of six steps: (1) labeling the skill, (2) providing a meaningful rationale for displaying the skill, (3) breaking the skill down into smaller components, (4) an interventionist demonstration, (5) learner role-play, and (6) providing feedback and reinforcement throughout. Along with these interventions and other behaviorally based procedures (e.g., activity schedules, script fading, pivotal response training), behaviorally based social skills groups are a common intervention strategy for individuals diagnosed with ASD.

All of the interventions mentioned above have empirical support and have a scientific evidence base to support their utility, as opposed to other commonly implemented interventions to improve social behaviors that have little to no empirical support and are not considered evidence-based (e.g., Social Thinking; Leaf et al., 2018).

It's Not All Good

Though I am thrilled to see more professionals entering into the field of ABA, it is not without its drawbacks. For a long time, I have been concerned with the state of the field and the direction it's heading. I am worried about the quality of treatment that individuals diagnosed with ASD receive and with the outcomes and progress of these individuals. All too often, interventionists are receiving sub-par training—not the same type of comprehensive training that has been provided at the University of Kansas, University of North Texas, or at UCLA on the Young Autism Project, to name a few.

I have four major concerns about where the field of ABA is headed. One is the adoption of rigid protocols. That is, interventionists all too often follow set "recipes" without understanding the underlying rationales, then fail to make needed adjustments based on a learner's performance and context. This proliferation of rigidity is occurring in all aspects of therapy. On a daily basis, interventionists implement formal preference assessments, rigid prompting hierarchies, strict counterbalancing of stimuli, predetermined order of presentation, and non-naturalistic discrete trial teaching (Leaf et al., 2019). I see interventionists strictly following these protocols even when they are ineffective for the learner; these interventionists do not have the flexibility or skills to make the needed adjustments.

I remember watching a video of an interventionist using script fading to teach two children how to play hide and seek. According to the script, the child diagnosed with ASD was intended to say, "I found you," when she found the peer who was hiding. In the video, the child instead said, "I got you," and immediately received corrective feedback for not saying, "I found you." I couldn't believe that a child would receive corrective feedback for an appropriate spontaneous comment just because it was not as written in the script they had been taught to follow. The interventionist was either following the protocol (which prohibited interventionist discretion) or did not have the therapeutic skills to determine that the two responses were equivalent. Generally, it's easier to train young professionals to follow protocols—this allows them to start working with clients as soon as possible. In some cases, interventionists may not be permitted to make adjustments to a protocol until a Board Certified Behavior Analyst (BCBA) returns for a consultation, which could be a month or more. Such a delay could result in lost time due to the learner having mastered a skill but not moving on to learn a new skill; or the ineffective protocol could result in inappropriate treatment being implemented.

The second area of deterioration I have witnessed in the field is the type of curriculum used to teach skills to children diagnosed with ASD. I remember one of the first cases I supervised. When I arrived at the child's house for the first time, the family and interventionists were so excited to show me the new social program they were working on, so I was curious to see it. It turned out that they were teaching a 5-year-old boy the difference between an Army man, a Navy man, and an Air Force man. I wondered, "How was this a social skills program?" My first question was, "Do you have family members in the military?" The answer was no. I followed up with, "Why are you teaching this skill?" They had no answer. This is just one of many examples of rigidity when it comes to selecting skills to teach an individual diagnosed with ASD that I observe all too often.

Children diagnosed with ASD are being taught state birds, dog breeds, and state flags as a part of their programming. This is occurring in research, but also within clinical practice. I see it when interventionists make basic social behaviors such as pleasantries and greetings the major emphasis of programming, while ignoring more natural and meaningful social behaviors (e.g., joint attention, joining into play). When we teach rote skills that lack social validity, children are not going to make the gains they are capable of.

The third area of concern is professionals not obtaining adequate training to provide behavioral intervention. As the demand for behavioral intervention has increased, so has the mass production and commercialization of intervention, as well as a lowering of the training criterion for all levels of staff within behavioral intervention agencies. Technicians who receive only 40 hours of training are considered "competent" to provide behavioral intervention. I have witnessed interventionists only receiving training for the procedures they are implementing and not receiving training on the principles behind those procedures. I also see professionals who are able to talk about a variety of procedures fluently using technical language and, as a result, are considered qualified even if they are unable to implement those procedures competently. The mass production of training to meet the demand for services has resulted in many professionals not receiving adequate training to provide quality intervention, yet these professionals work with and supervise children diagnosed with ASD.

Most certified behavior analysts believe they are implementing quality behavioral intervention. But my fourth area of concern about ABA is that I see many of these professionals implementing non-evidence-based procedures or procedures with no empirical support. I assume they implement these procedures for a variety of reasons: (1) these procedures have high "curb appeal" and may appease caregivers, (2) they like the information/procedures, (3) it allows them to work collaboratively with other professions, and (4) they do not understand the evidence, or lack of evidence, behind the procedures. I often hear that there is no harm when implementing these procedures (e.g., Social Thinking, Social Stories™), or that these procedures can be implemented in conjunction with behavioral intervention. Although these statements may seem reasonable, they are inaccurate. For one, research has made clear that an eclectic approach is not as effective as behavioral intervention alone (e.g., Howard et al., 2005). Second, any time spent *not* implementing ABA-based procedures takes away from valuable instructional time that should be dedicated to behavioral intervention. To be committed to implementing behavioral intervention is to be committed to not implementing non-evidence based, non-empirically supported, or pseudoscientific procedures.

The Autism Partnership Method

As I have observed these changes in the type and quality of behavioral intervention being implemented to individuals with ASD over the years, my colleagues and I have been vocal in advocating against this shift (Leaf, Leaf, et al., 2016). We have also attempted to disseminate an alternative approach (Leaf, Leaf, et al., 2016) in which quality intervention can be implemented so children diagnosed with ASD can make the significant improvements they are capable of making (Leaf et al., 2011). We first called this approach a structured yet flexible approach to ABA. More recently we have defined it as a progressive approach to ABA (Leaf, Leaf, et al., 2016). However, as more professionals claim they implement a progressive approach to ABA when they do not, we have begun calling our approach to ABA the *Autism Partnership Method*. By calling it the Autism Partnership Method, we are better able to provide training, guidelines, and feedback regarding correct implementation.

The main tenet of this method is that interventionists should be trained to use clinical judgment (Leaf et al., 2019). Rather than being bound by strict protocols, interventionists are trained to make in-the-moment assessments and decisions to provide treatment that is responsive to the learner they are working with. Often in the field of ABA, this approach is looked down upon—most assume that "clinical judgment" just means making decisions based on a gut feeling. This is not the case! When an interventionist is trained to use clinical judgment, they are trained to assess many factors based on a deep understanding of behavioral principles and strategies to inform decisions and changes.

There are many variables considered when using clinical judgment. One variable is the client's non-verbal behavior. What is the client's affect? What is the client's body language? A good interventionist will constantly evaluate these and other non-verbal client behaviors to determine how best to teach them. Another variable constantly evaluated is aberrant behavior. An interventionist needs to evaluate if aberrant behaviors are occurring and whether the aberrant behaviors are interfering with the learning process or social opportunities; analyze the functions of aberrant behaviors and determine if they are primarily operant (i.e., controlled by their consequences) or respondent (i.e., controlled by events preceding them); then intervene appropriately.

A third variable requiring assessment is the receptivity and attentiveness of the client. How long has the client been working? How is the rapport between the interventionist and client? How busy or distracting is the learning environment? The interventionist must also evaluate the data, including the client's recent performance and past performance. We believe that even direct-line staff should know how to interpret this data and make changes in the moment, not wait for a supervisor to make adjustments. A fourth variable is the client's health. This includes a client's sleep the night before, if the client may have stomach pain or a headache, if the client is on a new medication, or if the client's home life has significantly changed (e.g., divorce, new school, new sibling). All of these factors can affect the client's learning and need to be assessed by the interventionist. Finally, the interventionist must ensure that the reinforcers they are using are powerful. If a client does not have a variety of reinforcers, the interventionist must be able to adjust and condition new items to become reinforcers so learning can progress. All of these variables affect the client's learning process and need to be accounted for by the interventionist.

The Autism Partnership Method uses clinical judgment by incorporating in-the-moment decisions for all the variables mentioned above and more. The only way for an interventionist to achieve this level of expertise is through extensive training. Forty hours of training is simply not enough for a person to be considered qualified: That is, competence should not be measured in hours trained. Rather, training must continue until the interventionist implements procedures correctly and consistently—across time and with actual clients (i.e., not only within role-plays).

Within the Autism Partnership Method, the focus is on establishing learning-how-to-learn behaviors (e.g., attending, sitting calmly, understanding feedback, engagement, waiting, handling transitions, scanning materials) from the onset of treatment. Working on learning-how-to-learn behaviors can help expedite the learning process, not just teaching rote skills but how to be an active participant in the learning process. Within the Autism Partnership Method, interventionists focus on developing reinforcers such as social interactions, activities, and privileges (e.g., line leader, child who brings out the toys at recess, board helper), as opposed to the candy and tangible items that are often used by default. This requires time and effort, but doing so helps promote learning in more naturalistic settings and the maintenance of skills. Another hallmark of this method is making the teaching environment as natural as possible, which often involves teaching with distractions present so the client is ready to handle learning in the natural environment (e.g., school and community).

The Autism Partnership Method involves targeting the most meaningful, authentic, and pivotal skills for the learner so that they can be as independent as possible. The interventionists constantly evaluate which skills to teach and ensure that whatever skills they choose to teach, the learner will make meaningful progress. We do not simply teach joint attention so the learner will comment on a novel event—we teach it because it may improve language and permit access to more social opportunities.

Another feature of this method is that the interventionist is not just working with the learner but is often supporting parents, siblings, grandparents, and other family members. Finally, within this method, group teaching is used often and early in the learning process. Learners of all ages and functioning levels are exposed to group teaching to work on social skills, learning-how-to-learn skills in a group setting, and play skills. Within the Autism Partnership Method, group instruction, including social skills groups, are used frequently to increase learners' overall social behavior. This type of instruction will be the focus of this book.

References

Foxx, R. M., & Azrin, N. H. (1973). The elimination of autistic self-stimulatory behavior by overcorrection. *Journal of Applied Behavior Analysis, 6*(1), 1–14. http://doi.org/10.1901/jaba.1973.6-1

Howard, J. S., Sparkman, C. R., Cohen, H. G., Green, G., & Stanislaw, H. (2005). A comparison of intensive behavior analytic and eclectic treatments for young children with autism. *Research in Developmental Disabilities, 26*(4), 359–383. https://doi.org/10.1016/j.ridd.2004.09.005

Iwata, B. A., Dorsey, M. F., Slifer, K. J., Bauman, K. E., & Richman, G. S. (1982/1994). Toward a functional analysis of self‐injury. *Journal of applied behavior analysis, 27*(2), 197-209.

Koegel, R. L., & Covert, A. (1972). The relationship of self-stimulation to learning in autistic children. *Journal of Applied Behavior Analysis, 5*(4), 381–387.

Leaf, J. B., Cihon, J. H., Ferguson, J. L., Taubman, M., Leaf, R., & McEachin, J. (2018). Social Thinking®, pseudoscientific, not empirically supported, and non-evidence based: A reply to Crooke and Winner. *Behavior Analysis in Practice, 11*(4), 456–466. http://doi.org/10.1007/s40617-018-0241-0.pdf

Leaf, J. B., Leaf, R., McEachin, J., Taubman, M., Ala'i-Rosales, S., Ross, R. K., Smith, Tristram, & Weiss, M. J. (2016). Applied behavior analysis is a science and, therefore, progressive. *Journal of Autism and Developmental Disorders, 46*(2), 720–731. https://doi.org/10.1007/s10803-015-2591-6

Leaf, J. B., Leaf, J. A., Milne, C., Taubman, M., Oppenheim-Leaf, M., Torres, N., Townley-Cochran, Leaf, R., McEachin, J., & Yoder, P. (2017). An evaluation of a behaviorally based social skills group for individuals diagnosed with autism spectrum disorder. *Journal of Autism and Developmental Disorders, 47*, 243-259.

Leaf, J. B., Tsuji, K. H., Griggs, B., Edwards, A., Taubman, M., McEachin, J., Leaf, R., & Oppenheim-Leaf, M. L. (2012). Teaching social skills to children with autism using the cool versus not cool procedure. *Education and Training in Autism and Developmental Disabilities*, 165-175.

Leaf, R. B., Taubman, M. T., McEachin, J. J., Leaf, J. B., & Tsuji, K. H. (2011). A programmatic description of a community-based intensive behavioral intervention program for individuals with autism spectrum disorders. *Education and Treatment of Children, 34*(2), 259-285.

Leaf, J. B., Mitchell, E., Townley-Cochran, D., McEachin, J., Taubman, M., & Leaf, R. (2016). Comparing Social Stories™ to cool versus not cool. *Education and Treatment of Children, 39*(2), 173-185.

Leaf, J. B., Taubman, M., Milne, C., Dale, S., Leaf, J., Townley-Cochran, D., Tsuji, K., Kassardjian, A., Alcalay, A., Leaf, R., & McEachin, J. (2016). Teaching social communication skills using a cool versus not cool procedure plus role-playing and a social skills taxonomy. *Education and treatment of children, 39*(1), 44-63.

Leaf, R., Leaf, J. B., & McEachin, J. (2019). *Clinical judgement in ABA: Lessons from our pioneers.* Different Roads to Learning, NY: NY.

Lovaas, O. I. (1981). *Teaching Developmentally Disabled Children: The Me Book.* Austin, TX: PRO-ED Books.

Lovaas, O. I. (1987). Behavioral treatment and normal educational and intellectual functioning in young autistic children. *Journal of consulting and clinical psychology, 55*(1), 3-9.

Lovaas, O. I., Koegel, R., Simmons, J. Q., & Long, J. S. (1973). Some generalization and follow-up measures on autistic children in behavior therapy. *Journal of applied behavior analysis, 6*(1), 131-165.

McCoy, K., & Hermansen, E. (2007). Video Modeling for Individuals with Autism: A Review of Model Types and Effects. *Education and Treatment of Children, 30*(4), 183-213.

Risley, T. R. (1968). The effects and side effects of punishing the autistic behaviors of a deviant child. *Journal of Applied Behavior Analysis, 1*(1), 21–34.

Seiverling, L., Williams, K., Sturmey, P., & Hart, S. (2012). Effects of behavioral skills training on parental treatment of children's food selectivity. *Journal of Applied Behavior Analysis, 45,* 197-203.

Wolf, M., Risley, T., & Mees, H. (1963). Application of operant conditioning procedures to the behaviour problems of an autistic child. *Behaviour Research and Therapy, 1*(2-4), 305-312.

Chapter Three
An Overview of The Autism Partnership Method's Approach to Behaviorally Based Social Skills Groups

Like anything in the field of applied behavior analysis (ABA), it is important to objectively define what constitutes a social skills group. Across research and curriculum books, there does not appear to be a consensus. From study to study and clinic to clinic, the definition and approach to a social skills group changes greatly. For the purposes of this book, we define a behaviorally based social skills group as three or more learners coming together simultaneously to learn social behaviors using the principles of ABA. It is a pragmatic definition. It defines the minimum number of participants, the class of behaviors that should be taught (social), and the method of teaching (behavioral). When we conceptualize Autism Partnership Method's approach to behaviorally based social skills groups, there are at least 13 essential characteristics.

Behaviorally Based

One of the most important characteristics is that the social skills group is behaviorally based. This means that the group is conceptually systematic with the principles of ABA. The teaching must target changing observable behaviors using procedures that manipulate aspects of the environment for the learner to be successful. Within a behaviorally based social skills group, interventionists must only implement procedures based upon the principles of ABA (e.g., reinforcement, punishment) and not a mentalistic approach. Furthermore, interventionists should strive to only implement procedures with empirical support, published in peer-reviewed journals. It should be noted, however, just because a particular procedure that is rooted in the principles of ABA has not been specifically researched, that does not imply there is no empirical support. In fact, there is a plethora of research supporting the principles of ABA. So, what does this mean for the interventionist? It means that an interventionist should not implement many procedures that are commonly implemented today, such as various sensory activities (e.g., chewy toys, spinners, weighted vests, massages) or alternative teaching/social skills interventions (e.g., Social Thinking®, Rapid Prompting Method, Social Stories™, Floortime) as they do not meet the criteria for best research evidence.

Use a Variety of Teaching Strategies

There are a variety of behaviorally based procedures that have empirical support. Within the Autism Partnership Method, the types of procedures that have been implemented within the context of social skills groups have included discrete trial teaching, flexible prompt fading, video modeling, shaping, embedded instruction, systematic desensitization, observational learning, incidental teaching, communication temptations, the Cool versus Not Cool™ procedure, and the teaching interaction procedure.

The Autism Partnership Method, as it relates to social skills groups, has also included motivational systems such as levels systems, magic number token systems, and group contingencies. It should be noted that there are other behaviorally based interventions that have strong empirical support (e.g., script fading, matrix training, activity schedules); however, these interventions are not typically implemented within Autism Partnership Method's approach to social skills groups because they tend to be more rigid in their protocols.

One important characteristic of our approach is that within a social skills group, the interventionists do not implement just one teaching strategy–they implement many different teaching strategies throughout each session. For example, the interventionist may use group discrete trial teaching to take attendance, use video modeling to work on empathy, and use embedded instruction to teach social games. The interventionist may also use a variety of interventions to teach components of larger social skills such as friendships. For example, when teaching friendship development, the interventionist might start by using discrete trial teaching to teach classmates' names; move into using the Cool versus Not Cool™ procedure to discriminate between subjects you should talk about with a friend versus with an acquaintance; and, finally, end with using the teaching interaction procedure to discuss the importance of friendships and how to further develop relationships.

Teachable Moments

Regardless of the teaching procedures used within the social skills group, interventionists should strive to minimize downtime and capture every learning opportunity for each learner in the social skills group. The goal should be that every second a learner is present in the social skills group is a teachable moment. This is critical because our learners usually have multiple social deficits and we must provide as much teaching as possible to accelerate their learning to catch up to their same-age peers. This does not mean that every moment has to be direct teaching from the interventionists; interventionists also set up opportunities where indirect learning can occur, often referred to as incidental teaching. These indirect opportunities could be anytime during the group, but the key to these opportunities is that the interventionists plan for them and set them up in a natural manner. Interventionists can't merely show up and hope that opportunities occur so they can capitalize on them—though they should capitalize on any opportunity that happens without their setup.

Teaching this way requires a great deal of planning on the part of the interventionist, as well as systematic and flexible teaching skills. First, for each and every activity planned within the group, the interventionists must identify a variety of group goals as well as individual goals for each participant. For example, snack time is not just meant for the learner to eat a snack; rather, the interventionist arranges opportunities to practice communication goals (e.g., talking to peers, requesting, expanding language); social goals (e.g., orientating towards peers, sharing, turn taking); and behavior goals (e.g., waiting, refraining from self-stimulatory behavior, compliance with instructions). As the interventionist arranges these opportunities, they must use their clinical judgement to identify when indirect/incidental teaching is insufficient and when direct instruction for targeted social behaviors.

As Naturalistic as Possible

All too often, we observe ABA interventionists providing unnatural, robotic therapy—not what we would consider quality ABA-based intervention. Examples of rigid behavioral interventions include repeating the same instruction during every trial (e.g., "Do this," "Do this," "Do this."), using truncated language when a participant has good comprehension, using a robotic voice tone, or providing rote rationales for engaging in social behaviors (e.g., "Because your friends will like you."). By using these methods, they are implementing rigid behavior analysis—it's no wonder that people say ABA creates robots, when they are being taught robotically! Unfortunately, we see these types of interventions implemented in many behaviorally based social skills groups. It is important to note that all ABA-based intervention is not created equal.

Within the Autism Partnership Method, the interventionist interacts as naturally as possible. This means that an interventionist speaks to the group in a way that the learners would encounter in everyday life. An interventionist's body language and posture should be similar to how teachers, parents, and other adults would interact with the learners (e.g., bending down to talk to young children). Learning opportunities are arranged to be similar to opportunities that occur in the natural environment (e.g., a classroom). Teaching in a natural way helps learners generalize social skills learned in the social skills group to other environments and may result in increasing their enjoyment of the learning process.

Contingency Systems

Behavior intervention can only be successful if contingency systems are in place. Reinforcement systems must be established to increase desired social behaviors; likewise, behavior reduction procedures (e.g., corrective feedback, response cost, withholding reinforcement) should be in place to decrease undesired behaviors. Within the context of a behaviorally based social skills group, interventionists will often implement multiple contingency systems simultaneously. This includes a combination of individual (e.g., token boards for an individual learner) and group contingency systems (e.g., reinforcement systems that include all learners, such as a level system). Using contingency systems ensures the learner contacts reinforcement for engaging in desired behaviors and is corrected for engaging in inappropriate behaviors throughout the social skills group session. Another hallmark of the Autism Partnership Method is the interventionist fading contingency systems from the most assistive/intrusive contingency system (e.g., earning tokens for every occurrence of a target behavior) to the least assistive/intrusive contingency system (e.g., earning social reinforcement at the end of the day) as quickly as the learner's skillset allows.

Curriculum

We're often asked, "What do you teach as part of your social skills groups?" and "Where do you get your curriculum from?" It's important to note that there is no universal, comprehensive social skills curriculum. There is no one book, including this one, that includes all of the social skills you can or should teach. However, the curriculum we have developed for teaching social skills is included at the back of this book (Taubman et al., 2011). We encourage interventionists to use social skills assessments and curriculum from multiple sources to create an individualized curriculum for each learner's needs. It is important for interventionists to determine social skills targets by observing the learner's interactions and behaviors, assessing the learner's social skills strengths and weaknesses, then identifying the social behaviors needed for the learner to be successful in their everyday social interactions. After identifying the areas of need, if there is not a suitable program that already exists, the interventionist can create a curriculum for the targeted social skills and identify the appropriate interventions to teach these skills. One sign of a quality interventionist is the ability to independently create their own curriculum and materials as needed. This is essential because there may not always be an easy reference, curriculum, or book that encompasses all social behaviors that need to be targeted.

In the Autism Partnership Method, the curriculum is individualized and tailored to meet the needs of all learners within the group. We often see interventionists using only one curriculum (e.g., PEERS®) and following it step-by-step even when learners already have the skills in their repertoires—or when they don't have the necessary prerequisites to learn certain skills. And sometimes a learner urgently needs a skill that does not appear until late in a standardized curriculum guide. Interventionists must tailor the skills taught, as well as the order they are taught in, to maximize the benefits learners gain from the social skills group.

When teaching social skills in a group setting using the Autism Partnership Method, an interventionist does not simply teach one or two social behaviors per session, then move on to the next predetermined skill in the following sessions. Rather, the interventionists target as many social behaviors as are needed in any given session without a rigid curriculum sequence. This does not mean that there is no plan. Rather, the interventionists make changes to the plan as necessary based on learner performance. The interventionists may choose to address a social behavior immediately upon observing a concern—or they may address the observed social deficit in subsequent sessions. For example, if the interventionist brings in a new activity they think the learners will enjoy, but the learners have a difficult time engaging in the novel activity, the interventionist may decide that the next session will focus on developing the skills necessary for coming in contact with novel play activities (e.g., asking questions, observing others, imitating others).

Interventionists also create curricula based upon observations of the group. The interventionists may observe that the learners are exhibiting certain social or behavioral deficits or excesses within the context of the social skills group. But when they search through curricular books and research literature, interventionists might find no systematic method to target the social behaviors. As such, the interventionist will have to create their own programs, based upon the principles of ABA, to address these issues.

Finally, a good interventionist should think about the little picture as well as the big picture. Interventionists should not just teach and target specific social behaviors (e.g., observational learning, sharing, joint attention) out of context. They should also teach these social skills in context, so learners can generalize the skills which can lead to more important and global social behaviors (e.g., friendship development). ABA-based interventions, as they relate to autism intervention, are often criticized for only working on discrete, simple behaviors–as a field, we must strive to better address complex behaviors and disseminate this approach.

Aberrant Behavior

When individuals diagnosed with autism spectrum disorder (ASD) are engaging in aberrant behaviors (such as self-stimulatory behaviors, aggression, non-compliance, self-injury, or elopement), they are less likely to learn effectively. These aberrant behaviors interfere with attending to instructions, processing information, learning observationally, and, more generally, being ready to learn. Learners will not learn effectively when they are engaging in these behaviors and they may seriously hinder any opportunities for social interactions with peers. Imagine a learner who has a wide variety of prosocial behaviors yet aggresses toward peers. Any behaviors the learner might exhibit would not be maintained by the environment because peers are likely to avoid interacting with an aggressive learner.

This does not mean that the presence of aberrant behaviors should exclude an individual from participating in a social skills group. Rather, it indicates that reducing aberrant behaviors must be the first priority of intervention. When an interventionist is faced with learners who engage in aberrant behaviors, proactive and reactive strategies should be used to eliminate the behaviors. Proactively, interventionists should determine the function(s) of the behavior and systematically arrange evocative events that set the occasion for the learner to engage in replacement behaviors that will accomplish similar function(s) and ensure that replacement behaviors contact reinforcement. Reactively, if and when aberrant behaviors occur, interventionists should stay calm, continue to analyze the function(s) of the behaviors in the moment, minimize any potential payoffs for engaging in the behaviors (e.g., provide the least amount of attention necessary, do not allow access to preferred items and activities), and reinforce behaviors that are approximations toward calm, desired behaviors (Leaf & McEachin, 1999).

Data Collection

An essential element of ABA is *analysis*. For behaviorally based social skills groups, analysis means that we must take data to analyze and track the progress of our learners. More importantly, the data taken should be used to inform treatment decisions. Within the Autism Partnership Method, data need not be continuous (e.g., continuous recording of frequency or duration of a behavior) or bound by any particular measurement system (e.g., trial by trial data). Rather, it means that the data is collected in a manner that adequately tracks behavior and progress and informs possible intervention changes–

though not more than is needed, or done in a way that interferes with the teaching process or social opportunities for the learners.

Clinical Judgment

As you can see, there is a great deal of flexibility in Autism Partnership Method's approach to behaviorally based social skills groups. There are no set protocols interventionists must adhere to. Rather, interventionists have a general plan each and every session, but deviate from that plan to help meet the needs of the learners and take advantage of opportunities that occur during the session. Clinical judgment is used throughout all aspects of the Autism Partnership Method. As discussed in a previous chapter, clinical judgment is not a "gut feeling," but rather making in-the-moment decisions based on multiple variables to ensure maximum progress toward treatment goals.

Quality Staff

Running a behaviorally based social skills group is a difficult task. Implementing a variety of teaching procedures for numerous learners with different skillsets and abilities, all while using clinical judgment, is daunting. For a group to run effectively, it must be led and supported by well-trained staff. The interventionists have to be knowledgeable in the principles of ABA, social skills curriculum, ASD, and aberrant behaviors. They also need to work as part of a team and collaborate with families. Interventionists also have to be able to implement all procedures that may be used during a social skills group (e.g., group discrete trial teaching, embedded instruction, incidental teaching). They need to be able to work with a wide variety of learners with different strengths, deficits, and challenges. Within a social skills group, an interventionist might work with one learner who has limited language, one learner who has high levels of language but engages in non-compliance, and one learner who does not want to play with peers. These variables create an even bigger challenge for providing effective intervention.

Unfortunately, quality interventionists are not easy to come by; becoming a high-quality interventionist is not possible with limited training (e.g., 40 hours). It takes months to years of supervised experience specifically focused on running social skills groups to be able to run them independently and effectively.

Learners in the Group

Several variables need to be considered when starting a social skills group. Who are the learners participating in the group? Is the group going to be heterogeneous or homogenous? Will the group of learners have limited language? Will the social skills group consist of learners who display aberrant behavior? Will typically developing peers be included in the group? How many learners will be in the group? Within the Autism Partnership Method, there are no standard answers to these questions and interventionists must decide what is best for the group they are planning (see Chapter 5 for more details).

One important consideration is how the learners in the group fit together. Learners in the group need to have similar and complementary goals. For example, if you have a group of learners you are teaching play skills, they may all have a similar big-picture objective (e.g., sustained and shared engagement while playing), which could potentially mean they are a good fit. However, if each learner needs to work on leading play, it may not necessarily be a good fit: it would be more beneficial if you had some learners whose goal is to lead play, while others' goals include following the lead of others during play. These goals complement each other nicely because when it is time to practice "playing with a friend," the interventionist can easily pair up a learner who needs to work on leading play with a learner that needs to work on following play so both goals can be targeted simultaneously.

Along with complementary goals when selecting learners for the group, it is important that every learner selected benefits the whole group in some way. While all learners have social skills goals to acquire, they must also have skill strengths to contribute to the group. At the very least, there needs to be the expectation that they can learn, relatively quickly, some of the needed skills. If there is a learner who is likely to be highly disruptive, therefore taking teaching time away from the rest of the group, that learner may not be ready to be in a social skills group or another support staff may need to be added. However, the goal should be for the support staff to eventually be faded out. If this cannot occur, then a group setting may not be the best fit for that learner's needs and more one-to-one therapy sessions may be required for the learner to develop the necessary prerequisites to learn in a group setting.

Family Involvement

Another important component of the Autism Partnership Method, as it relates to social skills groups, is ensuring that families are involved in the treatment. The parents are not instructing the social skills group, but are included in other ways. It is important to build in periods of time when the interventionists can debrief with the parents and other times when parents can observe the social skills group. There might be times when interventionists will ask the parents to practice the skills learned in the group with their child at home, outside the group. Interventionists might also inform parents about particular skills being taught, so parents can recognize when they are being used and reinforce these behaviors outside of the social skills group. It is critical that the parents of the children in the social skills group are well informed and feel they are part of the team.

Although many social skills groups may include a learner's sibling, within this model we do not include siblings in the group. We believe that siblings should have their own identity outside of having a brother or sister diagnosed with ASD. Including them in the group may potentially even hinder their relationship with their sibling. We encourage families to enroll siblings in other activities or have special time with their parents while the sibling diagnosed with ASD participates in the social skills group (see Chapter 16 for more details).

Frequency and Duration

A final consideration is determining the number of sessions per week and the duration of each session for the behaviorally based social skills group. It stands to reason that the more times you run a social skills group per week, the more effective the results will be due to the higher dosage of treatment. Additional research is required to confirm optimal frequency and duration for various groupings of participants (see Chapter 4), but in the interim, here are considerations we have found helpful.

We have found social skills groups to be effective when the group is run at least two times per week. It is also recommended that a group be run for a minimum of 90 minutes per session, with the ideal time being anywhere between two to three hours (older learners can typically tolerate longer sessions than younger learners). The group should be long enough to practice several skills, but not so long that the session feels like it is dragging on or that there's a lot of downtime without clear skill targets. Learners should be excited to see each other each session. Long sessions that drag on could potentially cause learners to associate peers with boring, difficult, or tedious tasks. Ideally, learners should pair the social skills group with fun social activities, so they cannot wait to return for the next session.

References

Leaf, R. B., & McEachin, J. J. (1999). A work in progress: Behavior management strategies and a curriculum for intensive behavioral treatment of autism. New York, NY: Different Roads to Learning.

Taubman, M., Leaf, R., & McEachin, J. (2011). *Crafting connections: Contemporary applied behavior analysis for enriching the social lives of persons with autism spectrum disorder*. New York, NY: DRL Books.

Chapter Four
Research Supporting the use of
Behaviorally Based Social Skills Groups

Julia L. Ferguson

There is a relatively large body of research that supports the effectiveness of behaviorally based social skills groups to improve social behaviors for individuals diagnosed with autism spectrum disorder (ASD). The majority of this research has primarily been done investigating the effectiveness of social skills groups for individual participants (e.g., single-subject methodology, Matson et al., 2007), but more recently there have been studies which have looked at the effectiveness across a larger number of participants that is usually reported as an average gain (e.g., group designs, Laugeson et al., 2015; Leaf et al., 2016).

Given the research, behaviorally based social skills groups can now be considered an evidence-based practice according to several quality standards (i.e., Horner et al., 2005; National Autism Center, 2015). This chapter will be a brief overview of the existing literature on behaviorally based social skills groups as it applies to different populations, skills taught, teaching strategies, settings, length, duration, and the inclusion of parents or peers during social skills groups.

Populations

Behaviorally based social skills groups have been shown to be effective at increasing social behaviors, across a range of ages and cognitive functioning levels, of children diagnosed with ASD. Behaviorally based social skills groups have been implemented with individuals diagnosed with ASD as young as 3 years old (e.g., Leaf et al., 2010) and as old as 44 years old (e.g., Howlin & Yates, 1999). A large majority of the research on behaviorally based social skills groups has been conducted with young, school-age children (i.e., 6–11 years) and adolescents (i.e., 12–16 years) on the autism spectrum. Behaviorally based social skills groups have also been evaluated with individuals who have varying cognitive functioning levels along the autism spectrum. Research supports the effectiveness of social skills groups with individuals with IQ scores ranging from the average to superior range (i.e., 90–140) and in the low-average to borderline IQ levels (i.e., 65–89). Research on behaviorally based social skills groups supports the practice of grouping similar-age individuals with similar cognitive abilities together to create the social skills group. For example, Mackay and colleagues (2007) created two social skills groups based on the ages of the individuals seeking support from a behaviorally based social skills group. One group consisted of individuals diagnosed with ASD from ages 6–11 years and the other group consisted of individuals with ASD ages 12–16 years. Splitting individuals up by similar ages and cognitive abilities allows interventionists to have similar targets and curriculum across the individuals participating in the group.

Skills Taught

Within the research, there have been numerous social skills successfully taught to individuals diagnosed with ASD. Social skills taught through behaviorally based social skills groups range from prerequisite social behavior, such as joint attention, to more complex social behavior, such as developing and maintaining romantic relationships. The social skills taught within the research on social skills groups have been chosen from social curricula, interventionist observations, parent reports, and standardized assessments. Other factors researchers have used to determine which social skills to target are: ages of the individuals in the group, current level of social behaviors, frequency of challenging behaviors, and developmental norms for social behaviors. See Figure 1 for social skills commonly taught in the research on social skills groups separated by age. It should be noted this is not an exhaustive list of all the social skills that have been taught within the research on social skills groups. This research indicates that interventionists can teach a wide variety of social behaviors within the context of a social skills group.

Teaching Strategies

Within the research on behavior analytic based social skills groups, a variety of teaching strategies have been implemented. Social skills group researchers have used reinforcement, various prompting strategies, modeling, discrete trial teaching, shaping, role-play, and other behavior analytic approaches. These approaches have been used to decrease aberrant behavior and to increase prosocial behavior. The teaching strategies used in the research on social skills groups varies. For example, Leaf and colleagues

(2016) used the Cool vs. Not Cool™ procedure, shaping, discrete trial teaching, modeling, incidental teaching, reinforcement, flexible prompt fading, and the teaching interaction procedure to teach a variety of social behaviors. Laugeson and colleagues (2009, 2012, & 2015) use didactic lessons, role-play, modeling, performance feedback, and social discrimination training. Other teaching strategies that have been used in the research are a levels systems or behavioral charts (e.g., Cihon et al., 2019); self-management strategies (e.g., Coutugno, 2009); video modeling (e.g., Kroeger et al., 2007); and peer-mediated strategies (e.g., Banda et al., 2010). This research indicates that there is a broad range of effective behavioral strategies available for teaching social skills in a behaviorally based social skills group.

Figure 1. Skills to Consider

Age Level of Individuals	Social Skills Targeted	
Preschool age (3–5 years)	☐ Parallel play ☐ Taking turns ☐ Finding a partner ☐ Pretend play ☐ Imaginative play with a partner ☐ Showing appreciation ☐ Giving compliments ☐ Sharing ☐ Changing the game ☐ Making empathetic statements	☐ Interrupting appropriately ☐ Emotion recognition ☐ Appropriate greetings ☐ Cheering for friends ☐ Observational learning ☐ Conversation basics ☐ Joint attention ☐ Winning graciously ☐ Losing graciously ☐ Joining a group ☐ Social orientation
School age (6–11 years)	☐ Responding to greetings ☐ Initiating greetings ☐ Conversation skills ☐ Responding to offers to play ☐ Initiating others to play ☐ Joint attention ☐ Listening skills ☐ Perspective taking ☐ Compromise ☐ Cooperation ☐ Reading social cues	☐ Coping with bullying and teasing ☐ Social problem solving ☐ Keeping interactions going ☐ Giving and accepting compliments ☐ Sharing ☐ Taking turns ☐ Helping others ☐ Asking for help ☐ Emotion recognition and understanding ☐ Making and keeping friends

Adolescent (12–18 years)	☐ Conversational skills ☐ Electronic communication skills ☐ Choosing appropriate friends ☐ Good sportsmanship ☐ Handling teasing and bullying ☐ Handling disagreements ☐ Peer entry strategies ☐ Peer exit strategies ☐ Offering help	☐ Handling a bad reputation ☐ Handling rumors and gossip ☐ Perspective taking ☐ Conversation skills ☐ Eye contact ☐ Pleasant facial expressions ☐ Sharing ideas ☐ Complimenting others
Adult (18+ years)	☐ Identifying with others ☐ Identifying emotions ☐ Expressing emotions ☐ Conversational skills ☐ Assertiveness ☐ Problem solving ☐ Job interview skills ☐ Coping with stressful situations ☐ Developing and maintaining friendships	☐ Electronic communication skills ☐ Appropriate use of humor ☐ Organizing successful gatherings ☐ Handling teasing and bullying ☐ Conflict resolution ☐ Dating etiquette ☐ Showing romantic interest ☐ Asking someone on a date ☐ Handling rejection ☐ General dating guidelines

Settings

Behaviorally based social skills groups have also been found to be effective across multiple settings. The research supports behaviorally based social skills groups in school settings, clinic settings, afterschool programs, community-based programs, and hospital settings. Leaf and colleagues (2010) and Kamps and colleagues (1992) demonstrated the effectiveness of behaviorally based social skills groups in preschool and 1st grade classroom settings. Others have demonstrated the effectiveness of behaviorally based social skills groups in afterschool programs (e.g., Lavalle et al., 2005; MacKay et al., 2007). Many researchers have conducted behaviorally based social skills groups in behavior analytic clinical settings (e.g., Barry et al., 2003; Leaf et al., 2016). Other research on social skills groups has occurred in hospital settings (e.g., Howlin & Yates, 1999), university-based centers (e.g., Laugeson et al., 2009; Laugeson et al., 2012), and community-based programs (e.g., Weiss et al., 2013).

Length of Sessions & Number of Groups per Week

The research supporting social skills groups varies in terms of the length of each session and duration of the social skills group. Social skills groups within the research have ranged from sessions lasting from 20 minutes to 2.5 hours. The total duration of social groups within the research range from 8 sessions up to 16 months. Although the research on social skills groups varies in terms of session length and duration of the group, the majority of research supporting social skills group falls somewhere in the middle. Many research articles support group sessions lasting between 1 to 2 hours (e.g., Cotugno, 2009; Kroeger et al., 2007; Laugeson et al., 2009; Leaf et al., 2016; MacKay et al., 2007; Mathews et al., 2013). The average duration of social skills groups in the literature is between 12 and 16 weeks (e.g., Kroeger et al., 2007; Laugeson et al., 2009; Laugeson et al., 2012; Laugeson et al., 2015; Leaf at el., 2016; MacKay et al., 2007).

Parents and Peers

There are differing views among researchers on the role of parents and typically developing peers in social skills groups. Some researchers have not included parents or peers in the groups (e.g., Barry et al., 2003; Cotugno, 2009; Howlin & Yates, 1999; Laugeson et al., 2015; Leaf et al., 2016; MacKay et al., 2007; Rose & Anketell, 2009). Some researchers have used parents within the social skills group to help their children with social skills homework each week (e.g., Laugeson et al., 2009; Laugeson et al., 2012), while others have provided parent training on the principles of applied behavior analysis (e.g., Lavallee et al., 2005). Typically developing peers have been used as peer models in several social skills groups (e.g., Kamps et al., 1992; Kasari et al., 2015; Koenig et al., 2009; Kroeger et al., 2007; Lavallee et al., 2005; Leaf et al., 2010). Within the research, including peers or parents in social skills groups does not appear to significantly impact the effectiveness. The determination to involve peers or parents within a social skills group has depended on the resources available, the needs of the individuals in the group, and the skill levels of the individuals in the group.

Although the research on behaviorally based social skills groups varies (in terms of settings, the use of parents or peers, teaching strategies, population of individuals, and the length of sessions and groups), these social groups have all proven to be beneficial for the participants to increase social behavior and decrease aberrant behavior. The variations found in the literature prove that social skills groups are effective across a wide variety of populations on the autism spectrum, in a variety of settings, and using multiple behavior analytic procedures to teach social behaviors.

References

Banda, D. R., Hart, S. L., & Liu-Gitz, L. (2010). Impact of training peers and children with autism on social skills during center time activities in inclusive classrooms. *Research in Autism Spectrum Disorders, 4*(4), 619-625.

Barry, T. D., Klinger, L. G., Lee, J. M., Palardy, N., Gilmore, T., & Bodin, S. D. (2003). Examining the effectiveness of an outpatient clinic-based social skills group for high-functioning children with autism. *Journal of Autism and Developmental Disorders, 33*(6), 685-701.

Cihon, J. H., Ferguson, J. L., Leaf, J. B., Leaf, R., McEachin, J., & Taubman, M. (2019). Use of a level to improve synchronous engagement for children with autism spectrum disorder. *Behavior Analysis in Practice, 12,* 44-51.

Cotugno, A. J. (2009). Social competence and social skills training and intervention for children with autism spectrum disorders. *Journal of autism and developmental disorders, 39*(9), 1268-1277.

Horner, R. H., Carr, E. G., Halle, J., McGee, G., Odom, S., & Wolery, M. (2005). The use of single-subject research to identify evidence-based practice in special education. *Exceptional children, 71*(2), 165-179.

Howlin, P., & Yates, P. (1999). The potential effectiveness of social skills groups for adults with autism. *Autism, 3*(3), 299-307.

Kamps, D. M., Leonard, B. R., Vernon, S., Dugan, E. P., Delquadri, J. C., Gershon, B., Wade, L., & Folk, L. (1992). Teaching social skills to students with autism to increase peer interactions in an integrated first‑grade classroom. *Journal of Applied Behavior Analysis, 25*(2), 281-288.

Koenig, K., De Los Reyes, A., Cicchetti, D., Scahill, L., & Klin, A. (2009). Group intervention to promote social skills in school-age children with pervasive developmental disorders: Reconsidering efficacy. *Journal of Autism and Developmental Disorders, 39*(8), 1163–1172.

Kroeger, K. A., Schultz, J. R., & Newsom, C. (2007). A comparison of two group-delivered social skills programs for young children with autism. *Journal of autism and developmental disorders, 37*(5), 808-817.

Laugeson, E. A., Frankel, F., Gantman, A., Dillon, A. R., & Mogil, C. (2012). Evidence-based social skills training for adolescents with autism spectrum disorders: The UCLA PEERS program. *Journal of autism and developmental disorders, 42*(6), 1025-1036.

Laugeson, E. A., Frankel, F., Mogil, C., & Dillon, A. R. (2009). Parent-assisted social skills training to improve friendships in teens with autism spectrum disorders. *Journal of autism and developmental disorders, 39*(4), 596-606.

Laugeson, E. A., Gantman, A., Kapp, S. K., Orenski, K., & Ellingsen, R. (2015). A randomized controlled trial to improve social skills in young adults with autism spectrum disorder: The UCLA PEERS® program. *Journal of autism and developmental disorders, 45*(12), 3978-3989.

Lavallee, K. L., Bierman, K. L., Nix, R. L., & Conduct Problems Prevention Research Group. (2005). The impact of first-grade "friendship group" experiences on child social outcomes in the Fast Track program. *Journal of Abnormal Child Psychology, 33*(3), 307-324.

Leaf, J.B., Dotson, W. H., Oppenheim, M. L., Sheldon, J.B., & Sherman, J.A. (2010). The effectiveness of a group teaching interaction procedure for teaching social skills to young children with a pervasive developmental disorder. *Research in Autism Spectrum Disorders, 4,* 186-198.

Leaf, J. B., Leaf, J. A., Milne, C., Taubman, M., Oppenheim-Leaf, M., Torres, N., Townley-Cochran, D., Leaf, R., McEachin, J., & Yoder, P. (2016). An evaluation of a behaviorally based social skills group for individuals diagnosed with autism spectrum disorder. *Journal of autism and developmental disorders, 47*(2), 243-259.

MacKay, T., Knott, F., & Dunlop, A. W. (2007). Developing social interaction and understanding in individuals with autism spectrum disorder: A groupwork intervention. *Journal of Intellectual and Developmental Disability, 32*(4), 279-290.

Mathews, T. L., Erkfritz-Gay, K. N., Knight, J., Lancaster, B. M., & Kupzyk, K. A. (2013). The effects of social skills training on children with autism spectrum disorders and disruptive behavior disorders. *Children's Health Care, 42*, 311-332.

Matson, J. L., Matson, M. L., & Rivet, T. T. (2007). Social-skills treatments for children with autism spectrum disorders: An overview. *Behavior Modification, 31*(5), 682-707.

National Autism Center. (2015). *Evidence-based practice and autism in the schools* (2nd ed.). Randolph, MA: Author.

Rose, R., & Anketell, C. (2009). The benefits of social skills groups for young people with autism spectrum disorder: A pilot study. *Child care in practice, 15*(2), 127-144.

Weiss, J. A., Viecili, M. A., Sloman, L., & Lunsky, Y. (2013). Direct and indirect psychosocial outcomes for children with autism spectrum disorder and their parents following a parent-involved social skills group intervention. *Journal of the Canadian Academy of Child and Adolescent Psychiatry, 22*(4), 303.

Chapter Five
The Penguin Study

Justin B. Leaf, Jeremy A. Leaf., Christine M. Milne, Norma Torres, and Donna Townley-Cochran

For years, we have been running behaviorally based social skills groups at Autism Partnership and have seen tremendous clinical success. These social skills groups, and their results, have been informally replicated within our international offices and outside agencies (e.g., in university and school programs). We have shown that the specific teaching procedures implemented in our social skills groups were highly effective by conducting controlled research studies (Leaf et al., 2009, 2010, 2013, 2015).

Despite our work demonstrating the effectiveness of social skills groups, some professionals claimed there were still areas that needed to be addressed in the research (e.g., generalization, maintenance, blind evaluators; Rao et al., 2008; Reichow & Volkmar, 2010). We decided to address some of these areas by conducting a study evaluating the effects of a behaviorally based social skills group (i.e., Leaf et al., 2016). To fund this study, we were fortunate to receive a grant from the Organization for Autism Research (OAR). The purpose of the study was to use a randomized control trial to evaluate if the implementation of a behaviorally based social skills group would improve the social behavior of 14 children who were diagnosed with autism spectrum disorder (ASD).

This behaviorally based social skills group was aimed toward individuals with higher levels of communication and language skills who displayed lower levels of aberrant behavior. Due to limited time and resources, we created a homogenous group of learners that displayed similar behaviors, language, and social levels. The inclusion criteria were: 1) participants between the ages of 4 and 7 years and independently diagnosed with ASD; 2) participants could not have ever received services from Autism Partnership; 3) participants had to display low levels of stereotypic behaviors and other aberrant behaviors (e.g., aggression, property destruction, self-injurious behavior); 4) participants had to have age-appropriate expressive language and receptive language based upon standardized assessments (i.e., a score of in the average range); 5) participants had to have an IQ score of 80 or above; 6) participants had to demonstrate deficits in social behaviors as measured on the Social Responsiveness Scale (SRS; Costantino & Gruber, 2005) and Social Skills Improvement Scale (SSiS; Gresham & Elliott, 2008).

Once we received the OAR grant, we sent out recruitment fliers and notices through social media, local pediatricians, and local diagnosticians. As families reached out to indicate interest, we conducted formal interviews. We preferred to conduct interviews at our office, but we were willing to travel to parents' homes if needed. The interviews always included the lead researcher and another member of the research team. One researcher worked and played with the child to assess appropriateness for the group (e.g., limited aberrant behaviors, speaking in full sentences, answering open-ended questions), while the other researcher asked the parents questions about their child and described the study. The interview lasted 20 minutes, at which point the researchers informed the parents if their child qualified for the group. If the parents did not have testing information, the researchers had a blind evaluator conduct these assessments prior to determining qualification for the study. If the child did not qualify, the researchers informed the parents of alternative services that could be accessed. If the child qualified for the group, the researcher discussed informed consent and answered any of the parents' questions. Once the parents signed the consent form, the researcher informed them if their child would be in the first treatment group or the waitlist group (e.g., a group that received treatment at a later point in time). Group assignment was randomly determined prior to the interview.

Eight children participated in the treatment group (group A) and seven children were assigned to the waitlist control group (group B), for a total of 15 children who participated in the study. The average age of the participants in group A was 4 years and 7 months and the average age of the participants in group B was 4 years and 10 months. No significant differences were found between the groups prior to intervention in terms of IQ scores, Vineland Adaptive Behavior Composite scores (Sparrow et al., 2016), standard scores on the Peabody Picture Vocabulary Test (Dunn & Dunn, 2007), or standard score on the Expressive One Word Vocabulary Picture Vocabulary Test (Martin & Brownell, 2011).

Three interventionists were in charge of running the social skills group each session. Jeremy and Christine were the lead interventionists for groups A and B. At the time of the study, Jeremy and Christine each had 5 years of experience implementing behavior analytic intervention for individuals diagnosed with ASD, all of which occurred at Autism Partnership, and they each had previous experience running behaviorally based social skills groups. Donna was the third interventionist for group A and Norma was the third interventionist for group B. Donna had 5 years of experience implementing behavior analytic intervention for individuals diagnosed with ASD and did not have any experience with behaviorally based social skills groups. Norma had 3 years of experience implementing behavior analytic intervention for individuals diagnosed with ASD and did not have any experience with behaviorally based social skills groups.

There were four main measures used to evaluate the effectiveness of the behaviorally based social skills group. The first was the SSiS, which is an assessment where raters score specific social behaviors of each participant. The second measure was the SRS, which is an assessment where raters score specific social behaviors related to a diagnosis of ASD for each participant. The third measure was the Walker McConnell Scale of Social Competence (WM; Walker & McConnell, 1988) which is an assessment where raters score specific social skills and school readiness behaviors for each participant. These assessments provided standard scores for each participant. The final assessment was the Aberrant Behavior Checklist (ABC; Aman & Singh, 1986) where raters score how frequently the participant engaged in different aberrant behaviors. Each assessment was filled out by the lead researcher, the two lead social skills group interventionists, and a blind evaluator who did not know to which condition the participants were assigned. The raters filled out these assessments based on the participants' behavior during observation periods (described below) and based on the participants' behavior during observations in their natural environments (e.g., school, home, or community) while interacting with non-study peers.

There were four observation times throughout the study, during which the evaluators filled out the assessments based on the participants' behaviors during observation sessions and in the natural environment. Figure 2 provides a flow chart displaying the sequence of time periods that occurred in the study. The first observation period (T1) was prior to intervention for group A and group B. The second observation period (T2) occurred 17 weeks later; at this time intervention for group A had just concluded and intervention for group B had not yet begun. The third observation period (T3) occurred 17 weeks after the T2 observation period; at this time group A was in short-term maintenance and intervention for group B had just concluded. The fourth observation period (T4) occurred 17 weeks after T3; at this time group A was in long-term maintenance and group B was in short-term maintenance.

Each of the observation periods consisted of observations of each of the participants in their natural environment and during predetermined observation sessions. Each treatment group received two observational sessions per period of time. So, groups A and B received two observation sessions during T1, two observation sessions during T2, two observation sessions during T3, and two observation sessions during T4. When the observations were finished, each group had participated in a total of eight observation sessions, with each observational session lasting two hours, for a total of four hours of observation per assessment.

Observation sessions at the clinic were designed to simulate a play group. During this period of time, the interventionists could: provide instructions, but not provide any prompts; prime the participants for expectations during activities; reinforce appropriate behaviors; or provide corrective feedback for inappropriate behaviors. The interventionists were only allowed to stop or redirect behavior that put the participants or their peers in immediate harm (i.e., aggression or elopement). The purpose of the observation sessions was to assess the social skill strengths of each participant, the social skill deficits of each participant, and to complete the assessments mentioned previously. The general format of each observation session consisted of: (a) unstructured free play, (b) opening circle time, (c) structured games, (d) large group instruction, (e) outdoor structured games, (f) outdoor unstructured games, (g) large group instruction, (h) unstructured free play, and (i) dismissal.

Figure 2. Flow Chart of Penguin Study

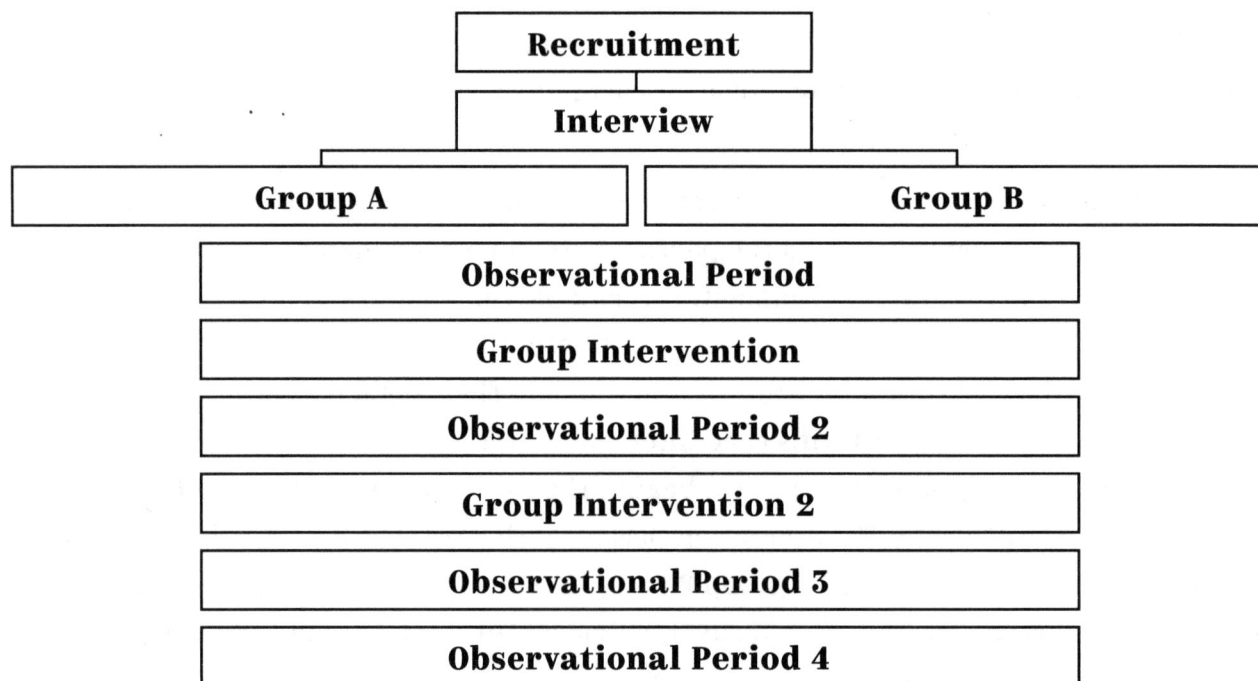

The study began with observation period T1. The blind evaluator, lead researcher, and social skills group interventionists made observations in each participant's natural environment (e.g., school and community). This was followed by two observational sessions for members of group A and two observational sessions for members of group B.

There is no easy way to describe what occurred during these initial sessions. It was chaos! We have compared it to the "Royal Rumble," a wrestling match where 30 wrestlers could be in the ring at one time. During these initial sessions, some participants were crying and wanted to leave, some were running around the room, and some refused to answer any questions. These participants were clearly not engaging in appropriate behaviors in this novel learning environment and likely had been engaging in these behaviors regularly prior to these observations. The participants were not under instructional control and the social skills group interventionists could not use the tools they were accustomed to using (e.g., prompting, reinforcement, corrective feedback, systematic teaching). These sessions were exhausting for the interventionists.

The observational sessions and evaluations in the participants' natural environments provided us with the ability to score the necessary assessments and gather information about each participant's social skill strengths and weaknesses. Participants, on average across both groups, scored in the 1st percentile on the SSiS, fell in the moderate range of social deficits on the SRS, scored in the 2nd percentile in social and school readiness behaviors on the WM, and displayed high levels of aberrant behavior based on the ABC. These scores indicated that the participants in the study had severe deficits in social behavior when compared to same-age peers. The results of these initial assessments confirmed that these participants needed intervention to improve their social behaviors.

After all observation sessions and evaluations in the natural environment were completed, participants in group B went back to their normal lives (e.g., school, whatever services they may have been receiving, time at home) for approximately 17 weeks and intervention began for participants in group A. The researcher provided clear instructions to the social skills group interventionists that they should teach the skills they thought were most important for the participants in the group, using the procedures they felt were best. The purpose of this instruction and format was so the behaviorally based social skills group resembled our clinical model as closely as possible. We wanted our talented interventionists to use their clinical judgment as opposed to following a strict protocol. The only interventions used during the social skills group were evidence-based procedures that were conceptually systematic with the principles of applied behavior analysis. Throughout the group, the interventionists implemented the Autism Partnership Method. The social skills group interventionists had a game plan for what skills to teach and how to teach the social skills every session, but could change their plans based on their clinical judgment. A goal for teaching was to minimize downtime so participants were constantly receiving direct or indirect instructions for a multitude of skills to maximize gains.

Each group met for a total of 32 sessions. Sessions occurred two times per week and were two hours long. Although the daily schedule of the sessions changed based on the needs of the participants, there was a general structure followed. The group usually started with a free play period, where there were two to three different free play centers available (e.g., dramatic play, game play, blocks). During this period, the interventionists typically did not provide direct instruction, but used shaping, prompting, and incidental teaching to help develop basic social skills (e.g., cooperative play, turn taking, joining in). This time was also used as an unofficial probe to identify what skills were learned and what skills still needed to be taught.

After the free-play period, the interventionists ran an opening group instructional circle time. The interventionists implemented a variety of teaching procedures during this time including shaping, group discrete trial teaching, the Cool versus Not Cool™ procedure, and the teaching interaction procedure. It was during the opening circle that the interventionists worked directly on basic social behaviors (e.g., joint attention, observational learning, auditory attending). Following the opening circle, the interventionists typically ran "Fun Games with Penguins," which was a time for the participants to play a variety of group games (e.g., fruit salad game, sleeping game). All games included embedded instructions and were an opportunity to work on shared excitement, cooperation, and other social behaviors. "Fun Games with Penguins" was usually followed by another large group instructional time, when the interventionists implemented the Cool versus Not Cool™ procedure or the teaching interaction procedure to teach the games that were just played or to work on other social behaviors (e.g. making friends, changing the game when someone is bored).

After this group instructional period, the interventionists took the participants outside to a park. The participants' time outside usually started with the interventionists implementing teaching procedures to increase appropriate participation in a variety of structured outdoor games (e.g., What Time is it Mr. Wolf?, Red Light Green Light, Freeze Tag). Following structured teaching, the participants were provided an opportunity to play on an outdoor play structure during which the interventionists used shaping, prompting, and incidental teaching to ensure the participants played with each other, engaged in sustained play, and followed their peers around the playground.

After outdoor time, the interventionists typically implemented another large group instruction period or split up the participants into smaller groups during which the interventionists implemented the teaching interaction procedure and/or the Cool versus Not Cool™ procedure to teach more advanced social skills (e.g., making friends, keeping friends, reading social cues). Finally, there was a closing group instructional circle time during which the interventionists said goodbye to the participants. If participants were on the top of the level system, they could cash in for a prize from the treasure box.

Since it was a behaviorally based social skills group, contingency systems were essential. The main contingency system in place was a superkid chart (i.e., level system, see Figure 3 for an example). The superkid chart consisted of five different levels. The bottom level was "miss a fun activity," followed by "warning," "ok," "awesome," and the top level, "superkid." Each session, the participants started on the "ok" level and the interventionists moved them up or down the chart, contingent upon their behavior during the social skills group.

There were no set criteria for moving up or down, instead, the interventionists used clinical judgment to determine when to move a participant up or down. In general, movement up occurred for appropriate social behavior, refraining from disruptive behavior, and responding correctly. Movement down occurred for not engaging in appropriate behavior or displaying inappropriate behavior. At the end of the day, if a participant was on "superkid," they got to take a small toy (e.g., a toy car) from a treasure chest home. Although the participants only received a little toy, getting to the treasure chest was a major accomplishment and the participants yearned to achieve this accomplishment. If at any point a participant moved down to "miss a fun activity," the interventionists had the participant sit out during a fun activity.

Figure 3. Picture of Level System

The second system in place was one where the participants took turns receiving a preferred item, regardless of their behavior. Each week one participant was chosen to take home a small stuffed animal (i.e., a penguin named "Puck"), a journal to write about what they did with Puck, and was encouraged to take pictures with Puck throughout the week. This was used as a way for participants to share stories about their lives with their peers, which allowed for more frequent and better conversations throughout the group.

In the initial stages of the group, some participants required an individual token system. For these participants, an interventionist provided the participants with a token for correct responding throughout each session. Once a participant earned all of the tokens, they raised their hand to inform the lead interventionist. The lead interventionist would then move them up on the superkid chart and allow the participant to have a break in a small area that included imaginative play toys (e.g., kitchen, pretend food, cars, Toy Story items) for no longer than five minutes. The interventionists faded this system as quickly as possible so that the only reinforcement system in place for all participants was the superkid chart.

Like the teaching procedures used in the structure of the group, the social skills group interventionists had flexibility in what to teach. They determined what to teach the participants based on many factors, including parents' responses on formal assessments, Autism Partnership curriculum books (e.g., Work in Progress, Leaf & McEachin, 1999; Crafting Connections, Taubman et al., 2011), other social skills curriculum books (e.g. Boys Town Curriculum; Dowd et al., 1994), and direct observations of the participants in social situations. Figure 4 lists a sampling of the skills taught to group A participants, which is by no means exhaustive.

Figure 4. Table of Skills Taught to Group A for Penguin Study

Skills and Games Taught to Group A

Behavioral Control	Mouse Trap	Asking for Help	Waiting
Frustration Tolerance	Sleeping Game	Joining In	Sitting
Recall	Duck-Duck Goose	Walking in a Line	Inferences
Contingencies	Positive Affect	Talking to a Friend	Joint Attention
Attending	Learning from Feedback	Responding	Starting a Conversation
Observational Learning	Flexibility	Being Silly	Conversation Rollers
Conditional Instructions	Delayed Instructions	Sportsmanship	Ending a Conversation
Receptive Instructions	General Knowledge	Losing Graciously	Turn Taking
Figuring it Out	Pop Culture Knowledge	Trying	Proximity
Fruit Salad	Playing with a Friend	Friendship Development	Environmental Awareness

After 32 sessions for group A, the T2 observations were conducted (i.e., school observations for each participant and two group observational sessions for group A and group B with no prompting, priming, reinforcement, or feedback). For participants in group A, a clear difference in their social engagement and aberrant behavior was observed. For participants in group B, these observations were once again very chaotic.

After the T2 observations, the participants in group A resumed their normal everyday activities but no longer attended the social skills group; intervention then began for the participants in group B. The social skills group for group B was 32 sessions long and lasted approximately 17 weeks. The intervention was designed similarly with respect to structure, teaching procedures, and curriculum. After the 32 sessions for participants in group B, the T3 observations were conducted. This time, participants in group B demonstrated clear improvements in their social engagement and decreases in aberrant behaviors and the participants in group A maintained their improvements. At this point, all participants took a break for 16 weeks until the T4 observations were conducted.

During T4, final observations in the participants' natural environments and final group observation sessions were conducted. Results from the T4 observations indicated that all participants in both groups maintained the social improvements and decreases in aberrant behavior.

We analyzed how the superkid chart was used across both groups. For groups A and B, the average amount of times the interventionists moved one or more participants up the chart within a session was 48 and 41, respectively. At any given moment, a single participant could be moved up, a few participants could be moved up, or all of the participants could be moved up simultaneously. On average, the interventionists moved one or more participants down the chart 10 times per session.

We also evaluated the number of target behaviors taught across the two groups. Within 32 sessions (64 hours of teaching), over 90 social behaviors were targeted for at least one of the participants. Our main measure, however, was evaluating any statistically significant improvements in social behaviors as measured on the formal assessment instruments. When we evaluated the data, there was no significant difference between the groups prior to the social skills group (T1), indicating that the two groups were evenly matched. Once group A received the social skills group and group B had not (T2), there was a statistically significant difference between the two. Thus, the social skills group was effective. Once group B received the social skills group (T3), there was no statistically significant difference between the two groups, as both groups were now demonstrating a similar degree of improvement. Also, the groups remained the same in the following weeks without the social skills group (T4), demonstrating the maintenance of the skills acquired in the social skills group. These findings demonstrate that the social skills group was effective at improving the social behaviors of the 15 children that participated and, we believe, improving their overall quality of life.

We also wanted to ensure the parents were satisfied with the social skills group and the results. To do this, we sent surveys to be filled out anonymously. The survey consisted of 13 questions asking parents to rate various aspects of the social skills group using a 7-point scale. The scale ranged from dissatisfied or great decline (a rating of 1) to very satisfied or great improvement (a rating of 7). We found, on average, the parents across both groups were satisfied with most areas of the social skills group and they were very happy with their child's outcomes. These sentiments were also reflected in an open-ended section of the survey:

☐ "We have loved being part of this study. Very impressed with the quality of teachers and instructions."

☐ "He has most definitely made huge leaps and gains in his social awareness and standing amongst his peers, especially the typical ones."

- "He has made significant strides, but he still has a little way to go and again many of those strides were because of you guys and for that we thank you!!!"
- "We have seen a BIG difference thanks to you and the THERAPISTS."

Overall, the results of this study showed that Autism Partnership Method's approach to behaviorally based social skills groups can be highly effective for improving social behaviors. Our analysis also showed that the procedures we used were effective in improving specific social behaviors. Based on our clinical and research experience with this study, we felt it would be beneficial to provide professionals and parents with information and guidelines on Autism Partnership Method's approach to social skills groups so this model can be replicated in clinical practice. We hope that if enough professionals and parents implement this method, more children diagnosed with ASD will make similar improvements in social behaviors and, in doing so, improve their overall quality of life.

References

Aman, M. G., & Singh, N. N. (1986). *Aberrant Behavior Checklist Manual*. East Aurora, NY: Slosson Publications.

Costantino, J. N., & Gruber, C. P. (2005). *Social Responsiveness Scale (SRS)*. Los Angeles, CA: Western Psychological Services.

Dowd, T., Czyz, J. D., O'Kane, S. E., & Elfson, A. (1994). Effective skills for child-care workers: A training manual for Boys Town. Boys Town, NE: Boys Town Press.

Dunn, L. M., & Dunn, D. M. (2007). *Peabody picture vocabulary test* (4th ed). Minneapolis, MN: NCS Pearson, Inc.

Gresham, F. M., & Elliott, S. N. (2008). *Social skills improvement system: Rating scales manual*. Minneapolis, MN: Pearson Assessments.

Leaf, J.B., Dotson, W. H., Oppenheim, M. L., Sheldon, J.B., & Sherman, J.A. (2010). The effectiveness of a group teaching interaction procedure for teaching social skills to young children with a pervasive developmental disorder. *Research in Autism Spectrum Disorders, 4*, 186-198.

Leaf, J. B., Leaf, J. A., Milne, C., Taubman, M., Oppenheim-Leaf, M., Torres, N., Townley-Cochran, D., Leaf, R., McEachin, J., & Yoder, P. (2016). An evaluation of a behaviorally based social skills group for individuals diagnosed with autism spectrum disorder. *Journal of autism and developmental disorders, 47*(2), 243-259.

Leaf, R. B., & McEachin, J. J. (1999). A work in progress: Behavior management strategies and a curriculum for intensive behavioral treatment of autism. New York, NY: Different Roads to Learning.

Leaf, J.B., Taubman, M., Bloomfield, S., Palos-Rafuse, L., Leaf, R., McEachin, J. & Oppenheim, M. L. (2009). Increasing social skills and pro-social behavior for three children diagnosed with autism through the use of a teaching package. *Research in Autism Spectrum Disorders, 3*, 275-289.

Leaf, J. B., Taubman, M., Leaf, J., Dale, S., Tsuji, K., Kassardjian, A., Alcalay, A., Milne, C., Mitchell, E., Townley-Cochran, D., Leaf, R., & McEachin, J. (2015). Teaching social interaction skills using cool versus not cool. *Child & Family Behavior Therapy, 37*, 321-334.

Leaf, J. B., Tsuji, K. H., Lentell, A. E., Dale, S. E., Kassardjian, A., Taubman, M., McEachin, J., Leaf, R., & Oppenheim-Leaf, M. L. (2013). A comparison of discrete trial teaching implemented in a one-to-one instructional format and in a group instructional format. *Behavioral Interventions, 28*, 82-106.

Martin, N., & Brownell, R. (2011). *Expressive one word picture vocabulary test*. Novato, CA: Academic Therapy Publications, Inc.

Rao, P. A., Beidel, D. C., & Murray, M. J. (2008). Social skills interventions for children with aspergers syndrome or high functioning autism: A review and recommendations. *Journal of Autism and Developmental Disorders, 38*, 353-361.

Reichow, B., & Volkmar, F. R. (2010). Social skills interventions for individuals with autism. Evaluation for evidence-based practices within a best evidence synthesis framework. *Journal of Autism and Developmental Disorders, 40*, 149-166.

Sparrow, S. S., Cicchetti, D. V., & Saulnier, C. A. (2016). *Vineland adaptive behavior scales* (3rd ed). Bloomington, MN: NCS Pearson, Inc.

Taubman, M., Leaf, R., & McEachin, J. (2011). *Crafting connections: Contemporary applied behavior analysis for enriching the social lives of persons with autism spectrum disorder*. New York, NY: DRL Books.

Walker, H. M., & McConnell, S. R. (1988). *Walker-McConnell Scale of Social Competence and School Adjustment: A social skills rating scale for teachers*. Austin, TX: Pro-Ed

Part Two

Running Behaviorally Based Social Skills Groups

Chapter Six
Group Composition

One of the most important aspects of a successful social skills group is the selection of the learners to participate in the group. In our experience, to have the most successful social skills group, the correct combination of learners is key. We understand there are variables that may limit the interventionist's selection of learners. For example, in some school settings, the members of a social skills groups may be determined by which students have it written in their Individualized Education Plan (IEP). Nonetheless, interventionists should strive to construct a social skills group that will be beneficial for all who participate.

We believe social skills groups can be beneficial for a wide variety of learners diagnosed with autism spectrum disorder (ASD). Within our model, we have conducted social skills groups for learners as young as 18 months to adults; for learners with little or no expressive language and those who have fluent language; for learners who display moderate rates of aberrant behavior (e.g., aggression, self-injurious behavior, self-stimulatory behaviors) and for those who have little to no aberrant behavior.

Having learners participate in social skills groups is an important component of the Autism Partnership Method—we make every effort to find a group for a learner when they are ready, and if no suitable group exists, one is often created to fill that need. However, there are behavioral repertoires that may prevent a learner from benefiting from a social skills group. Typically, these include serious aggression, self-injurious behavior, or severe deficits in learning-how-to-learn skills (e.g., paying attention, learning from feedback, being able to sit independently). Once these behaviors are mitigated (the learner is not a danger to self or others and demonstrates enough learning-how-to-learn skills in an individualized setting that it's likely they can learn in a group setting), then the learner may be a candidate for a social skills group. Below is a list of considerations for selecting learners diagnosed with ASD to participate in a social skills group. Although these considerations are discussed in more detail later, our purpose here is to provide interventionists with a form (see Figure 5) that can assist them to create appropriate social skills groups for their clients.

Group Considerations

Heterogeneous or Homogeneous Groups

One of the first considerations an interventionist must take into account is to create a heterogeneous or homogeneous social skills group. A heterogeneous group typically consists of learners who display different levels of communication skills, different rates and topographies of aberrant behavior, and different social skills deficits. For example, within a group, a few learners may have an expressive vocabulary of 50 words, while other learners may have communication skills typical for their age. In other cases, some learners in the group may display high rates of self-stimulatory behaviors while others do not. Within a heterogeneous social skills group, some learners may be learning how to label peers within the group, while others are working on friendship skills and learning what constitutes a friend.

The opposite of a heterogeneous group is a homogeneous group. Within a homogenous social skills group, the learners' skill levels are roughly the same. Learners in a homogeneous group are usually similar with respect to their language skills, rates of aberrant behavior, and share common social deficits as well as target skills. Of course, there will be some individual differences (e.g., some learners working on what constitutes a friendship while others working on discriminating a friend from an acquaintance), but these differences are minimal and would not result in major changes to the group's goals.

Figure 5. Social Skills Group Consideration Form

Domain	Ideal Learners	Potential Learner
Name		
Age		
Receptive Language Determined by _____		

Expressive Language Determined by _____		
Language Observed		
Social Behavior Determined by _____		
Social Behavior Observed		
Cognitive Functioning Determined by _____		
Adaptive Behavior Determined by _____		
Adaptive Behavior Observed		
Aberrant Behavior Determined by _____		
Aberrant Behavior Observed		
Other Notes		

In the early days of the Autism Partnership Method, our social skills groups were commonly heterogeneous. It was not uncommon to see learners with different language skills, different social needs, and various frequencies and topographies of aberrant behaviors in the same group. One of our earliest social skills groups was comprised of one learner who engaged in aggression toward adults, another who would flop to the floor whenever an instruction was provided, six learners who were considered to be higher functioning, and one who was from another country and spoke roughly 10 English words. This is what we still commonly see in our social skills groups and groups implemented elsewhere. However, over time, our model has evolved. We no longer run social skills groups with a heterogeneous composition; rather, our groups have a homogeneous makeup. Following are several rationales for using homogeneous social skills groups and recommendations for these groups.

Social Skills Strengths and Deficits

When learners have different social strengths and deficits, it is very difficult to find appropriate programming that would be relevant to every member of the group. The content or level of complexity required by one learner might be completely different from what is needed by other learners. When groups are heterogeneous, programming can only be targeted toward some group members at one time, which makes the activities less beneficial for the other learners. Heterogeneous group composition may also require more staff to ensure that each learner gets the support that they need.

In our experience, learners who are around similar peers (i.e., a homogeneous group) are more likely to develop meaningful relationships and friendships with the participants in the group. Ultimately, it is not easy to run a heterogeneous social skills group and many interventionists are not adequately trained or prepared to run this type of group. There are rare exceptions when one learner may be placed in a group who may not match the skill set of the group (e.g., more or fewer skills/deficits than the group). However, this learner will usually have their own support staff and may be working on a specific skill separately from the other participants. Although the learner may be proximal to the others, they are not truly engaged in group learning. Usually, the learner is pushed into the group for certain activities to address a specific skill, then pulled out of the group when it is not beneficial for the learner or the group. Therefore, one key component of Autism Partnership Method's approach to behaviorally based social skills groups is to construct the group with a homogenous population of learners.

Age

Frequently, we have observed social skills groups of predominantly 6-year-olds and one or two 13-year-olds. When we ask why the 13-year-old is in this group, we hear responses like, "His mental age is similar to the other group members," "He acts as a helper to these children," or "He likes being around children of this age." Whatever the answer, the simple truth is, it is inappropriate. For one, the targeted skills should be drastically different based upon age. Consider the skills required for play. The skills necessary for a 6-year-old to engage in appropriate play (e.g., duck-duck-goose, tee-ball, or child video games) are very different than the skills a 13-year-old would need (e.g., football, card games, or advanced board games). Pop culture and topics of interest are also different dependent upon chronological age (e.g., girls have "cooties" versus wanting a girlfriend). Finally, being in a group with varying ages could stigmatize learners in the group and may turn people away from using or seeking applied behavior analytic interventions, as it feeds into some negative stereotypes (e.g., it is seen as unnatural).

In general, we recommend the following age ranges for groups:

- ☐ 2 years old
- ☐ 3 to 4 years old
- ☐ 4 to 7 years old
- ☐ 7 to 10 years old
- ☐ 10 to 13 years old
- ☐ 14 to 16 years old
- ☐ 16 to 18 years old

Language/Communication Skills

When constructing a social skills group, interventionists should pay careful attention to the expressive and receptive language of each learner. Ideally, the group would comprise learners who have similar expressive and receptive language skills. If learners have limited receptive language, they may not be best paired with learners who have strong receptive language. For instance, when using a teaching strategy which has prerequisite skills of comprehending and responding to receptive language (e.g., the teaching interaction procedure), learners who do not have the prerequisite receptive language skills might not learn from the teaching strategy. It is important to implement the most effective procedures given the language and communication skillset of the group.

The same is true when evaluating learners' expressive language. If some learners have limited expressive language while others are able to have complex conversations, it may be difficult to arrange a context for all participants to have appropriate learning opportunities. For example, if one targeted social skill is changing the conversation when someone is bored, it might be difficult to have learners engage in a conversation when one learner has very little expressive language. Conversely, if the learners have similar expressive language skills, the curriculum can be beneficial for all learners.

There are several ways to evaluate language skills when determining group participation. A common, objective approach involves conducting formal assessments. For example, the Peabody Picture Vocabulary Test (Dunn & Dunn, 2007) and Expressive One-Word Picture Vocabulary Test (Martin & Brownell, 2011) can be used to help identify learners with similar receptive or expressive language scores (each of these assessments are described in further detail in Chapter 17). Formal observation of the learners and interviews with caregivers (described below) are approaches that provide the opportunity to evaluate a learner's language and obtain the caregiver's report of the learner's language skills. Finally, trial periods (described below) in which the learner participates in a current group provides the opportunity to observe language and other skills to determine their appropriateness for the group.

Cognitive Levels

Similar to evaluating learners' language skills, it is also important to evaluate learners' cognitive skills. Ideally, learners in a group are similar with respect to cognitive skills because it will determine what procedures an interventionist implements, the pace of instruction, and the skills targeted. For example, if the interventionist is implementing the teaching interaction procedure, learners with severe cognitive deficits are less likely to benefit. Additionally, teaching abstract social concepts (e.g., theory of mind) to learners with more cognitive deficits might be more difficult given the complexity of the skills.

As with the other skills, cognitive levels can also be assessed during interviews and trial periods. There are several standardized ways to evaluate cognitive skills when determining group participation. Similar to assessing language skills, formal intelligence quotient (IQ) tests can be used. IQ assessments such as the Wechsler Preschool and Primary Scale of Intelligence, Wechsler Intelligence Scale for Children, Mullen Scales of Early Learning, and Stanford-Binet Intelligence Scales are commonly used. Each has been standardized across ages and provides interventionists with full-scale IQ scores. Historically, we have used IQ scores as one factor when determining group placement. In our social skills groups, we have three general groupings based on IQ: 80 or higher, 50–79, and 49 or lower. It is important to note that these are guidelines and not rules, and many variables should be considered when selecting individuals to participate in a social skills group.

Social Deficits

Another consideration in determining appropriate group composition is ensuring that learners participating in the group demonstrate similar or complementary social skill deficits. Similar or complementary social skill deficits allow interventionists to ensure that learners are working on similar goals. Time spent in the social skills group is not going to be beneficial for all learners if some learners are working on early social skills (e.g., joining in, turn taking, sharing) while others are working on more advanced skills (e.g., responding to teasing, keeping secrets, social inferences). Although interventionists can divide learners into smaller groups, it is usually more beneficial for learners to be placed in a group with similar social skill needs.

We have incorporated three methods to evaluate social behavior to determine group placement. The first is to conduct formal social skills assessments such as the Social Skills Improvement System (SSiS; Gresham & Elliot, 1990) and Social Responsiveness Scale (SRS; Costantino & Gruber, 2005), both of which are described in further detail in Chapter 17. Typically, we have administered the SSiS and SRS in conjunction prior to starting a social skills group. Structured interviews are another method to obtain a caregiver's perspective on which social skills deficits are most prevalent and which skills should be prioritized. Perhaps the most informative method is direct observations to evaluate a learner's current social strengths and weaknesses in an environment where they have opportunities to engage socially.

Group Focus

It is also important to consider the overall purpose of the social skills group. What skills are going to be taught? What are the priority skills? What are the learner's current social skills, and where do you hope the learner will be in 10 weeks, 30 weeks, and one year from now? Considering these questions prior to starting the social skills group is critical. One option is for interventionists to run a traditional social skills group where the learners are primarily working on social behaviors (e.g., friendship development, theory of mind, turn taking, greetings). Another option would be a social skills group that targets learning-how-to-learn skills (e.g., sitting, waiting, developing reinforcers, attending, observational learning), as these are prerequisites to more advanced social behaviors. As the learners develop learning-how-to-learn behaviors, interventionists can more easily and frequently target social behaviors. Interventionists can also target reduction of aberrant behavior (e.g., self-stimulatory behaviors, non-compliance, aggression) prior to directly teaching social behaviors. Another option is running a social skills group targeting multiple behaviors (e.g., social skills, learning-how-to-learn, language, and reduction of any aberrant behavior).

Recruitment, Interview, and Observation

Once the focus of the social skills group is determined, the next task is recruiting potential learners—as previously described, this involves conducting interviews with the families and observing learners who might be part of the social skills group. In our experience, a recruiting process that involves assessment, structured interviews, and direct observation is more likely to place learners in appropriate social skills groups. There might be occasions where recruitment through interviews or direct observations is not possible, but, when possible, we highly recommend engaging in this process.

Recruitment

When Autism Partnership started recruitment for social skills groups, it was primarily done by providing fliers to local diagnosticians. Today, most of our recruitment occurs through social media platforms (e.g., Facebook, Twitter) and mass email services. Though there have been changes to our recruitment process over time, certain information has always been important to include. Two examples of recruitment fliers that we have used in the past are provided in Figures 6 and 7. We have found the following information useful when recruiting:

- ☐ Age range of participants
- ☐ Start Date
- ☐ Dates and times
- ☐ Description of skills targeted
- ☐ Description of the desired participant demographic (e.g., cognitive, language, social, aberrant behavior)
- ☐ Any costs associated with participation
- ☐ Location
- ☐ Contact information to set up an interview

Figure 6. Example of a Flier

Photo Credit:
Giedriius/Shutterstock.com

Social Skills Group

The Autism Partnership Foundation is sponsoring a 16-week social skills program as part of a research study looking at the advances in social skills development through evidence-based treatment. We are looking for children who are between the ages of 3-5 years old and have a current diagnosis of Autism Spectrum Disorder to participate in this study.

To Participate:
- Have a previous diagnosis of an Autism Spectrum Disorder
- Have the child be able to speak in full sentences

Group Details
- Two groups of 8-10 children will be participating in a 16-week program.
- Each group will meet 2 times per week for 2 hours each session.
- ABA-based intervention will be used to target specific social needs.
- Children will be taught variety of social, play, recreational and other adaptive skills based on their individual needs as well as group targets.
- The groups will be held at Autism Partnership Office in Seal Beach.

If you are interested in participating in an initial screening, please contact Dr. Justin Leaf at infoautismpartnership@aol.com

Figure 7. Example of a Flier

Photo Credit: Erwin Niemand /Shutterstock.com

We are pleased to announce the start of a new social skills group for individuals diagnosed with Autism Spectrum Disorder. We are in the middle of finding children to participate in a new social skills groups at Autism Partnership and wanted to share information about the social skills group. We are looking for children ages three to five years of age who have been diagnosed with autism spectrum disorder. The group will meet Tuesdays and Thursdays from 10:00 am to 12:00 pm. In the group, we will be teaching children a variety of social skills such as turn taking, waiting, sharing, talking to your friends, and different play activities. The group will be run by two behavior analysts. We are currently seeking a total of six children to participate in the group. For more information contact Jeremy at infosocialgroup@gmail.com.

Sincerely,
Justin

Interview

It is important to note that caregivers are often eager to access quality services, have their child improve their social skills, and to be part of a social skills groups. Even a very specific recruitment letter may result in respondents who do not meet the requirements for participation. We have not yet found an interview format or form that allows us to determine if a learner is appropriate for a social skills group with exact precision. Most of the time, some level of clinical judgment is required throughout the recruitment process. We have, however, provided an interview form with questions we have used in the past (see Figure 8), which can be a guide for interventionists.

There are several advantages for interviews to occur in the location planned for the social skills group or in a public place. First, we have found that caregivers feel more comfortable not having strangers come into their home. Second, when interviews happen outside of the home, caregivers tend to focus on the questions without the typical distractions (e.g., dog jumping on guests, doorbell ringing, siblings in the house). Third, interviews at the clinic or another public place can provide an indication of how committed caregivers can be to the social skills group. If caregivers are late without notification or cancel unexpectedly, it may indicate they might not be able to meet the commitment required by the social skills group.

Figure 8. Interview Question Form for Participants

Question	Response
Tell me about your child.	
How did you hear about the social skills group?	
What are you hoping to get out of the social skills group?	
What are the areas of need in terms of the social behavior for your child?	
What are your child's strengths in terms of social behavior?	
Does your child display any disruptive behavior?	
If so, what disruptive behavior do they display?	
Can you tell me when this disruptive behavior occurs?	
Can you tell me ways to stop this disruptive behavior from occurring (used for hypothesizing function)?	
What other goals do you have for your child in the social skills group?	
Does your child receive any other services?	
Can you tell me about those services?	
What questions do you have for us?	

During the interview, we prefer all caregivers be present when possible. It is also preferred for the learner to be present at the interview, so the interventionists can observe the learner. Usually when we conduct interviews, we have two interventionists present. One interventionist outlines the expectations of the group, asks the caregivers questions, and provides the opportunity for the caregivers to ask questions, while the other interventionist interacts with the learner.

It is important to remember that those interviewing caregivers should obtain as much information as possible to make an informed decision about the learner's participation in the group. This usually means asking a variety of questions that lead to accurate and useful information. It is possible that caregivers are not very accurate at conveying the prevalence rates of problem behavior such as aggression. Therefore, the interventionist might have to ask pointed questions to get this information (e.g., "So when Billy doesn't get the toy he wants, what usually happens?"). When asking caregivers questions, it is of great value to use a variety of questions, including open-ended, close-ended, and multiple-choice. Doing so provides the interventionist with a better picture of what the learner is like and more opportunities to assess consistent responses across questions.

The most important part of conducting an interview is to remember that these are not only caregivers, they are caregivers of a child diagnosed with ASD. This means they can have a range of emotions they may display during the interview, from happy to sad to angry. They may have frequently experienced their child being rejected from services or have had to fight for every service their child needs, making it even more important for the interviewer to be personable and professional. The interviewer needs to make sure the caregivers are at ease and comfortable, while also obtaining the necessary information. Most likely, the interviewer will also need to speak in friendly language (e.g., "We plan on teaching your child how to ask for things") as opposed to using jargon (e.g., "We plan on teaching your child to mand"). Interviewers should use their clinical skills to make the caregivers feel safe and that they can trust the interviewer. The interviewer should also remember that this is the first interaction the caregivers will have with the social skills group staff; a positive first impression is important.

In the interview format we've used, the interventionist not conducting the interview is interacting with the learner. The interventionist should set up a variety of activities for the learner and interventionist to engage in together to conduct informal probes to determine strengths, limitations, and common behaviors. The interventionist should set up situations and activities that allow for an assessment of social behavior, language skills, and possible aberrant behavior. Figure 9 provides a list of activities and skills that could be assessed during this time.

Figure 9. List of Activities to Play with Child During Interview

Activity	Skills to Assess	Skills Observed
Board Games	Sustained play, turn taking, sharing, attending, aberrant behavior, and sportsmanship	
Snack	Requesting, conversation, keeping up conversation, answering questions, sitting, aberrant behavior, and waiting	
Coloring	Requesting, waiting, language, coloring, gross motor, fine motor, and aberrant behavior	
Reading a Story	Comprehension, recall, visual attending, auditory attending, inferencing, sitting, waiting, conditional instructions, responding to instructions, and aberrant behavior	
Dramatic Play (e.g., dress up, blocks, Nerf™ guns)	Parallel play, cooperative play, staying with the adult, answering questions, language, and aberrant behavior	

We also recommend keeping the interview brief. We have found that a 20-minute interview is a perfect length to get the necessary information from caregivers and observe the learner. If both interventionists determine the learner is a good fit, we recommend offering inclusion in the group during the interview. Conversely, if both interventionists are unsure if the learner is a good fit, we recommend arranging an additional observation period (described below). If an additional observation period is not possible, the two interventionists should meet and contact the caregivers at a later time. If both interventionists determine the learner is not a good fit for the group, it is important to consider how this information will be presented to the caregivers. This can be upsetting information to deliver. We recommend having resources available for the caregivers regarding where they may be able to access other services and, if applicable, information about other groups (e.g., from the same clinic or school, other clinics or schools).

Observation Period

Another way to determine appropriateness for a social skills group is to conduct a trial visit where interventionists can observe a learner participating in a pre-existing group. This is an option when wanting to add another learner to a pre-existing social skills group, or to start a new group that is similar to an already occurring group. This also provides interventionists with an opportunity to observe how the learner interacts with the group.

When conducting a trial visit, it is important to keep the visit brief. We recommend that the observational periods be no more than an hour. During this observation period, the interventionists should use the time to assess how the learner responds to a variety of situations. The interventionists should arrange situations to assess the learner's receptive and expressive language skills, learning-how-to-learn skills, social strengths and deficits, and determine if there are situations that are more likely to evoke aberrant behavior. When arranging these situations, it is important the social skills group is conducted how it typically would occur (i.e., not making changes to the group). However, the interventionist should not push too hard with the new learner (e.g., creating events that make the learner uncomfortable or that would evoke severe problem behavior), as the learner does not have previous history of learning within the group, nor will their behavior be as sensitive to the contingency systems in place for the group. Additionally, if the learner engages in too many challenging behaviors, the caregivers or learner may not wish to return to the group.

Finally, when conducting these brief observation periods, we recommend having the learner's caregivers observe with an interventionist available to describe what is occurring and answer any questions. This will allow the caregivers to observe the group and get answers to any questions or concerns, which may lead to more trust in the intervention and process. This also allows the interventionist to better assess the learner's behavior, as the caregivers may provide additional information as they observe their child in the group. Once the hour has passed, the interventionist should answer any final questions the caregivers have and inform them of when they will be contacted.

References

Costantino, J. N., Gruber, C. P. (2005). *Social Responsiveness Scale (SRS)*. Los Angeles, CA: Western Psychological Services.

Dunn, L. M., & Dunn, D. M. (2007). *Peabody picture vocabulary test* (4th ed). Minneapolis, MN: NCS Pearson, Inc.

Gresham, F. M., & Elliot, S. N. (1990). *Social Skills Improvement System Rating Scales Manual*. Minneapolis, MN: NCS Pearson.

Martin, N., & Brownell, R. (2011). *Expressive one word picture vocabulary test*. Novato, CA: Academic Therapy Publications, Inc.

Chapter Seven
Staff and Staff Training

Whether in a school setting, one-to-one teaching, or social skills group, it is vital that intervention is implemented by well-trained, highly qualified interventionists. Our years of clinical experience and research have shown that learners make more progress when they are receiving intervention conducted by high-quality interventionists. The Autism Partnership Method will not be effective if interventionists adhered to rigid protocols or implemented protocols without considering the learners and the environment. Rather, quality interventionists use a systematic yet flexible approach that is responsive to the learner and to the environment. Quality interventionists are knowledgeable in the basic principles of behavior, know how to best implement a procedure, and know how and when to alter the procedure to maximize learner success.

These decisions are based on many factors, and well-trained interventionists must be able to quickly analyze these factors in the moment. Well-trained interventionists do not follow protocols as if they were following a recipe in a cookbook. Instead, they create their own recipes using their training, experience, and clinical judgment to make decisions. When well-trained interventionists run social skills groups, the results can be life altering (Leaf, Leaf, Milne, et al., 2016).

However, it might be difficult for parents, school administrators, and other professionals to determine the characteristics and skills that make up a quality interventionist—and how to train interventionists to develop these skills. This chapter will provide some guidelines on these very important topics. Figure 10 provides a quick, subjective assessment that can be used to determine the quality of a social skills group interventionist across many different characteristics.

Figure 10. Interventionist Assessment

Interventionist Behavior/Skill Observed	Rarely or Never	Sometimes	Almost Always
Dresses appropriately			
Works well with the team			
Seeks out information and educational opportunities			
Enthusiastic			
Relationships with caregivers are within appropriate boundaries			
Punctual			
Regularly attends sessions			
Communicates with supervisor and caregivers in a timely manner			
Follows through with commitments			
Establishes attending before an instruction is provided through shaping, waiting, or consequences but not by control statements			
Uses age-appropriate language			
Uses natural tone of voice			
Teaching sessions are an appropriate duration			
Materials are gathered prior to the teaching session			
Materials and reinforcers are in working order			
Attention is focused on learner and not on other events			
Has engaging style			
Rotates target stimuli as appropriate			
Intersperses tasks as appropriate			

Determines learner's health prior to and during the session			
Evaluates learner's nonverbal behaviors as they relate to tasks or reinforcement			
Evaluates learner's attentiveness			
Changes reinforcement systems in the moment to increase likelihood of correct responding			
Changes reinforcement systems in the moment to increase the likelihood of desired behavior			
Makes changes based upon recent performance			
Makes changes based upon past performance			
Energetic			
Displays patience			
Self-assessment of own behavior			
Maximizes number of teaching trials			
Captures all teachable moments			

What Makes a Quality Therapist for Behaviorally Based Social Skills Groups

In *It's Time for School! Building Quality ABA Educational Programs for Students with Autism Spectrum Disorders* (Leaf et al., 2008), the authors described some of the characteristics that make a quality teacher (referred to in this book as interventionists). Many of these characteristics apply to what makes a quality social skills group interventionist. Below are some additional characteristics that we look for in quality social skills group interventionists.

Fun. If you asked behavior analysts what the most important quality of an interventionist is, you might get answers like "they need to be behavioral" or "they must be technological." These are two important qualities, but for us they are not the most important indicators of a quality interventionist. One of the most important characteristics we see is that the interventionist is *fun*. The learners that attend social skills groups usually do not have a strong desire to engage in social interactions or develop meaningful relationships. Often, learners do not want to attend these groups and it is not uncommon in initial sessions to see learners crying, kicking, screaming, or trying to run out the door. Two of our most important goals are getting the learners to want to come to the group and for these learners to have a desire to make friends. To accomplish this, the interventionists need to be fun.

Too often, interventionists provide instructions in a monotone "therapy voice" or hand over a toy as a reinforcer with no social interaction or engagement with the learner. This simply will not cut it. The learners will not want to come to the group if the interventionists are boring—and if the learners do not want to attend the group, it is less likely they will learn the social skills needed for developing meaningful friendships and positive social relationships. There are many qualities that contribute to being fun; some of them may be subjective and difficult to define. As behavior analysts, subjective and difficult to define skills may be uncomfortable. Nevertheless, we have developed the Fun Assessment (Figure 11) that provides some behavioral indicators of a fun interventionist.

Figure 11. Fun Assessment

Behaviors/Skills Observed	Rarely or Never	Sometimes	Almost Always
Engaging style			
Naturalistic tone of voice			
Conditions themselves with preferred activities			
Warm and comforting to the learner			
Demonstrates pop culture knowledge of the learner's interests			
Contingent throughout			
Plays with games in a silly way			
Smiles			
Shows positive affect			
Uses positive affirming words			
Provides high-fives, tickles (when appropriate), and fist bumps			
Follows learner's lead with activities			
Plays in novel ways			

Social. Another important characteristic of a quality social skills group interventionist is that the interventionist has great social skills themselves. These are the interventionists that you want to hang out with after work or catch a game with after a long week of work. You wouldn't want a coach to teach you baseball who had no concept of the game, someone to teach you a foreign language who was not fluent in that language, or someone to teach you algebra who did not know basic math skills. Likewise, why would you want someone to teach social skills who is not socially adept? Often, we observe social skills groups run by interventionists who are not social themselves and much of the time it results in the participants in the group learning inauthentic or unimportant social skills. Given that social behavior is complex and nuanced, it is important for interventionists to understand these skills and their nuances of the skills, recognize appropriate and inappropriate social behavior, and model appropriate and authentic social behavior.

Innovative. A third important component of quality interventionists is they are innovative. There is an endless list of social skills that can be taught and not one comprehensive curriculum book that covers them all. Therefore, it is important for social skills group interventionists to be able to create their own curricula. This requires an interventionist to know and understand the principles of behavior analysis, identify the strengths and deficits of the learners, identify prerequisites, identify developmental norms, and create programs that target social deficits observed in the group. This book contains many programs that can be used to teach individuals diagnosed with autism spectrum disorder (ASD) a wide variety of social behaviors, most of which were created by social skills interventionists themselves.

Objective. Aberrant behavior does not occur because it is a full moon or because of astrological signs. Behavior is lawful and is the result of behavior–environmental relationships. The best interventionists are objective and use data to make their decisions. They rely on facts rather than speculation. The best interventionists take into account observable and measurable environmental variables and make decisions based on these variables. They do not rely on voodoo or superstitions to guide their behavior. Good social skills group interventionists can identify how to take data on social behaviors, analyze if a change is occurring, identify patterns in the data, and change their programming accordingly.

Complete Picture. When we are teaching social skills in a group, we should not only be concerned about the social skill we are teaching at that moment, but also the larger picture (e.g., creating meaningful friendships and relationships). The field of applied behavior analysis (ABA) has faced claims that ABA-based interventions cannot address advanced social skills or friendships—that it is more suited for simplistic social skills (Winner, 2008). This is simply not true. When ABA-based interventions are provided by quality interventionists, advanced social skills can be taught that can result in the development of meaningful friendships (Leaf, Leaf, Milne, et al., 2016). Unfortunately, when interventionists cannot see the complete picture, it can result in poorer outcomes.

Quality interventionists must know which specific skills are being taught and how they fit in the bigger picture. They have to know which skills are important to teach, which skills are not important to teach, how to prioritize skills, and when to teach skills. For example, a quality social skills group interventionist understands that we do not teach imitation just so a learner can learn to copy us; we teach imitation so that a learner can learn to copy their peers and engage in observational learning. Developing imitation skills can lead to parallel play, which is a prerequisite for more interactive play. An imitative repertoire can also lead to more advanced language. Further, a good interventionist does not just teach learners to imitate their peers, but teaches learners to problem-solve which behaviors they should or should not imitate. If an interventionist rotely teaches discrete imitation skills, learners will not progress and learn the more nuanced elements of imitation. Quality interventionists think beyond success within the social skills group, teaching skills that will be valuable in environments outside of the group (e.g., in the home, school, community) and teaching in a way that the skills will be maintained in those environments. The interventionist should not only be thinking about the success of the learner within the next week, month, or year but also thinking about the learner's success two or three years down the road and longer.

Systematic. Running a social skills group takes constant planning. Successful interventionists do not just go in and start teaching by the seat of their pants, which is unlikely to result in high levels of success. The best interventionists are highly systematic. They pay attention to every detail. They ensure that the presentation of a trial is correct, the type of instruction is appropriate, and the timing is spot-on. They break skills down to the learner's level and teach all component parts effectively. The best interventionists meticulously ensure they provide the proper amount of reinforcement and thin the schedule of reinforcement as quickly as possible. They provide prompts precisely, fade prompts, and evaluate multiple factors to know which prompt to provide and when to provide it. A systematic interventionist ensures the environment is setup to facilitate success (e.g., reinforcement only available when a learner has earned it) and have a game plan before teaching the learners in the group.

Flexible. A quality interventionist is like a great quarterback. Take Peyton Manning, Tom Brady, or Joe Montana, for example. They are given a play from their offensive coordinators, but prior to the snap these quarterbacks have the discretion to stick to the play they were given or call an audible (call a different play on the spot). They make the decisions based upon environmental factors (e.g., the defensive position), and, much of the time, these changes result in success.

A quality interventionist must have a game plan, but also be able to change that game plan based on environmental factors. These environmental factors may include the learner's receptivity, previous history of responding, attending, or how other learners are responding. There could be hundreds of factors that determine whether the interventionist should "call an audible." Being flexible does not mean not being systematic; you have a well thought out game plan, but are able to shift direction as needed to be responsive to the learners.

Dancer. Another important quality of a good social skills group interventionist is "dancing" well with the other interventionists. Within a social skills group, there are usually multiple interventionists running the group. These interventionists take on different roles (see Chapter 7) and it is important that they work collaboratively to ensure the instruction is implemented with the highest quality possible. Being a good dancer comes down to not only having a solid lesson plan, but also having good communication skills. All interventionists in the social skills group need to communicate constantly about what they observe, what they want to do next, what just occurred, and what changes they want to make. This communication needs to happen prior to, during, and after group time. It takes time for interventionists to develop rapport and learn to read each other's behavior, but with time this communication can be accomplished through simple nods, quick gestures, or a look of the eye. When the interventionists are "dancing" together, the social skills group is running at peak performance.

Staff Training

To be a talented social skills group interventionist, the individual must be well-trained. In the field of ABA, there have been changes related to training that have led to a watering down of what is accepted as competent. The effort to standardize intervention has changed the focus to defining a standard duration for training. How do we know how much training is enough for a person to become a competent social skills group interventionist? The truth is there is no magic number. It is not 40 hours, it is not 100 hours, it is not 1000 hours, it is not 10,000 hours. Interventionists should only be considered competent when they can understand and demonstrate the interventions based upon the principles of ABA with a high degree of fidelity. Training should not be time-based, but rather performance-based. The reality is that for an interventionist to be considered qualified, it will take many hours of initial training, followed by many hours of supervised practice and ongoing training.

Another mistaken notion is that if someone is a certified or licensed behavior analyst, they are qualified to practice in any area of specialty. Running social skills groups for individuals diagnosed with ASD is very specialized work. A person can be certified as a behavior analyst without ever participating in a social skills group. At best, certification means an individual has a degree that involved behavior-analytic content, has collected some experience or supervised fieldwork, and has passed a written examination. Although certification agencies may claim they meet minimal competency standards, they do not commonly attempt to measure whether an interventionist can effectively run a social skills group.

Another myth is that good training consists of teaching staff how to implement certain procedures with a high degree of fidelity. Although this is important, it is far from sufficient if the procedures evaluated are limited and basic. Good training is not just training staff how to implement procedures, but also teaching them to be experts in the principles of ABA (Leaf, Leaf, McEachin, et al., 2016).

When it comes to staff training, the main focus should be on which skills interventionists should be taught and how to most effectively teach those necessary skills. There is a wide range of topics that professionals should be taught. These include, but are not limited to: the principles of ABA (e.g., reinforcement, stimulus control); data collection methods; developmental norms; the characteristics of ASD; behavior management strategies; prompting strategies; respondent-based procedures; understanding caregiver concerns; and how to effectively work with caregivers, other staff, and supervisors. Most importantly, we have to train interventionists how to be critical analysts. Interventionists need to understand and critically analyze procedures that are working or not working with their learners. More importantly, they have to know *why* a procedure does or does not work. Training interventionists to critically analyze allows interventionists to make in-the-moment decisions of which procedures to implement, make assessments of the function(s) of challenging behavior, decide when to prompt and what type of prompt to use, and create meaningful programs.

For interventionists to become experts in all of these topics and procedures, training must consist of multiple modalities. First, there must be a strong didactic portion. It is important for professionals to learn the concepts; the best ways to do this include (but are not limited to) attending lectures and reading books and empirical studies. Interventionists should also attend workshops that further increase their knowledge of these topics. Second, training should consist of the trainee and the supervisor role-playing the various skills. Role-playing lets the supervisor set up occasions for the trainee to practice their skills and receive feedback without adversely affecting a client. Once proficiency is achieved in role-play, the training has to move on to working directly with a learner while receiving feedback from the supervisor. It is not enough to implement didactic training and role-playing with a supervisor: the majority of training must occur hands-on with the population the trainee will be providing intervention for.

Another effective way to train new interventionists is to use the teaching interaction procedure or behavioral skills training (BST). These procedures consist of several steps. First, the procedures the interventionist is to implement are described with a clear understanding of the objectives. Second, a meaningful rationale is provided to the interventionist (an optional step in BST) so they know why it is important to implement the procedure. Third, the trainer clearly describes the steps of the procedure, as well as the environmental variables that set the occasion for implementing the procedure. Fourth, the trainer models/demonstrates the procedure, then allows the interventionist to practice the procedure, ideally with an actual learner diagnosed with ASD. Finally, a good trainer provides contingent feedback throughout the training process. It should be noted that sometimes training does not look like a traditional teaching interaction procedure or behavioral skills training where all steps are conducted in one session. Rather, the trainer might spend days on the didactic portions (e.g., explaining each step of the procedure, providing rationales) and on subsequent days implement the hands-on training portion (e.g., modeling, practice, feedback).

Within the Autism Partnership Method, we have general guidelines and protocols for how to train staff, but these will differ depending upon the interventionists we are training. Each staff member comes in with different strengths and weaknesses and may take more or less time to develop certain skillsets. It is important throughout training to conduct frequent evaluations of an interventionist's progress, used to determine strengths and weaknesses, areas needing further instruction, and when interventionists may be ready to work in a social skills group (see Figure 12). These evaluations can help ensure that interventionists are well-trained and that their skills maintain over time.

Figure 12. Social Skills Group Procedure Assessment

Social Skill Group Procedure Assessment

Interventionists(s):   Scorer: Date:

Scoring Key

0	1	2
Rarely or Never	Sometimes	Frequently, Often, Always

	Skill	Score		
Reinforcement				
1	Paired socials with tangibles	0	1	2
2	Used age appropriate reinforcers	0	1	2
3	Used a variety of reinforcers	0	1	2
4	Demonstrated new and novel ways to interact with items	0	1	2
5	Maintained favorable affect when providing reinforcement	0	1	2
6	Incorporated learner's preference into new items or social activity	0	1	2
7	Responded and changed potentially reinforcing items/activities based on the learner's affect	0	1	2
8	Responded and changed potentially reinforcing items/activities based on the learner's non-verbal behavior	0	1	2
9	Attempted to condition novel/neutral items/activities as reinforcers	0	1	2
10	Allowed learner to sample potentially reinforcing items/activities free from direct instruction	0	1	2
11	Provided choices when providing potentially reinforcing items/activities	0	1	2
Group DTT				
12	Presented materials clearly and matched objective of task	0	1	2
13	Instructions were clear	0	1	2
14	Instructions were not repeated before completion of previous trial	0	1	2
15	Varied instructions	0	1	2
16	Tone of voice was appropriate (e.g., varied, not booming, natural)	0	1	2

17	Did not use readiness cues	0	1	2
18	Appropriate time was given for the learner to respond	0	1	2
19	Each trial included feedback (as appropriate)	0	1	2
20	Maintained an appropriate pace of trials	0	1	2
21	Consequences were contingent: only provided consequences that were deserved	0	1	2
22	Differential reinforcement was provided, and tone of voice matched the consequence	0	1	2
23	Timing of consequence: as immediate as needed by learner; delayed where appropriate	0	1	2
24	Quality of consequence: reasonably calculated to provide appropriate level of motivation and engagement (e.g., not unnecessarily lavish, not repetitive or boring, age-appropriate)	0	1	2
25	Consistency: was consistent in deciding what response to reinforce or correct	0	1	2
26	Feedback regarding learning how to learn behavior (e.g., attending, sitting) was informative and appropriate	0	1	2
27	Provided choral instructions	0	1	2
28	Provided sequential discrete trials	0	1	2
29	Provided nonsequential discrete trials	0	1	2
30	Provided overlapping discrete trials	0	1	2
Prompting				
31	Timing of prompts was optimal	0	1	2
32	Prompted trials were followed by unprompted or reduced prompted trials	0	1	2
33	Level of assistance was enough to ensure success but not more than necessary	0	1	2
34	Prompts were not used after an error or a failed attempt to respond	0	1	2
35	Prompts were used to avoid prolonged failure	0	1	2
36	Inadvertent prompts were avoided	0	1	2

Behavior Management

#				
37	Remained calm when problem behavior occurred	0	1	2
38	Provided minimal attention to problem behavior	0	1	2
39	Provided reinforcement for the absence of problem behavior (DRO)	0	1	2
40	The intervention provided matched the function of the problem behavior	0	1	2
41	Provided appropriate level of response blocking to address stereotypy	0	1	2
42	Provided positive reinforcement to strengthen and maintain appropriate on-task behavior	0	1	2
43	Shaped desired replacement behaviors	0	1	2
44	Used behavioral momentum to maintain high success rates and manage problem behavior	0	1	2
45	Timed onset of trials optimally to shape better attending	0	1	2
46	Followed plan to promote independent direction of attention	0	1	2

Incidental Teaching

#				
47	Maintained spatial control of reinforcers	0	1	2
48	Used descriptive praise	0	1	2
49	Provided reinforcement for the target response	0	1	2
50	Arranged environment to promote learning opportunities prior to learner arrival	0	1	2
51	Followed learner's lead	0	1	2
52	Anticipated learner responding	0	1	2
53	Provided models for targeted response(s)	0	1	2
54	Used time-delay to promote independent responding	0	1	2
55	Created several opportunities for the learner to respond	0	1	2

Shaping

#				
56	Determined terminal response	0	1	2
57	Determined learner's current level of responding with respect to the terminal response	0	1	2

58	Provided reinforcer contingent upon learner's current level of responding	0	1	2
59	Targeted expanding response class with respect to the terminal response	0	1	2
60	Maintained a high rate of reinforcement and learner success	0	1	2
61	Provided reinforcement contingent upon approximations leading toward the terminal response	0	1	2
62	Provided prompts when applicable	0	1	2
63	Withheld reinforcement to increase the probability of variability in responding	0	1	2
Teaching Interaction Procedure				
64	Provided a description of the behavior/skill	0	1	2
65	Provided a meaningful rationale	0	1	2
66	Task analyzed the targeted behavior/skill	0	1	2
67	Provided opportunities for learner to respond throughout didactic portion	0	1	2
68	Provided a demonstration of the targeted behavior/skill	0	1	2
69	Provided opportunities for learner to respond to demonstration	0	1	2
70	Provided opportunities for learner to role-play the behavior/skill	0	1	2
71	Attempted to include peers during role-play if possible/appropriate	0	1	2
72	Provided opportunities for learner to respond to the role-play	0	1	2
73	Provided appropriate consequences based on learner responding throughout didactic, demonstration, and role-plays	0	1	2
Cool versus Not Cool™ procedure				
74	Labeled the targeted skill	0	1	2
75	Provided a demonstration of the targeted skill	0	1	2
76	Provided an opportunity for the learner label the demonstration as cool or not cool	0	1	2
77	Provided an opportunity for the learner to label why the demonstration was cool or not cool	0	1	2
78	Provided opportunities for the learner to role-play the skill	0	1	2

79	Provided appropriate consequences throughout the entire Cool versus Not Cool™ procedure based on learners responding	0	1	2
80	Programmed for generalization throughout	0	1	2
81	Attempted to include peers during role-play if possible/appropriate	0	1	2

NOTES:

References

Leaf, J. B., Leaf, J. A., Milne, C., Taubman, M., Oppenheim-Leaf, M., Torres, N., Townley-Cochran, D., Leaf, R., McEachin, J. & Yoder, P. (2016). An evaluation of a behaviorally based social skills group for individuals diagnosed with autism spectrum disorder. *Journal of autism and developmental disorders, 47*(2), 243-259.

Leaf, J. B., Leaf, R., McEachin, J., Taubman, M., Ala'i-Rosales, S., Ross, R. K., Smith, T, & Weiss, M. J. (2016). Applied Behavior Analysis is a Science and, Therefore, Progressive. *Journal of Autism and Developmental Disorders, 46,* 720-731.

Leaf, R., Taubman, M., & McEachin, J. (2008). *It's Time for School!* New York, NY: Different Roads Learning.

Winner, M. G. (2008). *A politically incorrect look at evidence-based practices and teaching social skills: A literature review and discussion.* San Jose, CA: Think Social Publishing, Inc.

Chapter Eight
General Set Up

Christine Milne

When administering a behaviorally based social skills group, the planning that occurs prior to running the group is half of the work. Having a clear overall vision for the group and a thorough plan will make the group more effective. It is also important to have sufficient staff to effectively implement the various behavior plans and programs, appropriate grouping of participants with complementary skills and targets, clear long-term and short-term objectives, an organized schedule, and, most importantly, clear and consistent communication between staff. By following these guidelines, you are more likely to maximize the time you have during your social skills group.

Staff Roles

The social skills groups we have implemented have generally consisted of 8–10 learners and three interventionists who are regularly scheduled to assist with the social skills group. This number may fluctuate based on the level of assistance needed by the learners. Each staff role is important and contributes to the success of the group as a whole. It is essential that all staff know and understand their roles so that each session flows smoothly.

Lead. The lead interventionist is the role most similar to the teacher of a typical classroom. The lead interventionist should be the primary person who provides instructions, feedback, and reinforcement to the learners. The lead interventionist must also continuously communicate with the shadow interventionist(s). The lead interventionist may signal the shadow interventionist to step in and provide a higher rate of assistance with a learner, ask the shadow interventionist to prompt a response with a learner, or work with a learner individually in a brief one-to-one teaching session to rapidly teach a skill then bring the learner back into the group.

It is important that whenever possible only the lead interventionist provides the instructions. If a learner misses the instruction, the shadow interventionist should not re-issue the instruction, but instead signal to the lead interventionist that the learner missed it. This allows the lead interventionist to make the decision of whether to re-issue the instruction themselves or to allow natural consequences to occur for not listening. If the shadow interventionist re-issues the instruction, the learner may learn that they no longer need to attend to the lead and will rely on prompts from the shadow to respond. The learner could also only learn to follow direct individual instructions, as opposed to responding to group instructions. The main exception occurs when the lead is occupied with other learners. Ideally, the lead instructor should signal to the shadow interventionist to provide any necessary prompts. This allows the lead interventionist to keep track of which trials are independent versus those that are missed or prompted and therefore will be better able to adjust their plan.

Corrective feedback and reinforcement should also primarily come from the lead interventionist. It is important that the contingency involving instructions, learner responding, and feedback is established and remains with the lead interventionist; this helps the learners understand they should pay attention to the lead interventionist and the shadow interventionist can more easily be faded out. There may be learners who require a higher rate of reinforcement—in these cases, the shadow interventionist may provide additional reinforcement but always with the lead's knowledge. The terminal reinforcer should still come from the lead interventionist. For example, if a learner is earning tokens for specific target behaviors, the lead interventionist and the shadow interventionist could provide tokens. But when the learner fills up the token board, the learner should raise their hand and inform the lead interventionist. The lead interventionist will then provide access to the terminal reinforcer, whether it is a tangible item, moving up on a level chart, or excusing the learner from the large group to a play area.

Communication is not just the lead interventionist directing the shadow interventionist, but equally the shadow providing information to the lead interventionist. Sometimes it is beneficial to develop signals that may allow communication non-vocally (e.g., a thumbs-up above a learner to indicate praise should be given, or a thumbs-down to indicate corrective feedback is needed). Too many vocal responses between the lead interventionist and shadow interventionist(s) could distract the learners in the group. They can also draw attention to the shadow interventionist, which may make it more difficult to fade them out. The goal is for the learners to rely on the contingencies set by the lead interventionist, not by the shadow interventionist.

Shadow. The shadow interventionist's main role is to assist the lead interventionist in maintaining an appropriate level of reinforcement and feedback to meet the needs of the individual learners. As the lead interventionist can only attend to a certain number of learners at a time, the shadow acts as "extra eyes" to ensure that all learners are engaging in appropriate behaviors to be successful in the group. As discussed above, the shadow interventionists may cue the lead interventionist to provide reinforcement or feedback for individual learners. These cues are ideally non-vocal, such as a thumb up or down behind a learner. This is so the learners remain focused on the lead interventionist as opposed to attending to the shadow interventionist.

When acting as "extra eyes," it is important to check in with the lead to see which learners the lead is watching. If the lead interventionist is talking to Learner A, the shadow interventionist does not need to watch Learner A in that moment. The shadow interventionist should scan the rest of the learners in the group at this time. The shadow interventionist must also be aware of the targets for each learner. If an event occurs that sets the occasion for a target behavior for a learner in the group, the shadow may need to prompt the lead to provide reinforcement or feedback for the learner engaging in the target behavior. The shadow interventionist must also be knowledgeable about which learners may need a higher frequency of intervention (i.e., prompting or feedback). This does not necessarily mean the shadow interventionist will intervene more frequently, but rather more frequent visual attention may be needed for some learners.

There may be instances when the shadow interventionist needs to intervene directly with a learner without waiting for the lead interventionist. One instance may be when a learning opportunity has presented itself and the timing of reinforcement or feedback is critical for the learner. In this scenario, the delay of feedback from the lead interventionist may impact the effectiveness of the reinforcer or punisher, and the learning opportunity may be lost. Another instance where the shadow interventionist may need to intervene directly is when a high rate of disruptive behavior from a learner becomes a safety concern. In these instances, it is important that the learner is given the appropriate consequence immediately, for the safety of themselves and others. Additionally, if a learner frequently requires a high level of intervention directly from the shadow interventionist, the learner is most likely no longer learning or benefiting from the large group and may benefit more from small group or one-to-one intervention. The learner may not have the skills necessary to participate in a larger social skills group and other arrangements should be made (e.g., a different type of group or more one-to-one time).

We categorize two major types of shadow interventionists: 1) *velcro* and 2) *rubber band*. Velcro shadowing occurs when the shadow interventionist remains in close proximity to the learners, typically within three feet. A velcro support interventionist provides high rates of prompting, feedback, reinforcement, or even instructions to the learner directly. Learners become excessively focused on the velcro shadow, frequently checking in with them and diverting their attention away from the lead interventionist. If excessive intervention or close proximity is required from the shadow interventionist for the learner to perform the necessary behavior, the learner may not be appropriate for that particular social skills group and may need to find one that better meets their needs (e.g., a group with more frequent reinforcement breaks, major focus on learning-how-to-learn skills, higher adult:child ratio).

On the other hand, a rubber band shadow interventionist has the elasticity to move in as necessary, but never parks alongside the learner. When the group is doing well, the rubber band shadow interventionist is in the background by default. The shadow interventionist will continue to watch the learners and communicate with the lead interventionist but strives to be invisible. If the rubber band shadow notices that a learner needs assistance, the shadow interventionist will move in, provide support as needed, then bounce back out as quickly as possible. By reducing the proximity of the shadow support, the experience of the group more closely simulates a typical classroom. In addition, when less support is needed, the shadow may also help with taking data, though this is not their primary role.

Auxiliary. The auxiliary interventionist has several roles during each activity. One is to take data for individual learners. Given they are not usually providing intervention, they are more likely to take accurate data. The auxiliary interventionist also helps set up the next activity to make transitions more fluid and minimize learner downtime between activities. The auxiliary interventionist is likely to be the lead interventionist for the next activity, but this is not always the case. The auxiliary interventionist must also be prepared to step in as shadow support if the shadow has to pull out a learner for one-to-one instruction, grab materials for the lead, or if something unanticipated occurs. This allows the group to maintain flow and minimize learner downtime.

Flexible Staff Roles

Throughout a session, staff should change roles for each activity for several reasons. First, switching roles between activities allows for smoother transitions. If one staff leads the group while another staff sets up the next activity, there is less time between activities, allowing more time to implement teaching trials for the learners' target behaviors.

Second, given that the contingencies are consistent regardless of staff, learners are more likely to engage in target skills consistently throughout the session. All staff, lead or shadow, must be aware of all targets for all learners in the group. That way, reinforcement is more likely to occur consistently across staff and settings (e.g., treatment room, park, transitions to different settings). As learners continue to practice skills across different staff, the skills are more likely to generalize to other people as well. If, for any reason, novel staff are present (e.g., due to regular staff illness), it is a great opportunity to probe to see if skills generalize to the novel staff.

Third, by allowing all staff to engage in multiple roles, it provides an opportunity for experienced staff to train new staff in different roles. Experienced staff can model a specific role, then have new staff practice. Immediate feedback may then be provided, as well as another opportunity to practice again. Providing systematic training opportunities increases the number of skilled staff that may step in if needed in the future. It also prepares the staff to provide more effective support in other environments, such as the classroom.

Lesson Plans/Schedules

Developing a schedule prior to each session is critical for the learners' progression and success. The information on the schedule must be as thorough as needed to run a fluid session. All staff must know what is happening when and their role for each activity. Everything should be written on the schedule, including times, objectives, and materials needed for each lesson. This, again, helps maintain flow and keeps staff accountable for their roles throughout each session. There may also be smaller schedules within each group and activity to keep track of the progress made for each day, and to allow for the programs and skills targeted progress systematically. We've provided a sample schedule tracking sheet as well as a blank template sheet to help interventionists set up a group effectively (see Figures 12 and 13).

Figure 13. Example of Schedule for 2.5-hour Social Skills Group

Staff: Lauren, Steve, Jean

Students: James, Sarah, Cameron, Leslie, Ben, Sean

Time	Activity	Objective	Staff Assignments			Additional Notes
			Lauren	Steve	Jean	
2:45-3:00	Set-Up	Discuss session plan and set up materials	Set up materials for opening circle	Gathering materials for teaching	Gathering materials for teaching and data sheets	
3:00-3:10	Opening • Books available on carpet	Set up probes for generaliza-tion • Initiation with peers • Joint Atten-tion	Shadowing and Taking Individual Data: James: Initiating with peers Cameron: Staying with peers	Shadowing and Taking Individual Data: Sarah: Ini-tiating with peers Leslie: Re-sponding to peers	Shadowing and Taking Individual Data: Ben: Staying Calm Sean: Cool Body	
3:10-3:30	Large Group: • Attendance Song • Story with Felt Pieces	Learning-how-to-learn skills • Choral responding • Conditional Instructions • Visual and auditory attending	Lead Group	Shadow Students: Prompt rate of reinforce-ment for Sean	Auxiliary: Take Data/ Set up next activity	Individual targets: James: Not being called on first Sarah: Loud voice Cameron: Auditory attending Leslie: Novel comments Ben: Cool body and auditory attending Sean: Cool Body

Time	Activity	Col3	Shadow/Students	Auxiliary	Lead	Notes
3:30-3:40	Fun Games: • Boogie Walk • Musical Chairs	• Boogie Walk: Shared Excitement, Cool Body • Musical Chairs: Losing graciously, cheering on a friend	Shadow Students: Sean may need more support	Auxiliary: Take Data/ Set up next activity	Lead Group: Set up losing antecedents for James and Ben	James and Ben: Staying calm when losing Sarah and Leslie: Smiling and laughing Cameron: Sustained attention and smiling Sean: Cool body
3:40-3:50	Large Group: • Social Skills: Cool/Not Cool	Responding to Peers • Answering when a friend is talking to you	Auxiliary: Take data Set up next activity	Lead: Run full cool/not cool procedure	Shadow: Support as needed	Use "reading a book" as the activity for the role-play. Not cool examples: not responding, responding with an off-topic comment
3:50-4:10	Small Group: • Snack setting	Group A: Answering questions from friends:	Group A: Cameron, Sarah, Ben		Pull out with Sean: Work on statement/ statement Use snacks to make comments "look like is a fish!"	
		Group B: Asking questions based off information given by peer		Group B: Leslie, James		

4:10-4:20	Fun Games: • Fruit Salad • Who's Missing	Teaching Fruit Salad: • Conditional instructions • Keeping a calm body Who's Missing: • Attending • Social engagement	Lead: Introduce Fruit Salad Who's Missing: Have students set up the game	Shadow:	Auxiliary: Set up materials for walk and park activities	Sarah and Leslie: Smiling and laughing Cameron: Sustained attention and smiling Sean: Cool body
4:20-4:30	• Walk to the park	Walking in a Line Incorporate stop and wait	Shadow: Shadow second half of group	Auxiliary: Carry data sheets and materials for the park *May need to shadow Sean*	Lead: Put Sean in front Increase time students wait before walking about (Previous: 5 seconds, Goal: 10 seconds)	
4:30-4:45	Outdoor Game: • Obstacle Course	• Visual Attending • Waiting • Cheering on Friend	Auxiliary: Set up Obstacle course while Lead explains the game	Lead:	Shadow: Sean and James: Sitting and not playing with grass Leslie and Sarah: Cheering on Friend with loud voice	Materials for Obstacle Course: 8 Spots, 2 hula-hoops, 2 soccer balls
4:45-5:15	"Free Play" • Park Structure: swings, monkey bars, sand, slide, etc.	• Work on Individual Targets • Have students independently break into groups	Shadow: Pick 2 students to shadow	Shadow: Pick 2 students to shadow	Shadow: Pick 2 students to shadow	See individual Data sheets for targets

			Lead:	Shadow:	Auxiliary:	
5:15-5:30	Closing Circle • Check-in to superkid chart • Access reinforcers	• Feedback for Outdoor play • Debrief and access reinforcers	Lead:	Shadow: Inform Lead which parents are there	Auxiliary: Debrief with Parents	
5:30-5:45	Clean-up and Debrief					

Figure 14. Template of a Schedule for 2.5-hour Social Skills Group

Staff:

Students:

Time	Activity	Objective	Staff Assignments			Additional Notes
2:45-3:00	Set-Up					
3:00-3:10			Lead:	Shadow:	Auxiliary:	
3:10-3:30			Lead:	Shadow:	Auxiliary:	
3:30-3:40			Lead:	Shadow:	Auxiliary:	
3:40-3:50			Lead:	Shadow:	Auxiliary:	
3:50-4:10			Lead:	Shadow:	Auxiliary:	
4:10-4:20			Lead:	Shadow:	Auxiliary:	
4:20-4:30			Lead:	Shadow:	Auxiliary:	
4:30-4:45			Lead:	Shadow:	Auxiliary:	
4:45-5:15			Lead:	Shadow:	Auxiliary:	
5:15-5:30			Lead:	Shadow:	Auxiliary:	
5:30-5:45	Clean-up and Debrief					

Time

It is important to specify the time for each activity and adhere to this timeline as closely as possible. It is easy to get immersed in a program or activity and lose track of time, but doing so will affect other important lessons that are planned. This may also result in a snowball effect, where every session consists of trying to catch up to the next activity. If a pattern emerges where not enough time is allotted for a particular activity, take note and make adjustments to the schedule for the next session.

There may be circumstances where deviating from the schedule is appropriate. For instance, if one or more learners are on the cusp of achieving competency with a target skill, the interventionists may wish to spend more time on a specific social behavior to more quickly reach mastery criterion. In other instances, when natural learning opportunities arise, straying from the schedule may be appropriate. Reinforcing the first instance of a target behavior in a novel scenario increases the likelihood for the behavior to occur again in the future. It may also be beneficial to modify the schedule when encountering multiple challenging behaviors interfering with skill acquisition. In these cases, aberrant behavior targets must be prioritized over skill development.

When the predetermined plan isn't working, it may set the occasion for changing the schedule. The current lesson could be too difficult or easy for the group and adapting the lesson to the appropriate skill level requires additional planning. In these cases, it may be advantageous to end the lesson and engage in an activity that will be more beneficial. It is helpful to have one or two additional activities ready, like a large group activity targeting learning-how-to-learn skills or a fun activity targeting social engagement. Ideally, this situation does not occur often. By having clear program objectives and phases established ahead of time, it will be easier to make adjustments in the moment when needed (e.g. simplify or advance a program).

Activity/Objective

The objectives that will be targeted during that time frame should be listed. It is important to prioritize objectives over the activity, as the activity should only provide the context to practice the objectives. Therefore, when planning, snack does not occur because it is "snack time." Rather, snack is the context in which commenting can be targeted because snack time is a situation where commenting naturally occurs. In later sessions, the activity may change to playing with Playdough™ or drawing to use different contexts to target commenting (see Figure 15).

Figure 15. Example of possible targets

Activity	Possible Individual or Group Targets
Snack	☐ Initiating conversation ☐ Responding to peers ☐ Reading social cues ☐ Frustration tolerance ☐ Multiple step instructions ☐ Conversation ☐ Staying on topic ☐ Waiting ☐ Commenting
Art	☐ Multiple step instructions ☐ Compliments ☐ Conversation ☐ Frustration tolerance ☐ Initiating conversation ☐ Commenting ☐ Responding to peers ☐ Asking for help ☐ Material imitation ☐ Joint attention ☐ Perspective taking

Large Group

Large group lessons are beneficial as they provide an efficient way to target different skills by increasing the ratio of learners to interventionists. Ideally, one lead interventionist could provide a lesson for at least 8 learners at a time. During this time, there is usually a group skill target as well as individual learner skill targets. The large group skill target could include choral responding, problem solving, or specific social skills. Individual learner targets may include frustration tolerance, comprehension, or specific social skills.

Another benefit of teaching in a large group is the opportunity for observational learning. Through observational learning, learners can learn through the experiences of others in addition to their own experiences. Observational learning also allows a learner to indirectly experience which responses result in reinforcement rather than corrective feedback based on a peer's behavior, and may adjust their future responses based on this information.

Small Group

Small group lessons are also beneficial, allowing the interventionist to better tailor the lesson to the specific needs of learners in the group. For example, though the large group continues to work on talking with friends, individuals in the group may have different skillsets. In smaller groups, the lessons may be further tailored to address skills like making on-topic comments with peers or asking questions, depending on the deficits of the learners. Small groups also provide an opportunity for more trials to occur for each learner. In the large group, each learner may only get one trial to practice a new skill; providing more trials per learner could result in long periods of waiting for the other learners in the group.

One-to-one

One-to-one instruction is not ideal in a social skills group setting, but there are times when one learner may not be demonstrating a skill that others in the group are demonstrating. In these situations, an interventionist may pull the learner aside for intensive one-to-one intervention to develop that skill. The goal is to improve the skill in this one-to-one setting, then integrate the learner back into the group. One-to-one teaching can also be used when disruptive behaviors occur and cannot be appropriately addressed in the group setting. Again, the goal is to accomplish de-escalation, build behavior momentum, then integrate the learner back into the group. If a learner is spending more time in one-to-one teaching than in group teaching, a reassessment may be needed to determine if that social skills group is appropriate for the learner. Frequently tying up one staff member to serve a single learner will affect the group as a whole, since all staff are needed for the group to run effectively and efficiently.

Learner Targets

Throughout the social skills group, it is important to continue to target each learner's individual goals. These individual goals may change, based on the main objective of the group. The interventionist will be responsible for group targets and also individual goals that may not necessarily be shared by all learners. For example, one learner may be working on using a loud voice; therefore, the interventionist would set up multiple opportunities for the learner to display a loud voice. The interventionists need to know the individual learner targets as well as the overall group goals. Knowing all of the learners' goals is essential to being able to set up situations to practice their goals and know when to reinforce the learner's behavior if the learner engages appropriately within an activity.

Additional Notes

In this section, you can provide any additional information that would be useful for the session. This might include individual targets of learners, specific evocative events you want to arrange, or generalization probes for different skills.

Setup and Debrief

It is important to designate time for the intervention team to discuss what will occur in the next session and debrief about the current session. This is a time to go over how the learners are progressing, how the session went overall, and what changes will or will not be made for the next session. This time is especially important to debrief about the progression of small groups, as not all interventionists are able to observe the smaller group and may be able to provide suggestions for future sessions.

Chapter Nine
Contingency Systems

A good social skills group requires interventionists who are able to effectively establish motivation for learners to respond to instructions, display desired social behaviors with their peers, facilitate social engagement, and refrain from engaging in maladaptive behaviors. For interventionists to achieve these goals, they must effectively use reinforcement and punishment (described below) within their social skills group. There are many examples of items and activities that, when provided contingently, may increase the likelihood of desirable behaviors. These include, but are not limited to: food, drinks, toys, social praise, tokens, privileges (e.g., being the line leader, teacher helper, carrying the outdoor equipment), and social gestures (e.g., high fives, knuckles, secret handshakes). There are also many items and activities that, when removed contingently, may increase the likelihood of desirable behaviors. A break from instructions, reduction of the required work, or a homework pass are easy ways to reinforce target behaviors.

Although reinforcement is critical to behavioral intervention, there are often objections to using it. We often hear that learners diagnosed with autism spectrum disorder (ASD) should not need reinforcers, providing reinforcers is unfair to others, or that the learners should be intrinsically motivated. We all would like learners to be motivated to display appropriate social behaviors without needing any supplemental consequences, but that is not often the reality for individuals diagnosed with ASD. Just as typically developing children require supplemental reinforcement for things that require high response effort—whether it is ice cream for getting a good grade, getting the MVP ball after great effort in a baseball game, or going out to a favorite restaurant for doing an exceptional job helping out around the house—children with learning challenges require supplemental consequences to do things that they might find exceptionally difficult. The difference is that things that come easy for most children are not so easy for children diagnosed with ASD. There are many important guidelines to keep in mind when implementing contingency systems within social skills groups, many of which have been previously described by Leaf and McEachin (1999). Below are some guidelines for the effective use of reinforcement which come from Leaf and McEachin and our own clinical recommendations.

Age-Appropriate. Think about the social skills groups or special education classrooms you have seen. How many times have you seen a 10-year-old playing with a Thomas the Tank Engine toy or a 17-year-old listening to a Barney song? We strongly believe this is not appropriate. It is important for interventionists running social skills groups to use age-appropriate reinforcers within the context of the social skills group. If we give a 7-year-old a Wiggles guitar or a Bob the Builder truck, it can increase the social stigmas they may experience, which can also increase the likelihood of being teased or bullied. Also, when people see learners playing with toys that are intended for younger individuals, it may lower the expectations of the learner or lead to adults interacting with the learner as if they are younger than their actual age. The first guideline for using reinforcement in a social skills group is for interventionists to provide age appropriate reinforcers. If there are no age-appropriate items and activities to use as reinforcers for the learners in the group, there should be a large focus on conditioning and developing age-appropriate reinforcers.

Schedule of Reinforcement. Within our clinical observations, many interventionists provide reinforcement following every correct response. Reinforcement is also commonly provided based on time and not contingent upon a learner's behavior. Though there may be instances where these types of reinforcement schedules are appropriate (e.g., when just beginning to learn a skill), these schedules should be faded to a more natural rate of reinforcement within a social skills group. The second important guideline for using reinforcement in a social skills group is that interventionists should reinforce target behaviors on an appropriate schedule. If the schedule of reinforcement remains too dense for an extended period of time, it may be difficult to fade. If the schedule of reinforcement remains too thin for an extended period of time, behavior change may not occur or be maintained across time.

Variety. Interventionists also need to rotate reinforcers frequently within a social skills group. Without a variety of reinforcers, learners may become satiated, a phenomenon in which the reinforcing value is lost. In addition, a core diagnostic criterion of ASD is restricted and repetitive interests; this can manifest in getting stuck on one item or activity. Not providing many different reinforcers may actually feed into restricted and repetitive behaviors. The more reinforcers an interventionist has available for each learner, the higher the likelihood of the learner remaining motivated throughout the social skills group.

Conditioning. As previously stated, one of the diagnostic criteria for ASD is limited and restricted interests. It is common that a learner prefers to interact with only one or two items, resulting in a very narrow range of items that can be used as reinforcers. It is extremely important that interventionists have the skills to condition less preferred, or even non-preferred, items and activities to function as reinforcers and thereby expand the learner's repertoire of reinforcers. Conditioning reinforcers can be done in several ways, including: playing with these toys in fun, novel, and exciting ways; peer modeling; interacting with the item in ways similar to how the learner interacts with other preferred items; or pairing the less preferred item with the more preferred item and gradually fading the preferred item. The skills to condition new reinforcers ensure that a wide variety of items and activities are available as reinforcers within the social skills group.

Contingent. Finally, and maybe most importantly, the interventionist must provide access to reinforcing items contingent on the learner's target behavior(s). An interventionist should only provide a token, praise, or reinforcer when the learner has displayed a targeted behavior. We often observe learners getting the answer wrong or guessing at the answer and the interventionist still providing praise and giving the learner a toy. This ends up reinforcing incorrect answers and guesses, which will result in learners not really trying and not making meaningful gains in their social behaviors.

Identifying Reinforcers

Prior to the start of the social skills group and during the first group session, the interventionists should identify reinforcers that can be used for all learners in the group. There are a number of ways potential reinforcers can be identified. A simple method is asking caregivers, teachers, and other therapists familiar with the learners to provide a list of their favorite items, food, and activities. This provides the interventionists multiple items and activities that may serve as reinforcers to be used within the group. Figure 16 provides an example of a template that can be used to help interventionists identify potential reinforcers using interviews.

To use the template provided, the social skills group interventionist should ask caregivers, teachers, or other therapists to list a variety of items the learner prefers. The template has been divided into five domains (i.e., tangible, food, activities, privileges, and other). The interviewer should ask the caregiver, teacher, or therapist to rank each item in the domain. For example, a 1 would indicate highly preferred and a 3 would indicate minimally preferred. By creating a preference hierarchy, interventionists may be able to use differential reinforcement within the group (e.g., providing a higher level for better approximations). Once the interventionists have compiled a list of potential reinforcers, they should eliminate those that are not age-appropriate, cannot be provided within the group, or the learners have non-contingent access to at other times.

A second method for interventionists to identify possible reinforcers is observing the learners in their natural environments to determine with which items and activities they commonly interact with. During these observations, it is important to note how the learner interacts with those items and activities, how long the learner interacts with those items and activities, and the learner's affect. Figure 17 provides a data sheet that can help interventionists identify potential reinforcers through direct observation.

Figure 16. Interview to Identify Reinforcers

Reinforcer Identification Via Interview

Child: Age: Assessor: Date:

Item	Description of How the Item was Used	Rank in Domain	Overall Rank	Age Appropriate
Tangible Items				
				Yes No
				Yes No
				Yes No
				Yes No
				Yes No
Food Items				
				Yes No
				Yes No
				Yes No
				Yes No
				Yes No
Activities				
				Yes No
				Yes No
				Yes No
				Yes No
				Yes No

Privileges					
				Yes	No
				Yes	No
				Yes	No
				Yes	No
				Yes	No
Other					
				Yes	No
				Yes	No
				Yes	No
				Yes	No
				Yes	No

Figure 17. Data Sheet for Identifying Reinforcement Via Observation

Reinforcer Identification Via Observation Template

Item	How did the Learner Interact with the Item?	Duration of Play	Affect	Other Notes
			Happy Neutral Unhappy	
			Happy Neutral Unhappy	
			Happy Neutral Unhappy	
			Happy Neutral Unhappy	
			Happy Neutral Unhappy	
			Happy Neutral Unhappy	
			Happy Neutral Unhappy	
			Happy Neutral Unhappy	
			Happy Neutral Unhappy	
			Happy Neutral Unhappy	
			Happy Neutral Unhappy	
			Happy Neutral Unhappy	
			Happy Neutral Unhappy	

Interventionists should also be knowledgeable about current popular trends in games, toys, television, movies, and music. Knowing what typically developing, same-age children are buying in toy stores or watching on TV allows an interventionist to condition potential reinforcers that learners may also encounter outside of the social skills group. We recommend these three methods to identify potential reinforcers (i.e., interview, observation, pop culture trends) over formal preference assessments (e.g., paired-stimulus preference assessment). Formal preference assessments take a tremendous amount of time and could still result in identifying reinforcers that may not be age-appropriate or cannot be used within the social skills group (see Alcalay et al., 2019).

Overview of Punishment

In addition to using reinforcement procedures, interventionists will occasionally have to implement punishment procedures. Punishment, as used here, is defined as any item or event that occurs immediately following a behavior that decreases the likelihood that the individual will display that behavior in the future. There are a variety of punishers that can be used in a behaviorally based social skills group including corrective feedback, verbal reprimands, having the learner clean up the room after making a mess, taking away a toy, losing a privilege, moving down on the level system, or losing a token.

Today, many professionals in the field of ASD intervention, applied behavior analysis, and developmental disabilities discourage implementing punishment procedures (Burk, 2015; LaVigna & Donnellan, 1986). We do agree that more invasive types of punishment (e.g., shock, water misting, thigh slaps) should not occur unless in extreme cases (i.e., life threatening behaviors such as self-injury). In our social skills groups, we work with individuals who are responsive to less invasive forms of punishment (e.g., saying "no," removal of tokens, loss of a privilege) when those consequences are administered correctly and in conjunction with reinforcement for replacement behaviors. Research has consistently demonstrated that punishment decreases aberrant and incompatible behaviors, which can then help individuals diagnosed with ASD learn new skills through reinforcement procedures. It has been shown that implementing less invasive punishment procedures, such as saying "no" following an incorrect response, does not result in negative side effects (e.g. aggression, anxiety, stereotypic behavior), a common concern of other professionals (see Leaf et al., 2019).

Even these less invasive punishment procedures should only be implemented with careful guidelines. First and foremost, interventionists need to follow all ethical, legal, and certification guidelines. Second, the use of punishment must be done in conjunction with reinforcement-based procedures. Some professionals say that for every punishment implemented, an interventionist should provide reinforcement 10 times or even 100 times more. The truth is there are no set rules on the correct ratio of punishment to reinforcement. In the penguin study, we found that the interventionists used a 7:1 ratio of reinforcement to punishment (Leaf et al., 2016). We suggest that interventionists use a similar rate of reinforcement compared to punishment in instructional settings, including behaviorally based social skills groups. Punishment should not come from an emotional place—rather, it should be implemented systematically and by an interventionist who is thinking critically. The interventionist needs to be able to turn it on and off like a light switch. They must be able to provide corrective feedback in a firm voice, then immediately go back to being fun once the learner has turned their behavior around. Finally, if the punishment does not result in quick behavior decrease, the procedures should be terminated.

Range of Contingency Systems

There are a variety of contingency systems that can be used within the context of a social skills group. It should be noted that different learners in the social skills group may have different contingency systems simultaneously. Each individual learner could also be using multiple contingency systems simultaneously. The contingency systems described in this book are just some examples that can be used within a social skills group. It is important for interventionists to be able to create their own contingency systems based on the individual needs of each learner in the social skills group.

Direct Reinforcer Exchange

An example of a simple contingency system is one where an interventionist provides immediate access to a reinforcer following an appropriate social behavior, correct response, or a period of time the learner has not engaged in aberrant behavior. This type of contingency system is typically used with learners who are new to group intervention, may need a higher rate of reinforcement within the social skills group, and/or do not have a full understanding of contingencies.

There are some key components for the effective use of a direct reinforcement exchange. First, it is important that the interventionists have already determined which items or activities are potential reinforcers. It is also important for the interventionists to operationally define which behavior(s) will result in access to a reinforcer. During group instruction, ideally the lead interventionist provides access to reinforcers, but it is important that the shadow interventionists have potential reinforcers ready, in case the lead interventionist is preoccupied. When using this type of reinforcement system, it is also important that the learner is able to successfully transition away from the reinforcer (e.g., when time is up, they hand the item back to the interventionist or move away from the activity). If the learner cannot calmly transition, then this skill may need to be worked on proactively outside of the social skills group or as a one-to-one pullout session during the group.

Finally, interventionists should identify the desired schedule of reinforcement for the learners. The interventionist could provide reinforcement every time the learner engages in the target behavior, provides a correct response, or goes a period of time not engaging in aberrant behavior. The interventionist could provide reinforcement after so many instances (e.g., after every third instance) of the target behavior(s), a set number of correct responses, or a specific length of time not engaging in aberrant behavior. Alternatively, the interventionist can be more variable/unpredictable about when they provide access to reinforcement (e.g., sometimes after three responses and sometimes after seven responses). When implementing a direct reinforcer exchange, the general rule of thumb is to provide continuous reinforcement in the beginning of intervention and fade to a more variable schedule of reinforcement as quickly as possible.

As described above, using direct reinforcer exchange should typically be done with learners who are new to group intervention or need a higher rate of reinforcement within the social skills group. This type of reinforcement system should not be used with learners who have been in the social skills group for an extended period of time, are experienced in group learning, or do not need such a high rate of reinforcement. For those learners who are more impacted and initially require direct reinforcement exchange, fade reinforcement as soon as possible and transition learners to more natural reinforcement systems used in group learning environments.

Individual Token Systems

A token economy is a reinforcement system where learners receive tokens following engagement in a correct response, target social behaviors, or refraining from aberrant behavior. After the learner has earned all of their tokens, they hand the board to the interventionist and are awarded brief access to the terminal reinforcer.

There are a variety of ways an interventionist can implement a token economy. Figure 18 provides examples of token boards that have been used in our social skills groups. They range from basic (e.g., six tokens on a board) to elaborate and exciting (e.g., the token board forming a picture). If multiple learners are using a token board within the group, we have found it runs more smoothly if all tokens are the same. This way the interventionists can easily put a token on the board without having to search for the token that matches the learner. Similar to direct reinforcement systems, the interventionists can provide tokens on different schedules of reinforcement. Within a social skills group, it is important that the lead interventionist provides the majority of tokens during group instruction.

Figure 18. Picture of Token Boards

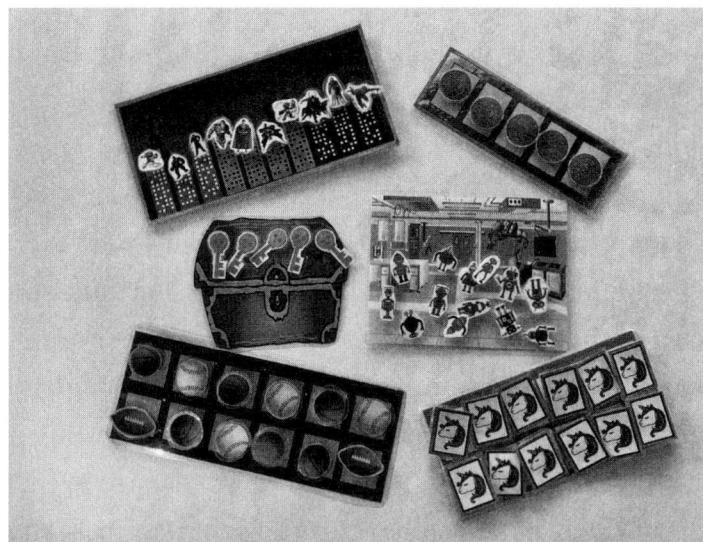

There are some important guidelines that should be considered prior to implementing a token system. One of the most important considerations is the earning requirement (i.e., how many tokens are required prior to exchanging). Interventionists should carefully analyze what schedule of reinforcement is required for the learner to be successful and acquire target skills at high rates. If the learner is only required to earn a couple of tokens, then the learner may become satiated with the terminal reinforcer. This can also interfere with the flow of teaching and reduce the amount of time available for teaching. If the learner is required to earn too many tokens, the learner may "give up" if the rate of reinforcement is too thin. Thus, it is important for an interventionist to select the optimal number of tokens. This should be a carefully considered requirement, not just defaulting to a commonly used number or basing it on whatever token board happens to be available. As the learner becomes more proficient and is able to rapidly earn tokens, the schedule of reinforcement should be thinned (e.g., by raising the number of tokens required before the exchange, by requiring more responses for each token earned). The goal is to eliminate the token system when the learner is motivated by naturally occurring contingencies (e.g., learning a new skill, peer approval).

A second consideration in determining how long the learner will have access to the item/activity and where the learner will engage with the item. In our social skills groups, we generally keep this duration between 2–10 minutes. If the duration is too brief, the learner may not be motivated to continue to engage in the target social behaviors. Conversely, if a learner receives more time than necessary, it decreases their number of learning opportunities, may result in satiation, and may make it harder for the learner to transition back to work. A good rule of thumb we've found for a social skills group is for a learner to receive no more than 5 minutes of access to a reinforcer. This ensures that the learner has enough time to engage with the reinforcer while also not missing out on learning opportunities within the social skills group. There is no magic number and this time should be individualized as necessary.

We've also found it to be beneficial to have a separate area for learners to access reinforcers. This area is a place within the room where there are a variety of reinforcers available. Figure 19 provides an example of what this area could look like in the context of a social skills group. When there is a separate area for accessing reinforcers, the lead interventionist does not need to provide the learner with a reinforcer directly, but can give the learner access to an area with multiple reinforcers that are available as long as they remain in that area. Once a learner receives all of their tokens, they are granted access to the separate area for a predetermined amount of time (e.g., 5 minutes). Another benefit to having this separate area is that multiple learners can be in the area simultaneously, allowing for more opportunities to engage in social interactions. Finally, interventionists do not have to carry around specific reinforcers for each learner in the group, as those items and activities are in the separate area. When using a separate area, it is important to practice transitioning from the break area back to the group quietly so that the group is not disturbed when the learner returns. It is also more natural, thereby helping to facilitate generalization.

Figure 19. Example of a Reinforcement Area

A final consideration is whether a response cost system should be implemented in conjunction with the token system. This would mean that in addition to the interventionist providing the learner tokens for appropriate behaviors, the interventionist would remove tokens when the learner engages in inappropriate behaviors. Some professionals have argued that removing tokens may impact the learner's self-esteem, lead to aggressive or other maladaptive behaviors, and is not an effective way to decrease unwanted behaviors. However, these concerns have not been supported by the research nor observed in our years of conducting social skills groups. Our experience has been that when interventionists provide tokens for desired behaviors and also (sparingly) remove tokens for carefully identified undesired behaviors, the learning process is accelerated. As always, it is important for interventionists to provide a higher rate of positive reinforcement (e.g., providing tokens) compared to response cost (e.g., removing tokens). It is also important for a learner to never go "into the red" (i.e., owe more than they can earn), but this should not happen if the tokens are meaningful and the behavioral expectations are reasonable. As long as these guidelines are taken into consideration, we recommend the use of response cost procedures within the context of a social skills group.

Level System (Behavioral Thermometer)

The contingency system we use most often in social skills groups is a level system (see Figure 20); also known as a behavioral thermometer (e.g., Cihon, Ferguson, Leaf, et al., 2019). A level system is a fluid contingency system in which a learner moves up the chart for appropriate behaviors (e.g., responding correctly to questions, displaying appropriate social behaviors, refraining from aberrant behaviors) or down the chart for inappropriate behaviors. At a minimum, a chart should consist of three levels (e.g., cool, okay, not cool) and, ideally, have multiple levels (e.g., superstar, excellent worker, ready to learn, turn it around, miss a fun activity). Each level can be differentiated with a color. Within each level, there should be enough space for the learner to move up or down within that level. This ensures that the learner engages in multiple appropriate behaviors to move to the next level. Within a level system, differential reinforcement can also be used. For example, if a learner engages in less effortful behaviors, they may only move up a little bit within their current level—but for more effortful behaviors or a newly learned social behavior, they may move up a whole level. This can also be done in reverse for inappropriate behaviors.

Figure 20. Example of a Level System

Similar to other systems, when using a level system, it is important to identify specific behaviors that are targeted for each learner in the group. Unlike other systems, however, the interventionist has the flexibility to determine the schedule of reinforcement and how much each learner can move up or down. An interventionist may move one learner up a level after every correct response and may use a more variable schedule for another learner.

We typically start the learners in the middle of the chart at the beginning of each session (e.g., okay). This way the interventionist can provide reinforcement (e.g., moving up the chart) or punishment (e.g., moving down the chart) contingent on each learner's behavior. We recommend that when an interventionist moves a learner up or down the chart, they provide specific praise or feedback (e.g., "Joe! I love how you are talking to Justin, I can move you up!"). Each level of the chart should also correspond to the consequence for the learner. The top of the chart (e.g., superstar learner) should indicate that the learner is displaying the best behaviors they are capable of displaying; this should mean that the learner earns their top-level reinforcer. Additionally, when a learner is at the top of the chart, the interventionist can pair privileges with being a "superkid" (e.g., line leader, teacher helper, gets to pick the song for musical chairs).

Alternately, if a learner is on the bottom level of the chart (e.g., miss a fun activity), this should signal that the learner misses out on an item/activity. If the learner finds it enjoyable to watch their peers engage in the activity, then they are only partly "missing out" and the consequence may not be effective. In this case, the learner should be relocated to an area where it is not possible to observe ongoing activity. At the first occurrence of appropriate behavior, once the activity is over, the interventionist should then move the learner up slightly and continue running the group.

Generally, the goal is a big "cash-in" (i.e., access a terminal reinforcer) to occur at the end of the social skills group for all learners. There may be impromptu opportunities along the way to pair something that is going to happen anyway with an individual's status on the superkid chart (e.g. "Joey, you're on excellent, so I can call on you first"). For newer learners in a social skills group, cash-ins may need to occur multiple times throughout the session. If a learner is receiving multiple cash-ins throughout the session, after each cash-in the learner should be moved back to the middle level of the chart. The goal should be to gradually increase the time between cash-ins until the learner is able to go the duration of the session prior to receiving the appropriate consequence for the corresponding level.

Like many contingency systems, the interventionists may have to specifically teach what each level on the chart means. This may require role-playing so the learners of the group know what will result in moving up and what will result in moving down. It is also important for the learners to buy-in to the system. Therefore, in the first couple of sessions, the interventionists should decrease the earning requirement to ensure that learners end on the top level of the chart so they can experience the top-level reinforcer. Once the system is established, a general rule of thumb is that learners should end on the highest level during approximately 80% of social group sessions. If learners are not meeting this level of reinforcement, then the interventionist may not be reinforcing behaviors frequently enough or the expected target behaviors may be too difficult. If a learner is consistently reaching the top level, but mild disruptive behavior is occurring during the session, this is an indication that the contingency is too lenient.

Self-Evaluation

One step toward a learner's independence in the absence of interventionist feedback and reinforcement is teaching learners to become self-evaluators (this differs from self-monitoring, described below). Self-evaluation occurs after a specified period of time when learners evaluate how they performed. To begin teaching this skill, we often have the learner evaluate the behavior of an actor engaging in a clear, discrete behavior (e.g., touching head). The learner tracks the behavior (e.g., writes a tally on a whiteboard) every time the actor engages in the predetermined behavior and the learner's accuracy is checked at the end of an interval (e.g., if the actor touched their head 10 times, the learner should have recorded 10 instances). Once this phase has been completed, the behaviors the learner is responsible for monitoring should become more subtle.

Following this step, the learner can start evaluating one of their own behaviors. This can be prompted by the learner marking down each time they get feedback on a specific target behavior. At the end of the time interval, the learner evaluates how often they engaged in a behavior. The learner would learn to associate how often they engaged in a behavior with how well they did during a specified time period. For example, if a learner engaged in an appropriate target behavior 6 or more times in a time period, they could evaluate this as doing a great job, 3–5 times as doing okay, and 0–2 as having a hard time. Initially, it is important to reinforce accuracy regardless of their behavior (e.g., if the learner accurately assessed that they had a hard time, they should access a reinforcer). Once the learner is an accurate evaluator, the instructors can provide differential reinforcement based on performance and accurate self-evaluation.

Self-Monitoring

A self-monitoring system should only be done when a learner has a complete understanding of the level system and can accurately self-evaluate their own behavior. Self-monitoring differs from self-evaluation in one important way. When a learner is self-evaluating, the learner does not need to change their behavior during the evaluation, they just need to know how they did at the end. Self-monitoring involves the learner actively self-evaluating *and* changing their behavior based on that evaluation—with the end goal that the learner can catch themselves being good.

When starting a self-monitoring system, it is important for the learner and interventionist to identify 1–5 specific behaviors. Initially, the target behaviors should be fairly concrete (e.g., sharing toys), but eventually more abstract concepts can be added (e.g., being a good friend). Next, the interventionist should set up a period of time when the learner has to monitor their own behavior. Initially, the interventionist should start with short periods of time, then increase the duration as the learner successfully monitors their own behavior(s). Much like self-evaluation, at the end of each interval the interventionist should ask the learner questions regarding each target behavior; the questions asked should be worded to highlight the positive behaviors being monitored.

For sharing toys, the interventionist may ask the learner, "Did you share your toys with a friend?" The learner then has the opportunity to say if they displayed the behavior correctly and the interventionist verifies whether the learner is accurate. The learner is awarded points for having engaged in the appropriate behavior as well as accurate reporting.

The interventionist may wish to set up a self-monitoring system that is differential so the learner gets more points for displaying the targeted behavior than for accurate self-monitoring. Like a token economy, the self-monitoring system can be used as a bridge for a terminal reinforcer. The interventionist should set it up so that after a learner receives a certain number of points, they can exchange for a reinforcing item or activity. However, given that this reinforcement system is meant to be implemented by the learner, there should be a plan to fade the use of supplemental reinforcers and transition to more naturally occurring contingencies. Figure 21 provides an example of a self-monitoring sheet.

Figure 21. Self-Monitoring Data Sheet Template and Example

Self-Monitoring Blank Template

Student: Date:

Behavior	Time Period 1	Time Period 2	Time Period 3	Circle:
	S: + –	S: + –	S: + –	+ = Displayed the Positive Behavior
	T: + –	T: + –	T: + –	
	S: + –	S: + –	S: + –	
	T: + –	T: + –	T: + –	– = Did not display the positive behavior
	S: + –	S: + –	S: + –	
	T: + –	T: + –	T: + –	
S = Student T= Teacher 2 points for displaying the positive behavior 1 point for accurate assessment				

Self-Monitoring Example

Student: Date:

	Time Period 1	Time Period 2	Time Period 3	Circle: + = Displayed the Positive Behavior - = Did not display the positive behavior
Listened to the teacher entire time	S: + -	S: + -	S: + -	
	T: + -	T: + -	T: + -	
Shared item with friends	S: + -	S: + -	S: + -	
	T: + -	T: + -	T: + -	
Kept hands to myself	S: + -	S: + -	S: + -	
	T: + -	T: + -	T: + -	
S = Student T= Teacher 2 points for displaying the positive behavior 1 point for accurate assessment				

Other Systems

These are just some examples of contingency systems that can be used effectively in a social skills group, but there are many others. Another type of contingency system is a group token economy. Within a group token economy, there are a few ways tokens could be delivered. One requires all learners to engage in a certain behavior to earn a token. Another allows the group to earn a token as long as one of the group members engages in a particular behavior. A third approach combines the previous two, where tokens could be earned either when the group as a whole or an individual in the group engages in a particular behavior. When all the tokens are earned, the entire group accesses reinforcement.

The method in which tokens are administered should be determined based on the behaviors being targeted and the rate that is most appropriate for the group. There is also a competitive token economy in which the learner and the interventionist earn tokens. The learners earn tokens for engaging in the desired target behaviors and the interventionist earns tokens when the learners engage in maladaptive behaviors or fail to engage in the target behaviors. Within this type of token economy, whoever gets all of their tokens first (i.e., interventionist or learner) earns the reinforcer. An interventionist could also implement the magic number token economy (e.g., Cihon, Ferguson, Milne, et al., 2019). The magic number token economy resembles a typical token economy (can also be a competitive token economy) with one major exception: The learner is unaware of the number of tokens required to access the terminal reinforcer. The great advantage of this system is that the interventionist uses clinical judgment and in-the-moment assessment to determine the exchange rate. In essence, the interventionist can shape appropriate behaviors without the constraints of a predetermined number of tokens required to earn reinforcement.

Conclusion

We consider the use of contingency systems to be a critical component of behaviorally based social skills groups. Without the use of contingency systems, the social skills group may turn into a play group and would not be considered behavioral. More importantly, without providing contingent reinforcement, it is very unlikely that the participants would learn the kind of social skills that can lead to lifelong positive outcomes.

References

Alcalay, A., Ferguson, J. L., Cihon, J. H., Torres, N., Leaf, J. B., Leaf, R., McEachin, J., Schulze, K. A., & Rudrud, E. H. (2019). Comparing multiple stimulus preference assessments without replacement to in-the-moment reinforcer analysis on rate of responding. *Education and Training in Autism and Developmental Disorders, 54,* 69-82.

Burk, C. (2015, May). *Errorless learning.* Retrieved from: http://www.christinaburkaba.com

Cihon, J. H., Ferguson, J. L., Leaf, J. B., Leaf, R., McEachin, J., & Taubman, M. (2019). Use of a level system with flexible shaping to improve synchronous engagement. *Behavior Analysis in Practice, 12*(1), 44–51.

Cihon, J. H., Ferguson, J. L., Milne, C. M., Leaf, J. B., McEachin, J., & Leaf, R. (2019). A preliminary evaluation of a token system with a flexible earning requirement. *Behavior Analysis in Practice, 12*(3), 548–556.

LaVigna, G. W., & Donnellan, A. M. (1986). *Alternatives to punishment: Solving behavior problems with non-aversive strategies.* New York: Irvington.

Leaf, J. B., Leaf, J. A., Milne, C., Taubman, M., Oppenheim-Leaf, M., Torres, N., Townley-Cochran, D., Leaf, R., McEachin, J. & Yoder, P. (2016). An evaluation of a behaviorally based social skills group for individuals diagnosed with autism spectrum disorder. *Journal of autism and developmental disorders, 47*(2), 243-259.

Leaf, R.B., & McEachin, J.J. (1999). *A Work in Progress: Behavior management strategies and a curriculum for intensive behavioral treatment of autism.* New York, NY: Different Roads to Learning.

Leaf, J. B., Townley-Cochran, D., Cihon, J. H., Mitchell, E., Leaf, R., Taubman, M., & McEachin, J. (2019). Descriptive analysis of the use of punishment-based techniques with children diagnosed with autism spectrum disorder. *Education and Training in Autism and Developmental Disabilities, 54*(2), 107–118.

Chapter Ten
Group Discrete Trial Teaching

One of the most commonly implemented teaching procedures for individuals diagnosed with autism spectrum disorder (ASD) is discrete trial teaching (DTT). DTT generally consists of three main components: 1) an instruction from the interventionist (sometimes referred to as a discriminative stimulus or S^D), 2) an opportunity for the learner to respond, and 3) the interventionist providing a consequence based upon the learner's response. Typically, if the learner responds correctly, the interventionist provides access to reinforcement (e.g., saying "good job" or providing a token) and if the learner responds incorrectly the interventionist provides corrective feedback (e.g., saying "no" or withholding a reinforcer).

An optional fourth component of DTT is the use of a prompt. A prompt can be conceptualized as anything the interventionist does to increase the likelihood the learner engages in a correct response. Prompts should occur after the instruction and before the learner responds. Prompts can take many forms, including but not limited to a verbal model, gesture, modeling, or physically guiding the learner to engage in the correct response. Finally, an interventionist should provide prompts only when needed and fade prompts as quickly as possible so the learner can respond correctly, independent of the prompt. There are several other important prompting guidelines within the Autism Partnership Method when implementing DTT. These guidelines should help ensure that interventionists are implementing high quality DTT and are discussed next.

The Instruction

The first component of DTT is the instruction. Today, there are many professionally recommended rules regarding the instruction. Some of these rules include using simple language–for example, saying "ball" instead of "find the ball." Another common rule is providing the same instruction each trial. So, instead of varying instructions between "Find Billy," "Where is Billy," and "Show me the picture of Billy," the interventionist would say "Find Billy" on every trial. Many of these rules lack empirical support and research does not show that following these guidelines results in the desired stimulus control and faster acquisition. They are also misrepresentations of what occurred at the UCLA Young Autism Project.

Within the Autism Partnership Method, we have guidelines with respect to instructions instead of protocols. The complexity of any instruction falls on a continuum (see Figure 22). On one end of this continuum are simple instructions (e.g., "Billy") and on the other end are complex instructions (e.g., "Hey, can you find the picture of Billy for me?"). The complexity of instructions may vary from learner to learner, program to program, and trial to trial. This helps ensure that the language is as natural as possible without confusing the learner. Within the Autism Partnership Method, it is important for an interventionist to vary the instructions as soon as possible (Leaf et al., 2016). Providing varied instructions can help prevent undesired stimulus control (e.g., only responding when one variation of an instruction is provided). Varying instructions also exposes learners to multiple exemplars which promotes generalization (Stokes & Baer, 1977), reduces learner boredom (Leaf & McEachin, 1999), and more closely resembles instructions provided within natural environments.

Figure 22. Continuum of Instructions During DTT

CONTINUUM OF INSTRUCTION

Beginning
"Batman"

Simple
"Find Batman"

Complex
"Where is Batman"

Advanced
**"Can you find where
the batman is?"**

The instruction provided by the interventionist should be based on variables that are assessed via in-the-moment assessment and clinical judgement. These variables include but are not limited to: the learner's previous history with the program or the task, receptive language skills, correct trials with a specific instruction, attending, and novelty or difficulty of the task.

Prompts

Prompting is one of the most important aspects of DTT: it is commonly how an interventionist teaches correct responses. Without systematic prompting, teaching just becomes a trial and error process. If the instructor provides too little assistance, the learner may become frustrated, stop responding to instructions, or engage in maladaptive behaviors. On the other hand, if the instructor provides too much assistance and fails to fade prompts quickly, the learner may become prompt dependent (i.e., only respond correctly in the presence of the prompt) and fail to respond correctly to the instruction alone. Poor timing of instructor prompts (e.g., prompting after an incorrect response) could create superstitious responding, undesired behavior chains, or attending to irrelevant variables.

It is difficult to become a good prompter, but prompting is critical to quality DTT. To help interventionists become good prompters, researchers and clinicians have developed numerous prompting systems. These prompting systems include but are not limited to: most-to-least, least-to-most, constant time delay, and flexible prompt fading. Each is common among interventionists and has been empirically evaluated. Most-to-least prompting is when the interventionist provides the most assistive prompt first, then systematically fades the level of assistance until the learner responds to the instruction alone. Least-to-most prompting is when the interventionist provides the instruction alone and systematically increases the level of assistance if the learner responds incorrectly.

A second category of prompting systems are time-delay prompting systems (e.g., simultaneous prompting, constant time delay, progressive time delay). Within these systems, the interventionist provides a controlling prompt (i.e., a prompt that ensures the learner will respond correctly) after a pre-specified duration following the instruction. For example, with constant time delay, the interventionist provides an instruction and gives the learner 5 seconds to respond. If the learner does not respond within 5 seconds, the interventionist provides the controlling prompt.

Within the Autism Partnership Method, interventionists implement flexible prompt fading (Leaf et al., 2016). Within flexible prompt fading, the interventionist has the flexibility to use any prompt and fade those prompts at their discretion. Though flexible prompt fading does not have strict protocols, there are five general guidelines. First, an interventionist can use any prompt type (e.g., gestural, verbal, positional) that is effective for the individuals they are providing intervention to. Second, the interventionist should aim to keep the learner responding correctly on 80% of trials (prompted or independent). This ensures that the learner remains successful and contacts a high rate of reinforcement, but still allows occasional errors. Third, the interventionist should provide the least assistive prompt necessary for the learner to engage in a correct response. Fourth, if the interventionist predicts a high probability of error without a prompt, then the interventionist should provide a prompt. Fifth, the interventionist should fade prompts as quickly as possible while still keeping the learner successful. This requires occasional unprompted trials (i.e., probes) to see if the learner can perform the skill independently. These guidelines should be followed using the interventionist's clinical judgment and in-the-moment assessment. Figure 23 provides a flow chart of some of the questions an interventionist should consider and how best to proceed depending on the answers.

Figuring 23. Flowchart of Prompting Decisions

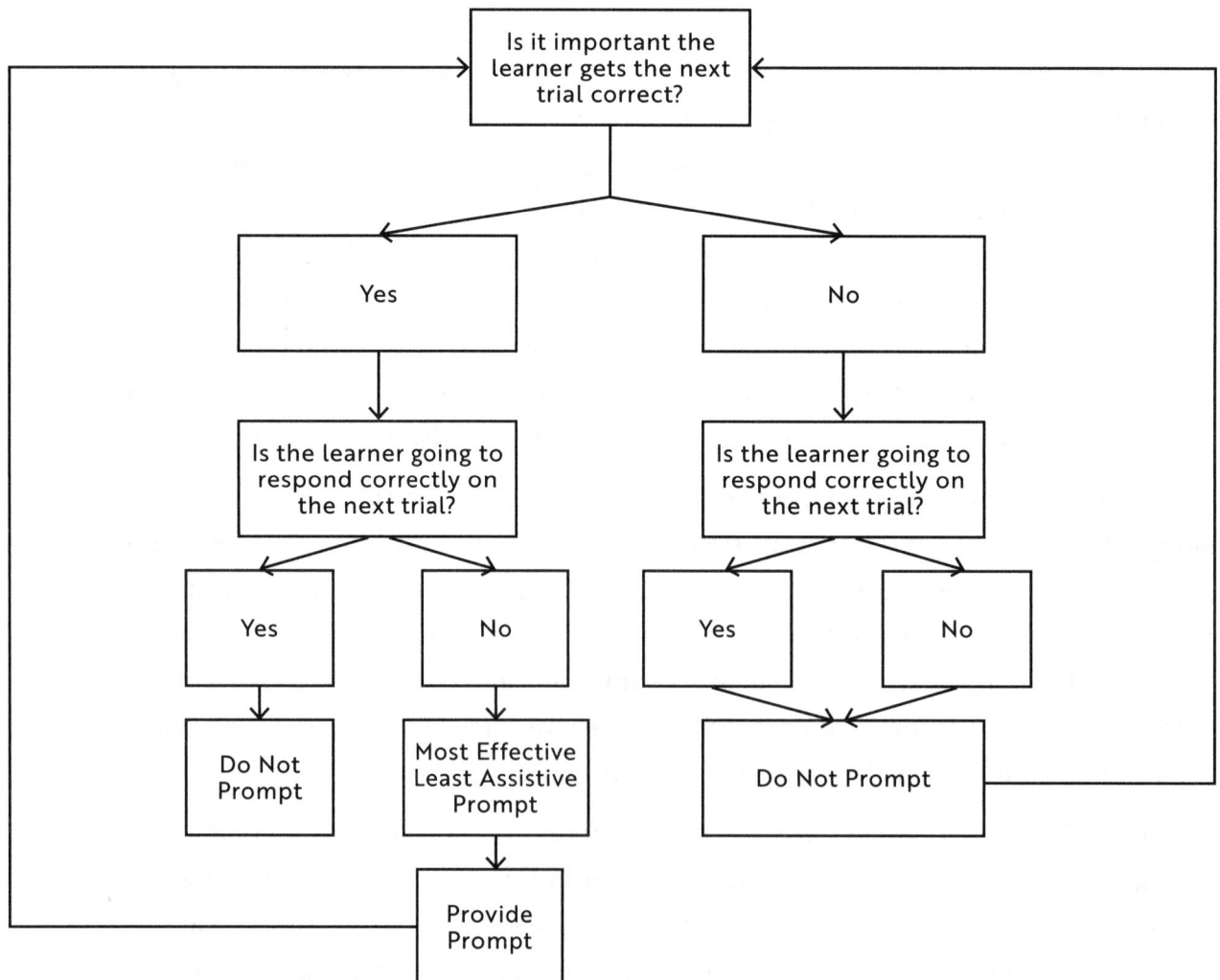

The Behavior

Within a DTT framework, interventionists often focus solely on the acquisition of the skill target. For instance, if the target is an expressive label, the interventionist's focus might be only on the learner's response to the label. In these situations, if the learner responds correctly (i.e., a correct expressive label) but also engages in stereotypy, the interventionist may still provide reinforcement based upon the correct expressive label. In the Autism Partnership Method, it is important to focus on the skill target (i.e., is the task response correct or incorrect) in addition to learning-how-to-learn behaviors (e.g., scanning, absence of stereotypic behavior, vocal disruptions, engagement). Similar to instructions from the interventionist, the learner's behavior is also on a continuum. On one end of the continuum, the interventionist may only be concerned with reinforcing the absence of aberrant behavior; on the other end, the interventionist may be concerned with reinforcing correct responding only in the absence of aberrant behavior. The interventionist's decisions on what behaviors to reinforce should be based on in-the-moment assessment of several variables, including but not limited to: how new the learner is to the teaching, the rates of aberrant behavior, and the type of task.

The Feedback

The final component of DTT is the provision of feedback following the learner response. As discussed above, if the learner responds correctly, the interventionist provides reinforcement. If the learner responds incorrectly or does not respond, the interventionist may provide feedback (e.g., "No, that's not it."). The tone of the feedback should correspond to the gravity of the error. Early in the learning process, we deliberately allow some errors to happen to see if learners can learn from mistakes. If there is good effort during the trial, feedback should be supportive while still clearly indicating that the response was incorrect. However, if scanning does not occur before the response, the response is careless, or stereotypic behavior occurs, there would be a sterner tone of voice and possibly removal of tokens or moving down on a level system. In this way, the corrective feedback is differential so that the "punishment fits the crime." The feedback should never be mean, emotional, or involve the interventionist yelling at the learner. But it does need to accurately convey the message to the learner.

A final consideration for providing feedback is whether the interventionist will include instructive feedback. Instructive feedback is additional information the interventionist provides during feedback. For example, if teaching superheroes, a trial might start with holding up a picture of The Flash and the interventionist saying, "Who is it?" Following a correct response, the interventionist provides general feedback (e.g., "That's right!")

as well as instructive feedback (e.g., "He is really fast."). Instructive feedback can be beneficial as it provides the learner with additional information that can be learned without direct teaching, in the same way that neurotypical children acquire new information.

DTT Misconceptions

Common misconceptions in the field are that DTT should occur in distraction-free areas, always include counterbalancing when teaching receptive labels, only occur with early learners, only be used with more impacted learners, not be used to teach complex skills, only be used to teach language or academic skills, and not be used to teach social skills. In reality, DTT is a systematic teaching procedure that can be used across all learners diagnosed with ASD to teach a wide variety of skills and can be implemented in many instructional formats. Unfortunately, the biggest misconception about DTT is it should only occur in a one-to-one teaching format, which is just not the case.

General Group DTT Guidelines

When implementing DTT in a group setting, there should always be one lead interventionist with the other interventionists providing support if necessary. Only the lead interventionist should provide the instruction and the support interventionists should not repeat the instruction. Doing so may result in the learners only attending to the support interventionists and not the lead. Ideally the lead interventionist should also provide all prompts when possible. If the support interventionist does provide a prompt, the prompt should occur from behind the learner in a manner that does not draw their attention away from the lead interventionist. Additionally, the lead interventionist should be the primary person to provide consequences (e.g., reinforcement, corrective feedback). It is the responsibility of the support interventionist to signal to the lead interventionist when a learner is doing well and reinforcement should be provided, or if a learner is not doing well and corrective feedback should be provided. If the lead interventionist cannot provide reinforcement at that time, then the support interventionist should provide the reinforcement.

One of the best ways we've found to prompt learners in a group setting is using observational prompts. When using an observational prompt, the interventionist provides feedback to the learner who responded incorrectly (e.g., "No, that's not it."), then immediately reissues the same instruction to a learner in the group who they know will respond correctly and provide reinforcement for the correct response (e.g., "Yes! You got it!"). At this point, the interventionist will reissue the same instruction to the learner who originally responded incorrectly. Figure 24 provides an example of how an observational prompt can be used.

Figure 24. Example of An Observational Prompt

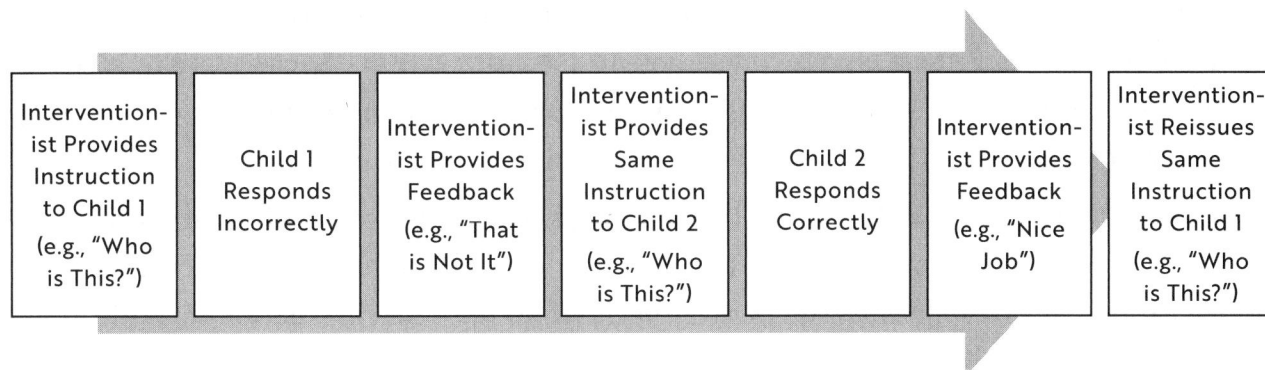

Interventionist Provides Instruction to Child 1 (e.g., "Who is This?")	Child 1 Responds Incorrectly	Interventionist Provides Feedback (e.g., "That is Not It")	Interventionist Provides Same Instruction to Child 2 (e.g., "Who is This?")	Child 2 Responds Correctly	Interventionist Provides Feedback (e.g., "Nice Job")	Interventionist Reissues Same Instruction to Child 1 (e.g., "Who is This?")

Trial Types

We use three different types of trials during group DTT. The first is sequential discrete trials. In sequential trials, the lead interventionist provides an instruction to one learner at a time and completes each trial before starting another trial. Each learner may receive the same instruction or the instruction may vary across learners to maximize the relevance of the trial to each learner's individual goals. For example, if the target is identifying activities available on the playground, the lead interventionist may start with, "Joe, what's something you do on the playground?" After Joe answers, the lead interventionist moves on to Henry, "Henry, can you think of something different?" Notice that this requires Henry to have been paying attention during Joe's trial, which helps promote sustained attention even when the lead interventionist is only directly interacting with a single learner. After Henry's turn, the lead interventionist turns to another learner with the same question or an entirely new question. Over time, all learners will receive a few turns, but not everyone has to answer every question. The instructor can provide more trials for learners who need it and less for learners who consistently demonstrate they are attending and learning from others' responses. Whenever possible, it is best to avoid going around the group in a predictable order, which can lead to inattentiveness—learners could begin to predict when it will be their turn and may not attend to group instruction before or after their turn.

The second type of trial that can be used in a social skills group is choral responding, where the lead interventionist provides one instruction for all learners to respond to simultaneously. For example, if the lesson is about changing the game when someone is bored, the lead interventionists may ask, "When do you change the game?" with the expectation of all learners responding simultaneously. A variation of choral responding is a discrete trial addressed to the group that uses a conditional instruction. The condition could be something that applies to none (e.g. "If you have an elephant as a pet, raise your hand"), some (e.g. "If you brought a snack from home, go get it now"), or all of the learners

("Everyone line up at the door"). Note that an instruction addressed to one individual by name occurring within a variety of instructions is a kind of conditional instruction, equivalent to "If your name is Joey, you can go to the story center." These types of trials require a greater level of attending and comprehension for learners in the group and may need to be broken down further before learners can be successful.

The final type of trial we have used in social skills groups is overlapping, where an instruction is provided to one learner (e.g., "Timmy go get a paper towel") and while that learner (Timmy) is responding, the instructor provides another instruction to a different learner. The overlapping trial can be related (e.g., "Susy, go help Timmy," "Billy, do you remember where we keep them?") or unrelated (e.g., "Joey, have you fed the fish today?"). Overlapping trials greatly increase the efficiency of instruction since more teaching trials can be completed in the same amount of time and it provides excellent opportunities for observational learning.

Skills That Can Be Targeted

There are a variety of social behaviors that can be taught using a DTT format in a social skills group. In the curriculum portion of this book, we have highlighted some of the skills that we have taught using DTT within the context of a social skills group such as joint attention, observational learning, identifying friends, making inferences, emotion identification, and joining in an ongoing activity. Interventionists could also teach advanced social skills such as identifying what makes a friend, ways to improve friendship, and identifying sarcasm.

References

Leaf, J. B., Cihon, J. H., Leaf, R., McEachin, J., & Taubman, M. (2016). A progressive approach to discrete trial teaching: Some current guidelines. *International Electronic Journal of Elementary Education, 9,* 361-372.

Leaf, R.B., & McEachin, J.J. (1999). *A Work in Progress: Behavior management strategies and a curriculum for intensive behavioral treatment of autism.* New York, NY: Different Roads to Learning.

Stokes, T. F., & Baer, D. M. (1977). An implicit technology of generalization. *Journal of Applied Behavior Analysis, 10,* 349-367.

Chapter Eleven
Cool Versus Not Cool™

One commonly implemented way to teach social behavior in the Autism Partnership Method is the Cool versus Not Cool™ procedure. The Cool versus Not Cool™ procedure is a social discrimination program to teach learners diagnosed with autism spectrum disorder to identify socially desired skills (cool) and socially undesired skills (not cool) and to engage in the socially desired behaviors. The procedure consists of five main components: (1) labeling the skill to be taught, (2) the interventionist modeling cool and not cool behaviors, (3) the learner answering questions following the models, (4) the learner role-playing, and (5) the interventionist providing reinforcement or feedback based on learner responding and the role-play. The procedure is generally used for intermediate to advanced learners who have an appropriate receptive and expressive language repertoire for their age.

The Procedure

Labeling. The first step of the Cool versus Not Cool™ procedure is for the interventionist to label the skill or behavior that will be targeted during the teaching session. For example, if the target skill is for the learners join into play, the interventionist might say, "Today we are going to practice how to join in with your friends the cool way." If the target skill is for the learners to go with the flow, the interventionist might say, "Today let's practice being cool when your friends want to do something different from you." After the interventionist labels the skill, it is important to ask comprehension questions with at least one member of the group to ensure learners were paying attention (e.g., "What are we working on today?"). If the learners in the group respond correctly, the interventionist should move on to the next step. If several learners in the group do not respond correctly, the lead interventionist should restate the target skill and check for comprehension again. After learners respond to comprehension questions, the lead interventionist should provide reinforcement for correct responses and corrective feedback for incorrect responses. During this time, the support interventionists should be taking data, helping manage aberrant behavior, providing reinforcement or corrective feedback when appropriate, or helping signal to the lead interventionist which learners to call on or not call on based on their behavior.

Modeling. After the lead interventionist labels the target behavior or skill, the interventionist will provide a model. In the Cool versus Not Cool™ procedure, the lead interventionist models the behavior correctly (i.e., cool) and incorrectly (i.e., not cool). Including examples of incorrect performance gives learners the opportunity to discriminate between appropriate and inappropriate versions of a behavior; when an example of inappropriate behavior is demonstrated, learners can demonstrate a better way to respond. Social behaviors are nuanced and missing one step could be the difference between displaying the skills appropriately or inappropriately. Because social behaviors are so nuanced, and often so difficult to learn, it may be hard for learners to understand what they are not doing correctly. As such, the interventionist modeling the behavior incorrectly can help highlight what the learners are doing incorrectly.

In the research evaluating the Cool versus Not Cool™ procedure, the interventionist has modeled the target behavior the cool way two times and the not cool way two times in a predetermined order (e.g., Milne et al., 2017). However, this can differ in clinical practice. We are currently evaluating variations on the ratio of cool to not cool examples, as well as the order. Preliminary findings suggest that the number and order of cool or not cool models should be based on what is necessary for the learners to successfully learn the target skill. If the interventionist determines that the learners need more examples of the cool way of responding (or more demonstrations of incorrect responses), they should provide additional trials of the type needed by the group. If the interventionist judges that having too many incorrect demonstrations may lead to undesired behaviors (e.g., the learners imitating the incorrect model), they have the flexibility to limit the number of incorrect demonstrations. Within clinical practice, the interventionist should also have the flexibility to determine the order of demonstrations based on the response of the learner(s) instead of predetermining the order.

The majority of social skills are easier to demonstrate with at least two people to model the target skill, though it is not always necessary. When modeling the target skill, it is preferable to include a lead and support interventionist(s). For example, if the target behavior is sharing, the model could include the support interventionist asking the lead interventionist to share a toy and the lead interventionist as the one who shares or does not share. It is important that the modeled examples are clear—initially it may be necessary to exaggerate the inappropriate example to make the discrimination as clear as possible. For this reason, it may be necessary to use adults as models in the role-plays. However, when there are group members who can clearly and reliably act out their roles, it may enhance generalization if the models are peers.

When the lead interventionist is setting up the modeling component of the Cool versus Not Cool™ procedure, the first thing they should do is inform the learners that the interventionists will demonstrate the target skill and the learners' job is to determine if the demonstration was cool or not cool (e.g., "Okay, you are going to watch me, then and tell me if I did it the cool or not cool way"). It is critical that the lead interventionist informs the learners which actor's behavior to monitor so they do not become confused when one actor's behavior is cool and the other actor's behavior is not cool. In early stages of discrimination training, it is helpful to specify which aspect of the actor's behavior to observe (e.g., "Watch to see if Jeremy is standing too close or just right."). As more components of a skill are combined, learners should develop the skillset to simultaneously monitor multiple components and each example may vary which component or components are not cool.

In the early stages of learning to evaluate an actor's behavior, it can be helpful to include a cue or signal that informs the learners that the demonstration is beginning (e.g., "Action!"). When the interventionists are demonstrating the skill correctly (i.e., the cool way), make sure they model all the steps that encompass the target skill correctly. When they are demonstrating the skill incorrectly (i.e., the not cool way), make sure they are missing steps, modeling steps incorrectly, or engaging in behaviors the learners typically demonstrate incorrectly in the natural environment. For example, if learners are struggling with sharing toys after being asked, this is what the interventionists should highlight in the "not cool" demonstration.

After each model, the interventionist should indicate the demonstration has ended (e.g., "Cut!"). For beginning learners, it is important to cut at the precise moment when the error is very clearly portrayed or when all aspects of the behavior are perfect. Next, the lead interventionist should ask the group to assess if the model was cool or not cool (e.g., "Was that cool or not cool?"). Typically, this is done chorally, although the lead interventionists could call on one of the learners (e.g., "Joe, was that cool or not cool?"). It's best to have the learners label specifically what was cool or not cool about the demonstration (e.g., "It was cool when you said 'sure' and handed over the toy to your friend"). The answers to the "why" question could be used to highlight steps of the task analysis for the skill being taught. For instance, "[The interventionist] was cool because he was looking at his friend when he asked for a toy." The lead interventionist provides appropriate feedback (e.g., "Yep! You're right, it was cool!" or "No, not quite. That one was not cool.") based on the responses.

Role-Play. After the modeling portion, the lead interventionist should have each learner role-play. Unlike the interventionist's portrayals, each learner should only role-play the skill the cool way. If it is the learner's first time practicing the target behavior in a role-play, it may be beneficial for the role-play to occur with the interventionist. As the learner progresses and consistently displays the target skill correctly with the interventionist, then it would be advantageous to have the learner role-play with a peer. Role-playing with a peer lets learners practice the target behavior closer to the context that they should ultimately engage in the social behavior. Finally, and similar to modeling, the interventionist should arrange the role-play to resemble the natural environment or situation where the skill should be displayed.

The interventionist should start by informing the group that it is time to practice. The interventionist then selects one learner to participate in a role-play. The interventionist should inform the learner of the expectations (e.g., "I want you to practice sharing with me the cool way.") and inform the rest of the learners that their job is watching the role-play to determine if it was cool or not cool—and what was cool or not cool about it. The interventionist should then inform the learners that the role-play is going to start (e.g., "Ready, set, action!"). The interventionist then engages in behaviors that set the occasion for the learner to display the target social behavior (e.g., asking the learner to share a toy). After the learner role-plays the skill, the interventionist should indicate that the role-play is over (e.g., "Cut.") and have the other participants assess if the role-play was cool or not cool. Then the interventionist should have them state why the role-play was cool or not cool. Throughout the process, the interventionist should provide feedback. The interventionist should also provide additional feedback to the learner who was role-playing about their performance.

If the learner displayed the targeted social behavior correctly, the next learner should role-play, continuing the process until each learner has had an opportunity. Note that the other learners observe the role-plays and will be asked questions about what they are observing to ensure all learners are continuously engaged. If a learner does not display the behavior correctly, role-play should continue until the learner displays the skill correctly. After 2–3 role-plays where the learner does not display the behavior correctly, it is recommended that the interventionist use flexible prompt fading (Soluaga et al., 2008) to ensure the learner displays the behavior correctly on the next role-play.

Common Misconceptions and Misuses

We have disseminated the Cool versus Not Cool™ procedure for years through conferences, workshops, consultations, books, and research. Many practitioners have begun to make use of this procedure, but several misconceptions and misuses of the procedure have occurred. One common mistake is not including a modeling or role-play component: interventionists simply ask the learner if a behavior is cool or not cool. For example, an interventionist might say, "Is it cool or not cool to share your toys?" and only require the learners to make a verbal response. Without the modeling and role-play, the teaching is incomplete.

Another misconception is that interventionists must use the words "cool" and "not cool." Those terms were used at the conception of the Cool versus Not Cool™ procedure because that was the vernacular of those particular learners–we wanted to ensure what the learners were being taught could generalize to the natural environment. That is, if one of the learners did something inappropriate and a peer told them, "That's not cool," the learner should change their behavior accordingly. Interventionists should determine which labels will be appropriate for the learners based upon their natural environment. For example, interventionists could use "wicked" or "not wicked" when running social skills groups in the east coast region of the United States.

Another misconception is that Cool versus Not Cool™ is a mentalistic procedure, in that we are only attempting to change the thought process. This is not the case, as the Cool versus Not Cool™ procedure is concerned with measuring and changing observable behaviors. This is why we believe that the role-play component is critical. Ultimately, the goal is for the learner to engage in the cool behavior in the naturalistic setting, not just to be able to describe a behavior as cool or not cool.

Another common mistake is teaching cool and not cool behavior in isolation without teaching the events that signal when to engage in the cool behavior (or not engage in the not cool behavior). These events should set the occasion for the learner to engage in the targeted behavior. When should you be gracious, give a compliment, ask a question, or offer help? The Cool versus Not Cool™ procedure is designed to not only teach the desired social behavior (e.g., losing graciously), but also the conditions under which one should engage in the social behavior (e.g., after losing a game to a friend).

Sometimes instead of determining a single target behavior, interventionists target multiple behaviors simultaneously. Targeting multiple skills simultaneously often results in slow or no acquisition. We recommend that during initial teaching, skills are targeted individually. For example, targeting "appropriate school behavior" includes sitting, waiting, and refraining from screaming and self-stimulatory behavior. Often, larger social skills, such as appropriate school behavior, require task analyses and targeting of individual skills. Once a learner is more successful with individual skills and familiar with the Cool versus Not Cool™ procedure, it may then be possible to teach multiple behaviors simultaneously.

Finally, too often we have seen the Cool versus Not Cool™ procedure used only as feedback to change behavior without any proactive teaching, demonstrations, task analysis, etc. Simply providing feedback when undesired behavior occurs is generally not sufficient to change the behavior. What is missing in this process is the opportunity to intensively practice the desired form of the behavior in advance of situations where the skill will be necessary. We believe that to most effectively produce change in behavior, it is necessary to provide proactive teaching with the Cool versus Not Cool™ procedure.

Skills That Can Be Targeted

A wide variety of social behaviors can be taught using the Cool versus Not Cool™ procedure in a social skills group. In the curriculum portion of this manual, we have provided numerous examples of social skills that can be targeted with the Cool versus Not Cool™ procedure. These skills range from simple skills, such as appropriate proximity to another person, to more advanced skills, such as joining into play. These examples are far from exhaustive and we encourage readers to recognize other specific social skills that would be amenable to Cool versus Not Cool™ discrimination training.

References

Milne, C., Leaf, J. A., Leaf, J. B., Cihon, J. H., Torress, N., Townley-Cochran, D., Taubman, M., Leaf, R., McEachin, J., & Oppenheim-Leaf, M. (2017). Teaching joint attention and peer to peer communication using the cool versus not cool procedure in a large group setting. *Journal of Developmental and Physical Disabilities, 29*, 777-796.

Soluaga, D., Leaf, J.B., Taubman, M., McEachin, J., & Leaf, R. (2008). A comparison of flexible prompt fading and constant time delay for five children with autism. *Research in Autism Spectrum Disorders, 2*, 753-765.

Chapter Twelve
The Teaching Interaction Procedure

Another intervention commonly used in the Autism Partnership Method is the teaching interaction procedure. The teaching interaction procedure is a multi-component intervention consisting of six steps, which include: 1) labeling the target behavior, 2) providing a meaningful rationale of why the learner should engage in the target behavior, 3) describing the steps of the target skill, 4) the interventionist modeling the target behavior, 5) the learner role-playing, and 6) feedback throughout.

The teaching interaction procedure is the most conversational and fluid of all of the formal procedures within our model. As such, the teaching interaction procedure is usually implemented to teach more advanced social behaviors (e.g., resisting peer pressure, what makes a friend, perspective taking) and used with learners that have age-typical expressive and receptive language. The teaching interaction procedure is similar to behavior skills training and skill streaming (see Leaf et al., 2015, for a detailed comparison), which have also been used to teach advanced social behaviors to individuals diagnosed with autism spectrum disorder. The main difference is that the teaching interaction procedure provides rationales to the learners about why they should engage in the behavior/skill being taught. The steps of the teaching interaction procedure typically occur in the same order in the literature (see Figure 25 modified from Cihon et al., 2017); however, the order of these steps should be viewed as guidelines only and the interventionist should remain flexible and modify as needed.

Figure 25. Flow Chart of The Teaching Interaction Procedure (modified from Cihon et al., 2017)

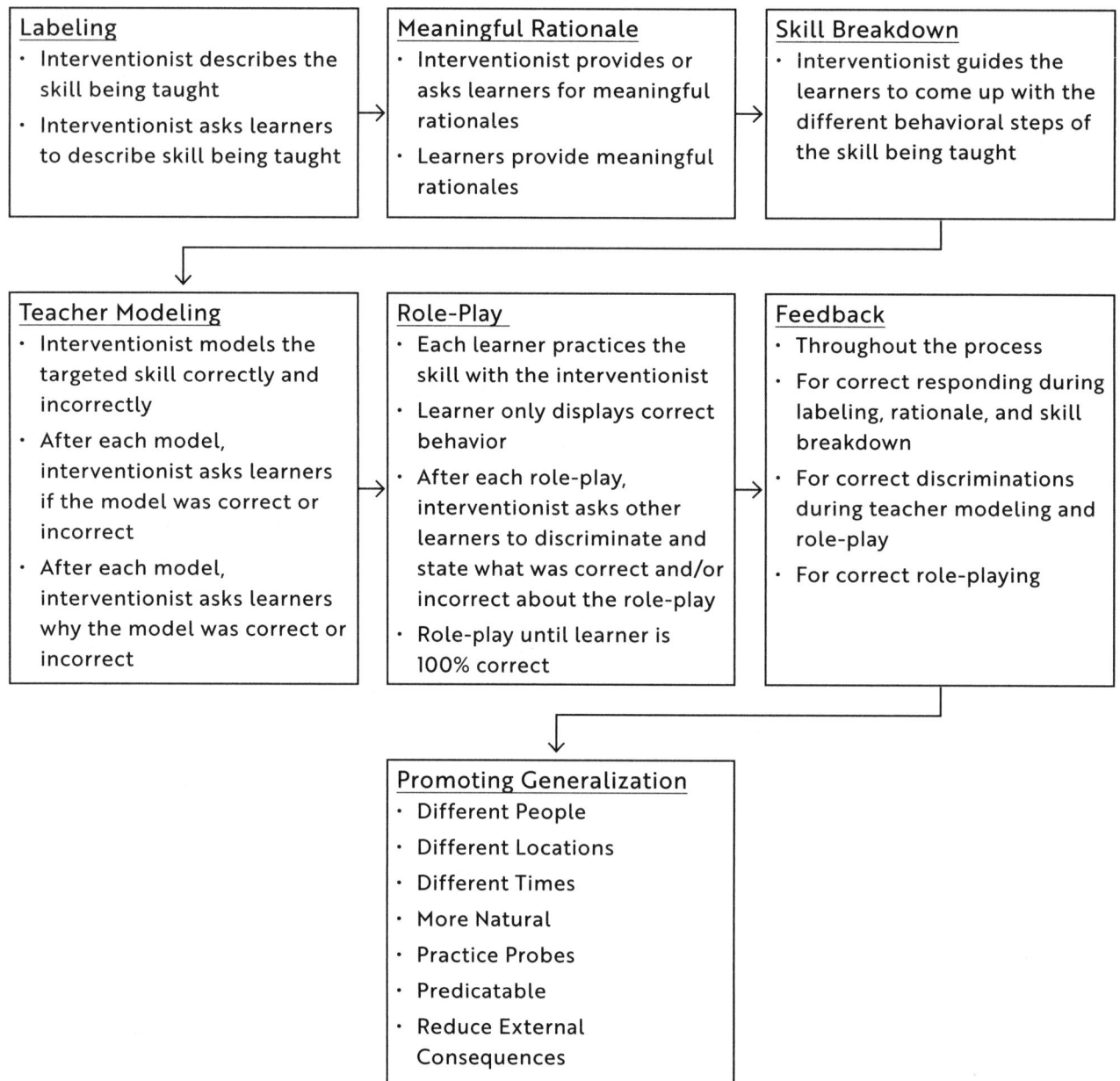

Labeling
- Interventionist describes the skill being taught
- Interventionist asks learners to describe skill being taught

Meaningful Rationale
- Interventionist provides or asks learners for meaningful rationales
- Learners provide meaningful rationales

Skill Breakdown
- Interventionist guides the learners to come up with the different behavioral steps of the skill being taught

Teacher Modeling
- Interventionist models the targeted skill correctly and incorrectly
- After each model, interventionist asks learners if the model was correct or incorrect
- After each model, interventionist asks learners why the model was correct or incorrect

Role-Play
- Each learner practices the skill with the interventionist
- Learner only displays correct behavior
- After each role-play, interventionist asks other learners to discriminate and state what was correct and/or incorrect about the role-play
- Role-play until learner is 100% correct

Feedback
- Throughout the process
- For correct responding during labeling, rationale, and skill breakdown
- For correct discriminations during teacher modeling and role-play
- For correct role-playing

Promoting Generalization
- Different People
- Different Locations
- Different Times
- More Natural
- Practice Probes
- Predicatable
- Reduce External Consequences

The Steps of the Teaching Interaction Procedure

Labeling

The first step of the teaching interaction procedure is labeling the target skill that will be the focus. The label of the skill is important, as it can be used later as an easy reference when providing feedback in the natural environment. The label can also be used for priming in a variety of situations to promote generalization from the teaching situation to everyday life. The interventionist should provide an age- and developmentally appropriate label and a simple description of the skill (e.g., "We are going to talk about answering our friends" instead of "We are going to talk about how to respond when a question is directed toward you"). Similar to the Cool versus Not Cool™ procedure, the interventionist should also describe when and where the target skill should occur.

After the interventionist labels the target behavior, they should provide an opportunity for learners to repeat the label. This allows the interventionist to determine if the learners are attending and comprehending the skill that is going to be taught. As teaching progresses across sessions, the interventionists may only ask the learners who are struggling with skill comprehension questions. Ultimately, the goal is for the learners in the group to demonstrate understanding of the skill that is being targeted.

Rationales

The second step involves providing a meaningful rationale for why it is important for the learner to engage in the skill. The provision of a meaningful rationale is one of the steps that distinguishes the teaching interaction procedure from other procedures, such as behavior skills training. A meaningful rationale is one that should be motivating for the learner. It is a rationale the learner finds important, something they are invested in and care about. It is neither a rationale that is important to the interventionist (e.g., "Because I said so.") nor a blanket rationale that can be used across all target behaviors (e.g., "Because it is cool."). When interventionists use adult or blanket rationales, it is unlikely that rationale will function as intended. Figure 26 provides examples of different types of rationales across different social skills. Rationales can also be used as a reminder for why it is important to engage in the targeted social skill. The goal of the rationale is to outline potential natural contingencies that may be contacted to engage in the behavior in the natural environment. Ultimately, the rationale should increase the likelihood the learner will engage in the targeted skill outside of the social skills group.

Figure 26. Different Types of Rationales

Potential Skill	Blanket Rationales	Adult Rationales	Potentially Meaningful Rationales
Playing with your friends	"It is cool."	"Because I told you so."	"If you play with your friends, you might have someone to play video games with."
Waiting your turn	"It is what big kids do."	"It is best for you."	"If you wait your turn, you might get to play for longer."
Sharing	"It is nice."	"It will make friends."	"If you share your toys, maybe you get to play with some of your friend's cool toys."
Sportsmanship	"It is doing a good job."	"It is important to me."	"If you don't cry when you lose, your friends might ask to play with you again."

When developing meaningful rationales, it is beneficial to provide multiple rationales when possible. This is especially true within the context of a social skills group, where meaningful rationales will likely vary across learners. When rationales are first being developed, an interventionist begins by stating two or three rationales of why engaging in the behavior is important. Then the interventionist provides the opportunity for each learner in the group to provide their own rationales. Developing meaningful rationales with learners in the social skills group takes a great deal of clinical skill to determine which rationales are appropriate and meaningful for learners, how to expand on rationales provided by learners, or how to shape rationales that may be inaccurate into more accurate and appropriate rationales for the learners. In the early stages of teaching, the interventionist may allow the learners to repeat rationales previously provided; however, as teaching progresses, the interventionist may require the learners to provide novel rationales.

An additional way to help develop the rationale for a target skill is to have the learners experience the contingencies the rationale describes. For example, if the target skill is taking turns, arrange a brief preferred game during which peers stop playing the game when the learner takes extra turns. In this case, the rationale could be that taking turns makes others happy and want to keep playing games you like. Having learners experience potential consequences does not need to happen in every session; when it's possible, or when a learner is struggling to learn new social skills, it may be helpful for them to experience the contingencies related to the rationale. Caregivers can also provide examples of situations they have observed when their child experienced a meaningful loss of opportunity due to behavior that peers did not appreciate. Such examples can provide powerful rationales for being willing to do things differently.

Description

After the rationale, the interventionist provides a description of the skill. The description is similar to a task analysis. How many steps are needed typically depends upon the complexity of the skill and the learners' prerequisite skills. More complex social skills will likely require a longer task analysis; less complex social skills will likely require a shorter task analysis. Some learners may need a skill to be broken into several steps with reinforcement occurring after each step to learn effectively, while others may learn effectively with fewer steps. Learners may also display deficits at different steps, requiring different steps of the skill to be emphasized. In the curriculum section of this book, we've provided potential task analyses for the skills we commonly teach. It is important to note that these task analyses are only guidelines, not rules, and they should be adjusted to fit the needs of each learner.

In the initial stages of describing the social skill, the interventionist typically states the first step and provides an opportunity for learners to repeat the step. The interventionist should provide access to reinforcement following correct responses and corrective feedback following incorrect responses. Additionally, interventionists should use flexible prompt fading to teach the steps of the skill. As learning progresses, the interventionists can ask the learners to state the steps without the initial verbal model. It is often beneficial to write or draw out the steps of the target skill (e.g., creating a list on a dry erase board). The interventionists might also elect to implement the Cool versus Not Cool™ procedure (see previous chapter) for individual steps as they are described.

Modeling

The next component of the teaching interaction procedure is modeling the targeted skill. This is similar to the use of "cool" (correct) and "not cool" (incorrect) in the Cool versus Not Cool™ procedure (see previous chapter). When modeling the target skill, the interventionist should model the skill correctly and incorrectly. This allows the learners to observe what the target skill should look like and what they may be doing wrong. To model the target skill, the interventionist should arrange a situation with an opportunity to engage in the targeted skill. After each model, the interventionists should provide an opportunity for the learners to determine if and why the model was cool or not cool.

Additionally, the learners should use the task analysis to describe what part of the skill was cool or not cool.

Role-Play

The fifth step of the teaching interaction procedure is role-playing. During the role-play, it is usually advisable that the learners only practice the correct social skill. Ideally, during initial teaching the learner should role-play with the interventionist. As teaching progresses with the learner successfully demonstrating the skill with the interventionist, the learner can then start to practice with a peer.

During a role-play, the interventionist should arrange situations that set the occasion to engage in the targeted social skill. For example, if the skill is losing graciously, the interventionist might arrange a game where the learner loses. After the role-play, the interventionist sets the occasion for the other learners (those not role-playing) to identify if and why the learner displayed the skill correctly or incorrectly. Then, the interventionist provides the learner with additional feedback regarding the role-play. Role-play should continue until all learners have had a chance to practice the skill (if it is a larger social skills group, this is a good opportunity to break into smaller groups for the learners to get more practice).

Feedback

The last step of the teaching interaction procedure is feedback (though it should be noted that feedback should occur throughout the teaching interaction procedure). During the didactic portion of the teaching interaction procedure (i.e., labeling, rationales, skill breakdown), the interventionist provides feedback for responding correctly. During the modeling portion, the interventionist provides feedback for identifying if the model was correct or incorrect. During the role-play component, the interventionist provides feedback while the learner is role-playing. Feedback, in the form of reinforcement and corrective feedback, is critical to the success of the teaching interaction procedure.

Promoting Generalization

To maximize the benefits of the teaching interaction procedure, interventionists should program for generalization. There are several ways to do this. One way is having *different people* implement the intervention, which will ensure that the learner is not just responding correctly to one interventionist. A second way to promote generalization is teaching in *different locations*. Similar to using different people, this helps ensure that correct performance is not controlled by the teaching environment (i.e., the learners are responding correctly across multiple settings rather than just in the social skills group setting). A third way to promote generalization is teaching at *different times* of day. A fourth way to promote generalization is exposing the learner to *varied antecedents* that set the occasion for the target skill. For instance, when teaching losing graciously, introducing different types of activities where a learner would encounter losing (e.g., a race, board game, completing a puzzle).

A fifth way to promote generalization is making the teaching interaction procedure and role-plays *more natural*. In the initial stages of teaching, the interventionists might make modeling and role-play very obvious, staged, or artificial. This typically makes teaching easier in the beginning, as learners will not be as distracted, cues to engage in the target skill will be salient, and the interventionist can really highlight the correct steps of the skill. As teaching progresses, role-play and modeling scenarios should more closely resemble the natural environment. More naturalistic role-plays in later teaching will help the learner display the skill in the natural environment.

A sixth way to promote generalization is to arrange *practice probes* after the teaching interaction procedure has concluded. Practice probes consist of setting the occasion for the learner to display the skill in a naturalistic setting. For example, for the skill of losing graciously, the interventionist might prime by letting the learners know that sometime soon they will need to lose graciously. The interventionist then sets up a situation where the learner will lose a game. Depending on how the learner performs, the interventionist should provide access to reinforcement or corrective feedback. As teaching progresses, the interventionist can increase the time between the prime and the cue and decrease the specificity of the prime (e.g., moving from, "You'll get a chance to lose gracefully" to, "Something will happen, and I want "you to think" about what to do.") until priming is completely eliminated.

A final way to facilitate generalization is to *reduce supplemental consequences* during the teaching interaction procedure. This means that the interventionists fade the schedule of reinforcement for correctly responding throughout the teaching interaction procedure.

References

Cihon, J. H., Weinkauf, S. M., & Taubman, M. (2017). Using the teaching interaction procedure to teach social skills for individuals diagnosed with autism spectrum disorder. In J. B. Leaf (Ed.), *Handbook of Social Skills and Autism Spectrum Disorder: Assessment, Curricula, and Intervention* (pp. 313–323). AG Switzerland: Springer International Publishing.

Leaf, J. B., Townley-Cochran, Taubman, M., Cihon, J. H., Oppenheim-Leaf, M. L., Kassardjian, A., Leaf, R., McEachin, J., Pentz, T. G. (2015). The teaching interaction procedure and behavioral skills training for individuals diagnosed with autism spectrum disorder: A review and commentary. *Review Journal of Autism and Developmental Disorders, 2,* 402-413.

Chapter Thirteen
Effective Group Teaching

Christine M. Milne

The beauty of running a social skills group is incorporating a variety of teaching procedures to consistently shape and improve multiple skills simultaneously in a group setting. However, to develop these skills, it is necessary to first determine the overall long-term objective of the group, as well as the short-term goals that will help lead to the overall objective. It is also important to be aware of each learners' individual goals and incorporate these goals into the group. Having a clear understanding of group and individual objectives can maximize the learning opportunities presented throughout the group. The way interventionists break down a skill, prompt a skill, teach a skill, make a skill more difficult, or even train toward generalization will all depend on the overall goals and objectives of the group.

To highlight quality group teaching, Drew, a learner, will be used as an example. Drew has an individual goal of losing graciously. While this skill has been taught proactively using a combination of the Cool versus Not Cool™ procedure and DTT in one-to-one settings, skill acquisition will continue to be incorporated during the social skills group. During the social skills group sessions, the interventionists will systematically manipulate situations presented throughout the group. First, they will present scenarios that are likely to result in low levels of problematic behaviors (e.g., losing in less preferred games). Following Drew's response, the interventionist will respond to two types of responses made by Drew: 1) the presence or absence of problem behaviors and 2) the appropriate skill currently being taught (i.e., losing graciously). Differential consequences will be provided to decrease the likelihood of problem behaviors occurring in the future, while a combination of shaping and differential reinforcement will be used to reinforce and increase the likelihood of displaying desired skills in the future. The interventionists will also need to determine whether a prompt should be provided, what type of prompt to use, when to fade the prompt, and how to fade it.

As Drew engages in the target skill more consistently, the interventionists will start to introduce situations that may evoke more problematic behaviors (e.g., losing a moderately or highly preferred game). In the meantime, the scenarios that were previously targeted will continue to occur, but the interventionist will begin to fade reinforcement quality (e.g., a quick high-five instead of verbal and physical praise), type (e.g., praise instead of tangible), or rate (e.g., every third occurrence instead of every occurrence).

When the interventionists plan how to promote the development of a skill, it is evident that many behavior analytic procedures will be used. Incidental teaching occurs when the environment is arranged in a way to increase the likelihood that the learner will have the opportunity to engage in a certain behavior. In Drew's case, the interventionist would arrange a variety of games Drew will lose. This means that the interventionist may manipulate some pieces in the game or determine who Drew will play against. The interventionist would also provide the opportunity for Drew to lose in a variety of ways (e.g., losing in board games, musical chairs, an outdoor obstacle course). This is important to ensure that not only one type of activity signals the need to remain gracious. Using multiple exemplars allows the learner to practice the skill across a variety of instances. Another variable the interventionist must consider is the level of difficulty of each scenario. Ideally, the interventionists will initially introduce low-level situations (i.e., situations in which the learner is likely to be successful and unlikely to display problem behavior), then progressively make situations more difficult, rather than setting the learner up for failure.

When the learner responds appropriately to the scenario described above, the interventionist must then determine how to respond. Given that the interventionist is evaluating appropriate and inappropriate behaviors, the interventionist is likely to use differential reinforcement. For example, if Drew lost a game and engaged in the targeted appropriate behaviors (e.g., "Aww man! Want to play again?") while refraining from inappropriate behaviors (e.g., throwing the materials and screaming), the interventionist should deliver a higher quality reinforcer (e.g., a favorite social reinforcer or moving up two levels on the level system). If Drew engaged in the targeted appropriate behaviors, but also some inappropriate behaviors (e.g., slamming a hand down prior to appropriate behavior), the interventionist would deliver a moderate or lower quality reinforcer (e.g., move up one level on the level system). If Drew engages in appropriate and inappropriate behaviors (e.g., "Aww man! Want to play again?" while pouting and yelling), the interventionist would not provide reinforcement or provide a punishing consequence instead. In this situation, the interventionist would simply provide corrective feedback (e.g., "You said something really cool, but it's not something to cry about."). If Drew only engaged in inappropriate behaviors, the interventionist is likely to respond with feedback and a negative consequence (e.g., moving down the color chart, missing a fun activity).

There will be times that unplanned situations occur, which is another reason why communication between interventionists is important and all interventionists must be aware of the current skill level and goals for each learner. If an unplanned situation occurs that is a current or previous goal for the learner, the interventionist has at least two options: (1) use the opportunity as a probe for generalization or (2) use it as a learning opportunity. If the interventionist uses it as a probe for generalization, the interventionist will not interfere and allow natural consequences to occur (though at a later time they may bring up the situation and provide feedback on how the learners responded). The response of the learner can provide valuable information for the interventionist about how the learner is likely to respond in the absence of direct intervention. This can help the interventionist determine how the learner is progressing toward the overall goal (i.e., progress to the next goal, stay at the current goal, or go back a step). If the interventionist decides to make the unplanned situation a learning opportunity, the interventionist should provide differential reinforcement based on the response of the learner.

If an unplanned situation occurs that is much more difficult than the learner's current goal and the learner responds appropriately, it is important to provide a high-quality reinforcer. And note that while the learner responded appropriately in that situation, it does not necessarily mean the learner is ready to jump to that type of scenario regularly. If the learner does not respond appropriately, it is important to maintain contingencies that result in decreasing the problem behavior. It is also important not to inadvertently reinforce inappropriate behavior, but rather provide consequences that will decrease the likelihood of that inappropriate behavior.

While differential reinforcement helps with increasing and decreasing the likelihood of certain behaviors, another approach—shaping —is beneficial in improving the quality of a response. Shaping is an approach that also involves differential reinforcement, but the criterion for reinforcement starts at a level that is currently in the learner's repertoire and is gradually increased to require successive approximations that are closer and closer to the terminal goal. While this sounds like a linear process, shaping is not linear, but rather an approach to expand response classes. For Drew, the quality of appropriate behaviors may be shaped by reinforcing variables such as tone, voice volume, non-verbal behaviors such as eye contact, and what Drew is doing with his body. Initially, reinforcement would be provided for Drew using the language, "Aww man! Want to play again?" even if his tone comes off as rude or angry. As Drew uses the language more frequently, reinforcement may be withheld until he engages in the targeted behavior with a calm tone. The next criterion for Drew could be to engage in the replacement behavior with a calm tone and a relaxed body. Shaping this new appropriate response will continue until the terminal goal is reached. Note that in a group context with multiple instructors, continual communication among the instructors about the current criterion for reinforcement is essential.

As the learner progresses with their individual skill goals, it is important to train for generalization. This can be accomplished by introducing the skill across a variety of settings and people, but can also occur by manipulating the rate of reinforcement. Fading supplemental reinforcement (e.g., extra praise, moving up on the level chart, earning toys) is critical for generalization. The ultimate goal is to expose the learner to a variety of situations and have the learner respond appropriately in the absence of supplemental reinforcement (i.e., responding appropriately based on the naturally occurring contingencies). Once a skill generalizes across people and environments, it allows for new skills to enter into skill acquisition.

So far, we have discussed using multiple procedures with one individual learner with one goal. However, these same techniques can, and should, be used across learners and for the larger group objectives as well. This will be illustrated in the next example.

The large group is working on joint attention. When a novel event occurs, the group is expected to initiate and respond to joint attention bids with peers. Initially, the scenarios set up will be very obvious. The interventionists will then provide consequences based on the learners' responses. The quality of responses will also be reinforced to improve the types of comments made, the latency between the event and the learners' responses, and the level of engagement with their peers (i.e., shaping). The types of events set up will become more subtle and levels of reinforcement will fade to more natural contingencies, leading toward generalization.

It is important to note that these teaching approaches for individual and large group formats do not occur in isolation. Teaching individual and group targets should be set up to run simultaneously. In the previous examples, the large group was working on joint attention. However, the learners must be engaged in an activity before the evocative event occurs. The interventionists will pick games that are likely for Drew to successfully engage in his target skill (i.e., losing graciously) while pairing him with a learner that may be working on commenting. Another pair of learners may play a game that requires turn taking, as those are individual goals for those learners. While the learners are practicing and accessing reinforcement for individual goals, the evocative event occurs. The learners are then expected to engage in the large group target (i.e., joint attention). The interventionist then provides access to reinforcement and/or feedback accordingly.

A major advantage to using a group format to teach social skills that observational learning can be an effective teaching tool. Observational learning is when learners can acquire skills through observation alone. This occurs when observing both the behavior of others and the contingencies connected to that behavior results in behavior change without having to directly contact the contingencies. This can make teaching more efficient. Initially, the skill of observational learning may need to be taught (Leaf & McEachin, 1999). Once the skill is established, it can be used as a method to teach multiple skills at once. For example, if the learner asks a question, some learners may shout out the answer while others raise their hand. By selecting learners who raise their hands and explicitly reinforcing doing so, other learners in the group should learn that they need to raise their hand if they want to say something. If the interventionist provides corrective feedback for a learner who shouts out the answer, the other learners in the group should they learn to refrain from shouting out.

Using observational learning can save time by not having to teach each learner or each skill individually. Observational learning allows the learners to learn from others in the group experiencing contingencies and provides a less intrusive way to prompt learners, which may also result in increased awareness of peers. For example, if Learner A has an individual goal of cheering on a friend, an interventionist may provide reinforcement to Learner B, who has already mastered the skill. The reinforcement provided to Learner B may function as a prompt for Learner A to cheer on a friend.

Overall, quality group teaching requires a good understanding of many behavior analytic procedures and the principles behind those procedures. In addition, it is important that all interventionists are aware of the overall group objectives and the current phase of programming that will lead to the terminal goal. This requires consistent communication between interventionists to systematically progress individual and group goals.

References

Leaf, R.B., & McEachin, J.J. (1999). *A Work in Progress: Behavior management strategies and a curriculum for intensive behavioral treatment of autism.* New York, NY: Different Roads to Learning.

Chapter Fourteen
Embedded Instruction Within Play

Christine M. Milne

Embedded instructions are when the interventionist provides direct or indirect instructions within the context of a larger activity. For example, providing instructions for the learner during a song would be an example of embedded instructions. Embedded instructions should occur in structured teaching settings but also may be used within play activities. Activities, games, and play can be a mechanism to target a variety of skills, from behavior reduction to skill development. Ideally, these should be activities that the learners will encounter within their natural environments such as school, home, camp, and playdates.

When using embedded instructions, the interventionist should provide reinforcement or corrective feedback not just for the main targeted social behavior, they should provide consequences for all target behaviors. This means that interventionists should observe and analyze all behaviors the learners are displaying at any given moment. Interventionists should use differential reinforcement and provide higher quality reinforcement for the main targeted behavior as opposed to the other embedded instructions.

Learning-How-to-Learn Skills

Numerous skills can continue to be targeted within a play or game format, especially learning-how-to-learn skills. These activities expose the learner to other opportunities and scenarios to practice behaviors such as sitting, attending, and scanning. Learners are expected to engage in these behaviors at all times, including transitions, and regardless of the activity.

One learning-how-to-learn skill targeted throughout play activities is sitting. Sitting is commonly targeted while learners are sitting in a chair and at a table. However, learners are likely to encounter a variety of situations where they need to sit and refrain from engaging in inappropriate behaviors, including sitting on the floor, in the grass, on a bench, etc. Each scenario requires a different set of skills, as each situation may evoke different behaviors that interfere with appropriate sitting. It is important to expose the learners to a variety of situations to ensure that the skill is fully generalized.

Within a session, certain games may be used as an activity to target the prioritized objective. It is important to note that activities should always be used to set the context for targeting specific objectives, not just activity for its own sake. Some activities that can be used to target sitting include, but are not limited to: Doggie Doggie, Obstacle Course, Spoon Game, Stare of Death, and Who's Missing (see curriculum section for more details). Many other skills such as attending, waiting, and frustration tolerance may be adopted as an embedded target within various activities.

Another learning-how-to-learn skill that can be targeted during play is attending. Learners must attend to the relevant stimuli to obtain the necessary information to play the game. Attending increases the learners' awareness of the environment, and, more specifically, the social environment. Some games that can create the context for targeting attending include, but are not limited to: I Like You But I Just Can't Smile, Obstacle Course, Sleeping Game, Snickers and Hoots, Statue Game, Stare of Death, and Who's Missing (see curriculum section for more details).

Reducing Aggressive Behaviors

Sometimes there are skills that a one-to-one teaching format may not set the context to target. For example, frustration tolerance with an adult in a one-to-one setting may not evoke inappropriate behaviors, as the interventionist may have stimulus control from a history of reinforcing appropriate behaviors. However, the learner may continue to engage in inappropriate behaviors in a peer setting. A social skills group is an ideal setting to practice these skills, as events may be manipulated by the interventionist to make it as structured, or unstructured, as needed for the learners.

Ideally, the interventionist will practice these skills in a structured way prior to embedding these types of targets into play settings. It is important that the learners identify potential situations that are likely to lead to problem behaviors and are taught alternative behaviors for those situations. Once these behaviors are taught, they can be embedded into more natural, play-like settings. It is important to arrange opportunities for the learners to practice multiple times within a session. Also, it is important to keep track of the progress of skill acquisition to fade prompts and reinforcement appropriately.

For example, if a learner tends to engage in aggressive behaviors whenever the learner loses, multiple opportunities will be presented to practice using appropriate coping skills. In early stages of practice, after proactively teaching coping skills, an interventionist may pull out the learner and prime by saying, "Something that may upset you will happen in the next few minutes." If the learner responds appropriately to the frustrating event, the interventionist will provide access to reinforcement. If the learner engages in inappropriate behaviors, the interventionist will provide feedback and possibly a punishing event (e.g., moving down a level on a level system). As the learner responds appropriately to frustrating antecedent events, the interventionist will fade the prime (by making it less specific and increasing the amount of time between the prime and the challenging event), as well as the schedule and quality of reinforcement. Eventually, no feedback or prime will be provided as the natural contingencies should maintain the performance.

Reducing Stereotypy and Stigmatizing Behaviors

It is also possible to target stereotypic behaviors during play activities. Similar to reducing aggressive behaviors, it is important to provide proactive teaching prior to implementing practice into more naturalistic activities such as play. Following proactive teaching, opportunities to practice maintaining a cool body (e.g., refraining from motor stereotypy) will be provided throughout the social group session. To truly provide opportunities to practice, make sure that the antecedent events introduced in sessions evoke self-stimulatory or stigmatizing behaviors. From there, the exposure to the antecedent events may be presented in a systematic way to promote success, progressing in difficulty as the learner engages in appropriate replacement behaviors.

For example, the entire group may be playing musical chairs and one of the learners tends to engage in arm flapping during certain types of songs. If the learner tends to arm flap for upbeat songs, the interventionist may first play music for short intervals and provide reinforcement or feedback following each interval. As the learner is successful, the interventionist may play the music for longer intervals. Initially, the interventionist may have the learners engage in a sitting activity to increase the likelihood of success. As the learner progresses, the next phase may involve standing up. The learner may require prompting to engage in appropriate replacement behaviors, but these prompts must be faded before progressing to more evocative situations. Again, this activity/program does not occur just for the individual learner but, rather, is embedded within an activity that benefits the entire group.

Other Social Skills

Many learners in social skills groups have individualized social skill targets that may not need to be taught to the rest of the group, or learners may be in different phases of social skill acquisition. Regardless, it is important to create opportunities for the learners to practice these skills within activities that are most appropriate for the learners' current stage of acquisition. For example, Learner A has a target of initiating play with others. Learner B has a target of responding to peers. It would be beneficial to pair these two learners in a game or activity, as these learners have complementary targets. While the overall group target may be "sticking with a friend," Learner A could access reinforcement for initiating play while Learner B could access reinforcement for responding to peers; both learners could access reinforcement for sticking with a friend.

Chapter Fifteen
Typically Developing Peers

Within the Autism Partnership Method as it relates to behaviorally based social skills groups, typically developing peers are commonly incorporated whenever available. Typically developing peers serve as models for the other learners in the group. They can model appropriate and age-typical learning, behavior, language, and social behavior. Having typically developing peers in the group also provides an opportunity for the learners to experience the responses and consequences that their peers are likely to encounter in environments outside the group (e.g., school, park, camp). Also, typically developing peers are often easier to coach for setting up antecedents for learners to display or refrain from certain behaviors. For example, an interventionist may tell a typically developing peer to grab a toy out of someone's hand to set the occasion for the learner to engage in appropriate assertiveness. Typically developing peers can also bring excitement to the group and learners of the group often form positive prosocial relationships with these peers.

Common challenges to including typically developing peers in a social skills group include, but are not limited to: (1) finding typically developing peers in the community who can join the group and (2) ensuring that the peers fit well into the group dynamic. One way we have found typically developing peers is asking coworkers or friends who have typically developing children of similar age if they could join the group. If we are unable to find children to participate in the social skills group from our coworkers or friends, we send recruitment notifications. As described in Chapter 5, interventionists should consider the same factors for typically developing peers as they do with individuals diagnosed with autism spectrum disorder (ASD) when determining fit. Peers should be the same age as the other group members and have average to above average age-typical language and social skills. Interventionists should ensure that the typically developing peer does not display any aberrant behavior (e.g., elopement, tantrums, noncompliance), which might interfere with the learning progress of the other group members. Finally, interventionists should ensure that the typically developing peer will be able to attend the group regularly. If a typically developing peer meets these criteria, it is advantageous to include them in the social skills group.

One difference between the Autism Partnership Method and other methods is the role of typically developing peers within the context of social skills groups. Frequently, typically developing peers are used as models and as peer mediators in a social skills group. In other words, they serve as mini-interventionists to help teach the learners diagnosed with ASD. Within the Autism Partnership Method, typically developing peers are used to help model appropriate language and social behavior, but not as assistant interventionists. As such, they are members of the group and are held to the same contingencies as every other learner. They move up and down the level system, earn the same types of breaks, and receive feedback if needed. The interventionists also work on improving the social behavior of the typically developing peers. That is, typically developing peers have their own goals and objectives and should be active participants during teaching, not just passive observers.

In the Autism Partnership Method, interventionists will not let typically developing peers know that the other members in the group are diagnosed with ASD—nor will they let them know that they are there to help. Doing so is counterproductive to the role they serve in the social skills group. Though caregivers might provide this information, interventionists should not. We also encourage caregivers to let the typically developing peers know that they are there to have fun, learn, and be a good friend (as all are there for the same purpose).

Chapter Sixteen
Families

Misty L. Oppenheim-Leaf

When any professional works with an individual diagnosed with autism spectrum disorder (ASD) they are not simply working with that individual; rather, they are working with the entire family unit. Frequently we hear behavior analysts say that our responsibility is to the child and we should not worry about the parents or siblings. This is just wrong! Individuals diagnosed with ASD do not live in a vacuum. They live with their mothers, fathers, grandparents, siblings, uncles, aunts, cousins, and other family members. Brilliant professionals discovered the importance of parent training (Lovaas et al., 1973) as well as the roles that siblings play in the intervention process (Knott et al., 2007). Parent training and working with siblings has long been a staple of quality behavioral intervention, though both are beyond the scope of this book (for more information see Leaf et al., 2017).

It is important to note that for an individual diagnosed with ASD to make meaningful gains, behavioral intervention usually relies on at least four factors: 1) what the learner brings to the table (e.g., language, social skills, aberrant behavior, cognitive skills); 2) the quality of intervention, in terms of the procedures implemented and the skills taught; 3) the quality of staff; and 4) the family's role. Ensuring caregivers provide a loving and caring environment—one where contingencies from therapy carry over and where a behavior analytic philosophy is embraced throughout the day—will lead to an even higher level of success. As such, training caregivers to be involved in behavioral interventions is extremely beneficial.

The Parents

In the Autism Partnership Method there has been a long history of parent involvement throughout comprehensive behavioral intervention. However, the expectations of parent involvement have evolved over the years. In the beginning, at the UCLA Young Autism Project, the expectation was that parents served as therapists (Lovaas, 1987). In fact, one parent had to give up a job to become part of the treatment team. At other points in time, parents were expected to simply be parents and have minimal involvement in the therapy process. Today, we expect parents to understand what is occurring in therapy, maintain consistent contingencies outside of therapy sessions, and fill their child's day with meaningful activities.

We also expect parents to be supportive of the Autism Partnership Method. That is, they should be on board with behavioral intervention being the priority, their child receiving only evidence-based treatments, and fully understanding that intervention is a process. We are also aware of the range of emotions that parents face and within the Autism Partnership Method we often recommend counseling for parents to help cope with these emotions. This is expected when we are providing comprehensive behavioral intervention, but when learners are only in social skills groups, parental involvement and expectations may be different.

There are many expectations for parents of children in the social skills group and many ways interventionists can build strong and collaborative relationships with the families. One expectation is that parents ensure their child is consistently attending the social skills group sessions. It is critical for their child's success (as well as the group's success) that children regularly attend and arrive on time. If attendance becomes an issue, the interventionists should address this concern with the parents and find solutions.

A second expectation is that parents fill out the formal assessments provided in an accurate and timely manner. Third, parents are recommended to not implement any procedure that would be counterproductive to the social skills group. This means parents are encouraged to not implement procedures with little or no empirical evidence, that are pseudoscientific, or that may cause harm to their child. Within the context of the group, these interventions should never be implemented, but it is also the interventionist's job to encourage parents to not implement these procedures at home or at other times outside of the group. It is also up to each interventionist to determine if there are any home-based interventions that will result in termination; for example those that signal conflicting values between the clinic and family. For example, if a child is receiving chelation therapy at home, the interventionist might elect to no longer serve the family if they choose to continue chelation therapy, due to the severe risk to the child's health.

More important than parent expectations are the ways interventionists can build strong and collaborative relationships with parents. This can happen in a variety of ways within the context of a social skills group. First, interventionists should collaborate with parents to select goals. This can be done using formal assessments such as the Social Skills Improvement System, which includes an importance rating for each skill. This can also happen through parent interviews. Interventionists should ask parents which skills are important to the parents and determine skill deficits at home. Collaboration with parents for goal selection, especially when a child first starts a social skills group, will help build a strong relationship.

Although interventionists should always listen to parents' suggestions about target goals, there are times when interventionists may not agree with the parent's priorities. For example, in the Penguins study (i.e., Leaf et al., 2017) some parents stated that having their child answer the telephone was very important to them, but the interventionists felt that the learners needed to work on other social skills (e.g., waiting, social conversation, observational learning). It is important that the interventionist does not ignore the parent or not talk to the parent about the child's current goals. Rather, the interventionist needs to meet with the child's parents and explain in a clinically sensitive way why those goals may not be targeted at the current time. Explain that the intervention team values the parent's suggestions and they would like to work on those behaviors, but there are other skills that have more immediate priority. Having these types of conversations, though sometimes difficult, will help build the relationship.

Another way to build a relationship with parents is having an open-door policy. A large part of the intervention for individuals diagnosed with ASD occurs behind closed doors. Frequently, parents are unable to observe the intervention their child is receiving. Parents may feel nervous, scared, unsure, or may not trust the system. These emotions are natural and it is the interventionist's job to help the parents feel comfortable with the intervention in the social skills group. We encourage an open-door policy where parents are always welcome to observe the social skills group. Giving parents the freedom to observe the group and knowing they can come and go as they please helps build a trusting, collaborative relationship between the parents and service providers. By not limiting the amount of time that parents can observe the group, they are reassured and can see that the interventionists are not hiding anything.

Some exceptions to the open-door policy include when the room becomes overcrowded with observers or when it may interfere with the session (e.g., practicing for a performance). There are also some rules provided for parents while observing the group, which include not talking to the interventionists while they are teaching, not interfering with the teaching and lessons, minimizing interactions with the children, not bringing guests (e.g., other professionals) without notification, not recording or filming any of the intervention, and keeping talking to a minimum.

A third way to build a relationship with parents is debriefing with parents about their child's goals and progress in the group as frequently as possible. The goal should be to debrief after every session to the greatest extent possible. When debriefing parents, the interventionist should discuss goals that were targeted during the day, areas in which their child did well, areas requiring improvement, and the upcoming plan of intervention.

It is important that when debriefing with parents, the interventionist does not come off as overly negative. Unfortunately, parents of children diagnosed with ASD hear about their child's deficits all of the time. Individual education program meetings, birthday parties, testing and assessment periods, prom, and sports activities are continual reminders that their child is not doing as well as others. It is critical for the interventionist to exercise clinical judgment and compassion while interacting with parents (see Taylor et al., 2019). Some professionals may recommend a "sandwich" approach that involves something positive, followed by what the child needs to work on, followed by something positive. We think this approach is overly prescriptive and can set the precedent that positive reports indicate something negative is coming. We recommend providing feedback in the style that works best for the parents. For some parents, a direct approach may work best, for others feedback may need to be provided softly, while others might not be able to hear any negative feedback. An interventionist must analyze the situation to determine what interaction style best suits the parents and debrief accordingly.

Along with debriefing, a daily report card may be helpful (see Figure 27 for an example). The interventionists should be equally mindful of their language when writing a report card as when they talk with parents. In the Autism Partnership Method, we also provide weekly group newsletters (see Figure 28 for an example). These newsletters are usually written more globally about the group overall as opposed to being learner-specific. Newsletters provide information about what has been worked on, future directions, exciting announcements, and updates on policies.

Another way to foster family relationships is to conduct team meetings. A team meeting is when we invite all parents to come without their children. To make the team meeting pleasant, the interventionists might have food and beverages available to the families. In the team meetings, the interventionists provide global group information and answer any questions the parents might have. There is also time for each parent to meet individually with interventionists. Doing this on a quarterly basis helps keep communication constant and fosters a positive relationship between the interventionists and parents.

The Siblings

Siblings are another important part of behavioral intervention. It has been reported that siblings of individuals diagnosed with ASD experience a broad range of emotions, which can range from happiness to anger, sadness, and jealousy. These emotions may change over time. It is important for interventionists to be compassionate toward siblings and be aware that siblings are going through stressors and hardships of their own.

In terms of social skills groups, it is our general rule to not include siblings for several reasons. First, we prefer siblings to have their own identity and not to be always associated with their brother or sister. Second, we prefer the sibling does not become a mini-interventionist or caregiver to their sibling. We also encourage parents to plan special activities with the siblings during social skills group times, so the siblings have their own activities with mom and dad. While the sibling diagnosed with ASD is attending the social skills group, it also allows siblings to attend their own activities. Encouraging independence will hopefully help siblings in their lifelong journey of having a brother or sister with ASD.

References

Knott, F., Lewis, C., & Williams, T. (2007). Sibling interaction of children with autism. Development over 12 months. *Journal of Autism and Developmental Disorders, 37,* 1987-1995.

Leaf, J. B., Cihon, J. H., Weinkauf, S. M., Oppenheim-Leaf, M. L., Taubman, M., & Leaf, R. (2017). Parent training for parents of individuals with autism spectrum disorder. In Matson J. (Eds). *Handbook of Treatments for Autism Spectrum Disorder. Autism and Child Psychopathology Series.* Springer, Cham.

Leaf, J. B., Leaf, J. A., Milne, C., Taubman, M., Oppenheim-Leaf, M., Torres, N., Townley-Cochran, D., Leaf, R., McEachin, J. & Yoder, P. (2017). An evaluation of a behaviorally based social skills group for individuals diagnosed with autism spectrum disorder. *Journal of Autism and Developmental Disorders, 47*(2), 243–259.

Lovaas, I. O. (1987). Behavioral treatment and normal educational and intellectual functioning in young autistic children. *Journal of Consulting and Clinical Psychology, 55,* 3-9.

Lovaas, I. O., Koegel, R., Simmons, J. Q., Long, J. S. (1973). Some generalization and follow-up measures on autistic children in behavior therapy. *Journal of Applied Behavior Analysis, 6,* 131-166.

Taylor, B. A., Leblanc, L. A., & Nosik, M. R. (2019). Compassionate care in behavior analytic treatment: Can outcomes be enhanced by attending to relationships with caregivers? *Behavior Analysis in Practice, 12,* 654–666.

Figure 27. Daily Parental Report Card

Social Skills Group Daily Report Card

CHILD NAME   TEACHERS   DATE

WHAT WE WORKED ON TODAY

CHILD GOALS	DAILY REPORT	NOTES
GOAL 1	☹ 😐 🙂	
GOAL 2	☹ 😐 🙂	
GOAL 3	☹ 😐 🙂	
GOAL 4	☹ 😐 🙂	
GOAL 5	☹ 😐 🙂	

OTHER INFO:

Figure 28. Weekly Group Newsletter Example

The

Penguins

Photo Credit: Giedriius/Shutterstock.com

Fun Games with Penguins!

We have had so much fun introducing and teaching different games to the Penguins. So far, we have taught the Sleeping game, Fruit Salad, and last week we started teaching Mousetrap. As we continue into the next few weeks, **we will continue to teach Fruit Salad and Mousetrap.**

Teaching Cool versus Not Cool

Talking to a friend

A few weeks ago we started teaching the Penguins what to do when a teacher is busy and walks away from the group (i.e., move toward a friend and talk). We have really enjoyed seeing the Penguins pick this up very quickly! It seems they really enjoy this time getting to chat with their friends.

Updates & Upcoming News

One of our main areas of focus for the group has been in their attending within both small and large groups. Attending can have a huge impact on a child's ability to learn in a variety of settings. To prepare for more natural settings, including our observation sessions (in which no praise or feedback will be provided), we are starting to *gradually* reduce the amount of praise and feedback the Penguins will receive. As such, we are starting to reduce the amount of times we refer to our Superkid chart. This week (September 9th and 11th) we will use the chart, but refer to it only a few of times during each activity. Next week, (September 16th and 18th) we will check-in after every activity. Although we intend to reduce the reinforcement systems gradually, it is possible to see some undesired behaviors increase (e.g., inattention). We will continue to target these behaviors on an individual basis. Please feel free to contact any of the Penguin's teachers if you have any questions or concerns.

Responding to peers

Throughout our group sessions, we have been practicing responding to peers. We have introduced a restaurant play center, and will be starting a fire fighter play center. In addition, we are excited to continuing to target engagement and responding to peers within both structured (e.g., duck, duck, goose) and unstructured (e.g., playing on the playground) play activities outside.

Chapter Seventeen
Measurement

Julia L. Ferguson

One factor that separates behaviorally based social skills groups from non-behaviorally based social skills groups is the reliance on objective data. The analysis of objective and observable behavior is a hallmark of applied behavior analysis (ABA). There are two ways in which data is commonly obtained in the Autism Partnership Method: 1) formal assessments and 2) informal assessments. We define formal assessments as commercial assessments which are standardized or normed across different populations and have been validated. We define informal assessments as data collection methods that interventionists are using during the social skills group sessions. It is imperative that standardized and informal assessments are used to evaluate a learner's progress while attending the social skills group.

Formal Assessments

Using formal assessments is standard practice outside the field of ABA. Psychologists, teachers, school administrators, speech-language pathologists, and occupational therapists all use formal assessments to track progress. If behavior analysts want to collaborate with others, we need to use formal assessments in conjunction with our other data collection methods. Additionally, formal assessments are widely used to measure outcomes in peer-reviewed journals outside of the field of behavior analysis. This makes the use of formal assessments critical if behavior analysts want to publish in peer-reviewed journals that reach a larger audience. Many third-party payers (e.g., insurance companies) now require the use of formal assessments for individuals diagnosed with autism spectrum disorder (ASD) to receive funding. Therefore, we consider it important for behavior analysts to report their findings in formats that will be understood and recognized by non-ABA professionals. Finally, and most importantly, formal assessments provide interventionists with a great deal of information on a learner's strengths, weaknesses, and progress over time—as well as the more global impact on intervention.

We use a variety of formal assessments in the Autism Partnership Method. One formal assessment conducted on a yearly basis is intelligence quotient (IQ) testing. Though we believe that IQ testing is critical, it is beyond the scope of this book, as interventionists need specialized training to conduct IQ tests. As such, we will not be describing IQ testing within this chapter. For the same reason, we will not provide any information on the Autism Diagnostic Observation Schedule (ADOS) or the Autism Diagnostic Interview-Revised (ADI-R), which are also commonly used.

We do provide information on eight formal assessments we typically use during social skills groups. Some assessments are completed by parents, some are completed by the social skills group interventionists, and some are completed by both. The section below describes each assessment, how they are administered, what information the assessment provides, and why these assessments are important.

Vineland-3 Adaptive Behavior Scales

The Vineland-3 Adaptive Behavior Scales is an assessment that measures adaptive behavior (Sparrow et al., 2016). Adaptive behavior for this assessment is separated into three domains including communication, daily living skills, and socialization. These domains are further separated into subdomains. Within the communication domain, the subdomains assessed are receptive communication, expressive communication, and written communication. Within the daily living skills domain, the subdomains assessed are personal daily living skills, domestic/numeric daily living skills, and community/ school daily living skills. The socialization domain is separated into interpersonal relationships, play and leisure, and coping skills subdomains.

Collectively, answers to the questions corresponding to the three main domains provide you with the Adaptive Behavior Composite score. The Vineland-3 also has two optional subdomains including a motor skills domain and a maladaptive behavior domain. The motor skills domain assesses gross and fine motor skills and the maladaptive behavior domain assesses internalizing and externalizing problem behaviors. These two optional domains do not count toward the Adaptive Behavior Composite score, but do provide additional information about the individual and separate standard scores that are obtained from the questions in these domains. Answers to the questions correspond with the numbers 0, 1, or 2. A score of 0 corresponds to "never," meaning the individual never engages in the behavior. A score of 1 corresponds to "sometimes," meaning the individual sometimes engages in the behavior, and a score of 2 corresponds to "usually," meaning the individual usually engages in the behavior. The Vineland-3 is a versatile assessment tool that evaluates multiple important domains, is comprehensive in scope, and is inclusive for individuals at any age (birth to 90 years and older).

The Vineland-3 can be administered in three different ways: an interview form, a parent/caregiver form, and a teacher form. Respondents for the Vineland-3 can be parents, caregivers, or teachers. With the exception of the interview form, which would be conducted by a professional in an interview format, the parent/caregiver form and the teacher form can be completed on paper or in an online format, making the administration of the Vineland-3 user-friendly.

Since the Vineland-3 is an age-referenced assessment, it provides interventionists with an accurate picture of how the learner compares to age-typical peers. The composite scores for the primary domains and the Adaptive Behavior Composite have a mean standard score of 100 which corresponds to the 50th percentile of others at the individual's age. Scores falling below the standard score of 100 indicate skill deficits in the corresponding domains compared to the individual's age; standard scores above 100 indicate skill levels above an individual's age for those domains. Increasing standard scores indicate an acceleration of progress. Since behaviorally based social skills groups primarily target social behavior, more progress may be expected in the socialization domain compared to other domains, such as daily living skills. Overall, the Vineland-3 Adaptive Behavior Scales is a good assessment to evaluate multiple aspects of an individual's overall behavior (i.e., social behavior, communication behavior, motor skills, daily living skills, and problem behavior).

Social Skills Improvement System

The Social Skills Improvement System (SSiS; Gresham & Elliott, 2008) is a standardized assessment of social behavior and problem behavior. Social skills in this assessment are divided into several subdomains, including social skills regarding communication, cooperation, assertion, responsibility, empathy, engagement, and self-control. Problem behaviors are divided into externalizing problem behaviors, bullying, hyperactivity/inattention problem behaviors, internalizing problem behavior, and an autism spectrum scaled score. To answer each question, the respondent uses a 4-point scale consisting of "Never," "Seldom," "Often," and "Almost Always." One unique feature of the SSiS is that respondents can also rate the importance of each social skill. Ratings for importance are "not important," "important," and "critical." For example, one question on the SSiS is "Says thank you," and a parent could rate that the child "never" engages in this skill, but they could also rate that this skill is "not important." This provides valuable information to the interventionist on which social skills are, and are not, important to parents/caregivers.

The SSiS can be administered to parents/caregivers, teachers, or individuals diagnosed with ASD. The SSiS is for individuals ages 3–18 years and is norm-referenced per age and gender. The social skills section of the SSiS provides an overall standard score for social skills and scores for each subdomain, which is further categorized into "average," "below average," or "above average" for each social skill subdomain. The problem behavior section provides an overall problem behavior standard score and scores for each subdomain categorized into "average," "below average," or "above average" levels of problem behavior. Overall, the SSiS is a great tool for research purposes, to assess social skills improvement throughout a learner's time in a social skills group, and to identify which social skill deficits are important to parents, caregivers, and teachers.

Social Responsiveness Scale

The Social Responsiveness Scale (SRS-2; Costantino & Gruber, 2005) is a standardized social skill assessment that measures social symptoms of an ASD diagnosis. The SRS-2 is comprised of 65 questions and each question corresponds to a different social subscale. The different social subscales for the SRS-2 are social awareness, social cognition, social communication, social motivation, and restricted interests and repetitive behavior. Each question corresponding to these subscales is scored on a 4-point scale. A score of 1 represents "not true," a score of 2 represents "sometimes true," a score of 3 represents "often true," and a score of 4 represents "almost always true." The respondent's scores to the 65 questions create an overall T-score to represent the individual's overall social behavior score. T-scores of 59 and below are considered within normal limits and are not generally associated with ASD (Constantino & Gruber, 2005). T-scores ranging from 60–65 represent social skills in the mild range of deficit for reciprocal behavior. T-scores ranging from 66–75 represent social skills in the moderate range of deficit for reciprocal behavior that considerably interfere with social interactions. T-scores of 76 and higher represent social skills in the severe range of deficit that significantly and severely interfere with social interactions. Scores in the severe range are highly associated with a diagnosis of ASD.

The SRS-2 has three different forms depending on the age of the individual being assessed; all forms are completed by a paper/pen administration. The SRS-2 has a preschool form (ages 2.5–4.5 years), a school age form (ages 4–18 years), and an adult form (ages 19 years and up). The preschool and school age forms are meant to be filled out by parents or teachers, but the adult form can be filled out by parents, spouses, relatives, friends, and also the adult themselves. A decreasing score on the SRS-2 indicates progress toward the normal range. Since this assessment is strongly associated with symptoms related to a diagnosis of ASD, the severity level of the symptoms of ASD can also be tracked.

Walker-McConnell

The Walker-McConnell Scale of Social Competence and School Adjustment is a standardized assessment that measures social competence within a school environment (Walker & McConnell, 1988). The Walker-McConnell has two forms: 1) the elementary version and 2) the adolescent version. The elementary version is for individuals in Kindergarten through 6th grade and the adolescent version is for individuals in 7th grade through 12th grade. The elementary version of the Walker-McConnell has a total of 43 questions and is divided into three subscales. The subscales include teacher-preferred social behavior, peer-preferred social behavior, and school adjustment. The adolescent version of the Walker-McConnell has four subscales to create a total score including self-control, peer relations, school adjustment, and empathy. Each question on the Walker-McConnell is rated by the respondent on a 5-point Likert scale. A rating of 1 represents "never" and a rating of 5 represents "frequently."

The Walker-McConnell is only filled out by teachers. The teacher that fills out the Walker-McConnell should be familiar with the learner and have had the learner in their classroom for a minimum of 6–8 weeks before completing the assessment. For the Walker-McConnell, average scores (i.e. 50th percentile) range from 116–118. Scores higher than 116–118 represent better social competence at school and scores falling below 116–118 represent lower social competence at school. For most school-age individuals, a classroom is where they spend the majority of their day and have the most opportunities for social interactions. Because of this, the Walker-McConnell is a good standardized assessment to evaluate generalization of the social skills learned within a behaviorally based social skills group to a school setting.

Aberrant Behavior Checklist

The Aberrant Behavior Checklist (ABC; Anman & Singh, 1986) is an assessment that measures aberrant or problem behavior. The ABC is meant to be used for individuals of ages 5 years to adult. The ABC has 58 questions and measures five different subscales of problem behavior including irritability, social withdrawal, stereotypic behavior, hyperactivity/noncompliance, and inappropriate speech. Each question on the ABC corresponds to one of the five subscales and is rated on a 4 point-scale. A score of 0 represents "not at all a problem," a score of 1 represents "the behavior is a problem but slight in degree," a score of 2 represents "the problem is moderately serious," and a score of 3 represents "the problem is severe in degree."

The ABC provides average scaled scores per age and sex that differ depending on the subscale. The average scaled scores differ due to the number of questions corresponding to each subscale, but in general, the goal is for scores on each subscale on the ABC to decrease as appropriate replacement behaviors are learned within the social skills group. This assessment can be filled out by teachers, caregivers, or anyone familiar with the individual, making this assessment versatile in who it can be administered to and scores for challenging behavior can be tracked across multiple respondents.

Parental Stress Index

Unlike the previous assessments discussed, the Parental Stress Index (PSI) does not measure child or student behavior, but the impact of the child's behavior on the parent. Within our social skills groups we use the PSI-Short Form. The PSI-Short Form includes 36 questions corresponding to three subscales that provide a total stress score. The separate subscales are parental distress, parent child-dysfunctional interaction, and difficult child.

The parental distress subscale asks questions relating to distress a parent may be experiencing and other personal factors that may be impacting parent distress. The parent-child dysfunctional interaction subscale asks questions pertaining to the parent's perspective on the extent the child meets the parents' expectations and if interactions with their child positively or negatively impacts their life. The last scale, difficult child, asks parents questions about the behavioral characteristics of their child and whether those characteristics are easy or hard to manage. Each question on the PSI-Short Form uses a 5-point Likert scale where the respondent can select "strongly agree," "agree," "not sure," "disagree," or "strongly disagree." The subscales on the PSI-Short Form each yield a percentile and the total stress score also yields a percentile rank. Percentile scores relate to responses from a normative sample. For example, a percentile score of 80 indicates the parent/caregiver's stress score is greater than 80% of the normative sample.

For this assessment, progress is indicated by decreases in percentile scores. This is a great assessment to use to monitor parent stress and can be used to make clinical decisions that could benefit the parent. For example, if stress scores from the PSI-Short Form are high, it could be an indicator that a parent needs more support and parent training services should be provided or increased, they should receive counseling, or seek help from other qualified professionals.

Peabody Picture Vocabulary Test

The Peabody Picture Vocabulary Test (PPVT; Dunn & Dunn, 2007) is an assessment for individuals ages 2.5 years and up that evaluates an individual's comprehension of spoken words. This assessment should be implemented by a qualified professional that is familiar with the assessment and assessment materials. The professional asks the individual being assessed to find the specified word. The individual then selects a picture that corresponds with that word from an array of four pictures. For example, when the examiner says, "Find running," the individual looks at a page with four pictures and points to the picture that corresponds with "running."

The PPVT is a standardized and norm referenced assessment with scores of 100 reflecting the average for the individual's age. Standard scores above 100 represent higher than average word comprehension for that age and standard scores falling below 100 represent lower than average word comprehension for that age.

Expressive One Word Picture Vocabulary Test

Similar to the PPVT, the Expressive One Word Picture Vocabulary Test (EOWPVT; Martin & Brownell, 2011) should be implemented by a qualified professional and can be administered to individuals 2 years and older. The EOWPVT assesses an individual's expressive naming vocabulary. An administrator of the EOWPVT shows the individual a picture and then asks, "What is this?" The individual responds with one word for the picture. For example, the examiner could show the individual a picture of an apple, ask "What is this?" and wait for the learner to respond with the answer "apple."

The EOWPVT is a standardized and norm referenced assessment with standard scores of 100 reflecting the 50th percentile of vocabulary for individuals of the same age. Standard scores above 100 represent a higher and more advanced expressive vocabulary compared to other individuals of the same age, and standard scores below 100 represent a lower expressive vocabulary compared to individuals of the same age.

Informal Assessments

Within the Autism Partnership Method, we also highly value ongoing assessments (i.e., data collection). The use of objective data allows the interventionist to assess progress on skills being targeted, the effectiveness of the procedures implemented, and, ultimately, inform if any changes are necessary.

The Autism Partnership Method's data collection differs from other behavioral models in several ways. First and foremost, within this model, collecting data should never interfere with teaching or momentum the interventionist creates during the teaching process. As such, we rarely will take trial-by-trial data or continuous frequency/duration data within a behaviorally based social skills group. These measurement systems are accurate and well established in the research, but they can be cumbersome and interfere with effective teaching. We've found that other less cumbersome data collection systems can be just as accurate (e.g., Ferguson et al. 2020)

A second difference in the Autism Partnership Method's approach to taking data is that we rarely collect reliability data during non-research intervention. Reliability data commonly involves two interventionists simultaneously, but independently, recording whether a learner engaged in the behavior of interest. We do take reliability data within our research but believe that doing so in clinical settings would be a waste of the interventionists' time. To make sure the data is reliable, interventionists communicate frequently about goals and the way the data is taken, then make adjustments accordingly.

A final difference between the Autism Partnership Method and other behavioral models is that within our behaviorally based social skills groups, we do not take formal treatment fidelity data. Though we think it is important for interventionists to implement procedures as planned, we expect a great deal of flexibility in implementation based on each interventionists' clinical judgment. As such, interventionists can make changes to the teaching based on in-the-moment assessments, which may make it difficult or impossible to take meaningful treatment fidelity. Additionally, within our model there is frequent supervision and oversight, so if learners are not meeting expectations, changes to teaching procedures can be made easily and training will ensure that the expectations are met going forward without the need for treatment fidelity data.

There are four types of data collection systems that we typically implement in behaviorally based social skills groups: 1) estimation, 2) task analysis, 3) time checks, and 4) social validity.

Estimation Data. Estimation data involves the interventionist estimating the duration, rate, or quality of the learner's behavior. Estimation data can be collected for skills targeted for increase (e.g., observational learning, joining in, telling jokes) and decrease (e.g., self-stimulatory behavior, aggression, non-compliance). Estimation data is collected using a Likert scale. Figure 29 displays scores on a Likert scale and how they can correspond across different behaviors that are commonly measured via other data collection systems (e.g., frequency, duration, percentage of opportunities). The interventionist takes estimation data after a teaching lesson, after a planned activity (e.g., outside game), when evaluating performance during portions of the group (e.g., the 1st half of the group), or at the end of the group. Ultimately, estimation data can be used in a variety of ways. Figure 30 provides an example of an estimation data sheet.

Figure 29. Example Likert Scale Across Different Measurement Systems

Estimation Score	Frequency	Duration	Percentage of Opportunities
0	Never Occurring	Never Occurring	Never or very rare (e.g., 0–20% of opportunities)
1	Infrequent (e.g., 1–4 times)	Brief duration (e.g., 1–4 mins)	Low occurrence (e.g., 21–40% of opportunities)
2	Moderately often (e.g., 5–9 times)	Moderate duration (e.g., 5–9 mins)	Moderately Often (e.g., 41–60% of opportunities)
3	Often frequent (e.g., 10–15 times)	High duration (e.g., 10–15 mins)	Frequent (e.g., 61–80% of opportunities)
4	Extremely often (e.g., 15+ times)	Extremely High duration (e.g., 15+ mins)	Very High percentage (e.g., 81-100% of opportunities)

Figure 30. Example Estimation Data Sheet

Date: Scorer:

Behavior	Child 1	Child 2	Child 3	Child 4
	0 1 2 3 4	0 1 2 3 4	0 1 2 3 4	0 1 2 3 4
	0 1 2 3 4	0 1 2 3 4	0 1 2 3 4	0 1 2 3 4
	0 1 2 3 4	0 1 2 3 4	0 1 2 3 4	0 1 2 3 4
	0 1 2 3 4	0 1 2 3 4	0 1 2 3 4	0 1 2 3 4
	0 1 2 3 4	0 1 2 3 4	0 1 2 3 4	0 1 2 3 4
	0 1 2 3 4	0 1 2 3 4	0 1 2 3 4	0 1 2 3 4
	0 1 2 3 4	0 1 2 3 4	0 1 2 3 4	0 1 2 3 4
	0 1 2 3 4	0 1 2 3 4	0 1 2 3 4	0 1 2 3 4
	0 1 2 3 4	0 1 2 3 4	0 1 2 3 4	0 1 2 3 4
	0 1 2 3 4	0 1 2 3 4	0 1 2 3 4	0 1 2 3 4
	0 1 2 3 4	0 1 2 3 4	0 1 2 3 4	0 1 2 3 4

Task Analysis Data. Task analysis data occurs when skills are separated into smaller component steps. At some point during the social skills group, the interventionist will set the occasion for the learner(s) to engage in the targeted social behavior. Simultaneously, the interventionist scores whether the learner displays each of the component steps. Typically, the interventionist marks either a "yes" (i.e., the individual displayed the step), a "no" (i.e., the individual did not display the step), or "n/a" (i.e., there was not an opportunity to display the behavior). A skill is considered mastered when the learner displays all component steps of the targeted behavior across multiple opportunities, sessions, materials, and people. This type of data collection is beneficial because it allows the interventionist to identify which steps of the targeted social skill the learner displays and does not display. Figure 31 provides a template for task analysis data.

Figure 31. Example Task Analysis Data Sheet

Date: Scorer:

Step	Behavior	Child 1	Child 2	Child 3	Child 4
1		Yes No N/A	Yes No N/A	Yes No N/A	Yes No N/A
2		Yes No N/A	Yes No N/A	Yes No N/A	Yes No N/A
3		Yes No N/A	Yes No N/A	Yes No N/A	Yes No N/A
4		Yes No N/A	Yes No N/A	Yes No N/A	Yes No N/A
5		Yes No N/A	Yes No N/A	Yes No N/A	Yes No N/A
6		Yes No N/A	Yes No N/A	Yes No N/A	Yes No N/A
7		Yes No N/A	Yes No N/A	Yes No N/A	Yes No N/A
8		Yes No N/A	Yes No N/A	Yes No N/A	Yes No N/A
9		Yes No N/A	Yes No N/A	Yes No N/A	Yes No N/A
10		Yes No N/A	Yes No N/A	Yes No N/A	Yes No N/A
11		Yes No N/A	Yes No N/A	Yes No N/A	Yes No N/A
12		Yes No N/A	Yes No N/A	Yes No N/A	Yes No N/A

Time Checks. Time checks (e.g., momentary time sampling) involve scoring if a behavior is occurring or not occurring at a specified time. Prior to the group, the interventionist determines time periods to observe the learner. At the specified period of time, the interventionist observes the learner in the group to determine if the learner is displaying the targeted behavior. For example, the interventionist might collect data on a learner playing with a peer every 5 minutes during outside play. In this example, every 5 minutes the interventionist will observe and record at the moment if the learner is playing with a peer. Time checks do not require interventionists to capture all behaviors that occur throughout the group—rather, they allow the interventionist to take a "snapshot" of the behavior. Although this type of data does not capture the target behavior continuously throughout the social skills group, it does provide a representative sample of what is or what is not occurring in the group. This type of data collection tends to be less cumbersome than continuous data collection systems. Figure 32 provides an example of how to take time check data.

Figure 32. Example Time Check Data Sheet

Date: Scorer:

Scoring Key

+	Engaged in the Behavior
-	Did Not Engage in the Behavior
N/A	Could Not Score

Learners Data

Time Period	Child 1	Child 2	Child 3	Child 4	Child 5
5 Mins					
10 Mins					
15 Mins					
20 Mins					
25 Mins					
30 Mins					
35 Mins					
40 Mins					
45 Mins					
50 Mins					
55 Mins					
60 Mins					

Social Validity

Finally, we collect data to see how caregivers feel about the group. We want to know if they are satisfied with the results, procedures, and interventionists. This information can be obtained by talking to the caregivers during debriefing or planned meetings, but more formalized systems may be useful. For instance, caregivers may not be comfortable directly discussing how they feel about the group with staff, especially if they have any concerns or are unhappy. We recommend collecting social validity data through a questionnaire analyzing caregivers' satisfaction of the group. The social validity questionnaire should ask caregivers a variety of questions about their experiences with the social skills group using a Likert scale and have space for any additional comments.

We recommend these surveys remain anonymous so the caregivers feel comfortable filling them out candidly. To make the questionnaires anonymous, the interventionist can hand out the questionnaires to caregivers in a pre-stamped, addressed envelope that can be mailed back without signing their name. We also recommend the social validity questionnaire be provided at least every 3 months. Based on the information gathered, interventionists can change portions of the social skills group, address any misconceptions, or improve areas caregivers are not satisfied with. Figure 33 provides an example of a social validity survey which has been used in our behaviorally based social skills group.

Figure 33. Example of Social Validity Survey

1. Overall how satisfied are you with the social skills group?

1	2	3	4	5	6	7
Very Dissatisfied	Dissatisfied	Somewhat Dissatisfied	Neither Satisfied or Dissatisfied	Somewhat Satisfied	Satisfied	Very Satisfied

2. How satisfied are you with your child's ability to learn social skills during the social skills group?

1	2	3	4	5	6	7
Very Dissatisfied	Dissatisfied	Somewhat Dissatisfied	Neither Satisfied or Dissatisfied	Somewhat Satisfied	Satisfied	Very Satisfied

3. How satisfied are you with your child's ability to learn play skills during the social skills group?

1	2	3	4	5	6	7
Very Dissatisfied	Dissatisfied	Somewhat Dissatisfied	Neither Satisfied or Dissatisfied	Somewhat Satisfied	Satisfied	Very Satisfied

4. How satisfied are you with your child's ability to learn school readiness skills (e.g., attending, observational learning, waiting, reduction of inappropriate behaviors) during the social skills group?

1	2	3	4	5	6	7
Very Dissatisfied	Dissatisfied	Somewhat Dissatisfied	Neither Satisfied or Dissatisfied	Somewhat Satisfied	Satisfied	Very Satisfied

5. Overall how satisfied are you with the teachers who ran the social skills group?0

1	2	3	4	5	6	7
Very Dissatisfied	Dissatisfied	Somewhat Dissatisfied	Neither Satisfied or Dissatisfied	Somewhat Satisfied	Satisfied	Very Satisfied

6. How satisfied are you with the teacher's ability to connect with your child?

1	2	3	4	5	6	7
Very Dissatisfied	Dissatisfied	Somewhat Dissatisfied	Neither Satisfied or Dissatisfied	Somewhat Satisfied	Satisfied	Very Satisfied

Figure 33. Example of Social Validity Survey (cont.)

7. How satisfied are you with the teaching procedures utilized within the social skills group?

1	2	3	4	5	6	7
Very Dissatisfied	Dissatisfied	Somewhat Dissatisfied	Neither Satisfied or Dissatisfied	Somewhat Satisfied	Satisfied	Very Satisfied

8. How much improvement do you feel your child has made with their social skills?

1	2	3	4	5	6	7
Great Decline	Decline	Slight Decline	Neither Decline or Improvement	Slight Improvement	Improvement	Great Improvement

9. How much improvement do you feel your child has made with their friendship development?

1	2	3	4	5	6	7
Great Decline	Decline	Slight Decline	Neither Decline or Improvement	Slight Improvement	Improvement	Great Improvement

10. How much improvement do you feel your child has made with their school readiness (e.g., attending, observational learning, waiting, reduction of inappropriate behaviors) skills?

1	2	3	4	5	6	7
Great Decline	Decline	Slight Decline	Neither Decline or Improvement	Slight Improvement	Improvement	Great Improvement

11. How much improvement do you feel your child has made in their ability to participate in group activities?

1	2	3	4	5	6	7
Great Decline	Decline	Slight Decline	Neither Decline or Improvement	Slight Improvement	Improvement	Great Improvement

12. How much do you feel your child has been able to generalize the skills taught in the social skills group to other environments (e.g., school or home)?

1	2	3	4	5	6	7
Great Decline	Decline	Slight Decline	Neither Decline or Improvement	Slight Improvement	Improvement	Great Improvement

Additional Comments:

References

Aman, M. G., & Singh, N. N. (1986). *Aberrant Behavior Checklist Manual.* East Aurora, NY: Slosson Publications.

Costantino, J. N., & Gruber, C. P. (2005). *Social Responsiveness Scale (SRS).* Los Angeles, CA: Western Psychological Services.

Dunn, L. M., & Dunn, D. M. (2007). *Peabody picture vocabulary test* (4th ed). Minneapolis, MN: NCS Pearson, Inc.

Ferguson, J. L., Milne, C. M., Cihon, J. H., Dotson, A., Leaf, J. B., McEachin, J., & Leaf, R. (2020). An evaluation of estimation data collection to trial⊠by trial data collection during discrete trial teaching. *Behavioral Interventions, 35*(1), 178-191.

Gresham, F. M., & Elliot, S. N. (1990). *Social Skills Improvement System Rating Scales Manual.* Minneapolis, MN: NCS Pearson.

Martin, N., & Brownell, R. (2011). *Expressive one word picture vocabulary test.* Novato, CA: Academic Therapy Publications, Inc

Sparrow, S. S., Cicchetti, D. V., & Saulnier, C. A. (2016). *Vineland adaptive behavior scales* (3rd ed). Bloomington, MN: NCS Pearson, Inc.

Walker, H. M., & McConnell, S. R. (1988). *Walker-McConnell Scale of Social Competence and School Adjustment: A social skills rating scale for teachers.* Austin, TX: Pro-Ed.

Part Three
Curriculum

Jeremy A. Leaf, Jonathan Rafuse
& Justin B. Leaf

Chapter Eighteen
Goal Selection

Jeremy A. Leaf

A social skills group could have the ideal learners for the group, caregivers who are invested, and the most talented interventionists, but if the goals selected for the learners and the group are not right, then the group will never achieve the best possible outcomes.

Selecting Goals for Individual Learners

Strengths and Weaknesses

Once a social skills group has been formed and the learners have been selected, it is the interventionists' job to start gathering information for choosing which goals to target for each learner in the group. Ideally, start gathering this information by asking the people who know the learner best. This generally means speaking to the learner's caregivers, teachers, and clinical supervisors if they are receiving other services. Each individual who has regular contact with learners can contribute valuable information, though this method is often subjective. Whenever possible, interventionists should observe the learner in a variety of environments or take the first couple of sessions to probe and gather more objective information. This process (i.e., talking to others, doing observations, and probing during the first sessions) leads to the question: what information should interventionists gather to select and create goals?

One of the first pieces of information to obtain is what the learner does well. Too often, interventionists are only interested in a learner's weaknesses and fail to take into account the learner's strengths. Knowing the strengths of the learners will help guide decision making in many ways. First, this information can help determine how goals will be targeted. For example, if the learner has strong language abilities, a teaching interaction procedure may be the best way to teach them skills. Having information about a learner's strengths will also help interventionists not waste time targeting skills that the learner already has. Another good reason to first get information about a learner's strengths to prepare for pairing learners together (discussed later in this chapter), when it will be necessary to know the strengths of each learner. One final reason is that often it will be possible to use a learner's strength to help teach a weakness. For example, if a learner has a sense of humor and enjoys telling jokes (i.e., a strength) but is also engaging in inappropriate attention-seeking behaviors (i.e., a weakness), it might be possible to teach the learner how to get people's attention appropriately by telling jokes. In this way, you have leveraged a strength to combat a weakness.

A learner attending a social skills group will also have areas that need improvement and it is of the utmost importance to find out as much information about these weaknesses as possible. When gathering information, make sure that caregivers, teachers, and other providers feel comfortable sharing the weaknesses of the learner. Too often, when trying to gather information, interventionists overlook that it might be difficult for those in the learner's life to be open about what is difficult for the learner. This is not done to deceive, but rather they want to make sure others know how wonderful the learner is, how much they have learned, and how hard everyone has worked to make improvements.

For these reasons, we recommend starting the conversation on with a discussion of strengths rather than weaknesses. We also recommend that interventionists gather this information in a free-flowing conversation as opposed to following a list of questions. This will help ensure the information obtained drives the conversation rather than an arbitrary checklist. Above all else, all conversation must be done in a clinically sensitive manner. Some important questions include what types of relationships the learner has with their peers, what are their areas of concern, the level of interest in others and/or friendships, and what are their biggest impediments to socializing with others.

When observing a learner or during the first sessions, be on the lookout for any areas that need improvement. One of the best ways to do this is seeing how the other individuals in their environment are behaving socially and if this aligns with how the learner is behaving. If the learner is behaving differently, it is important to note the ways these differences manifest. But it is also important to note the skills peers are displaying so that the learner can be taught the skills that will help them be successful in their natural environment. Keep in mind that the more you can observe a learner, especially when the group is underway, the more deficits might be noticed. This is to say that over time, when interventionists get to know learners better, they may identify previously unnoticed skill deficits.

Picking the Core Deficits

Once the information is gathered and a list of strengths and weaknesses for each learner has been made, determining where to start can feel overwhelming. Look for similarities across the identified targets. By doing this, interventionists will begin to see how the targets are inter-related and what core weaknesses most impact the learner's daily life. Core weaknesses are skills that the learner is not displaying that have an effect on many other skills. For example, a learner may have difficulty learning in group settings, knowing what to do in unfamiliar situations, contributing appropriately to conversations, and joining in play appropriately. Each of these is a skill that needs to be targeted; however, they all may share a common core deficit, which is the lack of observational learning skills. So, instead of targeting each skill individually, we've found it to be more efficient and effective to target the core deficit of observational learning. Often, we then see improvements in other skills that require observational learning without being directly targeted—and less teaching time required for those skills that still need to be addressed.

As an analogy, consider gardening. Each skill in the previous example is like a weed sticking up in the grass. A gardener could cut off each individual weed, but new ones will always continue to crop up. Instead, if the gardener pulled out the weed at the roots, the weed will be more effectively eradicated. Once core deficits for each learner have been identified, it is time to refine this list even further.

Not All Deficits Can Be Targeted

Learners often have many deficits that need to be targeted, but within a social skills group several factors will limit how many of these skills can be targeted for each learner. The first of these constraints is time. If a social skills group is only meeting two to three times a week, for two to three hours at a time, there may not be enough time to target everything (even core deficits). Another important factor that limits targeting all deficits is the nature of a group. Each learner in a group has unique deficits. If each learner has ten unique goals and there are ten learners in the group, then that would amount to 100 goals, which is simply too many. For this reason, we suggest limiting the goals being targeted for each learner to 3–5 at a time when running social skills groups. This number strikes a balance, allowing several goals to be targeted but ensuring each one can be targeted effectively. Limiting the number of proactive targets at one time also forces the interventionists to select the most important goals. Simply put, it is better to target a few goals fully than many goals incompletely.

One way to help decide which core deficits to target for each participant is to first eliminate any goal that can be targeted in other settings. For example, if there are goals that can easily be targeted in a one-to-one setting (assuming the learner has individual intervention sessions) and do not require a peer, these goals should be left out in favor of goals that can only be targeted in a group. Another way to decide on goals for the group is to see which goals the learners have in common. If multiple learners have a goal in common, it would be a great goal to target, helping multiple learners instead of just one.

In our experience with the Autism Partnership Method, learning to say "no" is a necessary part of running a social skills group. Sometimes a supervisor or caregiver asks for additional goals to be targeted after the lead interventionist has finalized the goals for the group. Such a request deserves consideration and if the new goal takes precedence, it may make sense to remove a previously selected goal. However, it might be necessary to tell the person requesting an additional goal that you are unable to add any more goals at this time but will keep it in mind for the future.

Sequence of Goals

After goals have been selected and teaching has begun, each goal will proceed through phases at different rates. At any given time, there will be goals that are being targeted, goals in generalization or maintenance, and goals that are waiting to be introduced. As discussed in previous chapters, it is important to know from the outset how a goal will be moved toward maintenance and generalization. Having this written in a lesson plan will help the interventionists in the group set up situations and reinforce behaviors appropriately—and will help the learner continue to grow. Interventionists should know the optimal sequence of goals and anticipate which skills are going to be targeted next. Knowing what is coming next allows planning to occur and also keeps the interventionists aware of those skills so if they occur naturally within the group, they can reinforce.

Goals for the Group

In Chapters 3 and 6, it was discussed that it's necessary to determine what type of group is being taught; it's also necessary to know what goals the group has as a whole. To make these decisions, the first question is which goals would be relevant to the greatest number of learners. For example, if only a few learners need to learn observational learning skills, but every learner needs to improve their play skills, improving play skills should be an overarching group goal. Selecting overarching group goals will help the entire group stay on track and help interventionists take into account the individual goals of the group and also the larger picture.

Activity Driven vs. Goal Driven

There are so many creative interventionists leading social skills groups who dream up wonderful activities that are fun, engaging, age-typical, and well thought out. What's often missing in these activities are the goals that help learners make progress. Interventionists can fall into the trap of activities as the end in itself and fail to consider how much real learning is occurring. This can happen when interventionists think of a fun activity then try to fit a goal into it, as opposed to the other way around.

Within the Autism Partnership Method, we recommend thinking of the goals you want to target during a part of a social skills group (e.g., circle time, play, snack), then coming up with an activity that will fit those goals. In the curriculum section of this book, you will see many activities and goals that have specific targets. When selecting curricula from this book, or any other source, we recommend you first find the goals and then read the programs to see if they fit for your learners or group.

Conclusion

Running a social skills group is one of the most challenging, time consuming, and exhausting tasks for interventionists. It can also be one of the most rewarding and fun. By gathering all the necessary information, finding the strengths and weaknesses of the learners, selecting the core deficits to be targeted, selecting group goals, keeping track of what is in maintenance and what is being targeted, and being goal-focused rather than activity-driven, you will ensure the best possible outcome for your social skills group.

Chapter Nineteen
Autism Partnership Method Social Skills Group Curriculum

In this section of the book, we provide a list of 92 skills that can be taught within the context of a social skills group. To help professionals, we have divided the skills into three different categories: 1) basic, 2) intermediate, and 3) advanced. This should help professionals determine which skills would be more appropriate for their learners based upon their social repertoires.

We further divided the social skills into five domains: 1) social awareness, 2) social communication, 3) social interaction, 4) social learning, and 5) social relatedness. These five categories make up Autism Partnership Method's social taxonomy as a way to help interventionists better conceptualize and teach social skills. This is described in detail in *Crafting Connections* (Taubman et al., 2011).

The first domain is *social awareness,* which encompasses reading and understanding social cues. The second domain is *social communication,* which focuses on social exchanges, such as conversation and nonverbal aspects of communication. The third domain is *social interaction,* which focuses on improving the interactions between learners and their peers. The fourth domain is *social learning,* which promotes the ability to learn social skills through everyday interactions. The final domain is *social relatedness,* which focuses on understanding how relationships develop and promoting friendship. It should be noted that the domains are not mutually exclusive and that social skills may fall into multiple domains.

We also divided the skills by our preferred or common method of teaching specific skills. It should be noted these skills do not need to be taught exclusively using these methods. We have provided different methods to teach social skills along with an operational definition of each skill, the purpose of teaching the skill, the suggested context for teaching the social skill, an example Individualized Education Program or treatment plan objective, and a recommendation for the data collection method.

It is important to note that these skills and methods are guidelines, not rules. Professionals should modify the skill definitions, procedures, and data collection methods based upon the needs of individual learners. This curriculum is not intended to be exhaustive. Rather, we have aimed to provide a substantial illustration of content and method which should be tailored to meet the needs of your learners. We trust that by providing multiple exemplars, you will be able to extrapolate, creating your own social skills programs and finding the best way to teach these social skills. This list of social skills requires the use of clinical judgment, probing within sessions, and task analyzing skills as needed. We encourage professionals to use this curriculum as a work in progress, changing where needed, adding where needed, omitting when not needed, and individualizing the curriculum based on your learners' social behavior.

References

Taubman, M., Leaf, R., & McEachin, J. (2011). *Crafting connections: Contemporary applied behavior analysis for enriching the social lives of persons with autism spectrum disorder.* New York, NY: DRL Books.

Chapter Twenty
Social Interaction Skills

Jeremy A. Leaf, Jonathan Rafuse & Justin B. Leaf

Social Interaction is one component of Autism Partnership Method's Social Taxonomy. This group of social behaviors focuses on those that help promote appropriate social interactions for individuals diagnosed with autism spectrum disorder. Within this domain, there are basic social interaction skills, intermediate social interaction skills, and advanced social interaction skills. We have also included a number of group games that provide opportunities to target multiple social skills as well as promoting shared enjoyment. There are 31 programs in this chapter that fall under the Social Interaction Domain, listed in the following table.

Basic Social Skills	Intermediate Social Skills	Advanced Social Skills	Group Games
Emotions	Winning and Losing Graciously	Joining Play	Doggie, Doggie
Basic Flexibility: Compromising	Ending Play	Don't Rub it in	Stare of Death
Changing the Game	Compromise	Rude vs. Polite	Snickers and Hoots
Alternatives to Being Silly	Bossiness		Hula Hoop
General Knowledge: Pop Culture	Sharing the Spotlight		Kids' Bowling
Turn Taking	Appropriate Places to Break Eye Contact		Mouse Trap
Sharing	Not Asking Silly Questions		Shark Game
Competing is Fun			Spoon
The Game of Tag: When it's Ok to Run Away			Statue Game
			Steal the Bacon
			Fruit Salad
			Sleeping Game

Emotions

Overall Goal	The learner will identify and label various emotional states, when experienced/demonstrated by others and when expressed by the learner. This enables the learner to more accurately read social situations and interactions, increases environmental awareness, promotes social inferencing, and allows greater access to social reinforcement and engagement.
Example Objective	The learner will correctly identify the emotions of peers in 80% of opportunities presented across 5 days.
Social Taxonomy Domain	Social Interaction, Social Relatedness
Teaching Methodologies	The Teaching Interaction Procedure, Discrete Trial Teaching, and The Cool versus Not Cool™ procedure
Data Collection	Trial-by-trial, Estimation, or Task Analysis
Prerequisite Skills	Matching, Receptive Language, Expressive Language, Expanded Language, Communication Temptations, and Beginning Social Skills

Phases

Phase 1	Identifying Emotional States	<ul><li>Teach the learner to identify a variety of emotional representations.</li><li>Use teaching methodology best suited to the individual learner and maximizing progress (i.e., beginning with picture matching or sorting might be appropriate for some learners, while demonstration and expressive labeling might be the starting point with others).</li><li>Use teaching material best suited to the level of the learner and the teaching methodology implemented.</li><li>Be sure to consider emotional age-typicality; for example, a 4-year-old would not understand "bored."</li><li>Examples of emotions to teach:<ul><li>Basic: Happy, sad, angry, and surprised</li><li>Intermediate: Scared, tired, hurt, silly, hungry, and thirsty</li><li>Advanced: Frustrated, nervous, bored, excited, confused, worried, stressed, jealous, and embarrassed</li></ul></li></ul>
Phase 2	Learner Demonstrates Targeted Emotional States	<ul><li>Teach the learner to accurately demonstrate emotions taught in Phase 1.</li><li>Teach a variety of verbal, facial, gestural, and bodily expressions of emotions.</li><li>Considerations are the same as Phase 1.</li></ul>

Phase 3	Incidental Identification of Emotions Presented by Others	• Teach the learner to recognize and label emotional states demonstrated by others (e.g., interventionist, peers, cohorts, in video) as they come up in everyday situations.

Phase 4	Learner Identifies Situations Associated with Emotions	• Learner identifies situations, activities, and events often associated with specific emotions.
		• For example:
		  - Access to favorite iPad App = "happy"
		  - Favorite toy snatched away = "angry"/ "surprised"
		  - Alone in an unfamiliar location = "nervous"/ "scared"/ "excited"
		  - Favorite toy broken or lost = "sad"

Phase 5	Learner Identifies Causes for Emotional Expression	• Learner identifies a variety of causes for emotional expression (e.g., "Why does Joe feel scared?") • Start with pictorial representation of scenarios then progress to incidental situations in everyday life.
Steps Towards Generalization		• Fade extrinsic reinforcers • Fade use of priming (including specificity and timing) • Fade interventionist presence • Practice with helpers/cohorts • Increase the variety of activities and levels of distraction • Move to more natural environments

Basic Flexibility: Compromising

Overall Goal	Because the nature of most play and socialization is based on shared experiences, new or novel ways of participating in interactions often arise. At times this can be difficult. This program works on the learner's ability to experience new thinking or new ways of doing things while remaining calm and "going with the flow." Specifically, the learner will learn to use a "fair" strategy to choose shared activities with a peer. Regardless of the activity chosen (the learner's or peer's preference), the learner will engage in the activity. The objective is to spend time with the peer, no matter the activity. This process can be repeated until the play opportunity ends.
Example Objective	During play, when the learner desires an activity or game different from a peer's choice, the learner will engage in a compromise strategy, then follow through with the outcome of that strategy with no disruptive behaviors in 80% of opportunities presented.
Social Taxonomy Domain	Social Interaction, Social Communication, and Social Relatedness
Teaching Methodologies	The Teaching Interaction Procedure, The Cool versus Not Cool™ procedure, and Discrete Trial Teaching
Data Collection	Task Analysis or Estimation
Prerequisite Skills	Comprehension, General Knowledge, Receptive Language, Expressive Language, Expanded Language, Beginning Social Skills, Frustration Tolerance, Stress Management, Beginning Play Skills, Basic Flexibility

Phases

Phase 1	Compromise Strategies	• Teach the learner a variety of compromise strategies. Possibilities include:
		  - Rock, paper, scissors
		  - Eenie, meenie, minee, moe
		  - Your choice, then my choice
		  - Combine activities

Phase 2	Systematic Exposure	• Teach the learner to remain calm and engaged with a game or activity, even when it is a peer choice, when the rules change, when you win or lose, or when a novel component is introduced. • Follow Frustration Tolerance/Stress Management procedural guidelines. • For each exposure, the learner first learns to remain calm, and then learns to respond in a socially appropriate manner when these situations occur.

Phase 3	Potential Scenarios	• Once Phase 2 is mastered, set up situations (e.g., with a cohort, another interventionist, a peer) where compromise skills are utilized. For example:
		  - Free time
		  - Play dates
		  - Group reinforcement opportunities
		  - Game time

Steps Toward Generalization		• Fade supplemental reinforcers • Fade use of priming (including specificity and timing) • Fade interventionist presence • Practice with helpers/cohorts • Increase the variety of activities and levels of distraction • Move to more natural environments

Changing the Game

Overall Goal	The learner recognizes the social cue when a peer is bored with a game and appropriately changes the play to something else.
Example Objective	When a peer is bored, the learner will recognize the social cue, ask the peer what they want to play, then go along with the peer's idea in 90% of opportunities presented.
Social Taxonomy Domain	Social Interaction
Teaching Methodologies	The Cool versus Not Cool™ procedure and the Teaching Interaction Procedure
Data Collection	Task Analysis or Estimation

Phases

Phase 1	Identify Bored Social Cues	Together with the learner, identify social cues that indicate boredom. Start with more obvious social cues, then move onto less obvious cues. More obvious social cue examples: • Turning away from the activity • Staring off • Saying "I'm bored," asking what other games you have, requesting something else, etc. • Yawning Less obvious social cue examples: • No positive affect • Moving slowly through the game • Making neutral or negative comments
Phase 2	Task Analysis of Changing the Game	Create a task analysis and go over it with the learner for the appropriate behaviors you would like the learner to engage in when their peer is bored. Example task analysis: • Accurately read the social cue of boredom • Ask the peer if they want to play something different • If the answer is yes, ask them what they want to play or make a suggestion • Go along and play the game the peer chose
Phase 3	Discrimination Training	Setup demonstrations of cool and not cool examples of the behavior and have the learner rate the demonstration. Example 1 (Cool):

Phase 3 (cont.)	Discrimination Training	• *Person A starts yawning and looking away.* • Person B: "Hey, want to play something different?" • Person A: "Sure!" • Person B: "What do you want to play? I have Go Fish, checkers, and Operation" • Person A: "Let's play Operation!" • *Person B gets the game and begins playing with Person A* Example 2 (Cool): • *Person A moves slowly with no positive affect.* • Person B: "Hey, want to play something different?" • Person A: "Yes please!" • Person B: "What do you want to play? I have Go Fish, checkers, and Operation" • Person A: "Hmm, I like Go Fish" • *Person B gets the game and begins playing with Person A* Example 3 (Not-cool): • *Person A starts yawning and looking away.* • Person B: "Hey, want to play something different?" • Person A: "Sure!" • Person B: "What do you want to play? I have Go Fish, checkers, and Operation" • Person A: "Let's play Operation!" • *Person B grabs checkers instead* Example 4 (Not-cool): • *While playing Jenga, Person A moves slowly with no positive affect.* • *Person B continues to play and comment on how much fun it is to play Jenga*
Phase 4	Role-Play	Set up role-play opportunities for the learner to engage in the appropriate behaviors. Reinforce the learner appropriately changing the game.
Phase 5	Real Life Situations	Set up more natural situations for the learner to practice responding to peers being bored. Use priming as a prompt (e.g., "remember to think about whether your friend is enjoying the game"). Fade the specificity of the prompt and the timing of prompt to promote generalization.

Alternative to Being Silly

Overall Goal	The learner will refrain from engaging in behaviors deemed as socially inappropriate. These behaviors likely interfere with the learner meaningfully engaging with others. Examples of these behaviors include off-topic or perseverative talking, non-congruent statements, and statements that would not be considered complimentary. Refraining from these behaviors (or, ideally, participating in socially appropriate alternatives) enables the learner to access more social opportunities, develop friendships, and increases exposure to other potential reinforcers in the more generalized environment.
Example Objective	When an opportunity to react or express emotion arises, the learner will refrain from defined "Silly" behavior in 80% of opportunities.
Social Taxonomy Domain	Social Interaction
Teaching Methodologies	The Teaching Interaction Procedure, the Cool versus Not Cool™ procedure, and Discrete Trial Teaching
Data Collection	Task Analysis and Estimation
Prerequisite Skills	Discrimination, Receptive Language, Expressive Language, Communication Temptations, and Beginning Social Skills

Phases

Phase 1	Discrimination Training of Silly (not cool) vs. Cool	· Together with learner, identify problematic examples of silly behavior (e.g., over the top, out of control behavior that is not congruent with the ongoing activity, stigmatizing stereotypic behaviors, jokes that are not funny) and common situations where silly behaviors often occur. It is important to zero on the silly behaviors that are exhibited by each learner, but examples may include:
		
		  - Free time within a group
		  - Transitions
		  - Walking
		  - Participating in conversations
		  - Joining into a conversation
		  - New or unfamiliar environments
		  - Situations eliciting excitement or emotionality that could go "over the top" rather quickly
		
		· Set up demonstrations of appropriate (cool) and silly (not cool) examples of the behavior and have the learner rate each demonstration.

| Phase 2 | Role-Play Appropriate Responding to Tempting Situations | • Together with the learner, for each silly behavior that was identified in Phase 1, brainstorm appropriate alternative behaviors. Examples of appropriate responding may include:

- Verbal alternatives to "silliness"
 • On-topic responses and comments
 • Non-perseverative speech
 • Expressive language best supporting the learner's social communication domain
 • Sounds and vocal embellishments supporting the conversation and social situation

- Non-verbal alternatives to "silliness"
 • Facial expressions matching the mood and context
 • Non-verbal expressions serving the purpose and not attracting undue attention

- Gross motor alternatives to "silliness"
 • Remaining still when lined up
 • Walking appropriately
 • Waiting with a still body

• Identify the hierarchy of least to most tempting scenarios. Beginning with a very mild level of temptation, role-play scenarios where the learner is tempted to engage in silly behavior. Early in the role-play, before silly behavior occurs, have the learner STOP (i.e., freeze) and THINK about the best choice to make.
- Refer to the initial phases in the Stop, Think, Act, Review (STAR) program

• Ask the learner to state what would be the cool way to continue the activity. If they can state a cool response, continue the role-play.
- If not, have the learner think further before continuing and provide assistance in identifying an appropriate alternative to being silly.
- At any time if the learner begins to act silly, direct them to stop and take as long as necessary for them to choose a suitable alternative to being silly.

• As the learner progresses, discontinue having them formally stop and state what they will do and allow the role-play to go from start to finish without interruption. |
| Phase 3 | The Learner Chooses the Best Alternative to "Silly" Behavior Based on the Situation | • Teach the learner to determine what response is best suited to the scenario.
• This requires further teaching. Examples of appropriate responding corresponding to the scenario may include:
- Expressive alternatives to "silliness"
 • On-topic responses and comments
 • Non-perseverative speech |

| Phase 3 (cont.) | The Learner Chooses the Best Alternative to "Silly" Behavior Based on the Situation | <ul><li>Expressive language best supporting the learner's social communication domain</li><li>Sounds and vocal embellishments supporting the conversation and social situation</li></ul>- Non-verbal alternatives to "silliness"<ul><li>Facial expressions matching the mood and context</li><li>Non-verbal expressions serving the purpose and not attracting undue attention</li></ul>- Gross motor alternatives to "silliness"<ul><li>Remaining still when lined up</li><li>Walking appropriately</li><li>Waiting with a still body</li></ul><ul><li>Refraining from "silly" behavior when free time occurs, or when the learner becomes bored/has nothing to do</li></ul>- Gross motor cool vs. not cool discrimination
- Fine motor cool vs. not cool discrimination
- Other stigmatizing behavior cool vs. not cool discrimination (e.g., movements, gestures, subtle SSB)
- Vocal cool vs. not cool discrimination
- Conversational fixation cool vs. not cool |
| Steps Toward Generalization | | <ul><li>Throughout the day there will be naturally occurring temptations. Initially, the learner can be primed in advance to remember to STOP and THINK. Priming just before the activity increases the likelihood of success. Over time the prime should occur further in advance and become less specific (e.g., "What are we working on today?").</li><li>Fade supplemental reinforcers</li><li>Fade interventionist presence</li><li>Practice with helpers/cohorts</li><li>Increase the variety of activities and levels of distraction</li><li>Move to more natural environments</li></ul> |

General Knowledge: Pop Culture

Overall Goal	This program develops a working knowledge of popular culture relevant to the learner. This relevance is dependent on the learner's age, where the learner lives, and includes the interests of the peer-group with whom the learner spends time (e.g., school, the community). Ultimately, this knowledge is what is generally popular or "cool" to the learner's generation. Having this knowledge increases social interaction opportunities and eventually, the development of learner-specific interests, hobbies, and leisure activities.
Example Objective	The learner will accurately identify characters from current or popular movies in 80% of opportunities presented.
Social Taxonomy Domain	Social Interaction and Social Relatedness
Teaching Methodologies	Discrete Trial Teaching and the Teaching Interaction Procedure
Data Collection	Trial-by-trial or Estimation
Prerequisite Skills	Comprehension, Categorization, General Knowledge, Receptive Language, Expressive Language, Expanded Language, Communication Temptations, Social Skills

Phases

Phase 1	Identify Current and Popular Characters and People	<ul><li>This phase focuses on celebrities that are part of pop culture, especially those specific to the peer group with whom the learner will be developing social ties.</li><li>Considerations for this teaching include age-typicality, where the learner lives, and what is currently "cool" and trending in the learner's peer group. From this knowledge base, collaborate with the learner to find elements of interest to the learner.</li><li>Examples include:<ul><li>Popular characters in televised series, movies, and animation</li><li>Characters from video games and apps</li><li>Characters from books, comics and magazines</li><li>Sport stars (depending on the community, might include athletes playing baseball, football, soccer, surfing, skateboarding, tennis, skiing, snowboarding)</li><li>Civic "heroes" or community "stars"</li></ul></li></ul>

Phase 2	Identify the Different Categories and Activities of Current and Popular Characters and People	• This phase pairs the above individuals with their areas of "expertise;" it develops more specific knowledge about the specific skills or talents these people possess and where they are used. For example: - Lionel Messi: soccer player, striker, goal scorer, play maker, Barcelona Football Club and Argentina - Aquaman: DC Comic superhero, King of the Sea, communicates with all sea creatures, Justice League, Atlantis - Mike Trout: baseball player, LA Angels, home runs, outfielder, all-star - Harry Potter: Book and movie character, powerful magician, good vs. evil, Hogwarts, book series, movies - Lindsey Vonn: Alpine skier, US Ski Team, Olympian, champion, fearless - Mia Hamm: Most famous American soccer player of all time, US Women's Soccer Team, striker, goal scorer, champion
Phase 3	Deeper Knowledge of Current and Popular Characters and People	• This phase teaches expertise in the subject matter. For example: - Lionel Messi: From Argentina, plays forward, on the club Barcelona team - Aquaman: Has trouble communicating with piranha, shows the ability to control any being evolved from marine life, grows weak if he remains on land for extended periods - Mike Trout: Bats right-handed, is number 27, has won 3 MVPs - Harry Potter: Is in Gryffindor, plays Quidditch, his best friends are Ron and Hermione - Lindsey Vonn: Has 3 Olympic medals, 1 gold medal, races in all disciplines of skiing - Mia Hamm: Two-time Olympic gold medalist, plays forward, was number 9
Phase 4	Deeper Knowledge of specific Broader Topics	• This phase teaches the specific activity, media, or skill categories and then the finer discrimination within categories for the previously mentioned famous people. For example: - Athletics – football – NFL teams – college teams – mascots and team names – developing fan base - Athletics – soccer – international sides – super leagues – La Liga, EPL, Bundesliga, etc. – teams – developing fan base - Marvel Comics universe – movies – Avengers – Iron Man, Spider-Man, Captain America, Black Panther, Antman, etc. – superpowers – secret identities – individual histories - Music – alternative – Imagine Dragons – musicians – albums and songs – histories

Phase 5	General Knowledge of Popular Games and Leisure Activities	• This phase teaches the play and leisure activities popular with the learner's identified peer group.
		• For each general topic follow teaching protocol promoted in Phase 4, increase the learner's specific knowledge of each area of expertise. For example:
		  - Video Games and apps
		  - Recess games and activities
		  - Free-time activities and sports
		  - Dancing, drama, movie making, storytelling, etc.

Steps Toward Generalization		• Fade supplemental reinforcers • Fade use of priming (including specificity and timing) • Fade interventionist presence • Practice with helpers/cohorts • Increase the variety of activities and levels of distraction • Move to more natural environments

Turn Taking

Overall Goal	The learner will participate in taking turns during a game or social opportunity. This skill includes remaining engaged with the game/process, initiating whose turn it is, and matching the mood with the others involved in the game/process until it is complete. Learning to participate in games is a key component of play and socialization. Teaching the learner to remain engaged during games provides opportunities for greater socialization opportunities and expansion of the learner's play and leisure repertoire.
Example Objective	During turn-taking games, the learner will remain attentive and respond and initiate whose turn it is in 80% of opportunities presented.
Social Taxonomy Domain	Social Interaction
Teaching Methodologies	Discrete Trial Teaching, the Teaching Interaction Procedure, and the Cool versus Not Cool™ procedure
Data Collection	Trial-by-trial, Estimation data, and Task Analysis Data
Prerequisite Skills	Comprehension, General Knowledge, Receptive Language, Expressive Language, Expanded Language, Communication Temptations, Beginning Social Skills

Phases

Phase 1	Taking Turns	• Teach the learner to remain engaged with a game or activity and actively take turns. Example task analysis:
		  - Learner sustains attention and cues in to turn-taking opportunities during a game or activity.
		  - Learner participates in the actions required to take a turn specific to game or activity. May include:
		    • The learner says, "My turn," and proceeds
		    • The learner simply proceeds with turn
		    • The learner pairs the turn with a typical comment (e.g., "Ha! Take that!" "Ooh, whatcha gonna do now?") while remaining appropriate to the situation
		• The learner ends turn and waits for peer to take their turn
		• If peer takes too long (depending on activity or game) or is distracted/inattentive, the learner appropriately informs peer (e.g., "Your turn," "Go!" "What are you waiting for?")
		• Repeat until game or activity ends
		• The learner ends game with good sportsmanship/appropriate comment/segue (e.g., "Good game," "Want to play again?" "Let's do something else now," "That was fun!")

Phase 2	Broaden Range of Turn-taking Activities	· Teach the learner to initiate/respond appropriately to a variety of turn-taking opportunities, including:
		  - Board games or activities that require sharing objects/pieces/implements
		  - Outdoor activities that require turn-taking
		  - Working with someone to complete a task/part of a team, etc.

Phase 3	Variations in Turn-taking	· Teach the learner to notice and appropriately respond to peers when turn-taking doesn't "follow the script." For example:
		  - Knowing when to end or continue an activity based on other's social cues (e.g., peer no longer interested in activity/game)
		  - Having to end a game/activity before it is completed
		  - Peer attempting to cheat (e.g., take more than one turn at a time, moving pieces in a board game incongruently with the die cast)

Steps Toward Generalization		· Fade supplemental reinforcers · Fade use of priming (including specificity and timing) · Fade interventionist presence · Practice with helpers/cohorts · Increase the variety of activities and levels of distraction · Move to more natural environments

Sharing

Overall Goal	Sharing things with others is commonly expected and appreciated. A person who does not share will be at a disadvantage and may be viewed unfavorably by others. Willingness to share is facilitated by promoting flexibility within play and tolerance of not having your own way.
Example Objective	When asked for an item by a peer the learner will engage in 100% of the steps of sharing appropriately across five consecutive days.
Social Taxonomy Domain	Social Interaction
Teaching Methodologies	The Cool versus Not Cool™ procedure, the Teaching Interaction Procedure, and Discrete Trial Teaching
Data Collection	Task Analysis or Estimation

Phases

Phase 1	What to Do and Say	• Choose a variety of alternative behaviors the learner can engage in based on their skill level and function of the not sharing. - For example: saying, "in a minute," handing over the item nicely, etc. • Use discrimination training (e.g., cool vs. not cool) if necessary.
Phase 2	Sharing a Non-Preferred Item	• Prime the learner that you are going to practice sharing a non-preferred item (e.g., "We are going to practice sharing this pencil"). • Set up situations to have the learner practice sharing the non-preferred item.
Phase 3	Sharing a Neutral Item	• Prime the learner that you are going to practice sharing a neutral item (e.g., "We are going to practice sharing this train"). • Set up situations to have the learner practice sharing the neutral item.
Phase 4	Sharing a Preferred Item	• Prime the learner that you are going to practice sharing a preferred item (e.g., "We are going to practice sharing this light saber"). • Set up situations to have the learner practice sharing the preferred item.
Phase 5	Sharing a Highly Preferred Item	• Prime the learner that you are going to practice sharing a highly preferred item (e.g., "We are going to practice sharing this iPad"). • Set up situations to have the learner practice sharing the highly preferred item.
Phase 6	Steps Toward Generalization	• Fade the use of priming • Practice with peers • Practice in a variety of locations • Practice without the interventionist present • Fade supplemental reinforcement for sharing

Competing is Fun

Overall Goal	Increase social awareness of other people. Increase social relatedness with peers. Regulating effort based upon observation of others. Cooperating and regulating actions with others to work as a team. Understand concepts of winning and losing. Provide motivation for games and activities that involve competitive concepts
Example Objective	During game play the learner will display an appropriate level of competitiveness as determined by a task analysis with 100% accuracy across five consecutive days.
Social Taxonomy Domain	Social Interaction
Teaching Methodologies	The Teaching Interaction Procedure and the Cool versus Not Cool™ procedure
Data Collection	Task Analysis

Phases

Phase 1	First to Get the Preferred Item	The learner should be seated face to face with "opponent" (e.g., interventionist, peer). A preferred item will be placed in front of both people. As soon as the preferred item has been placed in front of the opponents, the first person to reach and grab for the preferred item wins the round and can enjoy the preferred item. Different kinds of preferred item can be used including edibles, toys, or pieces of paper with pictures or words depicting the preferred item that is to be earned.
Phase 2	Increased Response Effort	The objective of this phase is to increase the effort of the learner. Examples of activities in this phase include: • The preferred item is placed farther away, and it is a race to get to it first. • The preferred item is placed under one cup and there are several cups on the table. The participants have to turn over the cups to find the preferred item first. • The preferred item is placed in boxes that need to be opened to find the preferred item.
Phase 3	Completing Assigned Tasks the Fastest	The objective of this task is to have the learner understand that the winner of an activity is the one who completes the task the fastest. Each participant should be given their own set of materials to complete or use. Examples of tasks include: • Running races

Phase 3 (cont.)	Completing Assigned Tasks the Fastest	· Scooter or bike races · Obstacle courses · Finishing puzzles/Lego sets · Tidying up · Stacking a tower · Egg and spoon races
Phase 4	Working with a Partner	The objective is still to complete the task the fastest; however, to complete the task, cooperation with a partner is necessary. There can be two teams of 2 people in each team competing against each other or 1 team competing against the clock. In teaching cooperation, it is important for a learner to recognize that helping their partner do their best improves success of the team. A learner should not be competing with their partner. Examples of tasks include: · One person has to put puzzle pieces together while the other person has to run up and down to retrieve the pieces from a place further away and give to their partner. · Tag team relay scooter, running, and obstacle courses. · One team member has to tell the other to get items from a list. · Pushing each other in a wagon or box to a finish line. · Team members hold a towel together and transport objects to a finish line. · A balloon is placed between teammates bodies and they have to transport the balloon to a finish line without touching it with their hands. If it drops on the floor, they start again. · Team members have to go to a finish line at exactly the same speed or they have to restart. · Three-legged races.
Phase 5	Productivity	The objective of this phase is to have the winner be the person who is able to produce the most in the given time. These activities could be done in teams of one to begin with but can also be done working with a partner once the concepts have been learned. Examples of tasks include: · Throwing balls into a basket and after a set period of time they are counted and the one with the most wins. This could be adapted to having the teammate hold the basket at a distance and try to also catch the balls thrown. · Balloon badminton using rackets or just hands. Count most rallies in a row. · List generation. Given a topic (e.g., animals, Star Wars characters), team members have to come up with the longest list possible in the time allocated.

Phase 5 (cont.)	Productivity	• Treasure hunt. Teams have to find as many items on the list as possible in the time given. • Pop as many balloons as you can in a specific time period.
Phase 6	Accuracy	The objective of this phase is to have the winner be the person who is the most accurate. Examples of activities include: • Throwing a ball nearest to a target. • Throwing darts at a board with the person closest to the middle being the winner. • Who can hit the ball the furthest?
Phase 7	Verbal Responses	Winning in this phase will be achieved by answering the most questions in a period of time or by being the first one to answer a certain number of questions correctly (e.g., first to 10). This can be run like a quiz show with each participant being offered opportunities to answer questions. While one is answering the other should wait their turn. It could incorporate some speed aspects by having the participants pressing a bell or buzzer to have the opportunity to answer the question.
Phase 8	Mixtures of All Rules	Mixtures of all the previously described rules. In this phase mixtures of rules will be applied to different games. This is often the case with games and activities in schools and sports. Examples include: • Duck, duck, goose • What's the time, Mr. Wolf?
Considerations		In the beginning of the training it is advised that reinforcement is provided to the winner immediately. However, it is also advisable to work toward tokens and points. This means that the learner may have to win numerous times to access reinforcement. It introduces the aspects of earning points which is very typical in competitive type activities. A competitive token economy might be developed where each team is earning tokens or points and the first team to get all their points or tokens accesses reinforcement.

The Game of Tag: When it's ok to Run Away

Overall Goal	Teach age-typical play skills. Reduce likelihood of elopement or other disruptive, dangerous behavior. Increase social interaction. Increase expressive abilities. Increase social cause and effect opportunities. Shared enjoyment.
Example Objective	The learner will perform 100% of the steps correctly when playing tag with a peer across five consecutive days.
Social Taxonomy Domain	Social Interaction and Social Relatedness
Teaching Methodologies	The Cool versus Not Cool™ procedure and Discrete Trial Teaching
Data Collection	Task Analysis or Estimation

Phases

Overview	• Initially, begin exposure to Tag in an enclosed area (even in a room at first if that assists the understanding and contingency development). Enclosed outdoor areas include tennis courts, fenced-in basketball courts, handball/squash courts, etc.
	• Move to a less enclosed area once the skill has been developed. The discrimination between chase being "ON" (available) and "OFF" (unavailable) is clearly understood and reinforcement has been successfully paired with the activity and associated behavior(s).
	• Be aware of safety, for the learner and peers, and any interventionists involved in the teaching.

	• Requisite skills may include:
	  - Go vs. Stop
	  - Walk with Me
	  - Follow a Friend
	  - Community Safety
	  - Other Individualized Reactive and Proactive Programs for Elopement

Phase 1	Teach the Discrimination Between Time to Play Tag (Chase) vs. Not Time to Play Tag (Chase)	• This phase is concerned with the practice required to teach when it is okay to run away from someone (during Tag, in this case) vs. when the learner should stay with the interventionist, friend, peer(s), or other adults.
		• Learner wearing the flag signals: Tag is "ON" and the learner can run away and be chased
		  - Setup may include:
		    • Statements: "Let's play tag. I'm it!" "Time to play tag. Run away!" "I'm it. you have to run!"
		    • A visual representing "Tag" when given to someone.
		  - Learner runs from chaser/person who is it until "caught."

Phase 1 (cont.)	Teach the Discrimination Between Time to Play Tag (Chase) vs. Not Time to Play Tag (Chase)	- "Caught" can be signaled by using flag football strips. Once the strip is pulled, the learner should be taught to stop running.
		- Individualize instruction. Task analysis and reinforcement should be based on the learner.
		  • Reinforcement could initially occur throughout steps. For example:
		    o Putting the flag on
		    o Chasing/starting to run away
		    o Stopping when the flag is removed
		  • Reinforcement should be faded to the most natural schedule, with the terminal reinforcer being the fun of the game.
		• Learner NOT wearing the flag signals: Chase/Tag is NOT AVAILABLE
		  - Flag off means staying with the adult/peer(s).
		    • For example, begin trials of Walk with Me or Stay with Your Friend
		  - Setup may include:
		    • Statements: "Vest off, no more Tag," "Let's practice staying with me" paired with flag taken off
		    • A visual representing "not available" placed over the picture of the representation of "Tag"
		  - Individualize instruction. Task analysis and reinforcement should be based on the learner.
		  - Follow appropriate reactive plan if learner attempts to elope.

Phase 2	Teach the Learner to Play Tag with Other Adults	Include continued discrimination practice (Tag "ON" = flag on; Tag "OFF" = flag off).
Phase 3	Teach the Learner to Play with Peers	Include continued discrimination practice (Tag "ON" = flag on; Tag "OFF" = flag off).
Phase 4	Teach Learner to Avoid Being Caught [if needed]	Create an incentive to avoid capture. One way to do this is to have the chaser grab the flag as the act of "tagging." By getting the flag, the game is over, and the tagger gets a preferred prize. The interventionist can reinforce keeping the flag by ending the game while the learner still has the flag and can exchange the flag for a prize.
Phase 5	Teach the Learner to Play with Peers in Less Structured/ Enclosed Areas	Include continued discrimination practice (Tag "ON" = flag on; Tag "OFF" = flag off).

Generalization		· Considerations include:
		- Varied settings/locations
		- Varied participants
		- Requesting Tag as a play/leisure activity
		- Discriminating when Tag is a good play activity vs. when something else would be more appropriate (e.g., location, time of day, weather, potential participants)

Doggie, Doggie Game

Game Instructions	1. Have all the learners sit in a circle.
	2. Have an item small enough that will be the "bone."
	3. Have one learner, or "doggie," leave the group so they cannot see what is happening in the circle, or sit in the middle of the circle and close their eyes.
	4. Give one of the learners the "bone."
	5. Have a learner hide the bone in their lap.
	6. Have all the learners pretend to also hide a bone in their lap.
	7. When everyone is ready, the group starts chanting: "Doggie, doggie, where's your bone? Somebody took it from your home!"
	8. The learner in the middle uncovers their eyes.
	9. The learner in the middle starts calling on learners in the circle, and asks if they have the bone (e.g., "Sam, do you have it?")
	    a. If the learner says "Yes," they reveal the bone go in the middle to be the "doggie."
	    b. If the learner says "No," the "doggie" must continue to call on peers until they find the "bone."

Purpose of Teaching Social Skill	To practice a variety of skills incorporated into a play-based setting.
Example Objective	The learner will respond appropriately based on the information provided by peers in 70% of opportunities presented.
Social Taxonomy Domain	Social Interaction and Social Relatedness
Skills that can be Targeted	Sustained attention, increased interactions, problem solving, responding to peers, frustration tolerance (not getting a turn), learning-how-to-learn skills (sitting, looking, waiting), learning peers names.
Materials Needed	Various items to be the "bone" (e.g., a bean bag, paper clip, toy bone)
Teaching Methodologies	Combination of: · The Cool versus Not Cool™ procedure · Discrete Trial Teaching · Shaping
Considerations	· Make this game fun and positive that the learners do together to promote shared enjoyment. · Try to limit the amount of corrective feedback. · If the activity evokes behaviors that interfere with participation, consider removing the learner until they are ready to participate appropriately.
Data Collection	Depending on the target skill: Estimation data, Trial by Trial, or Time Sample

Stare of Death Game

Game Instructions	1. Learners sit in a circle.
	2. The interventionist has the "stare of death."
	a. As the learners learn the game then they can have the "stare of death."
	3. When the interventionist makes eye contact with a learner, the learner must fall over.
Purpose of Teaching Social Skill	To practice a variety of skills incorporated into a play-based setting.
Example Objective	During a play-based activity, the learner will sustain visual attending for 90% of a 5-minute duration.
Social Taxonomy Domain	Social Interaction
Skills that can be Targeted	Sustained eye contact, joint attention, sustained learning-how-to-learn skills, sustained visual attending, conditional instructions, frustration tolerance, waiting, problem solving, winning/losing graciously
Teaching Methodologies	Combination of: • The Cool versus Not Cool™ procedure • Discrete Trial Teaching • Shaping
Considerations	• To make it more fun, change the actions the learner must engage in when looked at (e.g., make an animal sound, act like an animal, say their favorite ice cream). • To make it more challenging remove one learner from the room and tell all the other learners who will have "the stare of death." When the learner re-enters the room, start the game. It will then be their job to figure out who had the "stare of death."
Data Collection	Estimation data, Time Sample, Trial by Trial

Snickers and Hoots Game

Game Instructions	1. Play music – learners dance around freely at this time.
	2. Pause the music – learners must then find a partner.
	   a. Initially you can partner the learners up so that they are seeking out the same partner each time.
	3. Say "Snickers and Hoots" followed by an instruction such as "elbow to elbow."
	   a. Learners must then touch their partners elbow with their elbow.
	   b. Sample instructions include "back to back," "high five to high five," "toes to toes," etc.
	4. Learners continue following the instructions until the interventionist starts the music again. Then the learners can dance freely.
	5. Continue until song ends or finished with the game.

Purpose of Teaching Social Skill	To practice a variety of skills incorporated into a play-based setting.
Example Objective	During a group game, the learner will actively participate and maintain appropriate demeanor in 90% of opportunities presented.
Social Taxonomy Domain	Social Interaction
Skills that could be Targeted	Environmental awareness, conditional instructions, body parts, shared excitement, cool body, receptive instructions, matching the mood, observational learning
Materials Needed	· Music · Speakers
Teaching Methodologies	Combination of: · The Cool versus Not Cool™ procedure · Discrete Trial Teaching · Shaping
Considerations	· Provide fun instructions. · Manipulate time for learners to hold instructions (it may be more difficult for some if they have target behaviors around physical contact with peers). · May increase observational learning by giving instructions that some know and some do not know. Those who do not know must observe peers to figure out the answer (may need to plant some confederate peers or pre-teach). · Pair learners strategically (e.g., if one learner needs to practice seeking out peers do not place them with someone who will find them easily).
Data Collection	Estimation data, Time Sample, Trial by Trial

Hula Hoop Game

Game Instructions	1. Designate a play area (e.g., a marked basketball court) or use cones to mark the "play area." 2. One learner is given a hula-hoop. The other learners must run away from the person with the hula-hoop. 3. The learner with the hula-hoop tries to catch people by catching them inside the hula-hoop. 4. When a learner is caught, they join their peer as being "it" and help hold the hula hoop. 5. The game is over when everyone has been caught.
Purpose of Teaching Social Skill	To practice a variety of skills incorporated into a play-based setting.
Example Objective	During a play-based activity, the learner will sustain positive affect in 80% of opportunities presented.
Social Taxonomy Domain	Social Interaction and Social Relatedness
Skills that can be Targeted	Sustained attention, shared excitement, matching the mood, communication, teamwork
Materials Needed	• Hula hoop
Teaching Methodologies	Combination of: • The Cool versus Not Cool™ procedure • Discrete Trial Teaching • Shaping
Considerations	• May incorporate an additional hula-hoop for large groups. • May need to task analyze communication and planning between learners so that they are successful when multiple learners are holding the hula hoop.
Data Collection	Estimation data, Time Sample, Trial by Trial

Kids' Bowling Game

Game Instructions	1. One learner is a "bowler" with a large rubber ball and stands on one side of the room.
	2. The other learners are "pins" and crowd together or line up about 15 feet away from the bowler but must not move.
	3. The bowler rolls the ball at the pins.
	4. If a learner is hit, they get to fall down (and can fall down in a silly fashion).
	5. The bowler continues until they knock down all the pins.
Purpose of Teaching Social Skill	To practice a variety of skills incorporated into a play-based setting.
Example Objective	During a fun, play-based activity, the learner will match the mood of peers by displaying an appropriate level of excitement in 80% of opportunities presented.
Social Taxonomy Domain	Social Interaction
Skills that can be Targeted	Responding to peers, sustained attention, conditional instructions, waiting, positive demeanor, environmental awareness
Materials Needed	• Large rubber ball (ideally large exercise ball)
Teaching Methodologies	Combination of: • The Cool versus Not Cool™ procedure • Discrete Trial Teaching • Shaping
Considerations	• Another way to play is to allow the pins to run around and the bowler has to chase them with the ball to get them out. • Be mindful of learner safety.
Data Collection	Estimation data, Time Sample, Trial by Trial

Mouse Trap Game

Game Instructions	1. Lay a parachute open on the ground.
	2. Have the learners stand around the parachute (in a circle).
	3. Each learner grabs the edge of the parachute.
	4. As a group, wave the parachute up and down.
	5. As the parachute is moving up, the interventionist will call a learner's name.
	6. The learner must try to run across, under the parachute, and escape to the other side before the parachute comes down and "traps" the learner.
	   a. If the learner gets trapped, the learner is out.
	   b. If the learner escapes, they grab the edge of the parachute and keep playing.
	   c. The last learner to not get trapped gets to call out the names in the next round.

Purpose of Teaching Social Skill	To practice a variety of skills incorporated into a play-based setting.
Example Objective	The learner will correctly respond to conditional instructions during a play-based activity for 80% of opportunities presented.
Social Taxonomy Domain	Social Interaction
Skills that can be Targeted	Conditional instructions, cool body, matching the mood, cooperation, environmental awareness, peer awareness
Materials Needed	• Giant Parachute
Teaching Methodologies	Combination of: • The Cool versus Not Cool™ procedure • Discrete Trial Teaching • Shaping
Considerations	To make it more fun, call more than one learner at a time or even add conditional instructions (e.g., girls, boys, white shirts, 5-year-olds). Make sure to play in an area with plenty of free space so that learners do not bump into things.
Data Collection	Estimation data, Time Sample, Trial by Trial

Shark Game

Game Instructions	1. Lay out a large parachute.
	2. Have learners sit around the edge of the parachute with their legs straight under the parachute.
	3. One learner is the "shark" under the parachute.
	4. Learners sitting around the edge shake the parachute making "waves."
	5. The shark will "swim" under the parachute and "eat" a learner by grabbing the learner's legs under the parachute.
	6. The learner who was eaten then becomes a shark.
	7. The sharks will continue to eat all other people until everyone is under the parachute.
Purpose of Teaching Social Skill	To practice a variety of skills incorporated into a play-based setting.
Example Objective	During an exciting activity, the learner will match the mood of peers by displaying a level of excitement similar to peers in 80% of opportunities presented.
Social Taxonomy Domain	Social Interaction
Skills that can be Targeted	Shared excitement, responding to peers, positive demeanor, conditional instructions, waiting
Materials Needed	Large parachute
Teaching Methodologies	Combination of: • The Cool versus Not Cool™ procedure • Discrete Trial Teaching • Shaping
Considerations	• Make sure that learners do not get too rough when grabbing the other learners. • An interventionist might want to start as the shark to control the order of learners coming under the parachute.
Data Collection	Estimation data, Time Sample, Trial by Trial

Spoon Game

Game Instructions	1. Learners sit in a circle with spoons (or another object). spread out in the middle. There should be one less spoon than there are people.
	2. When the interventionist (or designated learner) grabs a spoon, all other players try to grab a spoon.
	3. Whoever does not have a spoon at the end is out.
	4. Remove one spoon each round. When only one player is left, they are the winner.
Purpose of Teaching Social Skill	To practice a variety of skills incorporated into a play-based setting.
Example Objective	When playing games that require visual attending, such as the "spoon game," the learner will sustain visual attending for 5 minutes on 4 out of 5 days.
Social Taxonomy Domain	Social Interaction
Skills that can be Targeted	Nonverbal Imitation (NVI), visual attending, shared attending, observational learning, frustration tolerance, winning/losing graciously
Teaching Methodologies	Combination of: • The Cool versus Not Cool™ procedure • Discrete Trial Teaching • Shaping
Considerations	• Make the game interesting by adding NVI movements the learners must imitate while they are waiting for the spoon to be taken. • To increase difficulty for sustained attention, increase the duration until you grab the spoon.
Data Collection	Estimation data, Time Sample, Trial by Trial

Statue Game

Game Instructions	1. Designate one place as the finish (e.g., small rug) where the "lead statue" must stand. 2. The lead statue must stand still, but will open and close their eyes. 3. All the other statues (learners) will stand on the other side of the room. 4. The statues can only move toward the finish when the lead statue's eyes are closed. 5. When the lead statue opens their eyes, all other statues must freeze. Anyone who does not freeze or is caught moving is out. 6. The first person to the designated finish/lead statue wins and can become the next lead statue.
Purpose of Teaching Social Skill	To practice a variety of skills incorporated into a play-based setting.
Example Objective	During a game that requires visual attending, the learner will maintain visual attending throughout the activity in 80% of intervals observed.
Social Taxonomy Domain	Social Interaction
Skills that can be Targeted	Visual attending, joint attention, excitement regulation, frustration tolerance, winning/losing graciously
Teaching Methodologies	Combination of: The Cool versus Not Cool™ procedure Discrete Trial Teaching Shaping
Considerations	The interventionist may want to start as being the lead statue to model the game. To make the game more fun the lead statue can blink their eyes rapidly. A variation of the game is instead of the learner getting out they have to start from the beginning again.
Data Collection	Estimation data, Time Sample, Trial by Trial

Steal the Bacon Game

Game Instructions	1. Have learners sit facing each other in two rows. 2. Assign each learner in one row a number and give the corresponding number to the other side (e.g., there should be a 1, 2, 3, etc. in each row). 3. Put the "bacon" (e.g., play food, bean bag, etc.) in the middle. 4. The interventionist calls out a number and the corresponding learner from each side needs to run to try and get the item in the middle first. 5. Whoever gets it first scores a point for their team. 6. The team with the most points wins.
Purpose of Teaching Social Skill	Practice a variety of skills incorporated into a play-based setting.
Example Objective	During a play-based activity, learners will respond to conditional instructions correctly in 90% of opportunities presented.
Social Taxonomy Domain	Social Interaction
Skills that can be Targeted	Conditional instructions, sustained attention, winning/losing graciously, shared excitement, teamwork
Materials Needed	• Item to be used as bacon (e.g., toy bacon, bean bag, tennis ball)
Teaching Methodologies	Combination of: • The Cool versus Not Cool™ procedure • Discrete Trial Teaching • Shaping
Considerations	• For older learners you can add a rule. If a person picks up the bacon, they need to get back to their seat without getting tagged to get a point. If they get tagged, then they do not get the point. • Call out multiple numbers at a time.
Data Collection	Estimation data, Time Sample, Trial by Trial

Winning and Losing Graciously

Overall Goal	After a game is finished, the learner will respond to the outcome of the game reflecting good sportsmanship: • If the learner won, the learner can engage in a small celebration (e.g., "Yes!" and high-five teammates) while refraining from gloating, bragging, and excessive celebration, then acknowledge the other team positively (e.g., "Good game") • If the learner lost, the learner can engage in a small act of disappointment (e.g., "Aww man") while refraining from derogatory words, statements, and aggression, then address the winner neutrally or positively (e.g., "Good game").
Example Objective	When a learner loses in a game, the learner will lose graciously by engaging in a small act of disappoint (e.g., whisper "Aww man") while refraining from derogatory words, statements, and property destruction, then acknowledge the winning team appropriately (e.g., saying, "Good game") in 80% of opportunities presented.
Social Taxonomy Domain	Social Interaction
Teaching Methodologies	The Cool versus Not Cool™ procedure and the Teaching Interaction Procedure
Data Collection	Task Analysis or Estimation

Phases

Overview		Focus of the skill depends on the need of the learner. Discuss opportunities where the skill may need to be used: • Organized sports or recess games • Competitive games with friends • Watching sports with friends
Phase 1	Develop Rationales	If you act inappropriately when you win or lose: • Friends will be annoyed, and it could affect your friendship • May get a reputation that could affect future friendships • People may not want to compete with you anymore. If they don't want to compete with you anymore then you can't win or play anymore
Phase 2	Task Analysis	Steps if the learner wins: • Engage in a small celebration (e.g., "Yes!" and high-five teammates) while refraining from gloating, bragging, and excessive celebration • Acknowledge the other team positively (e.g., "Good game") • If desired, the learner can ask to play again

Phase 2 (cont.)	Task Analysis	Steps if the learner loses:
		• Engage in a small act of disappointment (e.g., "Aww man") while refraining from negative words, statements, and aggression
		• Address the winner (e.g., "Good game") while maintaining a neutral to positive tone
		• If desired, the learner can ask to play again
Phase 3	Discrimination Training	Set up demonstrations of Cool and Not Cool and have the learner rate each demonstration.
		Example 1 (Cool): *Losing the basketball game.*
		• Actor whispers "Ugh" with head down. Walks over to the other team and high fives with a neutral face saying, "Good game" in a neutral tone and asks if they want to play again.
		Example 2 (Cool): *Winning the basketball game.*
		• Actor says, "Yes!" with a fist pump, walks over to a teammate and gives them a high five. Actor then walks neutrally to the opponent and says "Good game" in a neutral tone while giving a high five.
		Example 3 (Not Cool): *Losing the basketball game.*
		• Actor shouts, "UGH!" Then gets the ball and throws it.
		Example 4 (Not Cool): *Winning the basketball game.*
		• Actor says, "Yes!" with a fist pump, walks over to a teammate and gives them a high five. Actor then runs to the opponent, excessively celebrating and says, "We're so much better than you losers!"
Phase 4	Role-Play	Set up role-play opportunities for the learner to engage in the appropriate behaviors. Reinforce the learner's appropriate winning and losing.
Phase 5	Real Life Situations	Set up more natural situations for the learner to practice engaging in appropriate behaviors. Use priming as a prompt (e.g., "Remember what to do at the end of the game"). Fade the specificity of the prompt and the timing of prompt to promote generalization.
Considerations		Some learners will rely on continuing to play until they finally win to avoid ending on a loss. It is important to develop tolerance for not being able to win and arrange for play sessions to end without the learner being able to "redeem" themselves.

Ending Play

Overall Goal	The learner will end a game or play activity in a socially appropriate manner. This skill enables the learner to exit gracefully from activities or continue playing once a game or play has ended. Possessing this skill will open social and play opportunities for the learner.
Example Objective	When a play activity ends, the learner will close the activity in a socially acceptable manner (e.g., "Thanks for playing, that was fun," "Good game," "Do you want to play something else?") in 90% of opportunities presented.
Social Taxonomy Domain	Social Interaction and Social Communication
Teaching Methodologies	The Teaching Interaction Procedure, the Cool versus Not Cool™ procedure, and Discrete Trial Teaching
Data Collection	Task Analysis or Estimation
Prerequisite Skills	Comprehension, Joint Attending, Receptive Language, Beginning Social Skills, Beginning Play Skills

Phases

Phase 1	Teach Recognizing a Game or Activity has Ended	· The learner learns to notice when a game has ended or an activity is over (e.g., there is a clear end, there is a clear winner, the play script has run its course). · The learner learns to recognize when ending a game or activity may be a good idea (e.g., the learner is no longer enjoying the activity, the peers are bored, it is time to do something else). · The learner reads verbal and non-verbal cues indicating it is time to end the game or activity. This may require pre-teaching (refer to Reading Social Cues).

Phase 2	The Learner Learns to Respond When a Game has Ended or Should End	· Examples of responding appropriately if a game or activity has come to its natural conclusion include:
		  - "That was fun! Want to play again?"
		  - "Good game! I challenge you to a rematch!"
		  - "Well played! Should we do something else?"
		· Examples of responding appropriately if a game has run its course/ value or social cues demand an ending include:
		  - "Wanna play something else?"
		  - "Whew! Let's move on to something else."
		  - "What would you like to do now?"

Steps Toward Generalization		· Fade supplemental reinforcers
		· Fade use of priming (including specificity and timing)
		· Fade interventionist presence
		· Practice with helpers/cohorts
		· Increase the variety of activities and levels of distraction
		· Move to more natural environments

Compromise

Overall Goal	The learner will come to a compromise, using a fair strategy, and follow through when they want to do something different than what a peer wants to do.
Example Objective	When faced with a situation in which the learner desires something different from their peer, the learner will engage in a compromise strategy, then follow through with the outcome of that strategy in the absence of crying, whining, and aggression in 70% of opportunities presented.
Social Taxonomy Domain	Social Interaction
Teaching Methodologies	The Cool versus Not Cool™ procedure and the Teaching Interaction Procedure
Data Collection	Task Analysis
Prerequisite Skills	May need to teach the learner a variety of compromising strategies. Some strategies include rock paper scissors, eenie meenie minie mo, alternating who gets to choose, and combining parts of both ideas.

Phases

Phase 1	Possible Rationales if using the Teaching Interaction Procedure	· You may not get what you want this time, but a friend is more likely to go with your way next time. · Sometimes you do get what you want. · If you combine parts from both ideas, you may come up with a more fun way to play something.
Phase 2	Task Analysis	· Select and use a compromising strategy. · Follow through with the outcome. · Maintain a good attitude.
Phase 3	Discrimination Training	Set up demonstrations of cool and not cool examples. Have the learner rate the behavior. Example 1 (Cool): *Learner wants to play chalk and the other wants to do the swings.* Set up demonstrations of cool and not cool examples. Have the learner rate the behavior. Example 1 (Cool): *Learner wants to play chalk and the other wants to do the swings.* · Demonstrator: "Hey, let's do swings first, then chalk after?" · Peer: "Sure!" · Both proceed to swings.

Phase 3 (cont.)	Discrimination Training	Example 2 (Cool): *Learner wants to play ninjas and peer wants to play superheroes.* • Demonstrator: "What if we're ninja superheroes? Ninjas with superpowers!" • Peer: "What about super ninjas! I'm a super strong ninja!" Example 3 (Not Cool): *Learner wants to play chalk and the other wants to do the swings.* • Demonstrator: "Let's do rock, paper, scissors." • Demonstrator loses but proceeds to do their own choice anyway. Example 4 (Not Cool): *Learner wants to play ninjas and peer wants to play superheroes.* • Demonstrator: "No, let's play ninjas" • Peer: "We always play ninjas! I want to play superheroes" • Demonstrator: "I'm a fast ninja!" showing ninja moves.
Phase 4	Role-Play	Set up role-play opportunities for the learner to engage in the appropriate behaviors. Reinforce the learner's appropriate compromising.
Phase 5	Real Life Situations	Set up more natural situations for the learner to practice engaging in appropriate behaviors. Use priming as a prompt (e.g., "Remember what to do if you each want to do something different"). Fade the specificity of the prompt and the timing of prompt to promote generalization.

Bossiness

Overall Goal	Socially off-putting behaviors like being "bossy" can interfere with the learner getting along with others and may lead to developing a poor reputation or being stigmatized. At times, being bossy results from inflexibility, but sometimes these poor behaviors result from attempts to be social and engaged and doing so incorrectly. Refraining from these behaviors and exhibiting socially appropriate alternatives enables the learner to access greater social opportunities, develop friendships, and increases exposure to other potential reinforcers in the more generalized environment.
Example Objective	When engaged in play, the learner will refrain from bossiness (including instances of rudeness demanding tone, inflexible play, not listening to others' ideas) and instead play cooperatively (e.g., offering ideas once and letting it go, accepting others' ideas, being polite, showing flexibility when peers do not go along with the learner's ideas/directions) in 80% of opportunities presented.
Social Taxonomy Domain	Social Interaction and Social Relatedness
Teaching Methodologies	The Cool versus Not Cool™ procedure, the Teaching Interaction Procedure, and Discrete Trial Teaching
Data Collection	Trial-by-trial or Estimation
Prerequisite Skills	Discrimination, Receptive Language, Expressive Language, Play Skills, and Beginning Social Skills

Phases

Phase 1	Learner Learns Discrimination	• The learner learns the difference between "bossy" and "polite" or "cooperative" (i.e., "not cool" vs. "cool"). Defining these terms should be individualized and based on the learner's presentation and comprehension. Examples may include:
		  - During play, bossy can be defined as inflexible insistence, a rude or demanding tone, or a directing play that excludes others' ideas and participation.
		  - Cooperative can be defined as a willingness to share ideas and play mutually; a willingness to follow others' ideas.
		• Prior to introducing a peer, practice discrimination through modeling cool vs. not cool procedures, role-plays, or similar teaching methods best developing the understanding of these concepts.
		• It may be important to create a list of games and activities as a hierarchy, with a range of least to most likely to be bossy.

Phase 2	Starting Level of Hierarchy	• Practice games and activities least likely to provoke bossy behavior from the learner. • Keep duration brief.

Phase 3	Moderately Difficult Level of Hierarchy	· Practice games and activities that are moderately likely to provoke bossy behavior from the learner. · Increase duration of play activity.
Phase 4	Most Difficult Level of Hierarchy	· Practice games and activities that are most likely to provoke bossy behavior from the learner. · Intersperse less challenging play activities.
Phase 5	Incidental	· Maintain behavior for the full duration of naturally occurring play activities in a variety of settings with a variety of peers, especially those who are least inclined to placate the learner.
Steps Toward Generalization		· Fade supplemental reinforcers · Fade use of priming (including specificity and timing) · Fade interventionist presence · Practice with helpers/cohorts · Increase the variety of activities and levels of distraction · Move to more natural environments

Sharing the Spotlight

Overall Goal	The learner will share the spotlight, show interest in their conversation partner, and refrain from making the conversation only about themselves.
Example Objective	During a conversation with a peer, the learner will ask at least one question and make at least one statement about the peer with 100% accuracy across three consecutive sessions.
Social Taxonomy Domain	Social Interaction and Social Relatedness
Teaching Methodologies	The Teaching Interaction Procedure, the Cool versus Not Cool™ procedure, and Discrete Trial Teaching
Data Collection	Task Analysis or Estimation

Phases

Phase 1	Discrimination Training	· Have the learner discriminate statements and questions that make the conversation about another person versus making it about themselves.

Phase 2	Discrete Trial Teaching Setup	· Set up clear trials where the interventionist makes a statement and the learner must make a statement or ask a question that is about the interventionist and not about themselves. For example:
		  - Interventionist: "I went to Disneyland over the weekend."
		  - Correct learner response: "What rides did you go on?"
		  - Incorrect learner response: "I always go to Knotts Berry Farm because the lines are shorter."

Phase 3	Conversation All About the Interventionist	· Prior to having a conversation with the learner inform them they can only make statements or ask questions that are about the interventionist. · Keep the conversation short initially and then extend the length of time. · Reinforce statements or questions that are about the interventionist.
Phase 4	Conversation with Limited Amount of Statements/ Questions about the Learner	· Prior to having a conversation with the learner, inform them they can only make a limited amount of statements or questions about themselves. - You can set up a visual (e.g., tickets that go away) to show the learner how many statements/questions about themselves they have remaining. · Keep the conversation short initially and then extend the length of time.

Phase 4 (cont.)	Conversation with Limited Amount of Statements/ Questions about the Learner	• Reinforce statements or questions that are about the interventionist. • Reinforce the transition from making a statement/question about themselves and going back to talking about the interventionist.
Phase 5	Conversation with Equal amount of Statements/ Questions about the Learner	• Prior to having a conversation with the learner, inform them they need to talk an equal amount about the interventionist and themselves. – You can set up a visual (e.g., interventionist tally's and learner tally's) to represent how many statements/ questions have been about each individual. • Keep the conversation short initially and then extend the length of time. • Reinforce statements or questions that are about the interventionist. • Reinforce the transition from making a statement/question about themselves and going back to talking about the interventionist.
	Considerations	• The ultimate goal is for the conversation to be balanced, but to overcome self-centeredness it is beneficial to start out exclusively making the conversation about the other person. • To increase the difficulty level, the interventionist can make comments about the learner's special interests (e.g., if the learner is interested in Harry Potter and the interventionist says "I watched The Sorcerer's Stone last night," it would be more difficult for the learner to refrain from making a comment about themselves). • As the learner improves on the skill, use more natural cues to indicate if the learner is talking too much about themselves.

Appropriate Places to Break Eye Contact

Overall Goal	When the learner needs to break eye contact, they do so by looking at an appropriate location (e.g., not at a place that would distract them).
Example Objective	During a 5-minute conversation with a peer or adult, the learner will maintain a natural amount of eye contact and when looking away will refrain from focusing on a tempting or distracting item for 4 out of 5 days.
Social Taxonomy Domain	Social Interaction
Teaching Methodologies	The Teaching Interaction Procedure and the Cool versus Not Cool™ procedure
Data Collection	Ratio, Momentary Time Sampling, or Estimation Data

Phases

Phase 1	Pre-Teaching the Rationale	· Prior to running the program, provide and build meaningful rationales as to why the learner should not look at items that could be distracting.
Phase 2	Identifying Inappropriate Places to Look	· Set up environments where there are clear distractors (this will be different for each learner). · Have the learner identify inappropriate (i.e., distracting) locations to break attending/eye contact.
Phase 3	Identifying Appropriate Places to Look	· Set up environments where there are clear distractors. · Have the learner identify appropriate locations to break attending/ eye contact. - For example, the floor right above the person's head, or a spot to the side where there are no distractors.
Phase 4	Highly Engaging activities	· Set up high level engagement activities (e.g., favorite books, conversations of high interest, engaging school activities/lectures). · Reinforce instances of looking at appropriate locations and give corrective feedback for instances of looking at inappropriate locations. · As the learner is successful increase the duration of time engaged in the activity.
Phase 5	Moderately Engaging activities	· Set up moderate level engagement activities (e.g., interesting books, conversations of moderate interest, interesting school activities/lectures). · Reinforce instances of looking at appropriate locations and give corrective feedback for instances of looking at inappropriate locations. · As the learner is successful increase the duration of time engaged in the activity.

Phase 6	Low Level of Engagement	• Set up low level engagement activities (e.g., uninteresting books, conversations of low interest, uninteresting school activities/ lectures).
		• Reinforce instances of looking at appropriate locations and give corrective feedback for instances of looking at inappropriate locations.
		• As the learner is successful increase the duration of time engaged in the activity.

Not Asking Silly Questions

Overall Goal	The learner will ask appropriate questions or make appropriate comments while refraining from asking a question when the learner already knows the answer.
Example Objective	During a 15-minute observation period, the learner will refrain from asking silly questions across five consecutive days.
Social Taxonomy Domain	Social Interaction
Teaching Methodologies	The Teaching Interaction Procedure, The Cool versus Not Cool™ procedure, and Discrete Trial Teaching
Data Collection	Ratio, Task Analysis, or Estimation

Phases

Phase 1	Discrimination Training	· Provide examples of a cool question vs. a silly question. · Have the learner identify if the example was cool or not cool (silly).

Phase 2	Practice	· In a Discrete Trial Teaching format make a comment, the learner needs to then ask an appropriate question or make an appropriate comment.
		  - Examples:
		    · Interventionist: "I had pizza for dinner."
		    · Cool learner examples: "What kind?" "I love pizza," "I had chicken."
		    · Silly learner examples: "Did you have pizza?" "Did you eat it?"
		· Reinforce instances of appropriate questions/ comments and give corrective feedback for instances of silly questions.

Phase 3	More Natural Conversation Practice	· Set up conversations where the learner should ask appropriate questions/make appropriate comments. · At the end of the conversation reinforce if the learner refrained from silly questions. · Increase the duration of the conversation as the learner is more successful.
Phase 4	Incidental Practice	· At various times during the day set up a challenge to see if the learner can make it through the next period of time without asking silly questions.
Phase 5	Reactively	· If the learner is trying to engage by asking a silly question, model the correct language they can use. · Once the learner has the correct skills, put silly questions on extinction.

Fruit Salad Game

Game Instructions	1. Make two lines of chairs facing each other.
	2. Have the learners sit on the chairs.
	3. Assign a fruit name to each learner, there should be a learner with a matching fruit name in both lines.

Line 1 Facing	Line 2 Facing
• Banana • Strawberry • Mango • Peach • Grape	• Strawberry • Peach • Banana • Grape • Mango

	4. When you call a fruit name, the learners with that fruit name must meet in the middle to do something social (e.g., give the other learner a high five, make a silly face, make the other laugh). a. For example, when the interventionist calls "strawberry," both learners assigned "strawberry" run to the middle and give each other a high five. 5. When you call fruit salad, all the learners run to the middle and do something social (e.g., give the other learner a high five, make a silly face, make the other laugh). 6. As the learners are familiar with the game you can have a learner be the one to call out the fruit names. 7. During, or after, the game, you can provide consequences for group and individual targets.
Purpose of Teaching Social Skill	To practice a variety of skills incorporated into a play-based setting.
Example Objective	The learner will follow conditional instructions in a play-based activity in 70% of opportunities presented.
Social Taxonomy Domain	Social Interaction and Social Relatedness
Skills that can be Targeted	Conditional instructions, shared excitement, sustained attention, being silly
Materials Needed	• Chairs for each learner (though not necessary)

Teaching Methodologies	Combination of:
	• The Cool versus Not Cool™ procedure
	• Discrete Trial Teaching
	• Shaping
Considerations	• To make the game easier, predefine what action they should perform when called.
	• To make the game more fun, you can throw in random labels such as "pizza" or "shoe." This is great to increase shared excitement between peers.
Data Collection	Estimation data, Time Sample, Trial by Trial

Sleeping Game

Game Instructions	1. Present a stuffed animal.
	2. The learners listen for the animal's sound.
	   a. For example, if the stuffed animal is a pig, they should listen for "oink oink."
	3. Instruct the learners to "go to sleep" - all lie down and cover their eyes.
	4. Hide the stuffed animal.
	5. While you hide the toy, make different types of animal sounds (e.g., neigh, woof, meow).
	   a. Learners should remain "asleep" for all other animal sounds.
	6. When you finally make the stuffed animal sound (e.g., "oink oink"), the learners "wake up" and search for the toy.
	7. The first learner to find the toy is the winner.
	   a. The winner can then be the one to sit in the chair and make the animal sounds.

Purpose of Teaching Social Skill	Practice a variety of skills incorporated into a play-based setting.
Example Objective	During a 10-minute play-based activity, the learner will sustain attention throughout the activity by following instructions and maintain positive demeanor on 4 out of 5 days.
Social Taxonomy Domain	Social Interaction
Skills that can be targeted during game	Waiting, conditional instructions, environmental awareness, winning/losing graciously, responding to peers, auditory association, problem solving
Materials Needed	• Stuffed animal
Teaching Methodologies	Combination of: • The Cool versus Not Cool™ procedure • Discrete Trial Teaching • Shaping
Considerations	• Maintain interest by using a variety of sound making items and silly sounds (e.g., robots, cars, squish). • Increase difficulty by making sounds similar. • Increase difficulty by manipulating the number of sounds before the target sound occurs. • Hide the stuffed animal in novel places (e.g., on top of the interventionist's head) to increase shared excitement.
Data Collection	Estimation data, Time Sample, Trial by Trial

Joining Play

Overall Goal	The learner will learn to join play and leisure activities already in progress in a manner that furthers the play rather than slowing it down. In other words, the learner will join as seamlessly as possible, causing no undue attention. Joining in such a manner enables the learner to access activities and games they are interested in, as well as be around peers that share interests with the learner. This skill is best presented and taught using the Teaching Interaction Procedure and the importance of establishing meaningful rationales cannot be overstated.
Example Objective	The learner will determine whether a play or game opportunity allows for someone new joining, and, if so, joins in a manner that causes little to no disruption to the activity in progress in 8 out of 10 opportunities naturally presented.
Social Taxonomy Domain	Social Interaction, Social Awareness, and Social Relatedness
Teaching Methodologies	The Teaching Interaction Procedure and The Cool versus Not Cool™ procedure
Data Collection	Task Analysis or Estimation
Prerequisite Skills	Discrimination, Comprehension, Expressive Language, Beginning Social Skills, Environmental Awareness

Teaching Interaction Procedure Steps:

Pre-teach Concepts	Learner Evaluates Dynamic Play Opportunities	· Practice observation skills prior to introducing this skill for the Teaching Interaction Procedure practice. The learner should be able to evaluate play on several levels, including:
		  - Is it an activity I want to join?
		  - Is it an activity I know?
		  - Based on that, when is the best time for me to interject myself?

Identify/ Describe the Skill	Define the Skill the Learner will Use in the Generalized Environment	· "Joining well" can be defined as:
		  - Observing and answering the previous questions
		  - The learner determines if joining is something they want to do and is the best choice based on the peers involved and the game/play.
		  - Learner picks the right moment to join and best way to integrate with those already involved. For example:
		    · Tell?
		    · Ask?
		    · Simply jump in?
		    · Loudly?
		    · Quietly?

Identify/ Describe the Skill (cont.)	Define the Skill the Learner will Use in the Generalized Environment	• With accessories (e.g., game pieces)? • Is turn-taking a consideration? • Where can I add the most value (e.g., if a soccer game, does either team need a goalie? What are my strengths? My weaknesses?)? - Learner then participates in a manner that will be appreciated by peers.
Develop Rationale(s)	The Learner Participates in Developing Meaningful, Personalized Rationales for Participating	• Developing individualized rationales for and with the learner is essential. • Without personalized rationales that are also reflective of social expectations/norms, this teaching is less likely to generalize. • Generic discussion points may include: - There will be more opportunities to play/engage when you choose to join well. - Others will appreciate the value you bring to the play and will look forward to you joining again in the future. - You get to play the games you like more often when you join well. - Joining well gives you the confidence to play or try new activities.
Describe and Demonstrate Skill	Describe, Discriminate, Role-play, etc.	• Describe the skill to be taught • Offer scenarios to consider • Practice the skill with the learner (e.g., the learner can either observe and determine "cool" vs. "not cool," or participates in a systematic role-play demonstrating the target skill)
Practice Skill	Role-play	• Offer situations and scenarios allowing the learner to participate in practicing the target skill.
Feedback and further practice		• Provide feedback specifically describing parts of the skill performed well and parts of the skill requiring improvement. • Provide the opportunity for further practice to hone skill based on feedback.
Optional: Behavioral Contingency		• If needed, the learner can receive supplemental reinforcement for maintaining appropriate behavior during the Teaching Interaction Procedure. This can include token economies, bonus reinforcement, behavior contracts, point systems, or other supplemental reinforcement.
Steps Toward Generalization		• Fade supplemental reinforcers • Fade use of priming (including specificity and timing) • Fade interventionist presence • Practice with helpers/cohorts • Increase the variety of activities and levels of distraction • Move to more natural environments

Don't Rub It In

Overall Goal	To develop appropriate responses when the opportunity to demean or put someone down occurs. To further facilitate compassion and caring.
	To build requisite skills for responding to others' perspectives and emotions. To build requisite skills for making interpersonal choices.
	To build a foundation of understanding the learner's choices may impact positively another's life.
Example Objective	When the learner wins, they will refrain from rubbing-it-in behaviors in 100% of opportunities presented for 3 consecutive sessions.
Social Taxonomy Domain	Social Interaction and Social Relatedness
Teaching Methodologies	The Teaching Interaction Procedure, the Cool versus Not Cool™ procedure, and Respondent Conditioning
Data Collection	Task Analysis or Estimation
Prerequisite Skills	Joint Attention, Comprehension, Receptive and expressive understanding of emotions (may be run concurrently), Cause & Effect (including how one comes to "know" something), Recall, Environmental and Social Awareness, Inferences, Understanding the concept of "Perspective" (May be run concurrently)

Phases

Phase 1	Identification of "Rubbing it in"	• The learner learns to identify common iterations of the behavior. "Rubbing it in" consists of inappropriately and excessively calling attention to the shortcoming or inferior position of another person. When someone rubs it in, there is a quality of repetitiveness to the teasing or belittling. Unless something occurs that causes the behavior to stop – such as friends intervening, or an adult taking notice – it will likely continue unabated and possibly across several days or weeks. Another component of rubbing it in is the teaser is in a power position (i.e., has possession of something motivating that is out of reach or involves exploiting the other person's triggers). Iterations include but are not limited to:
		- Happiness with Hurt
		• For example, if a peer falls on the playground, the learner may gawk, point, laugh or say something referring to the hurt in a non-supportive way.
		- Stacking on Sadness
		• For example, if a peer expresses sadness or is clearly sad (e.g., crying, looking down, isolating), the learner may draw attention to that peer, or say something like, "Awwww, you're crying" or "Boo-hoo, crybaby!"

Phase 1 (cont.)	Identification of "Rubbing it in"	- Capitalizing on Competitiveness
		  • Rubbing in someone losing, especially if winning is important to that person (e.g., "Ha! I won, you lost!" "Man, I wasn't even trying").
		- Meddling in Misfortune
		  • For example, if a peer gets a poor grade after trying hard, the learner saying something like, "Bummer, you should have studied harder," "What? You didn't even get a C?", or "I got an A and I didn't even study."
		- I get to, you don't, or "Nah nah nah nah nah."
		  • Privileges or responsibilities important to someone can be used against them if they don't earn them, or if someone else gets them (e.g., "Too bad you don't get to take the attendance folder to the office" or "I'm going to Disneyland this weekend! Sorry you can't too")
		- Prodding Physically
		  • Repeatedly touching, poking, tapping, etc. Any uninvited, under the radar touch occurring over and over, with the goal of getting an escalated reaction.

Phase 2	Individualizing Rubbing it in	• The learner should be guided in discussing or coming to agreement on what their brand of rubbing it in looks and feels like. Questions to ask include: - What's the process? - How does the learner target someone to rub it in? - What are the signs the learner looks for? - What are the types of rubbing it in the learner tends to use? - How does it start? - How does it end? - Are there varying degrees? When to turn it up, when to back off a bit? - What is the payoff for the learner? • Self-reflection and definition of the learner's particular rub it in repertoire and the possible reasons the learner behaves this way, the motivation for continuing to rub it in.

Phase 3	Developing Rationales for Choosing NOT to Rub it in when the Opportunity to do so Presents Itself.	• Apply the same reasons/motivations for rubbing it in to choosing NOT to rub it in. These reasons likely include:
		- Selfish Reasons:
		  • Power
		  • Control
		  • Superiority
		• Over time, the interventionist should seek to develop more meaningful, social reasons:
		- Concern for Others

Phase 3 (cont.)	Developing Rationales for Choosing NOT to Rub it in when the Opportunity to do so Presents Itself.	- Reputation - Self-image - Applying The Golden Rule

Phase 4	Developing the Alternative Response System	· What should I say to myself? What's my process?
		- Noticing the antecedents and triggers typically resulting in rubbing it in
		- Noticing the target, the victim, the circumstances
		- Consider alternative including "letting it go"
		- Self-talk may include:
		  · I have control over this moment
		  · I have control over how this person will or will not feel
		  · I can prolong a feeling, or I can end it
		  · I am in charge
		- Noticing the opportunity has presented itself and I can choose to rub it in or not to rub it in
		  · If I rub it in, there will be consequences:
		    o Getting caught
		    o Inciting others to get even
		    o Losing hard earned privileges
		    o Mom disappointed and sad
		    o Damaging my reputation
		    o What goes around comes around
		  · If I refrain ("Be like Superman") there will be benefits:
		    o Improved self-control
		    o Opportunities to make someone feel less bad
		    o By being nice to others they are more likely to be nice to me.
		    o I am in charge
		- Other consideration based on the individual learner:
		  · Cost-payoff analysis:
		    o What was my initial goal?
		    o Did I achieve it?
		  · Competition system:
		    o With him or herself
		    o With the interventionist

Phase 5	Discrimination Training	Set up opportunities for learner to observe examples of rubbing it in (Not Cool) and examples of appropriate alternatives (Cool) and have the learner rate the behavior.

Phase 6	Role-Play	• Set up numerous opportunities and setting events typically leading to the learner rubbing it in and have the learner practice the Cool way.
Phase 7	Generalization (Incidental Application)	• Throughout the day when there are naturally occurring antecedents that have historically evoked rubbing it in, use priming as needed to ensure that learner will respond in a Cool way to the situation (e.g., "What would Superman do?"). As the learner is more consistently successful, fade the specificity and timing of the prompt and fade the reinforcement.

Rude vs. Polite

Overall Goal	· To assist the learner in getting needs met and opinions known in a socially appropriate manner. · To increase self-awareness and enable the learner to interact with others in a manner that others will appreciate. · To increase self-evaluation and eventually, self-monitoring skills.
Example Objective	The learner will discriminate between rude behaviors and polite behaviors with 100% accuracy across 3 consecutive sessions.
Social Taxonomy Domain	Social Interaction
Teaching Methodologies	The Teaching Interaction Procedure and the Cool versus Not Cool™ procedure
Data Collection	Trial by Trial, Task Analysis, or Estimation
Prerequisite Skills	Discrimination skills, Receptive Language, Expressive Language, General Knowledge and Reasoning, Advanced contingency understanding, Awareness of others' emotions and body language, Beginnings of empathy

Phases

Phase 1	Define Polite	This phase teaches the learner to clearly understand what polite means across a variety of examples. It begins to further establish how being polite can achieve meaningful goals for the learner without drawing negative attention or affecting the learner's reputation.
		"Polite" is defined as expressing yourself in a manner that is calm and respectful. Being polite can be illustrated with different presentations, sometimes alone and sometimes in combination, including:
		· Words used: Types of verbal expressions (e.g., "Please," "Thank you," "After you"), addressing someone by their given name (e.g., first name or title and name – Steve, Mr. Cooper, Interventionist Jane), answering questions in a timely manner, with relevance and on topic, adding to a conversation on topic, etc.
		· Tone/volume of voice: Not overly loud (i.e., volume matches the situation and what is being said), voice is not altered in a disrespectful manner, voice matches the "mood" (e.g., appropriately happy, sad, concerned).
		· Physical posture: Enough space between the learner and others, not invasive or threatening, and not aggressive.
		· Large and small body gestures: Keeps arms, hands, legs and body to self, uses supportive gestures to express empathy and when invited (e.g., pats on the back, hugs, hand-shakes), non-provocative, refrains from pointing in a demeaning manner, etc.

Phase 1 (cont.)	Define Polite	• Facial expressions: Face matches emotional expressions, facial expressions congruent with what is being said, refrains from demeaning expressions (e.g., sticking out the tongue, rolling eyes, silently mimicking). Use a variety of materials and presentations to teach the definition and iterations of "polite." For example, learner listens or watches as the therapist models above examples and the learner expressively labels, matches or receptively identifies which specific topic is being modeled. Stick with appropriate examples of the above topics; discrimination between "polite" and "rude" will come during a later phase.
Phase 2	Define Rude	This phase teaches the learner to clearly understand what rude means across a variety of examples. It further begins to establish how being rude can draw negative attention to the learner or affect the learner's reputation. "Rude" is defined as expressing yourself in a manner that is belittling and disrespectful. It can be clear and brash or confusing and passive-aggressive. Being rude can be illustrated with different presentations, sometimes alone and sometimes in combination, including: • Words used: Types of verbal expressions can be demeaning, sarcastic, demanding, or aggressive. Rude also describes not replying to a conversational opportunity or question or responding off-topic, inconsiderately changing the subject, interrupting, etc. • Tone/volume of voice: Sometimes loud and overbearing, using a voice in a demeaning manner, imitating or exaggerating other's voices and inflections, etc. • Physical posture: Overbearing, intimidating, invasive of other's space, walking away in the middle of a conversation, etc. • Large and small body gestures: Provocative, pointing in an aggressive manner, turning away from someone mid-conversation, etc. • Facial expressions: Grimacing, sticking out the tongue, "blowing raspberries" to interfere with someone's conversation, etc. Learner listens or watches as the therapist models above examples and the learner expressively labels, matches or receptively identifies which specific topic is being modeled.
Phase 3	Teach the Discrimination Between being Polite and being Rude.	Use modeling, role-play, cool vs. not cool, or the Teaching Interaction Procedure to develop a strong understanding of the reasons to avoid being rude. Develop meaningful rationales for appropriate demonstration of skill.

Phase 4	[Optional] When it is ok to not be so Polite	When politeness and assertiveness are exhausted, and the learner is stuck in an uncomfortable or non-preferred situation, using some of the aspects of rude behavior may be considered.
Phase 5	Generalization	Develop plans to expose the learner to more real-life situations requiring the ability to make a decision on how to behave. · Discuss scenarios during the Teaching Interaction Procedure · Develop role-plays focused on developing this processing skill · Arrange scenarios within more natural settings

Chapter Twenty-One
Social Communication Skills

Jonathan Rafuse, Jeremy A. Leaf, & Justin B. Leaf

Social Communication skills are behaviors that are concerned with the social aspects of communication, often referred to as pragmatics. These behaviors involve the use of language and nonverbal communication that will result in increased social opportunities. Within this domain there are basic social interaction skills, intermediate social interaction skills, and advanced social interaction skills. In this chapter, we provide two foundational listening programs and 13 social skills programs that fall under the Social Communication Domain.

Foundational Listening Skills	Basic Social Skills	Intermediate Social Skills	Advanced Social Skills
Auditory Attending	Commenting on Events	Do Not Echo	Initiating Conversation
Find the Message in the Chatter	Keep it Interesting	Follow the Conversation Thread	Gaining Attention
	Answering Questions	Inferences: Meaning of Words from Context	Proper Skepticism: You Can't Believe Everything You Hear
		Statement/ Elaboration	
		Conversation Movers and Stoppers	
		Handling Changes and Graceful Endings	
		Complimenting	

Auditory Attending

Overall Goal	The learner will listen to multiple parts/pieces of information in a sentence and receptively identify the corresponding card (e.g., find the monkey [1] swimming [2] with the yellow [3] star [4]).
Example Objective	When the learner hears an auditory stimulus, they will correctly respond with 90% accuracy across three consecutive days.
Social Taxonomy Domain	Social Communication
Teaching Methodologies	Discrete Trial Teaching
Data Collection	Trial by Trial or Estimation
Prerequisite Skills	Receptive labeling, a variety of receptive labels/actions

Phases

Phase 1	One Piece of Information	• Ask for the learner to receptively identify a card using only one piece of information (e.g., "Find the elephant.").
Phase 2	Two Pieces of Information	• Ask the learner to receptively identify a card using two pieces of information (e.g., "Find the elephant that is swimming."). - There should be another picture in the field where one piece of information is the same, but another piece of information is different (e.g., an elephant kissing).
Phase 3	Three Pieces of Information	• Ask the learner to receptively identify a card using three pieces of information (e.g., "Find the elephant that is swimming with a bear."). • There should be another picture in the field where two pieces of information are the same, but one piece of information is different (e.g., an elephant swimming with a crocodile.
Phase 4	Four Pieces of Information	• Ask the learner to receptively identify a card using four pieces of information (e.g., "Find the elephant that is swimming with a bear wearing pajamas."). • There should be another picture in the field where three pieces of information are the same, but one piece of information is different (e.g., an elephant swimming with a dog wearing sunglasses).
Considerations		• Number of distractors in the field • Degree of similarities across the distractors • Giving the information in the instruction in different orders (e.g., animal → action vs. action → animal)

Find The Message In The Chatter

Overall Goal	The learner will listen to auditory information with chatter and respond appropriately.
Example Objective	The learner will answer auditory comprehension questions correctly with 90% accuracy for three consecutive days.
Social Taxonomy Domain	Social Communication
Teaching Methodologies	Discrete Trial Teaching
Data Collection	Trial by Trial or Estimation

Phases

Phase 1	Responding to a Question Without Chatter	· Ask the learner a question (e.g., "What animal says oink?") or give an instruction (e.g., "Clap your hands.") free of any chatter.

Phase 2	Responding to an Instruction/ Question with Minimal Chatter	· Ask a question or give an instruction with minimal chatter
		  - Example: "Who can tell me...oh I really like this...tell me something that is a fruit?"
		· Do attending checks with the other learners to ensure that everyone is listening
		  - Example: "Who remembers what I really like?"

Phase 3	Responding to an Instruction/ Question with Moderate Chatter	· Ask the learner a question or give an instruction with a moderate level of chatter - Example: "Last night I ate fruit, which I really like a lot. Can you guess what I ate?" (requires inference) · Continue to do attending checks.
Phase 4	Responding to an Instruction/ Question with a High Level of Chatter	· Ask the learner a question or give an instruction with a high level of chatter - Example: "Last night I had a really yummy dessert, it was some fruit. Can you tell something that is a fruit? I really love fruit, it's so delicious." · Continue to do attending checks.
Considerations		· Vary where the question/instruction comes in the sentence (i.e., beginning, middle, end) · Vary the salience of the chatter · Questions may be more difficult than instructions

Commenting On Events

Overall Goal	The learner increases their spontaneous commenting by witnessing and then spontaneously commenting or retelling an interesting or unusual event. Examples of Events: • Unusual – someone dresses up as Spider-Man and runs around the room, a nerf gun fight breaks out in the room, a water balloon hits the window where a learner is working • Absurd – A shoe is in the refrigerator, someone has their face painted, someone has pretzels in their nose • Exciting – A birthday party in the classroom, someone brings their dog to school, snow day • High Interest – The learner gets to watch his favorite movie, a special snack is provided during snack time, they get to play their favorite game during group time
Example Objective	When asked what happened in the learner's environment, the learner will accurately retell an event that occurred within the past 15 minutes with 90% accuracy across three consecutive days.
Social Taxonomy Domain	Social Communication
Teaching Methodologies	The Teaching Interaction Procedure, the Cool versus Not Cool™ procedure, and Discrete Trial Teaching
Data Collection	Task Analysis, Estimation, or Trial by Trial

Phases

Phase 1	Absurd Events: Commenting in the Moment	• Setup an absurd event that the learner will easily notice. - To make the skill more difficult use a more subtle absurd event. • The event should serve as the occasion for the comment to occur. If the event does not evoke a comment, then use an instruction or a prompt to evoke an appropriate response. - Examples: "What happened?," "Wow!," "Look at that," "Tell me about it." - Try and fade any instruction or prompt so that the event itself evokes a comment. • Provide reinforcement for the learner telling you the absurd event they witnessed.
Phase 2	Absurd Events: Retelling with a Delay	• Setup an absurd event that the learner will easily notice. - To make the skill more difficult use a more subtle absurd event. • Setup a situation where the learner sees someone they know (e.g., another teacher, a peer, a parent).

Phase 2 (cont.)	Absurd Events: Retelling with a Delay	• Begin to tell the story and pause (e.g., as you would for a communication temptation) and wait to see if the learner fills in the rest of the story. If they do not provide a prompt (e.g., "What happened in the kitchen?") or provide feedback (e.g., "You didn't tell mommy what happened."). As the learner is more successful do not begin to start telling the story, have the learner be the storyteller. - Because we are going for spontaneous commenting, we do not want the person hearing the story to ask what happened. • Provide reinforcement for the learner telling the person the absurd event.

Phase 3	Exciting Events: Comment in the Moment	• Setup an exciting event that the learner will easily notice.
		  - To make the skill more difficult use a more subtle exciting event.
		• The event should occasion a comment. If not, then use an instruction or a prompt to evoke an appropriate response.
		  - Examples: "What happened?,", "Wow!,". "Look at that," "Tell me about it."
		  - Try and fade any instruction or a prompt so that the event itself evokes commenting.
		• Provide reinforcement for the learner telling you the exciting event they witnessed

Phase 4	Exciting Events: Retell with a Delay	• Setup an exciting event that the learner will easily notice.
		  - To make the skill more difficult use a more subtle exciting event.
		• Setup a situation where the learner sees someone they know (e.g., another teacher, a peer, a parent).
		• Begin to tell the story and pause (e.g., as you would for a communication temptation) and wait to see if the learner fills in the rest of the story. If they do not provide a prompt (e.g., "What happened in the kitchen?") or provide feedback (e.g., "You didn't tell mommy what happened."). As the learner is more successful, have the learner tell the story from the beginning.
		  - Because we are going for spontaneous commenting, we do not want the person hearing the story to ask what happened.
		• Provide reinforcement for the learner telling the person the exciting event.

Considerations		• Gradually increase the time delay between the event and the retelling. It is easier to retell the event moments after it happened versus hours later - To help with remembering, have the learner practice recalling throughout the day. • The specificity of priming (if necessary) before the event occurs (e.g., being very specific about what will happen vs. vague) • The timing of priming (if necessary) before the event occurs (e.g., priming right before the event vs. an hour before)

Keep It Interesting

Overall Goal	To increase the learner's rate of making interesting comments throughout their day (e.g., conversation, play). To decrease boring (e.g., narrating type) commenting. To teach the learner to identify what type of comments are "interesting," which are "okay," and what type of comments are "boring."
Example Objective	During a 1-hour period, the learner will make at least 1 interesting comment and refrain from boring comments across 10 consecutive days.
Social Taxonomy Domain	Social Communication
Teaching Methodologies	The Cool versus Not Cool™ procedure
Data Collection	Frequency

Phases

Phase 1	Discrimination Training	• Setup a continuum for boring, okay, and interesting things to say in a conversation.
		  - Examples:
		    • Boring – asking an unnecessary or inappropriate question, comment that is boring
		    • Okay – throw away comment (e.g., "cool")
		    • Interesting – a good question, a comment that furthers conversation

Phase 2	Practice Statement/ Statement	• Teacher makes a comment (e.g., "I saw the new Batman movie."). • Learner needs to make an interesting comment (e.g., "Me too. My favorite part was when he was driving the Batmobile.").

Phase 3	Priming Prior to Conversation	• Setup a clear prime (e.g., "We are going to talk, and you need to make sure you are making interesting comments.").
		  - As the learner is successful fade the specificity of your prime (e.g., "We are going to talk, remember what your job is.").
		  - As the learner is successful, fade the timing of your priming (e.g., prime 10 minutes prior to conversation as opposed to immediately before conversation).

Phase 4	Conversation without Priming	• Have a conversation without any priming. • Refer to feedback hierarchy to make skill more difficult.

Feedback Hierarchy – Move to Natural Contingencies as the Learner becomes more Successful	<ul><li>Giving positive or negative feedback immediately following the comment</li><li>Learner evaluates their own comments immediately following the comment</li><li>Interventionist gives feedback after the conversation</li><li>Learner evaluates after the conversation</li><li>Interventionist gives obvious social cues based on the learner's comments</li><li>Interventionist gives more subtle social cues based on the learner's comments</li><li>Interventionist gives natural contingencies (e.g., conversation ends or continues) based on the learner's comments</li></ul>

Answering Questions

Overall Goal	The learner will respond vocally and/or non-vocally when a question is asked. The learner's response should be congruent with what was asked, and given in a timely fashion (i.e., within 2–3 seconds). Developing the skills necessary to hear, interpret, and respond appropriately to questions is critical to ongoing social growth. Answering questions is a fundamental component of conversation skills. It increases a learner's knowledge base, expands environmental awareness, and affords greater socialization opportunities.
Example Objective	When asked a question regarding visual information during group activity, the learner will respond to the best of their ability (e.g., a correct response or "I don't know"), within 2–3 seconds, following the question in 80% of opportunities given.
Social Taxonomy Domain	Social Communication and Social Interaction
Teaching Methodologies	Discrete Trial Teaching, the Teaching Interaction Procedure, and the Cool versus Not Cool™ procedure
Data Collection	Trial-by-trial or Estimation
Prerequisite Skills	Comprehension, General Knowledge, Receptive Language, Expressive Language, Expanded Language, Communication Temptations, and Beginning Social Skills

Phases

Phase 1	Answering Questions with Visual Information Present	• Teach the learner to respond appropriately to a variety of questions based on information available through visual inspection of the immediate area (e.g., within the learner's sight, based on knowledge requiring the ability to see).
		• Considerations may include: topic preference, individualizing question complexity based on the learner's familiarity with the topic, paired social graces (e.g., looking at the person asking the question when responding), and age-typicality.
		• Learner responses and answers must be expressive (e.g., verbalized, communicated appropriately through gestures).
		• Examples include:
		  - Asking questions for the learner to answer while reading/looking at a book (e.g., "What's that?," "Where's the duck?," "What's the duck doing?," "How does the boy feel?")
		  - Asking questions for the learner to answer with materials out (e.g., "What's this?," "What do you do with this?")
		  - Asking questions for the learner to answer during snack time (e.g., "What's in your snack bag?," "Can we trade?," "What's your favorite snack?")

Phase 2	Answering Questions with Auditory Information Available	• Teach the learner to respond appropriately to a variety of questions based on information available through auditory inspection of the immediate area (e.g., within the learner's earshot, or based on knowledge requiring the ability to hear).
		• Considerations are the same as Phase 1.
		• Learner responses and answers must be expressive (e.g., verbalized, communicated appropriately through gestures).
		• Examples include:
		   - Asking questions for the learner to answer with sound provided (e.g., "What's that sound?," "Did you hear that?")
		   - Asking questions for the learner to answer with knowledge of sound and corresponding sources (e.g., "What sound does a pig make?," "What does an ambulance sound like?")

Phase 3	Answering Questions Based on Facts	• Teach the learner to use general knowledge, or information available through visual or auditory inspection of the immediate area and respond appropriately to a variety of questions regarding facts.
		• Considerations are the same as Phase 1.
		• Learner responses and answers must be expressive (e.g., verbalized, communicated appropriately through gestures).
		• Examples include:
		   - Answering questions based on basic truths (e.g., "What color is a banana?," "What do you do with a crayon?")
		   - Answering questions based on visual proof (e.g., "Where's your water bottle?," "Who is sitting in that chair?")
		   - Answering questions based on learner experience/knowledge base (e.g., "What city do you live in?")

Phase 4	Answering Questions Based on Abstract Information	• Teach the learner to use inferring, reasoning, or basic problem-solving to respond appropriately to a variety of questions.
		• Considerations are the same as Phase 1.
		• Learner responses and answers must be expressive (e.g., verbalized, communicated appropriately through gestures).
		• Examples include:
		   - Answering questions based on general knowledge (e.g., "Why do you brush your teeth?," "What would you do if you got chilly?," "How would you find directions to the beach?")
		   - Answering questions based on inferring (e.g., "What do you think is in this box?")
		   - Answering questions based on basic problem-solving (e.g., "What's the best way to clean this mess?," "I want you to draw a picture. What do you need?")

Steps Toward Generalization		• Fade supplemental reinforcers • Fade use of priming (including specificity and timing) • Fade teacher presence

Steps Toward Generalization (cont.)		• Practice with helpers/cohorts • Increase the variety of activities and levels of distraction • Move to more natural environments

Do Not Echo

Overall Goal	Some learners may exhibit a pattern of repeating aloud things they hear people say. Depending on the situation and the manner of speaking, this behavior can be stigmatizing. If this occurs frequently it may be necessary to make the learner aware that this behavior could be viewed unfavorably by others. Teaching the learner to discriminate when it is appropriate to repeat (e.g., when a teacher gives you an instruction) and when it is not appropriate to repeat (e.g., when a friend comments) will allow them to avoid undesirable peer interactions (e.g. teasing, annoying or upsetting your peers unintentionally, potential stigmatization). Learning to prompt yourself silently (i.e. "in your head") can build confidence while engaging in activities that require attending, comprehension, and recall.
Example Objective	The learner will refrain from inappropriately repeating aloud during a 30-minute period across three consecutive days.
Social Taxonomy Domain	Social Communication, Social Interaction, and Social Relatedness,
Teaching Methodologies	The Cool versus Not Cool™ procedure and Discrete Trial Teaching
Data Collection	Momentary Time Sampling, Trial by Trial or Estimation

Phases

Phase 1	Discrimination Training	Learner learns the fundamental difference between repeating and keeping it to yourself, and the many variables associated with this step.
		
		• Teach the learner to discriminate when it is okay to repeat (e.g., "tell your brain") and when it is not okay to repeat (e.g., "keep it to yourself").
		• Variables:
		  - What are "INSTRUCTIONS"
		    • Verbal directives given by teachers, parents, or other familiar adults
		    • Tell you to do something
		    • Okay to repeat: helps with retention, recall, comprehension, and compliance
		  - What are "COMMENTS"
		    • Can be said by anyone (e.g., peers, adults)
		    • Learner should say something different in response, or:
		      o Don't say anything at all (especially if the comment wasn't learner specific)
		    • Not okay to repeat, regardless of who says it

Phase 1 (cont.)	Discrimination Training	• WHO is talking: 　- NEVER okay to repeat: 　　• Familiar peers 　　• Unfamiliar peers 　　• Unfamiliar adults 　- SOMETIMES okay to repeat (only if an instruction is given, and with the intent to fade): 　　• Teachers 　　• Mom/Dad/Nanny 　　• Other familiar adults • Overhearing others 　- Not a time to repeat (e.g., interventionist and mom are debriefing about the session. The learner should wait, shouldn't be echoing what the interventionist and mom are saying) 　- May need to teach skills associated with appropriate waiting: 　　• Find something to do (e.g., draw on the whiteboard, read a book, play with a toy) 　　• Find a friend to play with 　　• Simply sit quietly 　- Waiting considerations 　　• Who is the learner waiting for (e.g., dad, a peer, a teacher)? 　　• How long? 　　• What items are available while waiting? 　　• Priming vs. no priming
Phase 2	Practice Appropriate Responding to Instructions vs. Comments.	• When the learner is given an instruction: 　- Learner can repeat the instruction and DO it (see Tell Your Brain program for more information) • When learner hears a comment: 　- Learner responds with another comment (e.g., someone says, "Disneyland is fun." Learner response is, "My favorite ride is the teacups.") 　- Learner stays quiet, doesn't say anything (e.g., learner is listening to someone else's conversation, comments aren't directed towards them) 　　• Note: We don't want the learner to think they are not allowed to join a conversation. If there is something to add, the learner should say it. But no repeating. • Variables to consider: 　- Who is delivering the instruction/comment? 　　• Practicing this program with familiar and unfamiliar peers will be essential due to provocativeness this creates (e.g., repeating peers at school, out in the community, less structured teaching) 　- Environment?

Phase 2 (cont.)	Practice Appropriate Responding to Instructions vs. Comments.	• Over time run this program out in the community (e.g., the park, stores) - Duration of commenting (e.g., one comment vs. a longer conversation)? - Complexity of commenting? - Tempting situations? - Comments directed towards learner vs. not (e.g., someone talking to learner vs. learner listening to a conversation)? - Structured vs. unstructured practice? - Priming vs. no priming?
Phase 3	Learner Reduces Reliance on Repeating Out Loud	For simplicity's sake, learner should be practicing this throughout phases. • "Tell your brain" by saying it out loud • "Tell your brain" by whispering it out loud • "Tell your brain" by mouthing the instruction but hearing the words in your mind • "Tell your brain" in your mind only
Phase 4	Generalization	• The learner accurately assesses when it is appropriate to repeat, when it is not appropriate to repeat, and responds accordingly across a variety of naturally occurring situations. • Variables to consider: - Expose the learner to a wide variety of situations eliciting the discrimination - Expose the learner to more natural environments (e.g., school, the community) - Reduce the structure of teaching as the learner demonstrates the skill - Reduce the level of priming as the learner demonstrates the skill

Follow The Conversation Thread

Overall Goal	The purpose of this program is to teach the learner how to stay on topic with similar words or sentences as part of conversation.
Example Objective	The learner will say a word or a sentence that is congruent with a statement that the interventionist makes with 90% accuracy across three consecutive sessions.
Social Taxonomy Domain	Social Communication
Teaching Methodologies	Discrete Trial Teaching, the Cool versus Not Cool™ procedure, and the Teaching Interaction Procedure
Data Collection	Estimation or Trial by Trial

Phases

Phase 1	Contingent Words	A word will be given (e.g., sand) and the learner will need to come up with a new word based on the previous word or the original word. There could be many acceptable words the learner could use, as long as it is contingent on the original word is acceptable (e.g. beach, waves, surf).
Phase 2	Multiple Contingent Words	Once the learner understands contingent words, begin using them back and forth with each other. · Example: - Interventionist – "Ocean" - Learner – "Fish" - Interventionist – "Salmon" - Learner – "Dinner"
Phase 3	Linking Contingent Words Together	While running Phase 2, write the words down so the learner can see them. After you have several words written down, draw an arrow between each word. Then have the learner tell you why the words go together. Write the explanation down on the arrow. · Example: - Ocean → Fish (because fish swim in the ocean) - Fish → Salmon (because salmon is a kind of fish) - Salmon → Dinner (because you can eat salmon for dinner)
Phase 4	Creating Contingent Sentences	Use the contingent words to create sentences with the learner. Take turns as you would in a normal conversation. · Example: - Interventionist – "I like the sand."

Phase 4 (cont.)	Creating Contingent Sentences	- Learner – "There is sand at the beach." - Interventionist – "The beach also has waves."

Phase 5	Connected conversation	Practice a conversation putting the sentences from Phase 4 together in a natural back and forth manner. See if this can be done without referring to the written sentences. Improvising should be encouraged as long as each new statement extends the thread. If the learner recalls verbatim what was previously practiced, see if the conversation can be extended for one or two further rounds, making it up as you go. When starting out on this phase do not allow the learner to use questions, limit them to statements. As they are more successful, questions can be allowed (but should not be the only form of response).
		
		· Example:
		  - Interventionist – "Yesterday I went surfing."
		  - Learner – "I never surfed before, but I like going to the beach and making sandcastles."
		  - Interventionist – "You need really wet sand to make a good sandcastle."
		  - Learner – "I dig a big hole and mix sand and water. When I'm done building, I bury myself in the hole."

Generalization		Work on this program in multiple locations, times, and while engaged in other activities, make sure to use different words and sentences. Reinforce when the learner expands sentences and when the learner uses the skill in naturally occurring situations. Make sure to reduce priming when working on Phase 5.

Inferences: Meaning Of Words From Context

Overall Goal	· To increase vocabulary and improve general knowledge · To improve conversational skills · To increase the skill of making inferences · To increase comprehension · To increase independence
Example Objective	The learner will state the meaning of an unfamiliar word with 90% accuracy for five consecutive days.
Social Taxonomy Domain	Social Communication
Teaching Methodologies	Discrete Trial Teaching
Data Collection	Task Analysis, Trial by Trial and Estimation

Phases

Overview		The goal is for the learner to learn how to infer the meaning of a word from the context in which it is used. Information regarding age-appropriate vocabulary should be collected before beginning the program. Initially, simple statements should be given directly to the learner which include one target word with which the learner is unfamiliar. The statement should also include several context clues. For example, for the target word "4x4," the sentence might be, "We drove my dad's 4x4 up the hill." The learner should be given several possible answers and then asked to figure out what the new word might mean. The answers can be pictures of items or written words depending on the learner's age. The possible answers should be in a similar category (in the above example, all types of transport) or to make it easier, unrelated items can be used. Once the learner has selected an answer, ask the learner to explain why they made that choice. The learner should relate the answer to the context clues given in the sentence.
Phase 1	Target Word in Simple Sentence, Visual Choices Available	The sentence should be said directly to the learner. The pictures or written words should be in front of the learner while hearing the sentence.
Phase 2	Target Word in Simple Sentence, Verbal Choices Given	After the learner hears the sentence, a list of choices should be presented verbally to the child (e.g., "Is it a football player, a singer or a TV star?).
Phase 3	Target Word in Simple Sentence, no Choices Given	After the learner hears the sentence, they should be asked to identify the meaning of the target word (e.g., "What's Mousetrap?").

	Target Word in Conversation	The learner should listen to a short conversation between two people in which the target word is used. For longer conversations the word may need to be used more than once.
e 5	Target Word used in Conversation with the Learner	Engage in conversation with the learner and use the target word.
ase 6	Words in Written Context	The target word should be included in a short text which the learner reads.
Phase 7	Words which have Less Concrete Meaning	Include words which may be more difficult to define (e.g., captain, poor, fasting).

Statement Elaboration

Overall Goal	The learner will elaborate on the statement of another person (e.g., Interventionist: "Look at that dog!" Learner: "It's so big!").
Example Objective	During a 10 minute interaction with a peer, the learner will make at least one on-topic elaboration across three consecutive sessions.
Social Taxonomy Domain	Social Communication and Social Interaction
Teaching Methodologies	The Cool versus Not Cool™ procedure, Discreate Trial Teaching, and the Teaching Interaction Procedure
Data Collection	Task Analysis or Estimation

Phases

Phase 1	Create a List of Descriptors	<ul><li>In collaboration with the learner, create a list of descriptors about and item/event that they are going to comment on.<ul><li>Example: Commenting on a dog<ul><li>It's a big dog</li><li>It's so pretty</li><li>It's a friendly dog</li><li>What do you think its name is?</li></ul></li></ul></li><li>If necessary for the learner, keep this list visible.</li><li>Write down comments as the learner says them or use pictures that represent the comments.</li></ul>
Phase 2	One Elaborative Statement	<ul><li>The interventionist makes a statement about an item (e.g., "Look at that dog!").</li><li>The learner uses the list to make one elaborative statement based on the interventionist's statement (e.g., "It's so big").</li></ul>
Phase 3	Taking Turns Elaborating	<ul><li>The interventionist makes a statement about an item (e.g., "Look at that dog!").</li><li>The learner uses the list to make one elaborative statement based on the interventionist's statement (e.g., "It's so big").<ul><li>When this statement is made, remove it from the options of statements to make (e.g., erase it, remove the picture)</li></ul></li><li>The interventionist then uses the list to make a different elaborative statement based on the learner's statement (e.g., "It's very pretty").<ul><li>When this statement is made, remove it from the options of statements to make (e.g., erase it, remove the picture)</li></ul></li><li>Continue taking turns elaborating on the statement until the list has been completed.</li></ul>

Phase 4	Fade the List	· Repeat phase 3 without making a list prior to the initial statement.
Phase 5	Steps toward Generalization	· Run the program in a variety of settings. · Have the learner comment first. · Use within a conversational context. · Practice with peers.

Conversation Movers And Stoppers

Overall Goal	The learner will continue a conversation by making statement or asking questions that keep conversation going. Definitions: • Conversation Movers – statements, questions, or actions that keep a conversation going • Conversation Stoppers – statements, questions, or actions that stop a conversation
Example Objective	During a 3-minute conversation with a peer the learner will make comments that will keep the conversation going in 90% of opportunities across three consecutive days.
Social Taxonomy Domain	Social Communication
Teaching Methodologies	The Teaching Interaction Procedure and the Cool versus Not Cool™ procedure
Data Collection	Task Analysis and Estimation

Phases

Phase 1	Description	• Collaborate with the learner to generate a list of comments or questions that are Movers and a list of Stoppers. Keep this list to refer to later.
		  - Examples of Movers:
		    • Questions or comments about the other persons preferred topic
		    • Short active listening comments (e.g., really? Cool! That's funny)
		    • Giving interested social cues (e.g., looking, smiling, nodding head)
		    • Short comments/questions
		    • Being on topic
		  - Examples of Stoppers:
		    • Questions or comments about your own preferred topics
		    • Off-topic comments
		    • Giving uninterested social cues (e.g., not looking)
		    • Talking for too long
		    • Doing "weird" things

Phase 2	Rationale	• Collaborate with the learner to generate rationales for using Movers and avoiding Stoppers during a conversation.
Phase 3	Discrimination Training	• Setup discrimination training for the learner to identify when someone has used a Mover or a Stopper.

Phase 4	Practicing Movers	• Make a comment or ask a question to the learner and the learner replies with a comment, after each comment give feedback on whether or not it was an appropriate Mover. - Differentially reinforce better Movers

Phase 5	Conversation with an Interventionist	• Setup a more natural conversation with the learner to practice using Movers.
		  - Initially use extrinsic reinforcers (e.g., points) or punishers (e.g., loss of points)
		  - Transition to more natural reinforcers (e.g., keep the conversation going or end it based on the quality of the learner's comments/questions)
		• At the end of the conversation have the learner evaluate their performance.

Phase 6	Conversation with a Peer	• Have the learner practice their conversation skills with a peer. • At the end of the conversation have the learner evaluate their performance.

Considerations		• Factors affecting difficulty level
		  - Topic of conversation
		  - Length of conversation
		  - Subtlety of social cues
		  - Naturalness

Handling Changes & Graceful Endings

Overall Goal	When faced with a change, something unexpected, or having to end a preferred activity, the learner should do so in an emotionally regulated manner appropriate to the situation. Applying the skill appropriately enables the learner to access greater social opportunities and increases exposure to other potential reinforcers in the more generalized environment.
Example Objective	When faced with a change or having to end something preferred, the learner will remain calm and make a graceful response following 80% of opportunities presented.
Social Taxonomy Domain	Social Communication, Social Interaction, and Social Relatedness
Teaching Methodologies	The Teaching Interaction Procedure and the Cool versus Not Cool™ procedure
Data Collection	Estimation or Task Analysis
Prerequisite Skills	Discrimination, Receptive Language, Expressive Language, Beginning Social Skills, Emotions

Teaching Interaction Procedure Steps:

Identify/Describe the Skill	Define the Behavior the Learner will use in the Generalized Environment	• Handling change well can be defined as: 　- Remaining calm 　- Taking in what is occurring without overreacting 　- Thinking of comments that will facilitate an upbeat mood (e.g., "Ok, I'll be right there" or "I Just need one more minute") 　- Remembering and using learned coping strategies 　- Responding in a manner that enhances reputation
Develop Rationale(s)	The Learner Participates in Developing Meaningful, Personalized Rationales for Participating in the Teaching Interaction Procedure and Subsequent Skill Display	• Collaborate with the learner to generate rationales that are meaningful for them. Without personalized rationales that are also reflective of social expectations, this teaching will not generalize. • Generic examples (these need to be personalized): 　- Change is unavoidable - might as well deal with it 　- It's an opportunity to make the best of a situation you have no control over 　- Change can bring good things. More opportunities to play/ engage arise when you choose to handle it well.

Demonstrate Skill		• Describe/role-play a scenario (e.g. instructor role-plays being in the middle of a favorite activity). Instructor models making a "Cool" response and contrasts that with a "Not Cool" response. Discuss with learner the specifics of what made the responses Cool and Not Cool.
Practice Skill	Role-play	• Present scenarios allowing the learner to participate in practicing the appropriate way to respond when it is time to change activity.
Feedback		• Objectively describe parts of the skill performed well (reinforcement) and also parts of the skill requiring more practice (corrective feedback). • Repeat role-plays as needed to provide opportunity to incorporate suggestions and refine performance. • Provide tangible reinforcement as needed for making improvement and for maintaining self-control during the Teaching Interaction Procedure. This can include token economies, bonus points, behavior contracts, or other reinforcement systems which provide access to preferred items, activities, or privileges.
Steps Toward Generalization		• Practice with different instructors and peers. • Increase variety of activities and levels of distraction. • Practice in a variety of environments/settings. • Fade interventionist presence. • In everyday situations that provide naturally occurring opportunities to practice handling change gracefully, provide formal and informal reinforcement as needed. To facilitate success, prime the learner in advance by providing reminders of the expected behavior and rationale. • Gradually fade tangible reinforcement and use of priming (including specificity and timing).

Complimenting

Overall Goal	The learner will learn what a compliment is and how to provide a compliment corresponding to the situation in which it is delivered.
Example Objective	When a peer experiences a positive event (e.g., gets a good grade, scores a goal in soccer), the learner will deliver a compliment specific to that positive event in 90% of opportunities.
Social Taxonomy Domain	Social Communication and Social Interaction
Teaching Methodologies	The Cool versus Not Cool™ procedure, the Teaching Interaction Procedure, and Discrete Trial Teaching
Data Collection	Task Analysis or Estimation
Prerequisite Skills	Discrimination, Receptive Language, Expressive Language, Communication Temptations, and Beginning Social Skills

Phases

Phase 1	Role-play	• Phase 1 provides the opportunity for the learner to learn what a meaningful compliment is and under what circumstances that compliment would be most appropriate. Teaching should be as structured as necessary (e.g., Teaching Interaction Procedure, role-plays, Discrete Trail Teaching).
		• Task analyzed example:
		- Learner observes (or listens to a scenario) an actor performing a skill or making an accomplishment
		- Thinks of congruent compliment
		- Approaches the actor
		- Establishes appropriate eye contact
		- Provides compliment with correct tone, emotion, expression, added social gesture (e.g., hi-five), personal space, etc.
		• Examples scenarios:
		- Getting a good grade
		- Doing a good job on an activity
		- Putting in a great effort
		- Wearing something nice or new
		- A stylish haircut
		- Overcoming an obstacle of some kind
		- Doing something nice for another person

Phase 2	Learner Learns to Assess Situation and Deliver Compliment to a Peer	· In naturally occurring situations with peers, the learner will recognize when special effort has occurred and will deliver a suitable compliment. - Prime the learner in advance as necessary · Introduce more subtle compliments, such as: - Hi-five in isolation, smiles and expressions signifying shared happiness, other hand gestures such as thumbs up, claps, etc. · Teach the learner to provide compliments that concur with what a peer experienced or what was observed. This will ensure the compliment makes sense to the peer receiving it, and that it demonstrates the learner's awareness of what has occurred.
Steps Toward Generalization		· Fade supplemental reinforcers. · Fade use of priming (including specificity and timing). · Fade interventionist presence. · Practice with helpers/cohorts. · Increase the variety of activities and levels of distraction. · Move to more natural environments.

Initiating Conversation

Overall Goal	This program teaches the learner to recognize opportunities to socialize and then respond by beginning a conversation with a peer. This skill enables the learner to maximize social opportunities when they arise, and to be the person initiating the interaction rather than waiting for, or simply responding to, someone else's initiation. This is a fundamental skill enabling the learner to access and take charge of social opportunities.
Example Objective	When presented an opportunity to engage with peers, the learner will appropriately begin a conversation (e.g., comment, ask a question, compliment) in 90% of opportunities.
Social Taxonomy Domain	Social Communication
Teaching Methodologies	The Cool versus Not Cool™ procedure, the Teaching Interaction Procedure, and Discrete Trial Teaching
Data Collection	Task Analysis or Estimation
Prerequisite Skills	Comprehension, Receptive Language, Expressive Language, Expanded Language, Communication Temptations, Beginning Empathy, and Beginning Social Skills

Phases

Phase 1	Steps to Teach in Order to Initiate a Conversation	Task analysis of skill (individualization should be considered based on the learner age, needs and skill set):
		
		 • Learner seeks out and observes opportunities to have a conversation; factors include:
		
		   - Is the environment conducive to conversation, or should the learner be occupied with something else (e.g., free time vs. work time)
		
		   - Is there someone the learner would like to have a conversation with in the area?
		
		   - Is there time to have a conversation?
		
		   - Is there a common topic/theme the learner can use to initiate a conversation with that person?
		
		   - Does the learner have prior practice with a "chat" or simple greeting exchange vs. a conversation?
		
		 • If appropriate, learner approaches peer(s).
		
		 • Learner uses best method available to initiate interaction with the peer(s):
		
		   - Walking towards peer(s) and establishing eye contact
		
		   - Getting the peer(s) attention correctly (e.g., age-typical greeting, non-verbal social cue, gesture)

Phase 1 (cont.)	Steps to Teach in Order to Initiate a Conversation	- Conversation starter (e.g., "howzit?," "hey there," "what's going on?," "good to see you!")
		• Learner determines if this will be brief or a more involved conversation; factors include:
		- How much time is available
		- Is this a peer the learner especially enjoys interacting with
		- Previous interaction history with the peer
		- Reading social cues provided by peer when the learner initiates
		- Knowing when to stop or move on from the initiation and ensuing conversation
		• Learner socializes appropriately; this may include:
		- Commenting to a peer
		- Asking a question of a peer
		- Complimenting a peer
		• Learner stops in a timely fashion with both participants benefiting from the interaction.
Phase 2	Practice During Exposure to Situations Allowing for Socialization	• Teach the learner to better notice and respond to opportunities to initiate conversations.
		• Based on the scenarios, the learner learns to recognize opportunities and smoothly segue into socialization with peers, and then to stop when the opportunity passes.
		• Teach the learner to choose when it is best to initiate, what level of socialization is optimal, and when it may be best not to initiate.
		• Even though an opportunity presents itself, it may be best to resist.
Steps Toward Generalization		• Fade supplemental reinforcers.
		• Fade use of priming (including specificity and timing).
		• Fade interventionist presence.
		• Practice with helpers/cohorts.
		• Increase the variety of activities and levels of distraction.
		• Move to more natural environments.

Gaining Attention

Overall Goal	· To teach the learner to gain attention appropriately. · To teach the learner to get attention from people in different relationship categories. · To teach the learner to get needs met and deal with urgent situations. · To increase the learner's persistence. · To increase the learner's problem solving and critical thinking skills.
Example Objective	When the learner wishes to make a person aware of their desire to speak to that person, they will perform 100% of the task analysis steps correctly in 4 out of 5 opportunities for 3 consecutive days.
Social Taxonomy Domain	Social Communication and Social Interaction
Teaching Methodologies	The Cool versus Not Cool™ procedure
Data Collection	Task Analysis or Estimation
Prerequisite Skills	Discrimination skills, Attributes, Social Awareness, Perspective taking, General Knowledge and Reasoning

Phases

Overview		This program teaches the learner to appropriately make it known that they would like to speak to another person and to be persistent when the initial attempt is not effective. The learner learns to identify possible ways to adjust attention seeking behavior and apply it to a variety of situations. This will involve problem solving skills and persistence. The types of problems should be individualized to the learner and be directly related to the type of errors the learner demonstrates.
Phase 1	Task Analysis and Discrimination Training	The desired steps for making a person aware that you would like to talk to them are as follows: · Approach and locate yourself not too close and not too far · Face listener · Be clear whose attention you are seeking (e.g., say their name) · At the right time, speak loud enough to be heard - Touch them if necessary and appropriate · Wait long enough for them to respond · Problem solve if there is no response Discrimination Training: · The instructor will present correct and incorrect examples for each step of the skill one-by-one and have the learner evaluate the step as correct (Cool) or incorrect (Not Cool). For the incorrect examples, invite the learner to demonstrate how the step should have been performed.

Phase 1 (cont.)	Task Analysis and Discrimination Training	• Once the learner can discriminate Cool vs. Not Cool for each individual step, present entire scenarios where there are sometimes one or more steps demonstrated the incorrect way. The learner will first identify if the example was correct or incorrect, and for each incorrect example the learner will identify which step was performed incorrectly and what should have been done instead.
Phase 2	Learner Practices Skill in Role-Play	Set up situations where the learner can practice getting another person's attention. The listener should be responsive if the learner is performing the steps correctly and unresponsive if the learner is not performing correctly. If the listener does not respond, this is a signal that the learner is performing a step incorrectly. Point out to the learner that something is going wrong and give them an opportunity to self-correct. Provide more specific feedback if necessary.

Phase 3	Problem Solving	In this phase the listener will sometimes be unresponsive even though the learner is performing the steps correctly. Have the learner problem solve what to do. Examples:
		• The listener walks away without acknowledging the learner.
		• Listener says, "I'm busy. Go back to your work."
		• Another person is in the way and it is not possible to approach the listener.
		
		Solutions vary based on the relationship the listener has to the learner. Additionally, the appropriate next step could vary by location (e.g., depending if communication occurs at school, home, community).
		
		• Peer as listener:
		  - Repeat peer's name
		  - Repeat communicative intent (e.g., question, request, comment)
		  - Talk even louder
		  - Tap peer on the shoulder (or some other non-verbal, physically appropriate method of getting attention)
		  - Use age-appropriate humor or sarcasm (for example, "Hey, I'm talking to you")
		  - Use a more insistent tone
		  - If warranted (due to urgency or safety), have another person intervene
		• Grown-up as listener:
		  - Say, "excuse me," or "pardon me"
		  - If target listener is talking to someone else, wait for a pause in conversation

Phase 3 (cont.)	Problem Solving	- If listener is busy, wait until a break occurs, or the "business" is completed - Repeat listener's name - Repeat communicative intent (e.g., question, request, comment) with a louder voice - Say, "When you're done, I have a question, and walk away - Find another available adult
Phase 4	Discriminating Emergency or Urgent Situations Requiring Attention from Those that Don't	Following a description of a scenario, the learner should indicate whether the situation is "urgent" or "not urgent." Examples: • Learner wants to show an adult a picture they drew (not urgent) • Learner wants to tell an adult they are hurt (urgent)
Phase 5	Problem Solving How to Best get Someone's Attention when a Situation is Urgent.	The learner learns how to get attention when in an urgent situation and practices this behavior in role-play situations. Once proficiency is displayed, the type of situation should be randomized between urgent and non-urgent situations. Examples of appropriate attention getting when the situation is urgent may include: • Interrupting the other person • Telling the person right away why you need attention • Persisting in giving information • Saying, "It's important!"
Phase 6	Program for Skill Generality	Create opportunities for the learner to practice this skill in the natural environment. It is important to provide opportunities to practice each of the variables learned in earlier phases, creating a whole skillset.

Proper Skepticism: You Can't Believe Everything You Hear

Overall Goal	The learner will determine when someone is telling them something that is true, something that is likely true, something that is likely false, and something that is false.
Example Objective	The learner will discriminate if a statement is probable or improbable with 90% accuracy across five consecutive sessions.
Social Taxonomy Domain	Social Communication
Teaching Methodologies	The Teaching Interaction Procedure, the Cool versus Not Cool™ procedure, and Discrete Trial Teaching
Data Collection	Task Analysis or Estimation
Prerequisite Skills	Fact vs. Opinion

Phases

Phase 1	Vocabulary for Trustworthiness of Information	· Learner will learn the meaning of "Expert" and "Knowledgeable." - Expert – someone who knows almost everything about a particular area/topic - Knowledgeable – someone who knows a lot about a particular area/topic - Basic Knowledge – someone who knows the basics about a particular area/topic - Lacking Knowledge – someone who knows very little to nothing about a particular area/topic · Depending on the learner you can introduce all or some of the labels.
Phase 2	Determine Areas of Expertise vs. Lacking Knowledge for Self and Others	· For various topic areas, have the learner identify what is their own level of knowledge. · For various topic areas, have the learner identify areas/topics and others level of knowledge in those areas/topics.
Phase 3	Introduce Likelihood Continuum	· Teach the concept of likelihood that an assertion is believable (could really happen). - Certain (i.e., well known fact) or obvious (i.e., readily observable phenomenon) - Likely – something you don't actually know but is plausible, you can easily imagine it, or is consistent with what we know is true - Unlikely – something that would be extremely rare, you have never seen, hard to imagine, and is not consistent with facts we know - Impossible – something that could never happen

Phase 3 (cont.)	Introduce Likelihood Continuum	• Depending on the learner you can combine Likely and Unlikely into a single category of "Possible or maybe."

Phase 4	Discrimination Training Based on Learners Area of Expertise	• Using the learner's area of expertise make comments and have them identify where within the likelihood continuum it falls.
		  - Example: The learner has expertise in Sharks
		    • Sharks eat other animals
		    • Sharks must always keep moving
		    • Sharks are herbivores

Phase 5	Discrimination Training Based on Learners Area of Knowledge	• Using the learner's area of knowledge, make comments and have them identify where within the likelihood continuum it falls.
Phase 6	Discrimination Training Based on Learners Area of Lacking Knowledge	• Using the learner's area of "lacking knowledge" make comments and have them identify where within the likelihood continuum it falls. - Because the learner does not have knowledge in the area it is important to make comments where it would be impossible for the comment to be true. For example, if the learner lacked knowledge about cars you could say "Toyota just came out with a new car that seats 70 people."

Phase 7	Responding to Assertions that are Questionable	• When someone makes a claim that is hard to believe, you have to decide what, if anything, to say or do about it. An important consideration is the reason why the person is giving the information (e.g., do they think they are correct, are they teasing, having fun). Examples include:
		  - Certain
		    • cool, I know, did you know that...
		• Likely:
		  - that's what I thought, neat, I didn't know that
		• Unlikely:
		  - are you sure?, I didn't think so, that doesn't sound right
		• Impossible
		  - there's no way, ignore, I think you're wrong because...

Phase 8	Practice within Activities	• Within a variety of activities, in structured practice (e.g., conversation, snack time, play time) make comments based on the learner's areas of knowledge along the likelihood continuum. Reinforce the responses to demonstrate the learner's ability to determine where the comment fell on the likelihood continuum with their related comment or question.

Chapter Twenty-Two
Social Awareness Skills

Jonathan Rafuse, Jeremy A. Leaf & Justin B. Leaf

Social Awareness encompasses the learner assessing the environment or reading the social cues of others, then responding accordingly. Within this domain there are basic social interaction skills, intermediate social interaction skills, and advanced social interaction skills. In this chapter, we provide 26 programs that fall under the Social Awareness Domain.

Basic Social Skills	Intermediate Social Skills	Advanced Social Skills
Socially Engaged Orienting	Recognizing and Responding to Social Cues	Keeping a Positive Outlook
Persistence	Who's Missing?	Social Awareness of the Group
Attending During Games	Matching the Mood	Recognizing Your Triggers
Hey, Learner	Joking vs. Provocation	Excitement Tolerance: The Right Amount of Silly
Personal Space	Achieving Your Desires	Say it or Keep it to Yourself?
Frustration Tolerance	Appearance Checks	Offering Help to Others
Impulse Control: Stop, Think, Act, and Review	Am I Splitting Hairs?	Responding to Bullying
Cheering For A Friend	Being a Big Kid	
Assumption Busting		
Asking For Help		
Talking When a Teacher is Busy		

Socially Engaged Orienting

Overall Goal	A basic component of social interaction is noticing and orienting toward others. Whether someone is speaking, has entered the learner's environment, or, conversely, when the learner enters a room, looking to see who is there and what is occurring is a critical stepping stone to further, more independent social opportunities.
Example Objective	During a large group activity, the learner will orient (e.g., turn and face, look at, notice) to the person speaking in 80% of opportunities.
Social Taxonomy Domain	Social Awareness
Teaching Methodologies	Discrete Trial Teaching, the Teaching Interaction Procedure, Role-Play, and the Cool versus Not Cool™ procedure
Data Collection	Trial-by-trial or Estimation
Prerequisite Skills	Comprehension, Joint Attending, Receptive Language, and Beginning Social Skills

Phases

Phase 1	Orient to Speaker	• Teach the learner to look at someone when that person is speaking. The skill includes: - Looking up, shifting body position, and focusing attention on the speaker • Secondly, introduce the skill in situations with more than one speaker (e.g. during a conversation or discussion.) It is socially acceptable to look at either the speaker or the listener.
Phase 2	Orienting and Determining Whether to Respond or Not	The learner learns to discriminate whether a response is required or not (e.g., answer a question, follow an instruction, do what peers are told to do, etc. vs. just listen or notice quietly)
Phase 3	Other Opportunities to Orient Meaningfully	• The learner learns to orient when someone enters the room or learner's environment. • The learner learns to orient to occurrences, oddities, and novelties in the environment (i.e., beginning joint attention). • When relevant, the learner orients to something the speaker is referencing (e.g. "Oh my, it's really windy outside."). • Before performing an action or activity, the learner learns to enter a space or room and meaningfully look around, take in what is occurring, or what possibly may be expected.

Steps Toward Generalization		• Fade supplemental reinforcers.
		• Fade use of priming (including specificity and timing).
		• Fade interventionist presence.
		• Practice with helpers/cohorts.
		• Increase the variety of activities and levels of distraction.
		• Move to more natural environments.

Persistence

Overall Goal	The learner learns to pay attention for longer periods of time. The learner develops better quality attending (e.g., coordinated looking, orienting, noticing, and then using this observation to better participate in activities, with peers, and with therapy). Increased productivity. Increased environmental awareness. Pre-requisite to better developed problem-solving strategies.
Example Objective	The learner will increase attending in natural environments to 75% of intervals (15 sec. partial interval recording) during a 10-minute observation for three consecutive days.
Social Taxonomy Domain	Social Awareness and Social Learning
Overview	• This program works on increasing the multiple subskills required for better overall attending and engagement. Interventionists should have a strong understanding of A Work in Progress, as each phase uses specific programs from that curriculum. Clinical judgement and in-the-moment assessment are critical across individual trials to determine the level of engagement and attending the learner is displaying. This is best taught using Discrete Trial Teaching and Discrimination Training. • Careful consideration of prompts and task sequencing will enhance the efficiency of this programming. – Use within-stimulus and programmatic prompting (e.g., teaching the "self-prompting" strategy of "tell your brain" may assist in multi-step programming and aid in information retention/memory). These prompts should be faded over time to increase independent responding and reduce any stigmatizing behavior (e.g., "tell your brain" may appear as "self-talking" and should be systematically faded).
Data Collection	Trial by Trial Data and Estimation Data

Phases

Phase 1	Self-Prompting	The learner learns to self-prompt – "tell your brain" – when given information or instructions to follow. For this phase, use multi-step receptive instructions, multi-element receptive discrimination, and multi-step Non-Verbal Imitation. • Instructions are multi-faceted and serve multiple objectives. If the interventionist says, "I want you to stand up and open the door; but first, tell your brain," the foremost objective is the learner learning the self-prompt of "tell your brain." Other objectives include actually doing what was asked, compliance, attending, comprehension, etc. • Instruction examples include: – "Stand up and open the door; but first, tell your brain"

Phase 1 (cont.)	Self-Prompting	<ul><li>Learner responds by repeating the instruction (i.e., "Stand up and open the door"), then doing what was asked (and repeated by the learner)</li></ul>- "Find the yellow school bus; [pause] What do you need to find?"<ul><li>Learner repeats the instruction, then retrieves the object</li></ul>- "We're going to color! Go get crayons and some paper. Remember, what do you need?"<ul><li>Learner responds, "crayons and some paper," then goes and finds the requested items<ul><li>It's okay if there are multiple opportunities to "tell your brain." If the interventionist accompanies the learner during material retrieval, ongoing prompts may include, "What were we getting?," "Remember what we need?," etc. These prompts should be faded over time and as the learner develops a stronger ability to remember and attend over greater distances and increased distractions</li></ul></li></ul><ul><li>Nonverbal Imitation examples</li></ul>- "Watch what I do, tell your brain, then do what I did." The interventionist performs two to three non-verbal actions – claps, then jumps, for example – the learner labels what the interventionist just did – "clap, jump" – then imitates the non-verbal imitation chain
Phase 2		<ul><li>Learner reduces volume of repeated information until the learner repeats the information privately and uses this template as a means to retain information, remain on-task, and complete instructions/ activities in a more independent manner.</li></ul>- This can be accomplished through shaping (i.e., differentially reinforce quieter vocalizations) and possibly the use of a gesture (e.g., interventionist places a finger to their lips to signify "quiet") - Once the learner is no longer repeating instruction out loud, intermittently probe to confirm that the learner is maintaining focus on the instruction<ul><li>Eliminate prompt to "tell your brain."</li><li>As learner demonstrates increased proficiency, discontinue probing to verify that they are retaining information.</li></ul>
Phase 3		**The learner participates in retrieval practice around the room.**<ul><li>The learner observes as you place items/objects/picture cards around the room, some in plain sight, some partially hidden. As the learner develops better attending and scanning skills, items can be placed completely out of sight, but they can see where you go as you move around the room hiding items. Ask the learner to retrieve the items until all are found.</li><li>As learner develops the skill, increase difficulty. This will require increased resolve, effort and perseverance</li></ul>- Vary the order of retrieval

Phase 3 (cont.)		- Run "interference" trials – instructions different than the retrieval instructions
		- Increase the distance of placement (e.g., out of the room, in different rooms, in different areas of the building)
		- Increase the number of items being retrieved per trial
		- Items are hidden in advance while learner is not present
		  • Learner is required to search without giving up or getting distracted
		  • Alternatively, the learner can ask for clues/hints in order to retrieve hidden items

Phase 4		• The learner participates in practice approximating school placements or other environments where this suite of skills is most applicable. Move toward generality of skills.
		- The interventionist issues instructions from a greater distance or away from the learner (e.g., as a teacher would; walking around the room; writing on the dry erase board)
		- Use the dry erase board as an instructional tool
		  • Increase visual and auditory attending
		  • Draw something memorable (i.e., within the learner's comprehension and labeling ability) on the dry erase board, then erase it
		    o Learner recalls what was there
		- Work on recall
		  • Color something with a certain color, circle a particular shape, read a story and point to a picture
		    o Then remove it from sight
		    o The learner recalls what color, what was circled, what picture was pointed to, etc.
		    o Or, the learner colors what you colored, circles what you circled, points to what was pointed to, etc.

Attending During Games

Overall Goal	The learner learns to pay attention for longer periods of time. The learner develops better quality attending (e.g., coordinated looking, orienting, noticing, and then using this observation to better participate in activities, with peers, and with therapy). Increased on-task behavior while sustaining attention. Increased environmental awareness. Pre-requisite to increased effort and persistence. Pre-requisite to better developed problem-solving strategies.
Example Objective	The learner will increase attending in natural environments by 25% from baseline levels for three consecutive sessions.
Social Taxonomy Domain	Social Awareness
Teaching Methodologies	Discrete Trial Teaching and the Cool versus Not Cool™ procedure
Data Collection	Trial or Trial or Estimation

Phases

Game 1	Slapjack Card Game	• Deal the deck of cards evenly across players.
		  - May be easiest to start with two players, develop the skill, then add players over time
		• Players take the dealt cards and without looking at what they have, place the cards in a neat pile in front of them, facedown.
		• The players simultaneously take the card on top of their piles and turn them face-up to form a new pile between them (in the middle).
		• Cards should be placed in the middle with a shared rhythm: each player puts their card down at the same time, then lifts the next card on their pile simultaneously and repeats this process
		  - Cards will start to pile up in the middle
		  - The middle cards don't need to be neatly stacked; it is just a place for the face-up cards
		  - It is more important that the game moves quickly and in a coordinated manner
		  - Players are responsible for keeping a watchful eye on the middle pile as it grows; they must look for Jacks!
		• When a Jack is played, the first player to slap the card wins the entire pile.
		• The player who slapped moves the middle pile to their side; play continues until all the cards in each players' initial stack are played.
		• The winner is the one with the most cards at the end.

Game 1 (cont.)	Slapjack Card Game	• Play can continue quickly with the next round if desired or required (e.g., for practice). • The "slap" card doesn't always have to be a Jack. – To foster greater attending, slap card can switch to another card

Game 2	Memory® (matching game)	• Begin with a smaller number of matches to teach the game.
		  – For example, begin with three to four matches – six to eight cards – and slowly work up to more matches as the learner learns the game and also an efficient process for playing the game:
		    • Turn the first card, remember it; turn the next card in sequence and if a match, keep it; if not, remember it
		    • Watch your opponent's turn to best remember where specific cards are
		    • Continue to turn cards in sequence until a match is found; repeat process
		• Initially, turn all memory cards over so they are face down and in even rows
		• Each player takes a turn flipping two cards over
		  – If no match, turn ends
		  – If there is a match, the player keeps the two cards and goes again
		    • Repeat until no match, then it is the next player's turn
		    • Continue playing in this manner until all the cards are matched
		    • Count matches to determine the winner
		• Once the learner has mastered the above steps, increase the field.

Hey, Learner

Overall Goal	• To increase the learner's responding when others say their name. • To increase the learner's environmental and social awareness. • To increase the learner's social motivation.
Example Objective	With intervals of 3 to 5 minutes between trials and during a variety of activities, the learner will stop and respond when their name is called in 100% of opportunities across three consecutive sessions
Social Taxonomy Domain	Social Awareness, Social Interaction, and Social Learning
Teaching Methodologies	Discrete Trial Teaching
Data Collection	Ratio, Trial by Trial, or Estimation

Phases

Phase 1	During Non-Preferred Activity or Lull	• In a structured setting, while engaged in a non-preferred activity or lull, teach the learner to stop and respond when their name is called (i.e., look at the person speaking). • Reinforcement will come from the person speaking. • Gradually increase difficulty by increasing the duration of intertrial interval.
Phase 2	During a Neutral Activity	• In a structured setting, while engaged in a neutral activity, teach the learner to stop and respond when their name is called (i.e., look at the person speaking). • Reinforcement will come from the person speaking.
Phase 3	During a Preferred Activity	• In a structured setting, while engaged in a preferred activity, teach the learner to stop and respond when their name is called (i.e., look at the person speaking). • Reinforcement will come from the person speaking.
Phase 4	Less Structured Activity with Neutral Activity	• In a less structured setting, while engaged in a neutral activity, teach the learner to stop and respond when their name is called (look at the person speaking) • Reinforcement will come from the person speaking.
Phase 5	Less Structured Activity with Preferred Activity	• In a less structured setting, while engaged in a preferred activity, teach the learner to stop and respond when their name is called (i.e., look at the person speaking) • Reinforcement will come from the person speaking.
Phase 6	Generalize	• Lengthen intertrial intervals to more closely approximate responding in natural environments. • Fade supplemental reinforcement.

Personal Space

Overall Goal	The learner should remain within appropriate proximity of peers when involved in conversation, play, socialization opportunities, and when "personal space" is a required component of shared interaction (e.g., standing in line, waiting in a group, walking with others). Being aware of personal space, and how individual that can be, is a critical social skill.
Example Objective	The learner will remain within appropriate boundaries of personal space (i.e., proximity to others) when interacting with peers in 90% of opportunities.
Social Taxonomy Domain	Social Awareness, Social Relatedness, and Social Interaction
Teaching Methodologies	The Cool versus Not Cool™ procedure, Discrete Trial Teaching, and the Teaching Interaction Procedure
Data Collection	Trial-by-trial, Task Analysis, or Estimation
Prerequisite Skills	Comprehension, General Knowledge, Receptive Language, Expressive Language, Communication Temptations, Beginning Social Skills, and Self-monitoring

Phases

Phase 1	Cool vs. Not Cool Discrimination	• The learner learns to discriminate what are "Cool" and "Not Cool" variations of individualized personal space.
		• Begin by teaching the learner their own comfort with personal space. Gently model being so close that the learner begins to show some uneasiness. Validate that it does not feel comfortable. Then validate how it feels better when you give more space.
		• Next, teach the learner others' perspectives on what is appropriate personal space.
		  - Too close? Too far? Just right?
		  - Demonstrate the need to be close enough that the other person understands you want to engage with them
		• Teach the learner the verbal and non-verbal social cues associated with Cool personal space and Not Cool personal space.
		  - COOL: conversation continues on topic; person doesn't attempt to move away, back up or lean in obviously; facial expression is calm, friendly, perhaps smiling, eye contact is appropriate; etc.
		  - NOT COOL: conversation feels awkward; person isn't focused on the topic; person says something clearly (e.g., "Hey, too close!," "Back up a bit!," "Gimme some space," "Come closer!,"

Phase 1 (cont.)	Cool vs. Not Cool Discrimination	"I can't hear you"); facial expressions seem bothered (e.g., frowning, eye contact broken); person raises arms/holds hands up; person backs away or turns sideways; etc.
Phase 2	Practice Potential Scenarios	• Teach the learner to evaluate whether their personal space is just right or needing adjustment based on verbal and/non-verbal cues provided by others. • Use situations/environmental setups the learner would likely contact. • Teach the learner to be assertive about their own personal space requirements without going over the top or acting in a stigmatizing manner. • If their personal definition of acceptable proximity is greatly beyond what peers would expect (e.g., well beyond arm's length), consider developing increased tolerance for proximity of peers. Use same format as Frustration Tolerance program.
Steps Toward Generalization		• Fade supplemental reinforcers. • Fade use of priming (including specificity and timing). • Fade interventionist presence. • Practice with helpers/cohorts. • Increase the variety of activities and levels of distraction. • Move to more natural environments.

Frustration Tolerance

Overall Goal	Frustration is an inevitable part of life. Being able to stay calm when challenging situations occur increases the opportunity for life-enriching experiences. The goal is for the learner to tolerate a broad range of potentially frustrating and disappointing events that are likely to occur in everyday life.
Example Objective	When presented with antecedents that have a history of causing frustration, the learner will maintain a positive demeanor in 80% of daily opportunities for five consecutive days.
Social Taxonomy Domain	Social Awareness
Teaching Methodologies	Discrete Trial Teaching, the Cool versus Not Cool™ procedure, and the Teaching Interaction Procedure
Data Collection	Ratio, Estimation, or Task Analysis

Phases

Phase 1	Identifying Stressors	• Identify the events that commonly precede the learner becoming frustrated, stressed, and/or upset. Creating a thorough list is critical, and as the program progresses, additional targets may be identified. Gathering information can be done in several ways:
		- Observe the learner
		  • Take ABC data
		  • Note the pattern of behavior
		- Ask for information from parents and teachers
		• Arrange the antecedents/stressors in a hierarchy, from least to most stressful.

Phase 2	Expose the Learner to Stressors	This must be done systematically and under specific conditions. • While the learner is as relaxed as possible (e.g., sitting in comfortable chair, dimmed lights, soft music) expose them to the least stressful situation contained in the hierarchy. - "Relaxed" or "Calm" should be clearly defined for the individual learner. What does it look like? - Provide praise and intermittent reinforcement contingent upon calm behavior - It may be necessary to gradually shape more appropriate responding (e.g., being sure "deep breaths" are actually deep and fulfill the physiological requirements, or making sure the reinforcement is truly contingent on defined calm behaviors and not inadvertently promoting extraneous, non-calm behaviors)

Phase 2 (cont.)	Expose the Learner to Stressors	- Be careful not to run this phase as a reaction to the learner appearing to get stressed (i.e., reactively). This could inadvertently teach a poor behavior chain ultimately leading to reinforcement · Gradually move the teaching to more natural environments and situations. · When the learner exhibits calm behaviors to the least stressful situation for five consecutive teaching sessions, move to the next level on the hierarchy. · Proceed through the levels of the hierarchy.
Phase 3	Teach the Relaxation Response	Depending on the learner, there are several choices for relaxation procedures, including, but not limited to: deep breathing, progressive muscle relaxation, visualization and guided imagery. · Teach the learner relaxation procedure(s). · Once the relaxation procedure(s) are learned, teach use of the procedure(s) when minimally stressed (i.e., lowest hierarchy level). · Fade prompts as quickly as possible. · Increase the naturalness of the environment in which the learner experiences stressors. The learner should use the relaxation procedure(s) to remain calm across structured environments and interventionists.
Phase 4	Generalize	The work is not complete until the learner is exposed to stressors/antecedents without warning, across as many environments as available, and can remain calm and use the relaxation procedure(s) to maintain a level emotional state.

Impulse Control: Stop, Think, Act, And Review (Star)

Overall Goal	Promote impulse control. Increase awareness of triggers in the environment. Develop self-monitoring behaviors and reactions in social situations. Identify and practice potential pro-social alternatives to disruptive behavior. Improve assessment of social situations. Develop skills to successfully participate in social interactions. Reduce occurrence of stigmatizing behaviors in social situations. Increase acceptance by peers. Improve self-confidence and self-concept.
Example Objective	The learner will refrain from engaging in any impulsive behaviors in 90% of opportunities across five consecutive sessions.
Social Taxonomy Domain	Social Awareness, Social Interaction, and Social Relatedness
Teaching Methodologies	The Teaching Interaction Procedure
Data Collection	Task Analysis Data
Prerequisite Skills	The learner should have a good receptive and expressive understanding of language, be able to comprehend simple stories and sequences of events, and enjoy reading books.

Phases

Phase 1	Stop	Present the learner with a situation that requires maintaining self-control. The learner should stop before responding to the situation presented. Use a visual cue to represent stopping. Begin teaching by using self-talk and then fade. When Phase 1 is mastered in a 1:1 teaching environment add Phase 2.

Phase 2	Think	Present the learner with a situation that requires maintaining self-control. After stopping, the learner will initiate thinking.
		
		· Describe what is happening (e.g., "I have seen my friend across the street").
		· Describe how you feel (e.g., "I feel excited").
		· State as many choices of how to respond as you can think of. For example:
		  - Become giddy, overexcited
		  - Walk over and say "hi" calmly
		  - Give him a high five
		  - Wave
		· Identify the likely outcome for each of the choices.

Phase 2 (cont.)	Think	- Become giddy = friend gets annoyed - Say "hi" calmly = friend is happy to see me
Phase 3	Act (Practice the Appropriate Alternative)	• Present the learner with a situation that requires maintaining self-control. After stopping and thinking about the options, the learner will state the best option or if no clear best option exists, any choice that is likely to produce a socially appropriate outcome. • If the instructor agrees with the plan, learner will then carry out the plan. If not, go back to previous steps and reconsider options. When learner has demonstrated a high rate of success, allow learner to carry out an inadvisable plan (as long as it does not have long term detrimental consequences) and proceed to the next phase. This will promote learning from trial and error.
Phase 4	Review	Present the learner with a situation that requires maintaining self-control. After stopping, thinking, and acting, the learner should review the outcome. • The learner gives an account of their friend's response (e.g., "My friend smiled and said 'hi' back."). • The learner should then assess their own feelings after the event (e.g., "My friend smiled and said 'hi' back, that made me feel happy.") • Finally, the learner assesses whether they made the right choice. If yes, great. If no, then what should he do next time?
Generalization		Once the skill has been mastered in a structured 1:1 session with immediate practice, have the learner practice the skill in a variety of situations. Practice the skill with immediate-delayed practice, fading the structure of the program. Fade self-talk. Practice the skill across settings and people. Fade the level of reinforcement. The goal is for the learner to demonstrate the skill in situations that occur naturally with no reminder and with no supplemental reinforcement.

Cheering For A Friend

Overall Goal	This program teaches the learner to show support and encouragement for peers or teammates during collaborative games and activities. This skill promotes good sportsmanship and allows the learner to experience these activities more fully, enhances the learner's reputation, and increases the likelihood that peers will reciprocate.
Example Objective	When engaged in a game or activity with a peer, the learner will show support (e.g., cheer on, encourage) for that peer in 80% of daily opportunities over 5 consecutive days.
Social Taxonomy Domain	Social Awareness, Social Relatedness, Social Interaction, and Social Communication
Teaching Methodologies	Discrete Trial Teaching, the Teaching Interaction Procedure, Role-Play, Modeling, and the Cool versus Not Cool™ procedure
Data Collection	Trial-by-trial, Task Analysis, or Estimation
Prerequisite Skills	Comprehension, Receptive Language, Expressive Language, Expanded Language, Communication Temptations, Beginning Empathy, Beginning Social Skills

Phases

Phase 1	Recognizing Opportunities to Cheer and Encourage a Peer	• Teach the learner situations when cheering and encouragement are expected. Examples may include:
		  - Team activities
		  - Sporting events
		  - When a peer is attempting something new or challenging
		  - When a peer could use a little encouragement (e.g., when things become hard, when further exertion is necessary, when it appears the peer may give up)
		  - When the peer's opponent has vocal support

Phase 2	Task Analysis and Role-Play	The learner role-plays the following steps:
		• The learner observes and determines whether cheering is appropriate or not (i.e., discrimination training).
		• If cheering is appropriate, the learner observes the activity/ game in which the peers are involved.
		• When the peer(s) do something noteworthy, the learner cheers and encourages. Examples may include:
		  - "Way to go!"
		  - "Nice shot!"
		  - "Great play!"
		  - "Keep it up!"

Phase 2 (cont.)	Task Analysis and Role-Play	· The learner uses a voice and tone commensurate with the situation, activity, and environment.
		· The learner remains engaged with the activity and continues to cheer as opportunities present themselves.
Phase 3	Generalization (Incidental Application)	· Throughout the day when there are naturally occurring opportunities to cheer for a friend, use priming as needed to ensure that the learner recognizes and acts on the opportunity. Over time, fade the specificity and timing of the prompt and use of supplemental reinforcement.
		· Practice with a variety of peers, instructors, activities, settings, and environments.

Assumption Busting

Overall Goal	The learner will respond according to the instruction given rather than an assumption about the instruction.
Example Objective	The learner will respond accurately to questions and/or instructions in 80% of opportunities per day for three consecutive days.
Social Taxonomy Domain	Social Awareness
Teaching Methodologies	Discrete Trial Teaching
Data Collection	Estimation Data or Trial by Trial
Prerequisite Skills	Receptive Labels, Receptive Instructions

Phases

Phase 1	Mix Multiple Programs	• While running one program (e.g., receptive labels) give instructions from another program unexpectedly (e.g., receptive instructions).
Phase 2	Conflicting Visual/ Auditory Stimuli	• Present visual stimuli (e.g., instructor bangs on drum) while giving a conflicting auditory instruction (e.g., "clap your hands").
Phase 3	Establish and Then Break the Pattern	• While running a program (e.g., receptive labels) give instructions that establish a pattern (e.g., always ask for the same item, or the item in a specific location). • Once the pattern is established unexpectedly give an instruction that breaks the pattern (e.g., ask for a different item, or an item in a different location).
Phase 4	Use Materials in a Different Manner	• Use materials in a way they are not intended (e.g., use a car as a crayon instead of rolling the car).
Phase 5	Use Materials from Other Programs Differently	• Use materials that have been used in previous programs (e.g., blocks for material imitation) in a new way (e.g., blocks for matching).
Considerations		• If priming is used, there should be a long delay between the prime and when the instruction occurs. • Any prompting that is done should be prompting that leads the learner to the process as opposed to giving them the answer. • Set up this program as if running another program (e.g., it should not be clear to the learner that they are about to run the assumption busting program).

Asking For Help

Overall Goal	Recognizing when assistance is needed and then communicating that need appropriately will instill appreciation for the "power of language." Sometimes our learners struggle with new material, or activities requiring ongoing effort. Teaching them to ask for help will increase the learner's ability to problem solve and become more independent. Ultimately, this will enhance the learner's quality of life through social interaction and relatedness, and reduce inappropriate behavior associated with confusion and frustration.
Example Objective	When an instruction cannot be completed due to inability or impossibility, the learner will recognize this and ask someone (e.g., a classmate, a teacher) for help in 80% of opportunities across three consecutive sessions.
Social Taxonomy Domain	Social Awareness, Social Interaction, Social Communication, and Social Relatedness
Teaching Methodologies	Discrete Trial Teaching, the Teaching Interaction Procedure, the Cool versus Not Cool™ procedure, and In-vivo Demonstration
Data Collection	Trial by Trial or Estimation Data
Prerequisite Skills	Comprehension, Receptive Language, Expressive Language, Expanded Language, Communication Temptations, Beginning Social Skills

Phases

Task Analysis		Example task analysis (individualize based on the learner's age, needs, and skillset):
		• Identify whether assistance is required or not (i.e., discrimination).
		• First, learner should try (e.g., exhaust possible solutions, put in more effort).
		• If assistance is required, learner should stop the activity.
		• The learner should seek out an appropriate "helper." This requires determining the characteristics of an individual who is capable of providing the needed assistance. For example:
		– If an object is truly too high to reach, should the learner ask a same-size peer, or a taller adult?
		– If an object is truly too heavy, should the learner request assistance from a smaller peer, or a bigger one? If still too heavy, what next?
		– The goal of this phase is increasing efficiency by being thoughtful and systematic when considering what kind of assistance is required

Task Analysis (cont.)		• Once that person is found, the learner gets their attention appropriately (this may need to be teased out and taught, depending on the learner). • Once attention is gained, the learner should appropriately ask for help (depending on the skill set, this may be verbally, through use of PEC icons, a communicative device, etc.). • The learner should identify the problem (e.g., gesture, tell, explain). • Helper assistance should be the reinforcer for appropriately seeking assistance.

Phase 1	Recognizing Situations Requiring Assistance	• Teach the learner to discriminate whether a situation requires assistance or does not require assistance.
		• Set up scenarios where the learner can either be successful alone or clearly requiring assistance to complete.
		• Create many scenarios to develop this discrimination. Examples may include:
		  - Obtaining an object completely out of reach vs. an object that can be reached with a bit more physical effort
		  - Moving an object completely too heavy to lift vs. an object that can be moved with a bit more physical effort
		  - Finding an object that the learner could never find vs. finding an object that requires a bit more problem-solving
		  - Putting things away in a container clearly too small for the job vs. exerting a bit more effort organizing what needs to be put away in an orderly fashion.

Phase 2	Expand to Functionally Different Scenarios	• The learner learns to evaluate what type of assistance is required based on the scenario presented.
		  - Needing help vs. Needing more information (i.e., "I need help" vs. "Tell me more") to figure out a problem
		  - Needing help vs. I should not do that (i.e., the learner learns that some tasks/requests should not be attempted, due to personal safety, confidentiality, social norms, etc.)

Steps Toward Generalization		• Fade supplemental reinforcers. • Fade use of priming (including specificity and timing). • Fade interventionist presence. • Practice with helpers/cohorts. • Increase the variety of activities and levels of distraction. • Move to more natural environments.

Talking When A Teacher Is Busy

Overall Goal	This program teaches the learner to recognize unstructured opportunities to socialize, such as when the interventionist is otherwise occupied and no specific instructions were given to the class/group or learner to follow or complete. Once this opportunity is recognized, the learner will look for a peer to interact with appropriately. This skill enables the learner to maximize social opportunities when they arise, even when they are not specifically arranged.
Example Objective	When presented an opportunity to engage with peers (e.g., unstructured/down time, no specific instruction or expectation, the interventionist is busy with something else), the learner will initiate peer interaction (e.g., comment, join in a conversation, ask a question) during 80% of opportunities.
Social Taxonomy Domain	Social Communication
Teaching Methodologies	The Cool versus Not Cool™ procedure, the Teaching Interaction Procedure, and Discrete Trial Teaching
Data Collection	Task Analysis or Estimation
Prerequisite Skills	Comprehension, Receptive Language, Expressive Language, Expanded Language, Communication Temptations, Beginning Empathy, Beginning Social Skills

Phases

Overview		Example task analysis (individualization should be considered based on the learner age, needs and skill set):
		• The learner observes and determines whether socializing is appropriate (i.e., discrimination training).
		• If appropriate, the learner seeks out a peer/peers.
		• The learner socializes appropriately. Examples may include:
		- Commenting to peer
		- Joining a conversation
		- Asking a question of a peer
		- Complimenting a peer
		- Appropriate non-vocal communication (e.g., smile, wave)
		- Learner approaches individual possibly requiring help
		• The learner stops in a timely fashion, such as when the interventionist calls the class back to order or becomes available again.

Phase 1	Recognizing Situations Allowing for Socialization	• Teach the learner to notice and respond to less structured opportunities to socialize, including: - The interventionist being called away by another adult - Center activity not set up yet - Group activity not set up yet - The interventionist being busy with another learner - Transitions between activities
Phase 2	Practice Socializing During These Situations	• Based on the scenarios, the learner learns to recognize opportunities and smoothly segue into socialization with peers, and then to stop when the opportunity passes. • Teach the learner to choose when it is best to socialize, what level of socialization is optimal, and when it may be best not to socialize. • Even though an opportunity presents itself, it may be best to resist. • Factors include: - Whether the learner is prepared for the next interaction with the interventionist - The learner may be finishing up something and the interventionist being busy is the best time to do that - No one else is taking the opportunity to socialize and the learner may draw negative attention - A simple smile and wave may be more powerful than a question, comment, or vocalized greeting - Determining the correct tone and volume of the interaction - Discriminating the difference between just right vs. too loud vs. too quiet vs. too long, etc.
Steps Toward Generalization		• Fade supplemental reinforcers. • Fade use of priming (including specificity and timing). • Fade interventionist presence. • Practice with helpers/cohorts. • Increase the variety of activities and levels of distraction. • Move to more natural environments.

Reading & Responding To Social Cues

Overall Goal	The learner will recognize social cues and respond appropriately. Developing the skills necessary to detect signals from others, interpret the signals and respond appropriately will foster increased receptiveness from those individuals.
Example Objective	The learner will respond appropriately to a variety of social cues provided by another person (e.g., peer, cohort, interventionist) in 80% of opportunities.
Social Taxonomy Domain	Social Awareness and Social Relatedness
Teaching Methodologies	Discrete Trial Teaching, the Teaching Interaction Procedure, Role-Play, In-vivo Demonstration, and Modeling
Data Collection	Estimation or Trial by Trial
Prerequisite Skills	Comprehension, Receptive Language, Expressive Language, Expanded Language, Communication Temptations, and Beginning Social Skills

Phases

Phase 1	Recognizing Social Cue with Minimal Distraction	• Start with obvious social cues that include a vocal and non-vocal/gestural component and move to more subtle social cues (this hierarchy may differ for each learner). All the learner has to do is signal they have spotted the social cue. In this phase they are not expected to adjust their behavior.
		
		  - Obvious verbal cues paired with non-vocal cue (e.g., "stop" + hand held out; "I'm bored" + exaggerated yawn; "no" + a finger wag)
		  - Obvious body cues paired with verbal description (e.g., turning your back + "I'm not listening to you;" walking away + "I'm finished talking;" high five stance + "give me 5")
		  - Obvious facial cues paired with verbal description (e.g., smiling + "I'm glad;" frowning + "I'm sad;" look of surprise + "what a shock!")
		
		• Progress to more subtle cues.
		
		  - Subtle body cues paired with a verbal description (e.g., turning your head + "losing interest;" backing away slightly + "whoa, you're too close")
		  - Subtle facial cues paired with verbal description (e.g., looking away + "I'm bored;" rolling your eyes + "I don't believe you;" crossing your arms + "I don't like that")
		
		• Adjust teaching based on the status/age of the person who is giving the cue (e.g., interventionist /parent vs. peer). Teach a variety of cues with the same meaning to foster generalization.

Phase 2	Dimension 2: Identify the Social Cue with Environmental Distraction	• Once the learner has mastered a variety of cues from Phase 1, this Phase introduces distractions during the teaching.
		• The objective is for the learner to notice and respond appropriately to social cues while engaged in a variety of activities that compete with attentiveness to social cues.
		• Trials should include some examples of obvious social cues and some examples of subtle social cues. The learner should report the social cue when it occurs.
		• The activity and distraction level should be organized as a hierarchy from least to most interfering.
		  - Initially, introduce low level distractors/activities that are not very captivating
		  - As the learner demonstrates proficiency with noticing and responding to social cues, expand to activities that are more captivating or that involve more distraction
		• Examples of distractions/activities to embed the teaching include, but are not limited to:
		  - While carrying out a simple task (e.g., putting books on a shelf)
		  - While explaining something to another person
		  - While engaged in play that does not involve toys (e.g., playing tag)
		  - While playing with toys (e.g., building with Legos™)
		  - During conversation about a highly preferred topic

Phase 3	Making Correct Adjustment Following the Social Cue	• Using a variety of teaching methodologies (e.g., role play, discrimination training, video modeling) teach the learner what response matches the social cue. For example:
		  - If someone isn't responding during a conversation change the topic
		  - If someone says no to an idea offer another suggestion

Generalization		• Fade supplemental reinforcers. • Fade use of priming (including specificity and timing). • Fade interventionist presence. • Practice with many different individuals. • Increase the variety of activities and levels of distraction.

Recognizing And Responding To Social Cues

Overall Goal	Teach the learner to discriminate a variety of verbal and non-verbal social cues. Teach the learner to recognize when someone is interested, not interested, bored, annoyed, upset, etc. and change behavior accordingly. Promote more successful peer interactions. Increase social attentiveness. Decrease occurrences of undesirable peer interactions (e.g., hurt feelings, evaluation, teasing, bullying). Help the learner respond reciprocally with peers. Begin developing social navigation (e.g., a template or sense of who to interact with and who to avoid).
Example Objective	During a 30-minute interaction, the learner will respond appropriately to a variety of social cues provided by a peer, a cohort, a teacher, etc. with 80% success over 5 consecutive days.
Social Taxonomy Domain	Social Awareness
Teaching Methodologies	The Teaching Interaction Procedure, The Cool versus Not Cool™ procedure, and Discrete Trial Teaching
Data Collection	Task Analysis or Estimation
Prerequisite Skills	More advanced contingency understanding (e.g., social contingencies, social cause and effect), familiarity with peer interactions, age-appropriate play skills, basic conversation skills, social interest.

Phases

Phase 1	Identifying Obvious Social Cues	Role-play a variety of play or social scenarios where obvious social cues occur and have the learner signal when they observe a sign of interest or disinterest. • Obvious verbal cue discrimination: positive comments, asking questions, etc. versus no comments, mean/negative comments (e.g., "stop," "I don't like that," "that's boring," "don't do that"), etc. • Obvious body cue discrimination: closer physical proximity demonstrating interest, facing the learner, physically staying in the interaction, open gestures (e.g., arms at side, reaching for the learner) versus appearing aloof or distant, turning body away, walking away, arms crossed, etc. • Obvious facial cue discrimination: laughing, smiling, eyes engaged with the learner, etc. versus frowning/upset/mad face, crying, looking away or down, etc.
Phase 2	Identifying Subtle Social Cues	Role-play a variety of play or social scenarios where subtle social cues occur and have the learner signal when they observe a sign of interest or disinterest.

Phase 2 (cont.)	Identifying Subtle Social Cues	• Subtle verbal cue discrimination: peer changing the subject but remaining engaged (e.g., topics overlap, reference each other) versus more ambiguous comments (e.g. "nah," "uh oh," "maybe"), silence/ignoring, etc. • Subtle body cue discrimination: peer beginning to fidget but stays engaged versus peer turning away slightly, orienting to something other than the learner, backing away slightly, etc. • Subtle facial cue discrimination: looking away but reorienting, less eye contact but still engaged versus rolling eyes, frowning, furrowing eyebrows, taking deep breaths, peer exhibiting subtler facial expressions, etc. During this phase, it is important to consider voice intonation (e.g. someone saying "stop" in a playful tone while smiling and laughing probably doesn't actually want the engagement to stop), as well as mixing social cues not typically congruent with each other (e.g., smiling, but saying a mean comment).

Phase 3	Responding to Social Cues	• The learner learns a variety of appropriate responses based on the social cue.
		• Positive social cue responses (e.g., the peer is interested or likes it):
		  - Keep playing, keep talking, continue engagement, etc.
		• Negative social cue responses (e.g., the peer is not interested or doesn't like it):
		  - Stop, don't say it again, say "I'm sorry," find someone else to play with/talk to, say something else, change topics, etc.

Phase 4	Practice Recognizing and Responding to Social Cues Within a Variety of Social Situations	• Possible social situations, mixing interest and disinterest from a peer:
		  - Offering someone food (e.g., "do you want a goldfish?")
		  - Offering someone a toy (e.g., "do you want this doll?")
		  - Offering a suggestion (e.g., "let's go on the monkey bars")
		  - Within play (e.g., knocking over someone's tower, building together, taking a toy from someone)
		  - Reading cues associated with something being an "accident" versus "on purpose"
		  - Conversation (e.g., sustaining peer's interest/engagement)
		  - Commenting (e.g., compliments – "I like your dress," commenting at inappropriate times – "look, the boy is crying")

Considerations		• Factors affecting degree of difficulty:
		  - Level of social engagement (offering someone a goldfish versus sustaining a conversation)
		  - Obvious versus subtle social cues
		  - Duration of activity

Considerations (cont.)		- Interaction with a peer or an adult
		- Familiarity of peer or adult
		• For some learners, below are comment examples that often get a negative reaction from peers, but the learner did not intend for that to occur (e.g., it is not the learner's intent to annoy, frustrate, or make someone uncomfortable, but what is said and the manner in which it is delivered may cause that to occur).
		  - Phrase repetition (e.g., the same comment or phrase over and over – even if it was a cool comment to begin with; disengaged – stimmy – repetitiveness)
		  - Imitating/echoing peers
		  - Timing issues (e.g., off-topic comments, incongruous comments, comments not matching the atmosphere – emotion, topic, location – comments said too loudly or softly)
		  - Narrating potentially stigmatizing or embarrassing occurrences (e.g., when someone is crying or upset, when someone receives feedback, noticing something idiosyncratic and comments loudly about it – "she's so BIG!")

Generalization		The learner assesses, recognizes, and appropriately responds to a variety of social cues in more natural situations. • Varied environments (e.g., school, home, clinic) • Variety of individuals giving the social cue (e.g., peer, adult, familiar, unfamiliar) • Varied materials/activities

"Who's Missing?" Game

Game Instructions	Have one learner go to another room while all other learners sit on the floor. Use a parachute (or another covering) to hide one learner. Have the learner from the other room come back and try to guess who is under the parachute.
Purpose of Teaching Social Skill	Practice a variety of skills incorporated into a play-based setting.
Example Objective	During a play-based activity, the learner will accurately identify something missing in the environment in 80% of opportunities.
Social Taxonomy Domain	Social Awareness
Level of Skill	Easy
Skills that can be Targeted	Memory, learning peers' names, process of elimination, problem solving, excitement tolerance, learning from feedback, waiting
Materials Needed	• Parachute or other covering
Data Collection Procedure	Task Analysis or Estimation
Teaching Methodologies	Combination of: • The Cool versus Not Cool™ procedure • Discrete Trial Teaching • Shaping

Considerations	• Make it more difficult for learners who are practicing problem solving by:
	  - Putting multiple people in the parachute
	  - Putting no one in the parachute, but maybe a stuffed animal instead
	• Putting more than one learner in the parachute could increase shared excitement for those learners.
	• Make sure that the learners do not shout out (give away) who is hiding.

Matching The Mood

Overall Goal	Improve the learner's regulating, varying, and adjusting emotional expression based on the emotion/activity level present in the peer group. Improve the learner's attending to social nuances, cues, and changing dynamics. Teach the learner to move more fluently through social occurrences (e.g., play, conversation, transitions between activities). Teach the learner to more accurately assess the group "mood" and then adjust behavior to fit with the group. Teach the learner to join in, participate, and sustain engagement with peers. Reduce occurrences of isolation, stigmatization, and potential bullying.
	Teach the learner to express emotion within the constraints of social environments (e.g., congruent emotion/activity level, body movements, talking versus not talking, proximity, volume, facial expressiveness matching emotion, knowing when to "dial it back in," when to stop, when to transition, when to break rules).
Example Objective	The learner will match their behavior with the behaviors that others are displaying within the environment in 100% of opportunities across five consecutive sessions.
Social Taxonomy Domain	Social Awareness and Social Interaction
Teaching Methodologies	The Teaching Interaction Procedure and the Cool versus Not Cool™ procedure
Data Collection	Ratio or Estimation

Phases

Phase 1	Learner Should be Familiar with a Variety of Emotions Commensurate with Age-Typical Norms	That familiarity should include the following:
		
		• Receptive understanding (demonstrates comprehension) of emotional states:
		  - Can "show" an emotion when asked (e.g., "show me what happy looks like," "let's see a sad expression," "what does mad look like?")
		  - Associates expressions (e.g., verbal or non-verbal/vocal) with corresponding labels (e.g., crying goes with "sad," "woo-hoo!" or smiling are happy expressions, "Grrrrr" or furrowed eyebrows are ways to express "mad")
		• Expressive understanding of emotional states:
		  - Can respond with corresponding emotion labels when asked, "How do I feel?" plus demonstration in-vivo; labels pictures, video representations, drawings in books, etc.

Phase 1 (cont.)	Learner Should be Familiar with a Variety of Emotions Commensurate with Age-Typical Norms	- Can answer questions about familiar scenarios (e.g., "your classmate intentionally knocked over the Lego castle you had spent all recess building and laughed about it. How would you feel?," "You just won the championship after all your hard work. You would feel…")
		• Other emotion features:
		  - How is emotion expressed, what does it look like?
		  - When might an emotion occur? Under what circumstances?
		  - What environments are associated with reduced emotionality? With loud expression?
		  - What activities are associated with reduced emotionality? With loud expression?
		  - Can the learner regulate emotionality/excitement?
		• A basic understanding of empathy (theory of mind):
		  - The learner can determine what peers might be feeling based on observation or vignette presentation
		• A basic desire to engage with others (e.g., has social motivation, wants to be around peers).
		• Other skill areas may include transitioning between a variety of activities, a range of play and leisure interests, and advanced matching.

Phase 2	Teach the Variability of Different Emotions	For example, "happiness" has a range of definitions. Those definitions have a general anchor, but vary according to "how they feel," and the intensity of the happiness. Understanding this will make matching the mood (i.e., emotional regulation) easier. Teaching as a range of intensity might help with clarity of emotional expression.
		
		• Possible emotion ranges might include:
		  - Happiness
		    • Joy, contentment, exhilaration, cheer, pleasure, etc.
		  - Sadness
		    • Feeling blue, down, upset, sorrow, grief, etc.
		  - Anger
		    • Mad, upset, furious, irate, enraged, irritated, etc.
		  - Excitement
		    • Enthused, thrilled, exhilarated, elation, etc.
		  - Mellow
		    • Chill, calm, cool and collected, peaceful, etc.
		  - Jealous
		    • Green-eyed, envious, wanting, desirous, spiteful, etc.
		  - Scared
		    • Fearful, frightened, terrified, mortified, afraid, etc.

Phase 2 (cont.)	Teach the Variability of Different Emotions	- Bored • Ho-hum, over it, uninterested, unenthused, etc. • Teach idioms and the emotional intensities with which they are associated.

Phase 3	Demonstrate the Variability of Emotion within One Activity or Environment	The learner should discriminate between different emotional expressions. They should also be familiar with a range of activities eliciting those emotions. Finally, the learner should be familiar with the social expectations associated with a variety of environments (e.g., the library versus classroom, recess outside versus board games inside, circle time versus lunch time). Now the learner will learn to sustain engagement with a peer or peer model (teaching staff included), switch between activities, and between the ranges of emotional expression during the teaching/practice session.
		
		• Initially, the learner matches the mood of a model/peer during brief opportunities.
		  - This may include 1 to 2 activities plus transitions
		  - Or a specified amount of time (short and successful initially)
		  - Transitions can include:
		    • Between activities (e.g., the peer moves from coloring at the table to reading a book in the library)
		    • Between emotions (e.g., the peer is initially excited about what is being colored but then becomes quiet and contemplative when reading)
		• As learner is successful, gradually increase the expected duration of engagement or the number of transitions described earlier. The learner becomes adept at discriminating between interaction topographies or matches. Further considerations include:
		  - Specific emotion congruence
		  - Range of emotion congruence
		  - Talking versus not talking
		  - Taking the opportunity to join in with others
		  - Activity congruence

Phase 4	Learner Learns to Suspend the Rules to Match the Mood	This phase concerns itself with doing what the peer group is doing, even if it breaks some usual rules. This should actually be encouraged to avoid becoming rule-bound and reduce any possible stigmatization from not being silly or over the top if that's what the peer group is doing.

Phase 4 (cont.)	Learner Learns to Suspend the Rules to Match the Mood	· Examples include:
		  - Everyone is talking when the interventionist leaves the room
		  - Everyone gets out of their seats and chats when the interventionist's back is turned
		  - Everyone gets "over the top" during an exciting activity, acting silly
		    · These last examples may require specific teaching focused on Emotional Regulation. The learner must be able to stop when everyone else does, reduce when everyone else does, and remain engaged with peers rather than disengaging, becoming self-involved, or preoccupied with self-stimulatory behavior.
		    · The learner should stay a little below the level of the peers to allow a margin of error, especially if the learner tends to underestimate how rowdy they are. The aim is to not be the loudest and not be the last one to stop. Avoid any lapse into potentially stigmatizing behavior.
		    · This may require specific practice in related skills such as observational awareness, self-monitoring, and timing from the learner. Practice should include taking the learner to the brink of overexcitement, allowing a small taste, and then regaining composure.

Phase 5	Teach Toward Greater Independence and Generalization	· Less structure, and more natural trials.
		· Fade priming:
		  - More subtle: "Remember what we're working on"
		  - Use of delayed priming: "Today's all about matching the mood throughout the session," then later in the session, present a transition opportunity (e.g., if you've been the model and talkative and happy, transition to a "calm time" trial, without warning, naturally and monitor response)
		· Longer duration trials.

Considerations		This program concerns itself with a learner assessing and responding to the variety of social opportunities presented in group situations. This can occur in school at any time as long as there is a group dynamic involved (e.g., in the classroom, on the playground, during instruction, during recess, within lunch and nutrition breaks). Teaching this skill set away from such a dynamic environment initially will help the learner better learn the information. It can then be applied in more natural situations. Techniques may include Discrete Trial Teaching, the Teaching Interaction Procedure, role-play, video modeling/assessment, or play dates (beginning with just one other peer).

Considerations (cont.)		• Practice self-monitoring and "bringing it down a notch" until it is muscle memory.
		• Motivate the learner by pointing out that not letting the fun get out of control means the fun activity can last longer.
		• Use priming systematically to promote success when the trials are challenging. Over time, fade the specificity and give the prompt further in advance.

		• Factors that may affect the difficulty level and therefore the likelihood of success:
		
		  - Higher preference for the activity = greater difficulty to match the mood
		
		  - The presenting level of excitement or prevalent mood
		
		  - Which peers are present and the emotions they evoke with the learner
		
		  - The level of structure versus the amount of downtime prior to teaching and practice sessions

Joking vs. Provocation

Overall Goal	To teach the difference between appropriate humor and being perceived as mean. To better understand the range of humor. To reduce unwanted attention from peers or correction from adults. To better understand ways to engage others. To capitalize on sense of humor without alienating others.
Example Objective	The learner will discriminate if an event was a joke or a provocation with 90% accuracy across five consecutive sessions.
Social Taxonomy Domain	Social Awareness
Teaching Methodologies	The Teaching Interaction Procedure and the Cool versus Not Cool™ procedure
Data Collection	Task Analysis or Estimation
Prerequisite Skills	Discrimination skills, Receptive Language, Expressive Language, General Knowledge and Reasoning, Advanced contingency understanding, Awareness of others' emotions and body language, Beginnings of empathy

Phases

Phase 1	Define Humor Versus Provocation	This phase teaches the learner to clearly understand what humor and provocation are, how they are similar, and how they are different.
		
		• Humor is defined as something that is designed to be comical or amusing, other people find funny, that causes people to laugh, etc.
		• Some types of humor:
		  - Self-deprecating humor:
		    • Doing/saying something about or to yourself to get a laugh
		  - Physical humor:
		    • "slapstick" humor, doing things to make others laugh
		  - Being able to tell a joke
		  - Shared humor:
		    • Retelling a funny experience to others that have an understanding of what you are talking about
		  - Practical jokes
		  - Sarcasm
		• Provocation is defined as to stir up on purpose, do something to get a response, cause embarrassment, cause a big reaction, or make someone uncomfortable.
		• Some types of provocation:

Phase 1 (cont.)	Define Humor Versus Provocation	- Verbal:
		  • Saying something you know will cause a reaction or bug someone
		- Physical:
		  • Pretending to choke someone, tripping someone, getting into someone's personal space, throwing things at someone, etc.
		- Gestural:
		  • Flipping someone off, blowing someone a kiss, etc.
		- Facial expressions/body language:
		  • Sticking your tongue out, getting too close to someone, getting in someone's face, staring at someone, etc.
		- Presenting or removing known triggers:
		  • Moving something out of its place, showing someone who hates spiders a fake spider, etc.

Phase 2	Discrimination Between Using Humor and Being Provocative	The learner will learn to discern what humor is during increasingly naturalistic teaching situations. Further, the learner will better understand what provocativeness looks like, sounds like, and the potential consequences for being provocative in different settings. Depending on the learner's skill level, appropriate teaching techniques may include Discrete Trial Teaching, The Teaching Interaction Procedure, role-plays, video observation, or naturalistic observation.
Phase 3	When to Use Different Forms of Humor	There are situations which call for certain types of humor. The learner will learn what types of humor are okay in different situations, why each is appropriate for the situation, and how to determine which form is appropriate for the situation. This can be taught using Discrimination Training in which the learner is presented with scenarios and will determine if the form of humor was appropriate for the situation.
Phase 4	When is Being Provocative Okay?	There are times when being provocative is okay, such as taunting the other team during a sporting event, or good-natured teasing between friends. The learner will learn what those situations are and what makes it ok during those times. This can be taught using Discrimination Training in which the learner is presented with scenarios and has to judge if being provocative is okay in that situation.
Phase 5	Option 3	Sometimes there is more to consider when deciding whether to use humor or be provocative. Sometimes it is best to simply stay quiet.

| Phase 6 | Option 4: Sarcasm as a Better Option to Provocativeness | In some situations, it is better to be sarcastic than provocative. The learner will learn what sarcasm is, what it looks and sounds like, and when it should be used through the following:

• Before doing the following scenarios, have a conversation with the learner about what sarcasm is:
  - Sarcasm can be: remarks that mean the opposite of what they seem to say and are intended to mock. In the extreme, it can be a bitter jibe.
  - Between good friends it can come off as a playful jab or joke. However, between strangers or acquaintances it can come off as mean or rude.
  - The problem with sarcasm is while the person using it may be trying to make a joke it can often come out as hurtful to the other person and be misinterpreted.
  - When you use sarcasm your tone of voice and facial expressions are different than when you tell a joke or are talking normally. When you are being sarcastic your inflection goes down, you keep a straight face, or your facial expression doesn't match your words. For example, if you are trying to joke around, you might smile while you are saying something that otherwise would be perceived as mean.
  - Examples include:
    • Seeing a peer in your math class got a D on his test and saying "Ooohh, good grade."
    • Someone has bad breath and you smell it, then say, "Someone needs to buy a toothbrush."
    • Someone says that they are ice skating in Mario versus Sonic Winter Olympic games, and you say, "Thanks for the info, Einstein." |
| Phase 7 | Generalization | Develop plans to expose the learner to more real-life situations requiring the ability to make a decision on whether to use humor, be provocative, or simply keep comments to themselves.

• Discuss scenarios during a Teaching Interaction Procedure.
• Develop role-plays focused on developing this processing skill.
• Arrange scenarios within more natural settings.
  - Prime in advance
  - Set up "check-in" times
  - Debrief with learner
  - Fade priming |

Achieving Your Desires

Overall Goal	Sometimes learners fail to recognize that there are reasons why their desires are not being met. Being able to evaluate the outcome of their actions and whether the choices they made promoted or interfered with achieving their desires will enable them to self-correct their social behavior.
Example Objective	The learner will independently and correctly identify the action of a central character and the reaction of others (i.e. cause and effect) in natural settings in 90% of opportunities across three consecutive sessions.
Social Taxonomy Domain	Social Awareness
Teaching Methodologies	The Teaching Interaction Procedure and the Cool versus Not Cool™ procedure
Data Collection	Estimation or Ratio
Prerequisite Skills	Expanded Expressive Language, Conversation Skills, Social Skills, Perspective Taking, Self-assessment, Familiarity with the Teaching Interaction Procedure

Phases

Phase 1	Identifying Desires of Others	· The learner identifies and discusses the apparent desires of others based on the choices they make. Use a variety of materials: - Watch movies and have the learner identify desires of the characters - Read books and have the learner identify desires of the characters - The interventionist narrates their own desires, so the learner can hear them
Phase 2	Identifying the Actions of Others	· The learner identifies and discusses the corresponding actions of others: - The interventionist can model behaviors the learner may have difficulty with
Phase 3	Identify the Reactions of Others	· The learner identifies and discusses the reactions of others (e.g., what others in a group do when the main character does a specific action).

Phase 4	Identifying Matching and Non-Matching Desires and Actions	• The learner identifies the apparent desires of others, the corresponding action(s), and whether the action(s) displayed by the actor helped support and achieve the hoped-for desire or if it got in the way. For example:
		
		  - Desire: Adam probably wants to keep playing with Mark
		  - Action: Adam is not answering Mark, but is making silly sounds
		  - Reaction: Mark goes to play with Kyle
		
		• If the person being observed did not engage in an action achieving the desire, the learner discusses what actions the person can take in the future to achieve the desire.

Phase 5	Practice Matching a Desire to an Action	• Set up situations and practice with the learner (e.g., playing a game, conversation) • Have the learner identify their desires (e.g., "I want to keep talking to Adam."). • Discuss actions helping the learner achieve their desire (e.g., answering Adam when he talks/asks questions). • Practice the situation. - Afterwards determine if the learner's actions corresponded with their desires. If so, reinforcement should be naturally occurring. If not, discuss what can be done differently and practice again
Steps Toward Generalization		• Fade supplemental reinforcers. • Fade use of priming (including specificity and timing). • Fade interventionist presence. • Practice with helpers/cohorts. • Move to more natural environments.

Appearance Checks

Overall Goal	Noticing and taking a measure of pride in appearance is one way to project the learner's "best self." In addition to confidence and a feeling of worth, appearance is part of a presentation package, what someone first notices when interacting with the learner. Depending on age, it is often how peers initially evaluate each other and make social decisions. This skill is best presented and taught using the Teaching Interaction Procedure. Participating in this teaching and then applying the skill appropriately enables the learner to access greater social opportunities and increases exposure to other potential reinforcers in the generalized environment.
Example Objective	The learner will accurately report on their grooming and overall appearance and, if necessary, make adjustments accordingly in 90% of opportunities.
Social Taxonomy Domain	Social Awareness and Social Interaction
Teaching Methodologies	The Teaching Interaction Procedure and the Cool versus Not Cool™ procedure
Data Collection	Task Analysis or Estimation
Prerequisite Skills	Discrimination, Receptive Language, Expressive Language, Self-monitoring, and Beginning Social Skills

Teaching Interaction Procedure Steps:

Overview		This program encompasses grooming, hygiene, style, and neatness. Be cognizant of how this information is presented; an underlying objective is to promote self-confidence and an individualized sense of style. Present opportunities to practice these concepts relevant to the learner: scenarios either from the learner's individual experience, or typical of the age and culture the learner is involved.
Identify/ Describe the Skill	Define the Behavior the Learner will Use in the Generalized Environment	• "Check yourself" means making sure you look your best for the situation: 　- Start at the top of the head and work your way down 　- Fix/adjust as the examination proceeds 　- End with a self-affirming statement (e.g., "Lookin' good," "Ready to rock")

Develop Rationale(s)		· Collaborate with the learner to generate rationales that are meaningful for them. Without personalized rationales that are also reflective of social expectations/norms, this teaching will not generalize. Here are some examples to get you started: - Checking yourself is a way to put your best out there - Taking pride in your appearance feels nice - Others will notice your appearance for the right reasons, not the wrong ones - Developing your own style allows you to find clothing and accessories you like and feel good wearing - Part of good health is good hygiene
Demonstrate Skill		· Describe/role-play a scenario that corresponds to the learner's everyday experience where their appearance would be especially important. (e.g., going on a date, giving a class presentation, meeting new people). · Demonstrate Cool and Not Cool examples of personal appearance. For Not Cool examples, have the learner identify what needs to be fixed.
Practice		· Have the learner practice doing the steps that are necessary to ensure a good appearance. This should include the things that need to be performed in advance (e.g., grooming at home in the morning) as well as things that need to be checked in the moment (e.g., "Are your pants hitched up?").
Feedback		· Objectively describe parts of the skill performed well (reinforcement) and also parts of the skill requiring more practice (corrective feedback). · Repeat role-plays as needed to provide the opportunity to incorporate suggestions and refine performance. · Provide supplemental reinforcement as needed for making improvement and for maintaining self-control during the Teaching Interaction Procedure. This can include token economies, bonus points, behavior contracts, or other reinforcement systems which provide access to preferred items, activities or privileges.
Steps Toward Generalization		· Practice with different instructors and peers. · Increase the variety of activities and levels of distraction. · Practice in a variety of environments/settings. · Fade interventionist presence. · In everyday situations that provide naturally occurring opportunities to show off your best appearance, provide formal and informal reinforcement as needed. To facilitate success, prime the learner in advance by providing reminders of the expected behavior and rationales. · Gradually fade tangible reinforcement and fade the use of priming (including specificity and timing).

Am I Splitting Hairs?

Overall Goal	Sometimes our learners lack the social understanding necessary to maintain balanced conversations. They can be literal, rigid, or "split hairs" when they correct others or make comments that could be interpreted as lacking respect, grace, and seem "know-it-all-ish." Reading social cues from others, refraining from off-putting comments and learning more polite ways to demonstrate knowledge, enables the learner to access greater social opportunities and increases exposure to other potential reinforcers in the more generalized environment.
Example Objective	The learner will refrain from critical comments and respond respectfully during naturally occurring conversations in 90% of opportunities.
Social Taxonomy Domain	Social Awareness, Social Relatedness, Social Communication, and Social Interaction
Teaching Methodologies	The Teaching Interaction Procedure and the Cool versus Not Cool™ procedure Data
Data Collection	Task Analysis or Estimation
Prerequisite Skills	Discrimination, Beginning Empathy, Expressive Language, and Beginning Social Skills, Think It vs. Say It, STAR

Teaching Interaction Procedure Steps

Identify/ Describe the Skill		• The skillset is the learner refraining from correcting inconsequential errors that others make (e.g., mislabeling something in casual conversation). • The learner should remain calm through the process/conversation.

Develop Rationale(s)		• Collaborate with the learner to generate rationales that are meaningful for them. Without personalized rationales that are also reflective of social expectations, this teaching will not generalize. Generic examples include (these need to be personalized):
		  - "Think it, don't say it" will keep you involved in conversations you really want to be a part of
		  - When you come across as polite and respectful, your friends will want to have more conversations with you
		  - When you learn to say things in a more respectful manner you can still say them, and the conversation will continue
		  - Sometimes it's better to let it go than "split hairs." It relieves you of stress and the responsibility of correcting others.

Demonstrate Skill		• Describe/role-play a scenario that corresponds to the learner's everyday experience where a person says something that is not correct:
		  - Provide examples that are clearly absurd (e.g., "the sun is blue today!")
		  - Provide examples that are incorrect (e.g., "San Francisco is the capital of California.")
		  - Provide examples that are incorrect specific to the learner (e.g., "Nice Vans [the learner is wearing Converse].")
		  - Provide examples that are incorrect about a highly preferred topic (e.g., "Harry Potter is a full-on Muggle.")
		• Demonstrate Cool and Not Cool examples of how to respond to incorrect remarks. For Not Cool examples, have the learner identify what needs to be fixed.

Practice Skill		• Have the learner practice disregarding the incorrect comment and carrying on with the activity or conversation.
Feedback		• Objectively describe parts of the skill performed well (reinforcement) and parts of the skill requiring more practice (corrective feedback). • Repeat role-plays as needed to provide the opportunity to incorporate suggestions and refine performance. • Provide supplemental reinforcement as needed for making improvement and for maintaining self-control during the Teaching Interaction Procedure. This can include token economies, bonus points, behavior contracts, or other reinforcement systems which provide access to preferred items, activities or privileges.

Steps Toward Generalization		· Practice with different instructors and peers.
		· Increase the variety of activities and levels of distraction.
		· Practice in a variety of environments/settings.
		· Fade interventionist presence.
		· In everyday situations that provide naturally occurring opportunities to refrain from splitting hairs, provide formal and informal reinforcement as needed. To facilitate success, prime the learner in advance by providing reminders of the expected behavior and rationales.
		· Gradually fade supplemental reinforcement and fade use of priming (including specificity and timing).

Being A Big Kid

Overall Goal	To have the learner engage in behaviors that are more age-typical. This is meant for older children who are displaying behaviors that would make them stand out as younger children.
Example Objective	During a 1-hour observation, the learner will display behaviors that make them look like a "fifth grader" in 90% of 1-minute intervals across three consecutive days
Social Taxonomy Domain	Social Awareness
Teaching Methodologies	The Teaching Interaction Procedure and the Cool versus Not Cool™ procedure
Data Collection	Ratio or Estimation

Phases

Overview		For each phase, introduce the target behavior, discuss the definition, and demonstrate examples and non-examples of "acting like a [grade level of learner]." If necessary, teach the discrimination with the Cool versus Not Cool™ procedure. Set up opportunities to practice the target behavior for a short period of time and then debrief. As the learner demonstrates consistent success, increase the duration of practice. Choose from phases below that are relevant for the learner and be sure to combine the behavioral expectation(s) from preceding phases and each new phase is mastered.
Phase 1	Talking Like a Big Kid	• Volume appropriate (e.g., based on environment, who she is talking to, activity). • Tone matches what is being said (e.g., serious). • Articulation is clear (e.g., no baby talk). • Proper syntax (e.g., no skipping words). • A "quiet mouth" (e.g., no tongue play).
Phase 2	Having a Strong Body	• Being in control of limbs, fingers, feet (e.g., not bumping into things). • Does not fidget excessively (be aware of age-typical norms!). • Standing tall. • Thumb where it belongs (i.e., not in mouth). • Keeping hands to self (e.g., not swiping surfaces, not picking up merchandise).

| Phase 3 | Being a Good Listener | • Age-typical attentiveness to adults, interventionists, peers, classmates, etc.
• Following directions like classmates (e.g., individual, choral, overlapping instructions).
• If distracted, reorients in an age-typical time frame.
• If inattentive, identifies why (e.g., "I was distracted," "I wasn't listening," "can you tell me again?").
• Antonym(s) for Cool versus Not Cool discrimination (e.g., "Oops, missed it!"). |
| Phase 4 | Willing to Give it a Go | • Tries new or challenging things.
• Attempts to respond, doesn't give up.
• Being brave.
• Risking.
• Showing effort and grit. |

Keeping A Positive Outlook

Overall Goal	Reduce negative assumptions. Increase flexible thinking. Expand possible explanations and alternatives. Increase thoughtful consideration of situations before reacting.
Example Objective	The learner will develop multiple ideas to deal with a novel situation with 90% accuracy across five consecutive sessions.
Social Taxonomy Domain	Social Awareness
Teaching Methodologies	The Teaching Interaction Procedure
Data Collection	Ratio or Estimation
Prerequisite Skills	Personal strengths (things you are good at) versus personal weaknesses (things you want to be better at)
Related Programs	Exploring/Understanding Emotional Triggers/Antecedents, Frustration Tolerance/Stress Hierarchy Development, Stress Management Procedures, Empathy, Self-evaluation

Phases

Phase 1	Increased Understanding of the Different Possibilities the Learner Should Consider Before Responding	• The Interventionist and learner should create a "bank" of examples/scenarios together to better practice the skills associated with assessing situations. Examples may include:
		  - Situations related to the learner's experiences, exemplars of similar situations, situations the interventionist has experienced, video/movie/television show examples, examples from books/stories/magazine articles, situations occurring in the moment
		• Prime: let the learner know you will be working on areas requiring practice, subject matter considered a personal "weakness."
		  - Discuss a situation in which the learner has assumed the worst and not considered alternative possibilities
		  - Teach the learner to expand on alternative possibilities
		  - The interventionist should have one or two already in mind to begin the conversation and guide it in the desired direction
		  - Work toward the learner providing one or two as well
		• Have the learner consider the alternatives to the initial assumption. Pair positive possibilities with associated emotions.

Phase 1 (cont.)	Increased Understanding of the Different Possibilities the Learner Should Consider Before Responding	- Teach the learner to look more fully at possibilities and not jump to negative thinking or assumptions. For example, the learner opens the door and walks into a lobby/waiting room. Those already there look up or stare. The learner assumes the worst, that judgement is occurring. Other possibilities include: • That's what typically happens in waiting rooms • Those already there may be looking up to decide how to greet you or whether to do so • They may be looking up because you are tall, or what you are wearing catches their eye • They may be looking forward to speaking with you • They may be looking up because they are expecting someone - There may be possibilities that truly are negative, but other possibilities should be explored so the learner has the opportunity to respond in a variety of ways
Phase 2	Practicing Responding Based on a Range of Possibilities	• Select a scenario previously discussed. The learner will practice considering alternatives, and then responding based on those alternatives. With the lobby/waiting room example, rather than glower and feel down, the learner responds based on one of the alternatives, such as, "They may be looking up to decide how to greet you..." - The learner discusses ways to respond based on that possibility • I can smile • I can look down and find an empty chair • I can look at them and say, "hello" • Repeat this process for other scenarios. • Debrief afterwards to better develop the contingency between the learner's response and the resulting emotion.
Phase 3	Learner Practices in More Natural Situations/ Environments	• The learner learns to recognize triggers/antecedents as they occur and verbalizes this to the interventionist. • As the learner develops a stronger sense of triggers/antecedents, therapy focuses on considering alternatives versus thinking negatively. • Learner learns to respond based on possibilities associated with more positive thinking and emotion. • Learner learns to take more control over how they respond to situations and, thus, control over the emotions felt.

Phase 4	Considerations for Generalization	• Fade priming and other artificial props associated with the teaching.
		• Fade interventionist feedback and reinforcement. Move toward a more naturally occurring reinforcement to practice the skills taught.
		• Move toward more natural environments with a variety of people.

Social Awareness Of The Group

Overall Goal	The learner will accurately read the social interactions, social cues, and the overall mood of a group of peers and match the group in order to join in appropriately.
Example Objective	The learner will display 100% of the steps of a task analysis for social awareness for five consecutive days.
Social Taxonomy Domain	Social Awareness and Social Relatedness
Teaching Methodologies	Role-plays, the Cool versus Not Cool™ procedure, Discrete Trial Teaching, and the Teaching Interaction Procedure.
Data Collection	Task Analysis or Estimation
Prerequisite Skills	Reading Social Cues, Matching the Mood, Joining in Appropriately, Play Skills, Conversation Skills, Observational Learning

Phases

Phase 1	Observing a Group	• Together with the learner, observe a group and have the learner identify all of the following dimensions of the group:
		  - What is the group doing (e.g., What game are they playing, What is the conversation about)?
		  - What is the mood of the group (e.g., excited, angry)?
		  - What role are others playing in the group (e.g., Is one person leading the group, Are all members joining in equally)?
		  - Should I join the group (e.g., Will I be successful, Are the peers welcoming, Do I know what's happening)?

Phase 2	Planning to Join in	• After the learner accurately evaluates the dimensions of the group, plan together how the learner will join in appropriately. You should plan for the following dimensions:
		  - What (if anything) should I say and to whom should I address my statement or question?
		  - What should I do (i.e., physically)?
		  - Where should I stand or sit?
		  - What mood should I have?
		• If appropriate or necessary, role-play joining in prior to the learner joining into the group.
		• As the learner gets better at planning with the interventionist the learner should take on the role of planning until this can be done independently.

Phase 3	Joining in	• Have the learner join into the group. • If the group is comprised of interventionists role-playing as peers, the interventionists should act as closely to peers as possible.

Phase 3 (cont.)	Joining in	- The interventionists should use the naturally occurring contingencies and reinforcers (e.g., keeping the game going or ending it, being responsive or unresponsive) based on the learner's behaviors

Phase 4	Assessment	· Either during (by pausing the role-play or pulling the learner from the group if appropriate) or after the social interaction, assess with the learner how the group social interaction went by discussing the following dimensions:
		  - Did the learner follow the plan?
		  - How did the group react?
		  - What did the learner do well?
		  - What should the learner have done differently?
		  - Was it reinforcing to the learner?
		· If the learner was unsuccessful have the learner plan again, factoring in the feedback they received from the previous attempt and join in the group again.
		· Follow up with another assessment after the second attempt.

Generalization		· Have the learner plan independently. · Fade planning out loud and have it become an internal process. · Practice in more natural settings. · Practice with peers. · Fade pre-teaching/priming. · Fade supplemental reinforcers.

Recognizing Your Triggers

Overall Goal	Helping a learner better understand the antecedents leading to inappropriate behaviors allows them greater independence, behavioral control, and control over the varied environments in which they may find themselves. This skill then affords the learner opportunities in the more naturalized setting and more access to potential social growth and reinforcement.
Example Objective	The learner will recognize/label known "triggers" prior to reacting and will then demonstrate emotional responding commensurate with age in 80% of opportunities.
Social Taxonomy Domain	Social Awareness and Social Interaction
Teaching Methodologies	The Teaching Interaction Procedure and the Cool versus Not Cool™ procedure
Data Collection	Task Analysis or Estimation
Prerequisite Skills	Discrimination, Frustration Tolerance, Stress Management, Beginning Social Skills, and Emotions

Teaching Interaction Procedure Steps

Identify/ Describe the Skill	Define the Behavior the Learner will use in the Generalized Environment	In this program the learner will learn to recognize "triggers" and respond appropriately when triggers arise.
		
		 • "Trigger" is defined as the following:
		   - Something you see/hear/feel/think that makes you want to do something
		   - A trigger typically results in a variety of behaviors individual to the learner, but may include checking out, wanting to hit something/someone, screaming, running away, etc.
		 • In collaboration with the learner, develop a trigger list of common antecedents that lead to undesired behavior.
		 • For each trigger help them identify appropriate alternative responses.
		 • "Handling it well" is defined as:
		   - Recognizing a trigger
		   - Remaining calm
		   - Remembering and using learned coping strategies

Develop Rationale(s)	The Learner Participates in Developing Meaningful, Personalized Rationales for Participating in the Teaching Interaction Procedure and Using the Skill in Everyday Life	• Developing individualized rationales for and with the learner that are also reflective of social expectations/norms is essential for this skill to generalize. Typical examples may include: - Recognizing triggers enables you to have more control over your environment - Reacting to triggers in a more socially acceptable manner allows you to maintain dignity - Others will be less likely to shy away or avoid you in specific situations - This is an effective way to take care of yourself and still have access to the things you like
Demonstrate Skill		• Role-play entering situations that correspond to the learner's everyday experience and include various triggers that have been identified. • Demonstrate examples and non-examples of identifying the trigger as soon as it is encountered. After each demonstration have the learner identify whether the actor correctly identified a trigger.
Practice Skill		• Using situations from the previous step, have the learner practice making an appropriate alternative response (e.g., distancing themselves from trigger and remaining calm).
Feedback		• Objectively describe parts of the skill performed well (reinforcement) and also parts of the skill requiring more practice (corrective feedback). • Repeat role-plays as needed to provide the opportunity to incorporate suggestions and refine performance. • Provide supplemental reinforcement as needed for making improvement and for maintaining self-control during the Teaching Interaction Procedure. This can include token economies, bonus points, behavior contracts, or other reinforcement systems which provide access to preferred items, activities or privileges.
Steps Toward Generalization		• Practice with different interventionists and peers. • Increase the variety of activities and levels of distraction. • Practice in a variety of environments/settings. • Fade interventionist presence. • In everyday situations that provide naturally occurring opportunities to recognize your triggers, provide reinforcement as needed. To facilitate success, prime the learner in advance by providing reminders of the expected behavior and rationales. • Gradually fade supplemental reinforcement and fade use of priming (including specificity and timing).

Excitement Tolerance: The Right Amount Of Silly

Overall Goal	The learner will actively monitor the way they express enjoyment and stay within an acceptable range of silliness given the situation.
Example Objective	The learner will accurately label what level of excitement that they are displaying with 90% accuracy across three consecutive sessions.
Social Taxonomy Domain	Social Awareness and Social Interaction
Teaching Methodologies	The Cool versus Not Cool™ procedure, the Teaching Interaction Procedure, and Discrete Trial Teaching
Data Collection	Ratio, Trial by Trial, or Task Analysis

Phases

Phase 1	Labeling Levels of Silly Behavior	<ul><li>Create a scale of Silly Behaviors:<ul><li>Too Silly/Over the Top – Out of control silly behavior</li><li>Silly – Having a lot of fun, but not over the top. Could become inappropriate if it continues for too long</li><li>A Little Silly – A moderate level of silly behavior that is easy to turn off</li><li>Calm – Baseline state of behavior</li></ul></li><li>Label the types of behaviors for the individual learner that show you and them where they fall on the scale (e.g., when you are too silly you repeat words over and over again, when you are a little silly you giggle a lot).<ul><li>Keep this list so that the learner can reference it later and make adjustments as necessary</li></ul></li><li>Label the antecedents (e.g., seeing someone fall down) that made the learner reach a new level on the continuum.</li><li>Label the locations where it is or is not appropriate to be at which level (e.g., it is never okay to be over the top, you can be silly with friends but rarely at the dinner table).</li></ul>
Phase 2	Discrimination Training	<ul><li>Using demonstrations (e.g., in-vivo, video clips) display silly behavior and have the learner determine where on the scale the actor's behavior falls.</li><li>Have the learner label how they knew (e.g., what behaviors made it that level).</li><li>Identify examples of other places where it would be appropriate and examples of places where it would not be appropriate to be at that level.</li></ul>

Phase 3	Self-Assessment	• Setup situations (or use naturally occurring opportunities) where you can get the learner to each level of silly behavior. • Have the learner self-assess where they fall on the scale, how they knew that's where they were on the scale, and what antecedent made them get there. • Reinforce accuracy of their assessment.
Phase 4	Teach a Replacement Behavior	• Determine a replacement behavior for the learner to engage in when they get to a level of silliness that is inappropriate. - Examples include: deep breath, excuse yourself from the area, change the topic of conversation, ask the other person to stop, squeeze your hands, etc.
Phase 5	Practicing Antecedents	• Using priming, set up clear situations (e.g., pretend we are at a restaurant) and antecedents for the learner to practice getting a little silly without getting too silly/over the top. Prompt the learner as necessary to use the replacement behavior. • Reinforce engaging in the replacement behavior(s) and remaining on the appropriate level of silly behavior. • Continue to increase the level of antecedent and decrease the level of priming to promote generalization.
Phase 6	Reactive Plan	• Create an effective reactive plan for what to do when the learner displays an inappropriate level of silly behavior. Use naturally occurring consequences (e.g., peers withdraw) and point out to the learner what the behavior cost them. Look for ways to mitigate problematic sources of reinforcement.

Say It Or Keep It To Yourself?

Overall Goal	Teach the discrimination between comments that are appropriate to say out loud versus those that should be kept private. Increase the understanding of specific social rules around what to say versus what not to say. Teach that it is okay to notice and think something, but learn when to say something versus not. Teach the discrimination(s) between different types of social appearances (e.g., a person's looks, hair styles, styles of dress, race, apparent disabilities, sexuality). Increase social awareness and grace.
Example Objective	The learner will make less than 10 inappropriate statements in a day for 10 consecutive days.
Social Taxonomy Domain	Social Awareness, Social Communication, and Social Interaction
Teaching Methodologies	The Teaching Interaction Procedure, the Cool versus Not Cool™ procedure, and Discrete Trial Teaching
Data Collection	Task Analysis or Estimation

Phases

Phase 1	Consider the Audience	When you notice things about a person:
		• It is ok to share your observation or ask a question with:
		  - Family members
		  - Trusted adults (e.g., interventionist)
		• You should keep your thoughts to yourself with:
		  - Strangers
		  - Peers

Phase 2	Take Note of Situations Out of the Ordinary	• Someone's physical appearance:
		  - Gender
		  - Race/ethnicity
		  - Height
		  - Weight
		  - Hair color
		  - Injury, deformity, etc.
		• Someone's clothing/dress/style.
		• Someone's behavior:
		  - Overt displays of togetherness/affection
		  - What they are eating
		  - Things they do differently than you would

Phase 3	Thoughts/ Comments to Say Versus Keep to Self for Each Category	<ul><li>Teach the difference between a thought and a comment:<ul><li>Thought:<ul><li>something private, something you think, something you initially keep to yourself</li></ul></li><li>Comment:<ul><li>a thought you say out loud, something you think that you express, something you say that others can hear</li></ul></li></ul></li><li>Teach the discrimination of what it looks like to comment versus simply have a thought.<ul><li>Show a picture, tell learner to say something (comment) versus think something. The learner should either speak or keep the thought private</li><li>After the discrimination, the learner can share the thought the picture evoked</li></ul></li><li>Teach the concept: you can think anything, but you should not say everything.</li></ul>
Phase 4	Okay to Say Versus Keep it to Yourself	<ul><li>Teach the differences between neutral comments, compliments, and rude comments:<ul><li>Neutral comments:<ul><li>Comments that have no opinion or social value, simply describing or descriptive things to say</li></ul></li><li>Compliments:<ul><li>Comments with a positive tone and social value, comments meant to make someone feel good, comments meant to show someone you notice, approve or like what you see</li><li>Synonyms:<ul><li>o Respectful, nice, friendly, etc.</li></ul></li></ul></li><li>Rude comments:<ul><li>Comments with a negative tone, derogatory comments; comments making someone feel judged, sad, or upset. It does not matter whether these comments were meant for that purpose or not. It is something said can be interpreted as rude</li><li>Synonyms:<ul><li>o disrespectful, mean, awful, judgmental, etc.</li></ul></li></ul></li></ul></li></ul>
Phase 5	The Learner Learns to Evaluate a Situation and Applies Previous Knowledge	<ul><li>Materials to use may include:<ul><li>Photos, videos, commercials, books, etc.</li></ul></li><li>Teaching techniques may include:<ul><li>Role-play, the Cool versus Not Cool™ procedure, the Teaching Interaction Procedure, Discrete Trial Teaching</li></ul></li><li>Within-program curriculum may include:</li></ul>

Phase 5 (cont.)	The Learner Learns to Evaluate a Situation and Applies Previous Knowledge	- Receptive Labeling - Matching - Sorting/Categories - Discrimination Training - Expressive Labeling - Expanded Language

Phase 6	Variety of Expressions	Teach a variety of appropriate comments to say based on the situation. For example:
		
		· The learner is shown a picture depicting a child having fallen off a bike
		  - Comments might include: "Ouch! Are you okay?" "Can I help you?" "Let's look at how you are" "That was a big spill!" "Shake it off, let's try again" etc.
		· The learner sees a peer with his zipper down
		  - Comments might include: "Hey, your zipper is down" "Oops, check your zipper" "Fly's unzipped" paired with a quieter tone, not drawing attention from others, etc.
		  - The learner wants to compliment someone's new sneakers: "Nice kicks!" "Hey, cool shoes:" "Ooh, those look good!" etc.
		· Teach synonymous phrases to be used based on each situation, increase fluency and variety.

Considerations		· Expose the learner to a wide variety of situations evoking the discrimination. · Be sure the situations are age-typical. · Expose the learner to more natural environments. · Reduce the structure of the teaching as the learner demonstrates the skill. · The learner uses this skill with other adults. · The learner uses this skill with peers, classmates, and friends.

Offering Help To Others

Overall Goal	This program teaches the learner to recognize when someone else may require assistance, and then offer it. Ultimately, this will enhance the learner's quality of social interaction and relatedness, and increases skills like environmental awareness, empathy, and self-assessment (e.g., what am I good at, how can I offer help).
Example Objective	When presented an opportunity to help a peer (e.g., with a task, with a problem), the learner will offer assistance and provide commensurate help based on the peer's response (e.g., determine what to do when the peer responds "yes" versus "no") in 80% of opportunities.
Social Taxonomy Domain	Social Awareness, Social Interaction, and Social Communication
Teaching Methodologies	Discrete Trial Teaching, the Teaching Interaction Procedure, Role-Play, In-vivo Demonstration, and Modeling
Data Collection	Task Analysis, Trial by Trial, or Estimation
Prerequisite Skills	Comprehension, Receptive Language, Expressive Language, Expanded Language, Communication Temptations, Beginning Empathy, Beginning Social Skills

Phases

Phase 1	Teaching the Response	• <u>Task analysis of skill</u> (individualization should be considered based on the learner age, needs and skill set):
		  - The learner observes and determines whether assistance is required (discrimination training)
		  - The learner determines whether they can assist, or if another person may be required
		  - If assistance is required and the learner can help, the learner stops what they are doing
		  - The learner approaches individual requiring help
		  - The learner gets the individual's attention appropriately
		  - The learner asks, "Can I help you?" (or some equivalent phrase, such as, "do you need help?" "how can I help?" etc.)
		  - The learner assesses the individual's response and proceeds accordingly:
		    • If "yes," the learner assists
		    • If "no," learner says "Okay," and moves away

Phase 2	Recognizing Situations Requiring Assistance	• Teach the learner to discriminate whether a situation requires assistance or not.
		• Create scenarios to develop this discrimination. Examples may include:
		  – Seeing someone struggle with carrying objects (e.g., too many for one trip, too heavy to do alone, too awkward to do alone)
		  – Someone appears lost (e.g., can't find a location, needs help navigating an environment)
		  – Someone cannot find something (e.g., misplaced item, not sure where items are kept, not sure where to look)
		  – Someone struggling with a task (e.g., can't figure out a problem, requires help with a Lego construction, can't read or make sense of instructions)
		  – Someone is hurt
		  – Someone is in emotional need

Phase 3	Based on the Scenario, the Learner Learns What Kind of Help Will Solve the Problem, and Whether They are Capable of Assisting	• Based on the scenarios, the learner learns what support will solve the problem.
		• This requires further discrimination. Considerations include:
		  – Do I have the time to help?
		  – Am I capable?
		  – Is there someone that is better at helping in this case that I can find?
		  – Is this a case where offering support is better than not, even if the problem does not get solved?
		  – If I try to help and it does not work, do I know what the next steps are?

Steps Toward Generalization		• Fade supplemental reinforcers. • Fade use of priming (including specificity and timing). • Fade interventionist presence. • Practice with helpers/cohorts. • Increase the variety of activities and levels of distraction. • Move to more natural environments.

Responding To Bullies

Overall Goal	The learner will recognize, avoid, and act appropriately when they have been bullied.
Example Objective	When faced with a person who is bullying, the learner will appropriately leave the situation in 100% of opportunities across seven consecutive days.
Social Taxonomy Domain	Social Awareness, Social Relatedness, and Social Interaction
Teaching Methodologies	The Teaching Interaction Procedure and the Cool versus Not Cool™ procedure
Data Collection	Trial by Trial, Task Analysis, or Estimation

Phases

Phase 1	Exposure	• While watching age-appropriate videos (e.g., cartoons, kids shows) where bullying takes place, point out times where bullying occurs in a natural way (e.g., "Roger doesn't seem like a nice kid.").
		• After the learner has been exposed to videos where bullying is portrayed, start to label the behavior as bullying.
Phase 2	Discrimination	• While watching age-appropriate videos have the learner identify when bullying is occurring.
		• More difficult discriminations will be when somebody is teasing in a friendly manner versus when someone is being bullied.
		• As the learner is successfully discriminating bullying in videos, move toward having the learner discriminate in-vivo with and without the learner being part of the in-vivo role-play.
Phase 3	Perspective Taking	• While watching age-appropriate videos pause the videos and ask the learner perspective taking questions (e.g., "How do you think he is feeling?") about the person who is being bullied, the bully, and the other people in the scene.
		• As the learner is successful in accurately identifying the perspectives of others in videos, move towards having the learner identifying the perspectives of others in-vivo.
Phase 4	Recognizing Causes	• While watching age-appropriate videos have the learner identify the reason (if any) the bullying occurred.
		• As the learner is successful in accurately recognizing the causes (if any) of bullying in videos have them identify the causes of bullying in-vivo.

Phase 4 (cont.)	Recognizing Causes	- Causes to expose the learner to may include: saying inappropriate things, doing odd/silly things, one-upping others, joining an inappropriate peer group, joining into play/ conversation incorrectly - Later these causes can help to build rationales for the learner for not engaging in those behaviors
Phase 5	Response to Bullying	• While watching age-appropriate videos have the learner identify the responses to being bullied and how it affected the outcomes (e.g., did the bullying continue, get worse). • As the learner is successful in accurately recognizing responses and their effects of responding to a bully in videos have them identify the responses and their effects in-vivo.
Phase 6	Role-Play	• The learner will participate in role-plays where they are being bullied, and where they are being teased in a friendly manner. • Begin with frequent pauses within the role-play to allow the learner to evaluate their behavior as they are occurring (similar to Stop-Think-Act). As the learner is successful, pause less often, until a whole role-play can be done without the need to stop. • Debrief with the learner following the role-play on how their behavior affected the bullying, what they could do to avoid future bullying, how they felt, and how they reacted.
Phase 7	Avoiding Being Bullied	Come up with strategies with the learner on how to avoid being bullied. Examples may include: not engaging in inappropriate behaviors that make the learner stand out and become an easy target for bullying, coming up with a list of peers to avoid, etc.
Phase 8	Debriefing	• As situations in the learner's life occur where they are being bullied, discuss with the learner what happened, and go through Phases 2–6 (as necessary to the situation) to help the learner see why the bullying may have occurred. • As appropriate, add to the list of behaviors the learner needs to avoid to stop being the target of bullying, and add to the list of unapproachable friends.
Considerations		• This is a sensitive subject and needs to be done in a sensitive manner. Be careful about who is present while working on this program. Do not push the learner too much in the discussions of their own experiences and include role-plays that reflect behaviors they do not engage in, so as not to over-personalize. • Discrimination between bullying and friendly teasing is critical. Some peers often tease each other in a friendly manner, which can be misinterpreted as bullying if the discrimination is not clear enough. • Phases can be worked on concurrently.

Considerations (cont.)		· Role-plays should be done in a variety of environments to help with generalization. · If the learner tends to act impulsively when working on role-plays, make sure the learner is taking time to think about their behaviors and reactions.

Chapter Twenty-Three
Social Relatedness Skills

Jeremy A. Leaf, Jonathan Rafuse & Justin B. Leaf

Social Relatedness encompasses how well the learner connects with their peers. These social behaviors dive deeper than basic social skills and work toward authentic and meaningful relationship and friendships. Within this domain there are basic social interaction skills, intermediate social interaction skills, and advanced social interaction sills. In this chapter, we provide 11 social behaviors that fall under the Social Relatedness Domain.

Basic Social Skills	Intermediate Social Skills	Advanced Social Skills
Peer Social Interest and Engagement	I Like You, But I Just Can't Smile	Feel the Feeling
Empathy: Responding to The Emotional States of Others	Don't Be Silly: Making "Cool Kid" Choices	Living in the Gray
	Friend Fluency	What Would Superman Do?
		Reputation Building
		Perspective Taking
		Goal Setting and Self-Management

Peer Social Interest And Engagement

Overall Goal	Increase environmental awareness. Increase attention to others. Increase the reinforcing value of peer interactions. Increase interest in and desire to be around peers. Increase overall social motivation. Enhance quality of peer interactions. • Develop prerequisites for group peer experiences. • Build requisites for relationship development.
Example Objective	During a 30-minute observation, the learner will appropriately engage with peers in 90% of intervals for 5 consecutive days.
Social Taxonomy Domain	Social Relatedness, Social Interaction, and Social Awareness
Teaching Methodologies	Shaping
Data Collection	Time Sampling, Trial by Trial, Estimation
Prerequisite Skills	Social Tolerance, Basic Environmental Awareness, Basic Peer Awareness, Basic and Intermediate Observational Awareness, Observational Learning Skills

Phases

Phase 1	Arrange Situations and Activities Enhancing Interest and Reinforcement Value of Specific Peers	Situations could include: • A peer selects or plays with preferred object or toy. • A peer has, hides, or finds needed item (e.g. straw for juice box). • A peer provides access to reinforcement (i.e., end of trial reinforcement). • A peer provides the necessary prompts. • A peer serves as observational model (e.g., shows a novel way to use a toy, provides non-vocal observational prompt). • A peer engages in an extended novel activity. • A peer builds anticipation for an activity or outcome (e.g., excitedly saying, "This is going to be great!," "I can't wait for recess!"). • Competitive or cooperative activities with a peer that evoke excitement (e.g., winning a three-legged race). • The peer participation enhances play activity (e.g., the peer can help merry-go-round spin faster, plays hide and seek with the learner). • Activities are selected requiring two people to fully enjoy; thus, the learner must engage with a peer to participate. • Several highly preferred activities are kept off-limits unless the learner has a peer to play with (e.g. watching a specific video, making cookies, throwing water balloons).

Phase 1 (cont.)	Arrange Situations and Activities Enhancing Interest and Reinforcement Value of Specific Peers	Each situation provides opportunities for increasing the reinforcing value of peers and sets the occasion for the reinforcement of socially engaged behavior. Although the situations often involve naturally occurring reinforcement, for some learners, providing supplemental reinforcement may be necessary. The idea is to not only create opportunities, but to reinforce the engaged and interested responses the opportunities create.
		• Instances of engaged and interested learner behavior in response to peers warranting reinforcement include, but are not limited to:
		  – Extended tracking
		  – Approach
		  – Anticipatory response
		  – Attention and contact seeking
		  – Extended proximity or interaction
		  – Joint attention
		  – Preference

Phase 2	Increase Quality (Including the Affective Component) of Engagement and Interest During Peer Interaction	Increased degrees of social engagement are differentially reinforced with feedback and higher value reinforcers as appropriate. As in Phase 1, situations and activities increasing the opportunity for more engaged interaction are carefully planned. Over time, efforts should move from supplemental to naturally occurring reinforcers, and from work in contrived to more naturalistic and ultimately to naturally occurring situations. Examples of enhanced levels of social engagement with peers include, but are not limited to: • More enthusiastic participation in activities. • More consistent social referencing (i.e., joint attention). • More consistent and increased breadth in imitation of peer or reciprocity toward peers. • Amplified competitive drive. • Displays of enhanced anticipation. • Excitement with the appearance of a peer. • Responses which indicate disappointment with the absence of a peer. • Active and preferential selection of, or request for, peers. • Approval seeking. • Disapproval avoidance.
Phase 3	In This Phase Work Moves from Developing Interest in Specific Peers to Groups of Peers	The goal is to promote greater interest and engaged participation in group social experiences. As with Phases 1 and 2, efforts are initially directed at developing the reinforcing value of group experiences and creating opportunities for interested and engaged responding during carefully planned activities. Pre-teach any unfamiliar

Phase 3 (cont.)	In This Phase Work Moves from Developing Interest in Specific Peers to Groups of Peers	activities to the learner individually before exposure in the group. Set-up situations could include: • The group is involved in activities of high value to the learner. • The group is engaged in novel, eye catching, or mysterious activities. • The group is involved in high energy and exciting interactive, cooperative, or competitive activity (e.g. relay race). As with earlier phases, efforts are directed at reinforcing the interest and engaged participation such as: • Tracking of group activity. • Curiosity about group goings-on. • Gravitation toward group. • Engaged participation in group. Finally, as in Phase 2, reinforcement fades to naturally occurring (ideally social) consequences and effort is moved from contrived situations to naturally occurring opportunities to engage with a group of peers.

Empathy: Responding To The Emotional State Of Others

Overall Goal	To increase the quality of social relationships. To teach the learner to share emotional experiences with others. To teach the learner to respond to the emotional needs of others. To increase social awareness and sensitivity. This program can be run individually or in a small group. Small groups allow for opportunities for immediate practice with peers.
Example Objective	When someone else is in distress, the learner will display empathy by engaging in 100% of a task analysis for five consecutive days.
Social Taxonomy Domain	Social Relatedness
Teaching Methodologies	The Teaching Interaction Procedure
Data Collection	Task Analysis or Estimation
Prerequisite Skills	The learner recognizes a variety of emotional states in self and others, Cause & Effect Inferencing, Understanding the contingency of "why – because"

Phases

Phase 1	Situations that Create Emotional Arousal and Why	• The learner learns to identify situations likely to create emotional arousal, the likely emotional state, and why. Examples may include:
		  - "The boy will be happy because his team is going to win."
		  - "She's going to be upset because she fell off her bike."
		  - "He may become jealous because his classmate won a prize."
		• Strategies may include:
		  - Watching a video of familiar individuals or scenes from movies
		  - Role-playing
		  - Observing real-life events
		  - Looking at picture sequences

Phase 2	Responding to Emotional Situations	• Considerations may include:
		  - Whether an immediate response is appropriate or possible; if not, learner further determines when is the best time to respond.
		  - The learner should identify multiple responses, taking into consideration what they can do to make the other person feel better, how they can demonstrate a shared understanding, or show support (e.g., "That's happened to me," giving a smile or comforting gesture, asking the person, "What can I do to help?").
		• Discuss gender differences, age appropriateness, "saving face" concerns, issues of privacy, and timing may be helpful during this phase. Examples may include:
		  - What should you do if you see a classmate fall down?
		    • Learner responses: "Ask if he's ok," "go get an adult."

Phase 2 (cont.)	Responding to Emotional Situations	- What happens if your brother can't find his homework and seems worried about it?
		  • Learner responses: "Can I help you look for it?" "Let's retrace your steps."
		- What about if your friend won a game?
		  • Learner responses: "Give him a hi-five;" "Say, congratulations!"
		- Your buddy gets scolded by the teacher.
		  • Learner response: "Check in with him after class."
		• Strategies may include:
		- Discussion
		- Watch video clips and evaluate whether a response was socially appropriate or not. If not appropriate, the learner should describe an alternative response. If appropriate, the learner could describe additional appropriate responses.

Phase 3	Role-Play Emotion-Evoking Scenarios	• Role-play scenarios the learner typically encounters during the day, such as sibling issues, having to stop to check-in with an interventionist during a highly preferred activity, or when something expected does not occur. Switching roles during these scenarios can enhance the experience of giving and receiving social support and understanding. • Sometimes an appropriate response to an emotional situation will result in an inappropriate response from the recipient. It may be helpful to address these types of situations with more advanced learners at this time. For example, someone might not be receptive to you asking them if they are ok when they are feeling very embarrassed.
Phase 4	Practice in Staged Situations	• Present the learner with situations throughout the instructional session requiring a response to another's emotional state. The learner should stop whatever they are doing, orient, and identify what situation has occurred. Examples my include: - The interventionist pretends to slip down a few steps on the stairs and drops their books - After working on a building project, someone comes over and crushes the person's structure - After trying and trying to figure something out a classmate becomes frustrated, pushes their seat back and says they needs a break from the project
Phase 5	Learner Engages in an Appropriate Response when Situations Occur Throughout the Instructional Day	• Prime the learner as needed so that whenever a situation comes up in everyday life where another person displays an emotional state the learner will make an appropriate empathic response. • As noted previously, situations do not always warrant a specific response from the learner, but they should be aware of the event. Be sure to acknowledge such instances of refraining from inappropriate responses (e.g., laughing at the person, lengthy staring at someone who is upset, talking to someone who wants to be left alone).

I Like You, But I Just Can't Smile

Game Instructions	1. The "king/queen" sits on a "throne" (could be the interventionist's chair for fun).
	 2. All the other learners stand in a line, facing the king/queen.
	 3. The first learner in line has 5 seconds to make a face, say a joke, anything to make the king/queen smile.
	 4. The king/queen will attempt to not smile. They must then say (with an attempted straight face), "I like you, but I just can't smile."
	
	     a. If the king/queen does not smile, the first learner goes to the back of the line, and the next learner takes their turn.
	
	     b. If the king/queen smiles at any point, even during their given phrase, the learner who induced the smiling becomes the new king/queen.

Purpose of Teaching Social Skill	Practice a variety of skills incorporated into a play-based setting.
Example Objective	When given a social cue from a peer, the learner will respond appropriately in 80% of opportunities.
Social Taxonomy Domain	Social Relatedness and Social Interaction
Skills that can be Targeted	Initiating with peers, responding to peers, shared excitement, over the top, positive affect, responding based on social cues, emotions, matching the mood, problem solving, observational learning, waiting, standing in a line
Materials Needed	· Throne (any chair will do).
Teaching Methodologies	Combination of: · The Cool versus Not Cool™ procedure · Discrete Trial Teaching · Shaping
Considerations	Waiting in line may need to be targeted to ensure the game runs smoothly. You should not choose a learner as the king/queen if they have low affect as this could inadvertently reinforce their low affect.
Data Collection	Estimation or Trial by trial

Don't Be Silly: Making "Cool Kid" Choices

Overall Goal	The learner will learn to interact with others in a socially typical manner and refrain from engaging in behaviors deemed socially inappropriate. These behaviors likely interfere with the learner engaging with others in a meaningful way. Examples of these behaviors may include off-topic or perseverative talking, non-congruent statements, and statements that would not be considered complimentary. Refraining from these behaviors and displaying socially appropriate alternatives will enable the learner to access greater social opportunities, develop friendships, and increases exposure to other potential reinforcers in the more generalized environment.
Example Objective	When a high risk antecedent occurs, the learner will behave in an age-typical "cool" manner (i.e. will demonstrate appropriate emotion to the situation) and will refrain from defined "Silly" behavior in 80% of opportunities over 5 consecutive days.
Social Taxonomy Domain	Social Relatedness
Teaching Methodologies	The Teaching Interaction Procedure, the Cool versus Not Cool™ procedure, and Discrete Trial Teaching
Data Collection	Task Analysis and Estimation
Prerequisite Skills	Discrimination, Comprehension, Beginning Social Skills

Phases

Phase 1	Discrimination Training of Silly (i.e., Cool versus Not Cool)	• Together with the learner, identify problematic examples of "silly" behavior (e.g., over the top gross motor activity/out of control behavior that is not congruent with the ongoing activity, stigmatizing gestures and vocal stereotypic behaviors, jokes that are not funny, negativity/sarcasm) and common situations where silly behaviors often occur. It is important to zero in on the silly behaviors that are exhibited by the learner. Consider a wide range of situations that might evoke silly behavior including, but not limited to: - Free time within a group - Transitions - Walking - Participating in conversations - Joining into a conversation - New or unfamiliar environments - Situations evoking excitement or emotionality that could go "over the top" rather quickly

Phase 1 (cont.)	Discrimination Training of Silly (i.e., Cool versus Not Cool)	• Setup demonstrations of appropriate (Cool) and silly (Not Cool) examples of the behavior and have the learner rate each demonstration.

Phase 2	Role-Play Appropriate Responding to Tempting Situations	• Together with the learner, for each silly behavior that was identified in Phase 1, brainstorm appropriate alternative behaviors. Examples of appropriate responding may include:
		– Verbal alternatives to silliness
		  • On-topic responses and comments
		  • Non-perseverative speech
		  • Expressive language best supporting the learner's social communication domain
		  • Sounds and vocal embellishments supporting the conversation and social situation
		– Non-vocal alternatives to silliness
		  • Facial expressions matching the mood and context
		  • Expressions serving the purpose and not attracting undue attention
		– Gross motor alternatives to silliness
		  • Remaining still when lined up
		  • Walking appropriately
		  • Waiting with a still body
		• Identify the hierarchy of least tempting to most tempting scenarios. Beginning with a very mild level of temptation, role-play scenarios where the learner is tempted to engage in silly behavior. Early in the role-play, before silly behavior occurs, have the learner stop (i.e., freeze) and think about the best choice to make.
		– Refer to the initial phases in the Stop, Think, Act, Review (STAR) program
		• Ask the learner to state what would be the Cool way to continue the activity. If they can state a Cool response, continue the role-play.
		– If not, have the learner think further before continuing and provide assistance in identifying an appropriate alternative to being silly
		– At any time if the learner begins to act silly, direct them to stop and take as long as necessary for them to choose a suitable alternative to being silly
		• As the learner progresses, discontinue having them formally stop and state what they will do and allow the role-play to go from start to finish without interruption.

| Phase 3 | Learner Chooses Best Alternative to Silly Behavior Based on the Situation | • Teach the learner to determine what response is best suited to the scenario.
• This requires further teaching. Examples of appropriate responding corresponding to the scenario may include:
  – Verbal alternatives to silliness
    • On-topic responses and comments
    • Non-perseverative speech
    • Expressive language best supporting the learner's social communication domain
    • Sounds and vocal embellishments supporting the conversation and social situation
  – Non-vocal alternatives to silliness
    • Facial expressions matching the mood and context
    • Expressions serving the purpose and not attracting undue attention
  – Gross motor alternatives to silliness
    • Remaining still when lined up
    • Walking appropriately
    • Waiting with a still body |
| Steps Toward Generalization | | • Throughout the day there will be naturally occurring temptations. Initially, the learner can be primed in advance to remember to stop and think. Priming just before the activity maximizes the likelihood of success. Over time the prime should occur further in advance and become less specific (e.g., "What behavior are we working on today?").
• Fade supplemental reinforcers.
• Fade use of priming (e.g., reduce specificity and give prompt further in advance of problematic situations).
• Fade interventionist presence.
• Practice with helpers/cohorts.
• Increase the variety of activities and levels of distraction.
• Move to more natural environments. |

Friend Fluency

Overall Goal	The learner will actively think about their friends and make spontaneous comments about a friend's interest in naturally occurring situations.
Example Objective	The learner will increase comments about friend's interest by 40% in the natural environment.
Social Taxonomy Domain	Social Relatedness
Teaching Methodologies	The Teaching Interaction Procedure
Data Collection	Rate, Estimation

Phases

Phase 1	Interests of Others	The learner writes and/or verbally describes the interests of a friend. This will help the learner start to identify and think about a friend's interest.
Phase 2	Items that Correspond to Interest	The learner is given options of different games, television shows, movies, etc. (e.g., Star Wars™, Monopoly®, Pokémon®) and identifies an activity their friend would enjoy based on the previously identified interests.
Phase 3	Role-Play	With the interventionist acting in the role of a peer, have the learner practice initiating activities that the peer would enjoy.
Phase 4	Structured Practice	Set up situations where a friend's interest will be seen (e.g. a Star Wars game is out, the learner walks by a baseball poster). • Have the learner practice making a comment based on the friend's interest (e.g., "Look at that Darth Vader mask, my friend Adam would really like that").
Phase 5	Conversation Practice	Engage in conversation with the learner and steer the conversation to arrive at a topic of interest to one of the learner's friends (e.g. "I saw a new Avengers comic book yesterday). • Prime the learner in advance as needed so that when the learner hears the topic or statement, they should comment about it being something the peer would be interested in (e.g., "Sam would be happy to know that it's out").

Phase 6	Natural Practice	Use priming and reinforcement so that in naturally occurring situations the learner will comment on events or topics of a friend's interest when they are seen or brought up in conversation. For example, "This morning, see if you can remember to notice and comment whenever things that come up that [peer's name] would be interested in."

Generalization		• Initially it may be necessary to use supplemental reinforcement for spontaneous comments they make about their friends. This reinforcement should be differential and thinned over time.
		• Immediate priming will need to occur for the learner at the beginning of each phase.
		• Systematically increase the amount of time between the priming and the skill being worked on.
		  - Immediate prime
		  - Prime with a 5-minute delay
		  - Prime with a 10-minute delay
		  - Continue systematically until the priming can be removed completely.

Feel The Feeling

Overall Goal	To facilitate a range of emotional knowledge. To better recognize individual emotion, emotional expression, and the physiological correlates of those emotions. To facilitate compassion and caring. To build requisite skills for empathy: (a) increased attending to others, (b) better understanding of perspectives that are different from their own; and (c) learn what others may see, understand, think, feel, believe or desire differently than the learner does. To experience the emotions others are feeling. To build requisite skills for responding to others' perspectives and emotions. To build a foundation for understanding that the learner's choices may positively impact another person's life.
Example Goal	The learner will identify the emotion that they are feeling when a salient event occurs with 100% accuracy across five consecutive sessions.
Social Taxonomy Domain	Social Relatedness
Teaching Methodologies	The Teaching Interaction Procedure, the Cool versus Not Cool™ procedure
Data Collection	Estimation or Task Analysis
Prerequisite Skills	Imaginative Play, Joint Attention, Comprehension, Receptive and expressive understanding of emotions (may be run concurrently), Cause & Effect (including how one comes to "know" something), Recall, Environmental and Social Awareness, Inferences, Perspective taking

Phases

Phase 1	Video Review	Learner watches videos of themselves in situations evoking various emotional responses and labels emotions. The goal is to evoke the same emotional response the learner experienced when the event actually occurred. Be sure to include positive and negative emotional experiences. Some examples may include: · Gum in your hair (sad) · Receiving an award (proud, happy) · Acting in a play (proud, happy) · Getting hit with a ball and being laughed at (angry, embarrassed) · Going to the amusement park (excited)
Phase 2	Remember the Feeling (Real History)	Recall and re-experience the feeling. · This phase helps the learner experience an emotional response to a prior incident. The interventionist has the learner remember specific

Phase 2 (cont.)	Remember the Feeling (Real History)	events from their past experience. The memory must have a strong potential to evoke an emotion in the present. The learner then feels the emotion (in the present) corresponding to the memory (from the past). For example:

		- "Think of a time when you felt something strongly"
		
		- "Think of a time you were the most [emotion] you have ever been"
		
		    · Emotions could include but are not limited to: Happiest, Saddest, Most Excited, Most Scared, Most Nervous, Maddest/Angriest
		
		    · While being careful not to lead the learner or possibly influence the recall/memory, use emotion "heighteners" to assist the learner to remember. These multi-sensory assists may include:
		
		        o "What did you see?"
		
		        o "What were the smells?"
		
		        o "Do you remember what you heard?"
		
		        o "What did it taste like?"
		
		        o "Describe what your body was doing."
		
		        o "How was your breathing?"
		
		        o "What was the weather/temperature?"
		
		- The learner immerses themselves in the feeling associated with the memory

Phase 3	Imagine the Feeling	Imagined occurrence and conjuring of emotion.
		
		· The learner listens to a description of an event (fictional) and attempts to capture the feeling it conjures up. For example, "Close your eyes and pretend..."
		
		    - "...someone pushed their way in front of you and got the last toy. How is that making you feel?"
		
		    - "...you've just opened a birthday present and it's the one toy you wanted more than anything else in the world."
		
		    - "...you are riding your skateboard and wipe out and skin your knee badly."
		
		    - "...you are just falling asleep in the most comfortable, coziest bed you've ever slept in."
		
		    - "...you see your mom after she's been away from you for three days and she is smiling and holding her arms out for a huge hug."
		
		    - "...you have been working so hard to learn how to surf and you finally catch a wave and stand up all by yourself."
		
		· "Imagine something that makes you feel [emotion] and live it/tell me about it." (Refer to already established emotion foundation from Phase 1). Work learner through the following hierarchy:
		
		- Imagined occurrences that have a lot of similarities to Phase 1 memories and corresponding emotions
		
		- Imagined occurrences that have some similarities to Phase 1 memories and corresponding emotions

Phase 3 (cont.)	Imagine the Feeling	- Imagined occurrences that have little similarity to Phase 1 memories and corresponding emotions - Goal is for learner to feel the feeling associated with the imagined occurrence

Phase 4	What's the Feeling?	• The learner watches someone experiencing a salient event and reports what those people are feeling. This phase takes the work into a more natural environment, where the learner now must apply their emotional knowledge to real people and real situations.
		- Possible iterations:
		  • Video examples
		  • Role-Play examples
		  • Actual observations of others

Phase 5	Predict your own Feeling	• The Learner anticipates how they will feel prior to going through a salient event and practices describing how it likely will feel.
Phase 6	Predict Someone Else's Feeling	• The Learner anticipates how they will feel prior to going through a salient event and practices describing how it likely will feel.

Living In The Gray

Overall Goal	To reduce adherence to rigid self-imposed rules about how to act, how to respond, how to interpret what is happening. To disrupt rule-bound thinking templates preventing entertaining differing perspectives. To develop an appreciation for flexible thinking. To encourage greater use of flexible thinking. To encourage greater social engagement. To increase self-evaluation and self-monitoring. To better recognize, understand and adjust to other's beliefs, opinions and truths.
Example Objective	The learner will display flexibility in their decision making by coming up with different alternatives in 70% of opportunities across five consecutive sessions.
Social Taxonomy Domain	Social Relatedness
Teaching Methodologies	Discrete Trial Teaching, the Cool versus Not Cool™ procedure, and the Teaching Interaction Procedure
Data Collection	Task Analysis, Estimation, Trial by Trial

Phases

Phase 1	Discrimination	Define the concept of black and white thinking (e.g., only one right answer) versus living in the gray (e.g., being ok with multiple possible answers). Then collaborate with the learner to generate responses to a variety of situations. Focus on examples that are relevant to the learner and represent typical examples of where they get into trouble because of black and white thinking. Provide differential reinforcement for increased flexibility and shape further understanding and use of "Gray" concepts. Examples may include: • Where something goes (e.g. where it usually goes versus where else we could put it). • What to use as a substitute when something is not available. • Where to stand or sit. • What to wear. • Order of completing daily routines.
Phase 2	Application	Present antecedents typically resulting in rigid responding and practice responding in a more flexible manner. Incorporate tolerance strategies if the lesson evokes anxiety (or some other form of unpleasant respondent behavior/emotion). • Note: The learner should have basic frustration tolerance skills prior to this Phase.

Phase 2 (cont.)	Application	• Situations/opportunity examples may include:
		  - Practice forced choices:
		    • Choosing between two highly preferred activities/toys
		    • Deciding upon ranked, top five lists
		    • "My favorite" lists
		  - Ask questions with several correct answers
		  - Give instructions that could be interpreted in a variety of ways. For example:
		    • "Go find the best thing to have for a snack today"
		    • "Make a rocket with these Lego pieces"
		    • "Use a blue block, a red block, and a yellow block and build a tower"
		    • Receptive Instructions with dry erase boards (e.g., "Everyone draw a fish," "Draw 3 flowers," "Draw me a house" – color, shape, type of final product can vary)
		    • Receptive Labels with multiple response examples available (e.g., "Find me an animal" – a variety of figurines or pictures available to choose from across a variety of categories)
		    • Expressive Labels (e.g., "Tell me an animal that swims," "How about a vehicle that flies?," "Who would you see at the beach/supermarket/Disneyland?")
		  - Guessing games (e.g., "I'm thinking of an animal that swims")

Phase 3	Increased Generalization, Comprehension, and Application of Flexibility and Empathy	This curriculum encompasses skills that evolve over time. Considerations include:
		• The changing nature of facts, opinions, and beliefs and how they can simultaneously differ and overlap.
		• Experience, contact with reinforcement and punishment, individual viewpoints, and history shape beliefs.
		  - Sometimes the beliefs of others jibe with your own, sometimes they conflict
		  - Others' beliefs and opinions are not negative reflections of the learner's beliefs and opinions
		  - Navigating this complexity while remaining civil, calm, and respectful requires greater restraint and perhaps more varied coping and stress management procedures
		    • These are all benefits of more thoughtful, flexible thinking

Considerations		• All techniques should be modified for age and comprehension levels. Use supplemental token economies or other reinforcement system as needed.

Considerations (cont.)		· This teaching addresses skill deficits in processing, thinking, and interacting with others, with the environment, with materials, etc. Thus, this teaching will also touch upon respondent behaviors. When someone believes strongly in and relies solely on a strict decision-making protocol to navigate decisions or social interactions, any disruption can elicit emotional responses. - Those feelings may include anxiety, sadness, or anger, and may result in withdrawal, escape or avoidance. · Refrain from arguing about differences in thoughts, opinions, and beliefs unless doing so is a mutually agreed upon exercise. · Help the learner learn when to "let it go" and when to "agree to disagree," those decisions can lead to increased mutual respect. · Explore how differences in opinions, beliefs, and history benefit the learner's experience. · Build a "why it's worth it" list · Explore how beliefs affect a person's life, how they evolve, etc. · Is this person worth my time? Do we share common beliefs? Are our beliefs a possible hindrance to a shared, respectful relationship? Is there room for friendship development? Etc. · Sometimes expression of a belief or opinion is okay but other times it is better not to speak up. This requires reading social and environmental cues, and being thoughtful before speaking up.

What Would Superman Do?

Overall Goal	To facilitate a stronger sense of right versus wrong. To encourage a range of emotional knowledge and experiential feeling. To further facilitate compassion and caring. To build requisite skills for empathy, and to: (a) gain an increased attending to others; (b) better understand other perspectives, those typically different from the learner's; (c) better learn others may see, understand, think, feel, believe, or desire differently than each other and the learner; and (d) care about the above. To build requisite skills for responding to others' perspectives. To build requisite skills for making interpersonal choices. To build a foundation for understanding that the learner's choices may positively impact another's life.
Example Objective	The learner will answer questions about the right thing to do when challenges arise with 100% accuracy (i.e., chooses the right thing to do) across five consecutive days.
Social Taxonomy Domain	Social Relatedness
Teaching Methodologies	The Teaching Interaction Procedure and the Cool versus Not Cool™ procedure
Data Collection	Trial by Trial, Task Analysis, or Estimation
Prerequisite Skills	Imaginative Play, Joint Attention, Comprehension, Receptive and expressive understanding of emotions (may be run concurrently), Cause & Effect (including how one comes to "know" something), Recall, Environmental and Social Awareness, Inferences, Understanding the concept of "Perspective" (May be run concurrently), Respondent Development ("Feel the Feeling") (May be run concurrently), a familiarity with Teaching Interactions

Phases

Phase 1	Define and Learn About Heroics	• Introduce the characteristics of a hero. In this phase, the learner uses imaginative play to act out heroics. At first, the goal is for the learner to identify with and want to emulate the actions and adventures of a character who possesses strong, exciting, and compelling powers and/or attributes and who consistently prevails heroically in their quests. However, the character should also have strong moral character, as the ultimate goal is for the learner to identify with and want to emulate those attributes as well. To best drive the point of the teaching home, the emulated hero should not be conflicted or dark. Good choices include Superman©, Shazam, or Mighty Mouse™; poor choices include Batman™, Darth Vader©, or many of the X-Men™. • Have the learner identify an appropriate hero. - Read comics depicting the hero in exciting adventures

Phase 1 (cont.)	Define and Learn About Heroics	- Watch video depicting the hero in exciting adventures - Read chapter books depicting the hero in such adventures

Phase 2	Action Play with a Hero	• The learner learns to identify with and emulate a hero, through action/adventure play. Play should be in multiple modalities:
		  - action figure play
		  - role/pretend play
		  - dress-up/costume play
		• Emphasis should be on fun, power, success, etc., so that being the hero is attractive and identification is promoted. Emphasis should be on acting like the hero in role-play; that is, using powers in a way that is consistent with the character, so the emulation is facilitated.

Phase 3	Moral Play with a Hero	Once identification and emulation have been achieved, play gradually includes situations where moral decisions must be made. The learner has the opportunity to emulate and ultimately identify with the hero on this level. Such choices and good deeds are heavily reinforced within the play in manners illustrating how those choices contributed to saving the day/prevailing.
		
		  - The following hierarchy may be indicated:
		  - Clear problem/predicament with clear resolution
		    • The learner identifies a clear problem with a clear resolution for the hero to tackle. For example:
		      o Rescue someone from a burning building
		      o Stop a robber from stealing an old lady's purse
		      o Stop a runaway train from crashing into a stalled vehicle with the driver stuck inside
		      o Hero catches a person who has stumbled and fallen off a tall bridge
		  - Clear problem/predicament with several resolution options:
		    • The learner identifies several resolution options for the hero in the above scenarios
		    • Which powers can be used to resolve the above scenarios?
		    • Identify best solution or choose among equally effective courses of action
		Use several heroic figures through the various phases. In time, the definition and sense of hero can be expanded beyond the super-powered to real life heroes.

Phase 4	Generalization	• The learner takes the capacities gained from the above Phases and applies the hero template to everyday (e.g., non-hero, non-fantasy) scenarios and ultimately everyday events. This takes the work into a more natural environment, where the learner now must apply problem-solving skills.

Phase 4 (cont.)	Generalization	- Start with stories, scenarios, or paused videos and ask, "What would [name of hero] do?"
		- Gradually move to, "What would you do?" Possible iterations:
		· Video examples
		· Stories
		· Role-Play with the interventionist
		· Observations of others, accompanied or followed by narration/ discussion with the interventionist
		- In-vivo situations are orchestrated, and the learner making the heroic choice is heavily reinforced
		- Provide meaningful reinforcement in naturally occurring situations throughout the day, when the learner makes morally strong choices.

Reputation Building

Overall Goal	The learner will understand the meaning and importance of their reputation and make decisions that will better their relationships with others.
Example Objective	The learner will identify five important traits of a positive reputation with 100% accuracy for five consecutive days.
Social Taxonomy Domain	Social Relatedness
Teaching Methodologies	The Teaching Interaction Procedure and the Cool versus Not Cool™ procedure
Data Collection	Trial by Trial, Task Analysis, Estimation
Prerequisite Skills	Empathy, Expressive Language, Cause and Effect

Phases

Phase 1	Defining Reputation and Identifying Traits	· In collaboration with the learner, define reputation (e.g., what other people think about you). · Identify common reputation traits (e.g., funny, smart, annoying, bossy) and be sure to include traits that are present in the learner (i.e., positive and negative traits targeted for change).
Phase 2	Identifying Reputation Traits in Others	· Using the traits list created in Phase 1, have the learner identify people in their lives that have those traits (e.g., Mom is nice, Dad is funny, Sister is bossy) - You may also use TV shows, movies, books, etc. and watch together to have the learner identify the reputation traits in the characters (e.g., Sheldon from The Big Bang Theory is nerdy) · Make sure that each person has multiple traits (positive and negative) associated with them. · It is also important to note that people may have different reputations with different people.
Phase 3	Identifying Effect of Reputation	· Using the reputation traits of others have the learner identify their own reaction to those people (e.g., "I wouldn't want to play with Tommy because he is mean," "I would tell a secret to Sally because she is trustworthy.") · Describe scenarios where the learner's reputation affects the behavior of others (e.g., "Tommy and Sally want you to sit with them for lunch. Why do you think they asked you to join them?"). · Alternatively, you can use videos from TV shows, movies, etc. to show these situations and analyze the motivation behind the characters' actions in terms of reputation.

Phase 4	Building Rationale of Having a Good Reputation	• In collaboration with the learner identify meaningful rationales as to why having a good reputation is important. • This is a phase that you should always revisit. In later phases, rationales are an important part of the feedback and motivation.
Phase 5	Identifying Their Own Reputation: What Builds Their Reputation up? What Tears it Down?	• Use examples from the learner's behavior in a variety of situations, have them identify the effect of their actions on their reputation. - Remember that the learner may have different reputations with different people (e.g., their teacher might think they are nice, but their sister might think they are mean) • Give situations to the learner from their own behaviors and experiences and have them identify what character trait they were exhibiting, and what it did to their reputation. Examples may include: - "When you shared your snack at lunch today, what trait was that? How did that affect your reputation with Tommy?" Then tie it back into the rationale. "Next time Tommy has a snack; do you think he might share it with you?" - "When you yelled at your Mom, what trait was that? How did that effect your reputation?" Then tie it back into the rationale. "Next time you ask Mom for a favor, what do you think she will say?"
Phase 6	Role-Play Reputation Building Situations	• Setup role-plays with the learner where they get the opportunity to practice building up their reputation. - Example: "Let's pretend we are at home and your sister takes your toy, let's think about what you can do to help build up your reputation with your sister and your Mom" • Make sure to practice situations that the learner typically struggles with and needs help building up their reputation. • When the learner behaves in ways that build their reputation let them have the chance to experience the rationale. - Example: When the learner doesn't hit their sister, have the person in the role-play pretending to be the sister share something different with the learner
Phase 7	Generalization	- When situations arise in the learner's everyday life, point out their reactions and how it affected their reputation. - Whenever possible, have the rationale be delivered by the person who contacted the behavior (positive or negative) from the learner (e.g., if the learner yelled at Mom, have her make them miss something later on, and mention their reputation).

Perspective Taking

Overall Goal	To gain increased attending to the details of others' behavior. To learn that others often see, understand, think, feel, believe or desire differently than oneself. To better understand and ascertain when others have knowledge different than the learner's knowledge. To build requisite skills for responding to others' perspectives. To build requisite skills for empathy.
Example Objective	The learner will correctly answer questions from another person's perspective with 100% accuracy across five consecutive sessions.
Social Taxonomy Domain	Social Relatedness
Teaching Methodologies	The Teaching Interaction Procedure
Data Collection	Task Analysis, Estimation
Prerequisite Skills	Imaginative Play, Joint Attention, Comprehension, Receptive and expressive understanding of emotions, Cause & Effect (including how one comes to "know" something), Recall, Environmental and Social Awareness, Inferences, Understanding the concept of perspective

Phases

Phase 1	Differing Perspectives	Differing vantage points: "what do you see?" versus "what does someone else see?"
		• Arrange a number of people including the learner sitting in various places around the room. Hold up a picture so one person can see it, but not another. Ask the learner "Can (Person A) see the picture?" "Can (Person B) see the picture?"
		- The learner should discriminate who can see the picture based on who is oriented toward it. If necessary, have the learner stand next to the person to gain the same perspective. Then have them return to original spot and repeat the questions
		• Turn the picture away from the learner and ask, "Can you see the picture?"
		- Once they can correctly answer the question, ask them, "Where would you need to go so you can see it?"
		The learner shows own work.
		• The learner should orient the page, so the person can see it, rather than the learner orienting it toward themselves.
		- Have a number of people around the room. Tell the learner "Now show it to Person C. Next, show it to Person D"
		- The learner should turn the picture, orienting it to each person's point of view
		Use objects and photographs of objects to teach how something can look different depending on the point of view.

Phase 1 (cont.)	Differing Perspectives	• In this exercise, the learner learns two people may see the same object differently. Take photos of objects having different attributes when viewed from different angles.
		
		  - For example, a toy car looks different when viewed from the front, the back, the side, from above and from below. This is also true with a chair, a doll, a teddy bear, a model airplane or a doll house. For each object, take two or three photos from different angles
		
		• Place the object in the middle of a table. Place the learner so their view of the object (e.g., the back of the car) is different from Person A. Place all the photos in front of the learner. Ask the learner "Which photo shows what you can see?" versus "Which photo shows what Person A can see?"
		
		• Use features within rooms (e.g., large furniture) to further demonstrate the concept. The learner stands in front of one object in the room. Person A stands in front of another object. Each person is looking at the object in front of them. Show the learner photos of the two different objects, along with some distractor photos. Ask the learner "Which one can you see?" versus "Which one can Person A see?"
		
		• Have the learner stand in front of an object, looking at it, and Person A standing in front and facing an object but looking at a different object. Have pictures of all the objects out (including the object in front of the learner, the object in front of Person A, and the object Person A is actually looking at). Repeat the previously mentioned questions, teaching the learner to discriminate what can be seen in a room versus what someone is actually looking at.
		
		• Have the learner stand in front of an object, looking at it, and Person A standing in front and facing an object but looking at a different object. Have pictures of all the objects out (including the object in front of the learner, the object in front of Person A, and the object Person A is actually looking at). Repeat the previously mentioned questions, teaching the learner to discriminate what can be seen in a room versus what someone is actually looking at.
		
		• Have the learner and Person A walk together from one room (Room 1) to another room (Room 2). Once they are in Room 2, have the learner return to Room 1. Have Person A stay in Room 2 (e.g., initially the two were in the living room, and then they both walked to the kitchen. The learner returned to the living room while the cohort stayed in the kitchen).
		
		  - Offer photos of objects from each room for the learner to choose from. Ask the learner "Can Person A see this?" The learner should be able to predict what Person A can see, based on the room that Person A is in. For example, Person A might be able to see the refrigerator but cannot see the television in the living room.
		
		Blocked view.
		
		• Set up a situation where a small item (e.g., toy car) is blocked from the view of Person A by a larger item (e.g., box). The learner's view of the small item is unobstructed. Have Person A look in the direction of the car. Ask the learner, "Can Person A see the car?" The answer is "no," even when Person A is looking in the direction of the object. Move the box away and ask the same question. The answer is now "yes," Person A can indeed see the object. The

Phase 1 (cont.)	Differing Perspectives	learner is now learning to discriminate between a blocked view – even if the learner can see the object, that doesn't mean the other person can – versus one that is no longer blocked – now both can see the object.

Phase 2	What a Person Knows	• Knowing as a function of sensory perception.
		  - Arrange a variety of situations involving a range of sensory modalities. Have the learner observe someone doing a specific activity causing them to "know" something. For example, a friend watches as their mother takes a cake from the refrigerator and puts it on the table. Ask the learner, "Does (your friend) know the cake is on the table?" The learner should answer "yes." Then ask, "How does (your friend) know?" The answer is, "because (the friend) saw her put it there."
		  - Use variety of situations that demonstrate a wide range of modalities for gaining knowledge
		    • Seeing
		    • Hearing a sound directly
		    • Touching/feeling
		    • Tasting/smelling
		    • Being told about something
		
		Do they know what you know?
		• The learner learns to discriminate between things they know versus things another person knows. There are a number of discriminations the learner must learn:
		  - Learner knows, person does not know
		  Learner and person know
		  - Learner and person do not know
		• Examples could include:
		  - The learner and person go to separate rooms and perform an action written down in each room. After performing the action, they both return to the interventionist. Ask the learner, "Do you know what (person) did?" and "Does (person) know what you did?"
		  - Person A and learner go outside to play soccer, and Person A kicks the ball over the fence. Person B stays inside to watch TV. Ask the learner, "Does Person A know the soccer ball went over the fence?" and "How does he know?" Also ask, "Does Person B know the ball went over the fence?" and "Why not?"
		  - The learner receives an award at school assembly. The learner's mother did not attend. Ask the learner, "Does your mom know what you got at assembly today?" and "Why not?" Then, "Does your teacher know?" and "How do they know?"
		  - Person A looks into a bag to see an object within. The learner does not watch this. Ask the learner, "Do you know if Person A knows what's in the bag?" (Answer is, "no"). In contrast, the learner then watches Person A look into the bag. Ask the same question (Answer is now "yes").
		• Use the similar examples as described here, but this time the question is, "Do you know if Person A knows?" There are four possible types of situations:
		    • Person A does not know, the learner knows they don't know

Phase 2 (cont.)	What a Person Knows	• Person A knows, the learner knows they know • Person A does not know, the learner does not know they don't know • Person A knows, the learner does not know they don't know

Phase 3	Identify Desire	**What is important to you?**
		
		• Provide the learner with a worksheet listing 15–20 desires common to all of us. Have the learner indicate how important each desire is to them (e.g., low, medium, high interest level). It is helpful to stress there is a middle ground for individuals with regard to preference of desires and preference is typically not all or nothing. Desires may include:
		
		  - Control
		  - Family Time
		  - Sports
		  - Learning New Things
		  - Drawing
		  - Eating
		  - Fame
		  - Getting Good Grades
		  - Acceptance
		  - Being the best
		  - Being first
		  - Video Games
		  - Power
		  - Popularity
		
		• For younger learners, listing tangible items or familiar games and activities may be more helpful with this lesson. Older learners may better understand abstract concepts such as control or independence.
		
		• Next, have the learner survey one or more people to see how they rate each of the items. Then have the learner compare their own choices with those of other people. Explain that for the most part, no two people are going to have the exact desire profile, and that is what makes us unique. Further, the interventionist may have the learner provide possible rationales for why another person would have high desire for an area they indicated as a low desire, and what the learner's rationales may be for their choices.
		
		Observing and assessing desire in others
		
		• Determining what a person wants or desires is possible by simply asking or observing them. The learner should observe a person who demonstrates examples of wanting versus not wanting an object. Have the Person A act in a manner that reveals the desirability of an item. Ask the learner, "Does Person A want the chips?" and "How do you know they want them?" or "How do you know they don't want them?"
		
		  - How does someone demonstrate whether they have a preference for something or not? Some helpful hints to teach the learner might include the following:
		
		    • Does the person look at it?

Phase 3 (cont.)	Identify Desire	· Does the person reach for it?
		· Does the person ask for it?
		· If offered, does the person choose it?
		· Is the person happy when they get it (e.g., smile, laugh, say something positive)?
		· Does the person spend time with it?
		· Does the person talk about it?
		· Does the person do these things often when in the presence of it, rather than just once?
		- Over time, the learner can get to know what another person wants through observation. Knowing – or inferring – what a person wants by watching their actions can assist the learner in understanding the person's general desires. This in turn can assist the learner to interpret intention based on the relevant actions and words someone uses.
Phase 4	Identify Emotions: Affective Perspective Taking	· Affective perspective taking refers to understanding another person's emotions and feelings. Identifying the emotions of others is described in detail in the Emotions program.
		· It is important for the learner to understand how to interpret verbal and non-verbal cues about emotions. The learner should learn to answer questions such as, "How do they feel?," "How do you know they feel sad/angry/happy?," "Why are they sad?," etc.
Phase 5	Identifying Thoughts and Beliefs: What is Someone else Thinking?	Predicting what a person might be thinking.
		· Use pictures, videos, or role-plays to illustrate situations involving clear actions or events. Ask the learner to determine what each person might be thinking. The learner should base their answers on the knowledge built from previous Phases, and the context (e.g., setting, event, person's words, body language).
		Other people may have differing beliefs from your own.
		· The learner learns their beliefs may differ from those of others. Teach the learner many different examples where their own beliefs vary from the beliefs of others.
		· Examples could include:
		- Person 1 puts a hat on a table and walks away. Person 2 picks it up and puts it in Person 1's school bag, then walks out. Ask the learner "Where does (Person 1) believe the hat is?" (i.e., "On the table") and "Where Person 2 believe the hat is?" (i.e., "In the school bag")
		- Show the learner a box of chocolates where the chocolates have been replaced by pencils. Have another person enter the room and look at the closed box of chocolates. Ask the learner, "What does (Person 1) think is inside the box?" and "What do you think is inside the box?"
		- Hide an object in a box. Have the learner and another person try to guess what is inside. The person should indicate what they think is in the box (e.g., saying, "maybe it's a ball," "it might be a donkey"). Right before the interventionist discloses the answer, ask the learner "What do you think is inside the box?" and "What does (Person 1) think is inside the box?"

Phase 5 (cont.)	Identifying Thoughts and Beliefs: What is Someone else Thinking?	Advanced perspective taking.

Advanced perspective taking.

- In time, the learner should learn individuals may come away from the same event with differing beliefs (potentially based on different vantage points).
- Additionally, "second order" belief can be addressed. Second order beliefs occur when a person has a perspective about what someone else believes. For example, "Rick believes that Sally thinks she won't get invited to the party."
- Further complexity can be added to perspective taking. For example, the learner can learn differing beliefs and values occur not only based on viewing the same event. Differing beliefs can also occur when two people hear the same content, topic, or issue. Or, having read a story, people can have different answers to the question, "What is the main idea?" However, it is important to be able to judge whether the answer that was given truly captures the main idea. In this case the interventionist is really asking, "What would most people consider to be the main idea?"
- Finally, working towards better inferring intent, based on observing someone's actions, gestures, or body language can occur. Essential elements of this level of perspective taking effort include: remembering and using specific situational context, having previous observational history, knowing the person whose actions are being evaluated, and a firm understanding of non-verbal cues.

Examples of Perspective Taking Exercises

- Giving directions to others.
  - Have the learner guide you toward an item by giving instructions. Initially, the learner may walk with you. Eventually, the learner should be able to give directions from a stationary location and modify their instructions to suit the perspective of the accomplice
  - Tell someone on the phone how to get to your location
  - Progress to learner giving directions based on memory. For example, if the learner and accomplice are watching television in the living room, have the learner get the accomplice to go to the kitchen (i.e., a different room) and retrieve sodas (i.e., the learner not having the benefit of being in the same room to watch the accomplice and modify instructions)
- Keeping Secrets.
  - Games such as I Spy, Guess Who, Charades, Kids on Stage, Secret Square and Secret Forest are good for teaching learners to keep answers secret. All these games have in common a reliance on the players giving meaningful clues without revealing the answer
- Practical Jokes/ Magic Tricks
  - Playing harmless tricks on other people can be a great way of understanding another person's perspective. For example, go with the learner and secretly hide a toy snake in the pantry out of view of Person A. Ask the learner, "What does Person A think is in the cupboard?" and "What might they do when they see the snake?"
  - Many magic tricks also involve perspective taking. Objects that are placed in a magic hat often turn into different things, so you can ask the learner, "What do the observers think is in the magic hat?" and "What is the magician going to do?"

Phase 5 (cont.)		· Deception
		- Understanding deception is another way to teach perspective taking. An added bonus may be the development of a learner who is less naive, and more circumspect. Deception is the understanding that someone can produce false belief in another person A note of caution here:
		· Rather than teaching deception, examples of other's deception can be used as perspective taking exercises. This is the development of deception recognition
		- Fairy tales such as Snow White, The Gingerbread Man, and Little Red Riding Hood include themes of deception. These examples can be used to illustrate themes relating to deception. Questions such as, "Who does Snow White think the lady is?," "Who is the lady really?," "What do you think the wolf hopes to gain dressed up as granny?," and "Why did the witch dress up as a lady selling apples?" can guide the learner to a better understanding of other's motives. The final step is being able to explain why the deception occurred.

Goal Setting And Self-Management

Overall Goal	To increase the understanding of "self-advocacy." To increase the learner's ability to emotionally support themselves. To better promote a learner's unique point of view. To increase the learner's ability to appropriately stand up for what they want. To assist the learner to better assert themselves. To assist the learner in obtaining what is rightly theirs. To increase the learner's ability and desire to be involved in their own education and development. To be able to define their own personal goals and engage in thoughtful planning. To improve ability to discuss their situation with peers and trusted adults.
Example Objective	The learner will demonstrate appropriate assertion during 90% of intervals observed.
Social Taxonomy Domain	Social Relatedness
Teaching Methodologies	The Teaching Interaction Procedure and the Cool versus Not Cool™ procedure
Data Collection	Ratio or Estimation
Prerequisites	Assertiveness, Appropriately expressing displeasure, Keeping rightful place or object, Appropriate conviction, Correcting others when the learner is wrongly accused, Displaying appropriate competitiveness, Understanding the concepts of winning, losing and sportsmanship

Phases

Phase 1	Learner Develops Own Goals	The learner can be taught to participate in selecting the goals they need to work on at school or in-home sessions. These goals can be academic in nature, but can also include stronger development in areas of social or leisure skills, independent living skills, behavioral control, etc.
		
		 • Multiple choice:
		   - Examples include: "What do you think you should work on first – catching the ball with two hands, or joining in a game of soccer with a group of kids?"
		   - The learner should access reinforcement for: 1) making a choice and 2) selecting appropriately challenging goals. That is, the goals should be easy enough for the learner, but enough of a challenge that the learner will need to put in some effort. Reinforcement should include pointing out the advantages of choosing something a little more difficult
		 • Self- initiated:
		   - The learner picks a skill to work on
		   - The learner is then taught to break this task down into smaller steps

Phase 1 (cont.)	Learner Develops Own Goals	· The interventionist may need to spend time systematically teaching this objective to further promote the learner's ability to achieve goals independently. This should be considered a critical component to the learner's ability to best promote themselves and their work - The learner then sequences the steps leading to completion and begins to work - The learner should access reinforcement for: 1) developing an appropriate goal and 2) participating in learning the new goal · Skill assessment: - When a learner is aware of their own skills and abilities, they can be taught to assess their own performance in different areas (e.g., socially, physical skills in sports, academic abilities) and advocate for special consideration within that area, if required - For example, the learner can be taught to approach the physical education instructor to ask for accommodation (e.g., more time to dress, easier version of physical skills to work on in class). · Sets own agenda: - Older learners can be taught to create an agenda for important meetings where the learner's welfare and education are discussed - This will allow the learner to advocate for themselves, and share the responsibility for their own education
Phase 2	Self-Reward	The learner learns to evaluate their performance and provide themselves appropriate reinforcement based on effort. · Independent tasks: - Set up a task (with a distinct end point) for the learner to complete independently - Tell the learner, "Once you finish your work, you can help yourself to something you'd like to play with" - The learner should stay on task, complete the task, and then initiate finding a preferred activity to reward themselves for their efforts - The teacher should monitor unobtrusively, then fade that presence - To promote the development of independence, it is better not to provide assistance or verbal redirection. If the learner is not successful, end the trial, make any necessary adjustments (e.g., prime the learner, or reduce task difficulty) or simply allow learning to progress by trial and error. · Choice of reinforcement level based on performance: - Categorize reinforcers into three levels, based on learner preference - Sort the reinforcers into three boxes, labelled "Best work/effort" (i.e., A level), "Ok work/effort" (i.e., B level), and "Poor work/effort" (i.e., no reinforcement). - Depending on the learner's abilities and the mobility of potential reinforcers in each level, other methods of division can be employed: · For example, the learner can select appropriately from a divided photo album with picture representations

Phase 2 (cont.)	Self-Reward	<ul><li>Use a list with the titles written out, contained in three levels; the learner can pick accordingly, based on the written labels</li><li>- Regardless of how the levels are represented, the potential reinforcers should be rotated and updated regularly<ul><li>This is another process in which the learner can participate. Helping create the levels based on what is currently a favorite versus what no longer is</li></ul></li><li>- Have the learner complete a task</li><li>- Upon completion, ask the learner to rate their own performance: "What do you think you should have?" If the learner believes they did a fantastic job, they can select something from the A level. If the learner feels they performed averagely, they can choose something from the B level. If the learner believes they did poor work, they should recognize they did not earn reinforcement, or can request to try again</li><li>- It is critical at this point to teach the concept of "agreement"<ul><li>For example, if the learner believes they did a "fantastic" job on a task, Initially, the work should be checked to determine the accuracy of their belief</li><li>During this stage, the learner and the interventionist come to agreement on what "fantastic" work looks like, as well as what constitutes "Ok" work and "Poor" work</li><li>If the interventionist and the learner reach the same conclusion, then the learner chooses from the level of reinforcement representing their work.</li><li>If there is disagreement between the interventionist and the learner, then the interventionist and the learner need to better define the terms representing quality</li></ul></li><li>- As the learner learns to better assess their work and effort, the interventionist can fade from this interaction and occasionally do spot checks to be sure the quality is not slipping<ul><li>We expect our learners to perform according to their abilities. Anything less than what they are capable of should be called exactly that</li><li>This will further assist them in understanding and assimilating the concepts included in self-advocacy, including pride and promotion</li></ul></li><li>- The learner should receive social praise for completing the task</li><li>- They should access reinforcement from the choice levels for accurately assessing their own reinforcement level</li><li>- In this phase, and many others, the learner's reinforcement can be based not only on work product, but also on effort<ul><li>That is, if the learner tries really hard to complete the task, but that task is actually quite difficult for them, they can receive high levels of reinforcement for their effort</li></ul></li><li>Spontaneous reward:<ul><li>- The learner should be encouraged to recall positive things they have done throughout the day, and reward themselves for excellent effort and work</li><li>- Once the learner initiates wanting to self-reward, encourage the learner to explain what they believe they deserve as a reward. This will assist the learner to link their behavior to the reinforcement accessed</li></ul></li></ul>

Basic Social Skills	Intermediate Social Skills
Handling Corrective Feedback	It's Okay to Be Wrong
Excitement Thermometer	Nobody's Perfect
Delayed Gratification	Get Your Head in the Game
Perseverance	Decision Making
Extended Secret Word	

Handling Corrective Feedback

Overall Goal	The learner will learn to remain calm and continue to participate in an activity when given corrective feedback. Learning to accept corrective feedback is a critical skill, and a basic requirement for participation in more naturalized social environments such as school, team sports, and games. Corrective feedback is a learning opportunity benefiting the learner, and requires the learner to remain calm and engaged.
Example Objective	When presented with corrective feedback, the learner will respond in an age-typical manner (e.g., remain calm, refrain from disruptive behaviors), and then apply the feedback in 90% of opportunities.
Social Taxonomy Domain	Social Learning
Teaching Methodologies	Discrete Trial Teaching, the Teaching Interaction Procedure, the Cool versus Not Cool™ procedure
Data Collection	Trial-by-trial or Estimation
Prerequisite Skills	Comprehension, Receptive Language, Frustration Tolerance, Stress Management, Beginning Flexibility

Phases

Phase 1	Graduated Exposure	· Create a list of examples of corrective feedback that the learner commonly encounters and tend to evoke an inappropriate response. Rank the items based on the intensity of learner's reaction to the feedback.
		  - The learner should have some basic coping strategies (e.g., can take a break or deep breaths)
		  - The learner should be able to discriminate "calm" versus "not calm"
		· Begin in a highly controlled setting by exposing the learner to the lowest level/intensity of corrective feedback (e.g., absence of praise, shaking head to communicate "no," quietly saying "mm-mm").
		· Differentially reinforce remaining calm after receiving feedback. Be sure to pause long enough so that this additional feedback is not confused with the original feedback. Make it very clear that the original response was incorrect, and this new feedback pertains to the subsequent behavior.
		· As the learner demonstrates tolerance for very mild instances of corrective feedback, gradually move up the hierarchy.

Phase 2	Constructive Responses to Feedback	· Continue the expectation of remaining calm, but start putting more emphasis on changing behavior based on the corrective feedback. · Consider the ways a learner can respond appropriately to corrective feedback and create another list of constructive response options.

Phase 2 (cont.)	Constructive Responses to Feedback	• For example:
		
		  - Learner exhibits calm in a non-verbal way (e.g., just do it, deep breath)
		
		  - Learner exhibits calm, plus added Cool comments. Consider age-typicality (e.g., "Okay," "Got it," "Makes sense")
		
		  - Learner determines whether feedback was clear or not. For instance, the learner remains calm and asks for clarification (e.g., "What do you mean?," "I don't get it," "Can you give me an example?")

Steps Toward Generalization		• Fade supplemental reinforcers. • Fade use of priming (including specificity and timing). • Fade interventionist presence. • Practice with helpers/cohorts. • Increase the variety of activities and levels of distraction. • Move to more natural environments.

Excitement Thermometer

Overall Goal	The learner will get to a state of excitement and go back to a baseline state without getting over the top.
Example Objective	During exciting events the learner will engage in appropriate behavior in 90% of opportunities across three consecutive sessions.
Social Taxonomy Domain	Social Learning
Teaching Methodologies	Discrete Trial Teaching and the Cool versus Not Cool™ procedure
Data Collection	Trial by Trial and Estimation

Phases

Phase 1	Create a Hierarchy of Antecedents	• Create a hierarchy of levels of excitement through observations, reports, and discussion with the learner.
Phase 2	Create a Self-Awareness Thermometer	• Create a "thermometer" with the learner that has anchor points at each level of excitement and describes what their body (and mind, if learner is capable of expressing these thoughts) is doing at each "temperature."
Phase 3	Discrimination Training	• Using the self-awareness thermometer created in Phase 2, the interventionist demonstrates different actions the learner engages in when calm/silly/very silly/over the top. The learner should then identify the corresponding level on the thermometer.
Phase 4	Self-Assessment	• While antecedents are present, ask the learner where they are on the thermometer. Ensure that check-ins occur equally often for each level on the thermometer. Reinforce accurately self-assessing.
Phase 5	Creating/Practicing Coping Strategies	• In collaboration with the learner, identify coping strategies that the learner is capable of using (e.g., deep breaths, cognitive lists, taking a break). • Without antecedents for excitement present, practice the coping strategies in isolation. • Do not move onto Phase 6 until the learner successfully engages in a coping strategy without antecedents present.
Phase 6	Introduction of Antecedents	• Starting at the lowest end of the hierarchy to evoke excited behavior (e.g., being silly), introduce antecedents. Prime the learner about what antecedents will be presented (e.g., "I'm going to make some silly noises…"). • The learner should be allowed, and even encouraged, to get excited. When the learner behaves in a way that shows they are at a silly level of excitement, withdraw the antecedent and prompt the learner to engage in a coping strategy to get back to baseline levels.

Phase 6 (cont.)	Introduction of Antecedents	• Continue this process at the lowest level until the learner is consistently able to get to a low level of excitement and then get back to a baseline level. Then move onto the next level of the hierarchy.
Phase 7	Generalization	• Increase the time between the prime and the antecedent (e.g., "In the next 30 minutes I'm going to make some silly noises"). • Increase the vagueness of the prime (e.g., "Sometime coming up I'm going to do something that might make you silly."). • When antecedents occur in the natural environment and the learner is able to get excited without getting over the top provide a high amount of reinforcement.

Delayed Gratification

Overall Goal	The learner will forgo an immediate reinforcer for a better reinforcer later, eventually setting up their own schedule of delayed gratification.
Example Objective	When presented a choice between a smaller reinforcer provided immediately and a larger reinforcer provided at a later point in time, the learner will select the larger reinforcer provided at a later point in time in 70% of opportunities across five consecutive days.
Social Taxonomy Domain	Social Learning
Teaching Methodologies	Discrete Trial Teaching and the Cool versus Not Cool™ procedure
Data Collection	Ratio or Estimation
Prerequisite Skills	A basic sense of time concepts, Less and more, Cause and effect.

Phases

Phase 1	Short Duration	• Present two options to the group. Option 1 is a small amount of a potential reinforcer (e.g., 1 cookie, playing with a toy for 10 seconds, watching 10 seconds of a movie). Option 2 is a large amount of a potential reinforcer (e.g., 3 cookies, playing with a toy for 3 minutes, watching 3 minutes of a movie) that the group has to wait a short duration to access (e.g., one minute).
		• If the group selects option 1:
		- Give a small amount of the potential reinforcer to the group immediately
		- Set a timer for the short duration (e.g., one minute), when the timer goes off show the group what they missed out on by not waiting. You should now rub it in, but the group should be made aware of what has been forfeited. Just show them what they missed out on, and then retrial the same or similar setup
		• Possible adjustments include increasing the value of option 2, or reducing the duration required to delay gratification
		• If the group selects option 2:
		- Provide praise for making a good choice for waiting to get something better
		- Set a timer for the short duration (e.g., one minute), when the timer goes off immediately give the group the larger amount of the potential reinforcer that they waited for
		- Point out to the group how much more they received by waiting (initial rationale building). Try to build up how proud you are of the learners for waiting for something better (initial building of intrinsic motivation rationale)

Phase 2	Moderate Duration	• Same set up as in Phase 1, but the amount of time the group has to delay gratification if they choose option 2 is a moderate duration (e.g., 3–5 minutes).
Phase 3	Longer Duration	• Same set up as in Phases 1 and 2, but the amount of time the group has to delay gratification if they choose option 2 is a long duration (e.g., 10–15 minutes).
Phase 4	Longer Duration with Mystery Prize	• Present two options to the group. Option 1 is a small amount of a specified potential reinforcer. Option 2 is a mystery potential reinforcer that they will need to wait a longer time to gain access. • Mystery: - Initially the mystery prize should be a highly preferred potential reinforcer every time - After several times of the group selecting the mystery prize, thin the schedule so that the mystery prize is sometimes a little less preferred potential reinforcer and sometimes highly preferred • The mystery prize should never drop below a little less preferred than the most desired potential reinforcer
Phase 5	Bringing in the Group's Behavior	• Prior to the onset of a teaching round, and prior to the occurrence of any maladaptive behaviors, go over the group's reinforcement system with them (e.g., token board, response-cost system, magic number) • Go over some of the maladaptive/immediate gratification behaviors they have exhibited in the past (e.g., avoidant behavior, self-stimulatory behavior), and point out how it might seem good in the moment, but the price they pay is missing out on better things. • If the group refrains from maladaptive/immediate gratification type behaviors: - Throughout the teaching round, point out what a good decision they are making by not engaging in those behaviors - When the teaching round ends, provide a highly preferred potential reinforcer (the reinforcer can be thinned over time) and point out how much more they got by "waiting" (i.e., refraining from immediate gratification) • We refer to the desired behavior as waiting, but in essence, the goal is that they continue to refrain from immediate gratification • If the group engages in maladaptive/immediate gratification type behaviors: - Point out to them the decision they are making to engage in those behaviors now instead of waiting - When the teaching round ends, provide a low level or no reinforcer and point out how they missed out on something better, because they chose to engage in those behaviors during teaching

Phase 6	Building Naturally Occurring Motivation	• Set up a work round where the two options are closer together (e.g., 1 cookie now vs. 1 ½ cookies later).
		- If the group selects option 2 then provide the larger amount of the potential reinforcer as well as an activity that builds pride (e.g., going around to tell people that they waited, a certificate to show parents)
		• Set up a work round where the two options are identical (e.g., 1 cookie now or 1 cookie later).
		- If the group selects option 2 then provide the larger amount of the potential reinforcer as well as an activity that builds pride (e.g., going around to tell people that they waited, a certificate to show parents)
Phase 7	Group Makes Up Their Own Break Schedule	• Give the group all the items in the schedule that need to be completed and a time limit. Have them plan when they want to take breaks with a goal of taking the breaks later in the period. Examples may include: school practice, working on speaking clearly, a scooter ride, snack, counting practice.

Perseverance

Overall Goal	The learner will learn the value of continuing to try and feel the accomplishment when they persevere.
Example Objective	When faced with difficult tasks the learner will keep trying in 90% of opportunities across five consecutive sessions.
Social Taxonomy Domain	Social Learning
Teaching Methodologies	Discrete Trial Teaching
Data Collection	Ratio, Trial by Trial, or Estimation

Phases

Phase 1	Create a List	• Create a list of skills the learner would like to (and be proud to) learn.
		 - Examples may include:
		  • Blowing a bubble
		  • Tying your shoes
		  • Riding a bike
		  • Shuffling cards
		  • Making paper airplanes

Phase 2	Create a Hierarchy	• After creating the list put it on a hierarchy of what will take the least amount of time to master to the most amount of time to master.
		 - An example may be:
		  • Shuffling cards
		  • Making paper airplanes
		  • Tying your shoes
		  • Blowing a bubble
		  • Riding a bike

Phase 3	Introduce the Rationale	• Introduce the rationale of how challenging it is going to be to learn the new skill, but how great it is to learn something new that is really cool. - You can give examples of other times they had to work hard to learn something new, but were able to succeed - Share times you learned something new with hard work
Phase 4	Teaching Easy Skill	• Select the easiest skill on the hierarchy (and work your way up) and start teaching the learner how to perform the skill. • Allow them to struggle a little, providing minimal assistance (enough to make sure they are not getting excessively frustrated, but not so much that they are becoming dependent). The goal is for them to learn to persevere on their own. • While the learner is learning the new skill provide lots of encouragement of how hard they are working and how much better they are becoming.

Phase 4 (cont.)	Teaching Easy Skill	• Take videos frequently so that you can later review the progress they made on the skill.
Phase 5	Review the Process	• When the learner has mastered the skill, go over how hard they worked and make sure to highlight how much they have improved, how proud you are of them, and how proud they should be of themselves. • Review video clips with the learner to show them all the progress they have made. • Have the learner show off their new skill to others.

Extended Secret Word

Overall Goal	The learner will increase attending to what people say in their environment throughout their day.
Example Objective	When a secret word is provided the learner will engage in the target response in 90% of trials for five consecutive sessions.
Social Taxonomy Domain	Social Learning
Teaching Methodologies	Discrete Trial Teaching
Data Collection	Trials or Estimation

Phases

Phase 1	Secret Word with Increased Delays	<ul><li>Select a word for the group that becomes the secret word (e.g., monkey).</li><li>Assign an action the group is to perform when they hear the secret word (e.g., clapping).</li><li>Start reciting words with the secret word coming up quickly. Systematically increase the number of intervening words with the goal being several minutes between trials of the secret word.</li><li>Additionally, systematically increase the amount of chatter within trials.</li></ul>
Phase 2	Secret Word within Conversation	<ul><li>The group will listen to a conversation between a minimum of two people. When the secret word is said, they perform the corresponding action.</li></ul>
Phase 3	Secret Word While Engaged in an Activity	<ul><li>Give the group a task to perform (e.g., matching) and say the secret word while they are engaged in the task.<ul><li>Start with a task that does not require language (e.g., matching) move to a task where language is involved (e.g., receptive instructions)</li></ul></li></ul>
Phase 4	Secret Word While Traveling	<ul><li>Start to move throughout the environment (e.g., office, classroom) when the secret word is said the group should perform the action.</li></ul>
Phase 5	Secret Word for Increasing Durations Throughout the Group	<ul><li>Start by giving a short duration of time where the group knows they are responsible for the secret word (e.g., 10 minutes).<ul><li>This can be visually represented by a timer if necessary</li></ul></li><li>Systematically increase the time the group is responsible for listening to the secret word (e.g., 10 minutes/30 minutes/1 hour/half of a session/ whole session).</li></ul>

It's Okay To Be Wrong

Overall Goal	The learner will remain calm when giving an answer that may be wrong.
Example Objective	When the learner does not know the answer, they will make a guess in 100% of opportunities across five consecutive sessions.
Social Taxonomy Domain	Social Learning
Teaching Methodologies	The Teaching Interaction Procedure, the Cool versus Not Cool™ procedure
Data Collection	Task Analysis, Estimation Data, or Trial by Trial Data Collection
Prerequisite Skills	Knowing what a guess is

Phases

Phase 1	Making Absurd Guesses	• Prime the learner by letting them know they will be taking crazy guesses and there is no way they will know the answer, and you do not know it either. • Ask the learner to take a guess about something there is no way they could know, but something you can look up together (e.g., how many miles from the earth to the moon). - Reinforce willingness to take a guess • You can take turns where the learner asks you to take a guess about something both of you do not know.
Phase 2	Making Less Absurd Guesses	• Prime the learner by letting them know they will be taking guesses and you know the answer but there would be no way they could know the answer. • Ask the learner to make a guess about something they would not know but you do know (e.g., your middle name). - Reinforce willingness to take a guess • You can take turns asking questions so that the learner get to ask you about something you do not know, but they do know.
Phase 3	Making a Guess about Information they can Reasonably Estimate	• Ask the learner to make a guess about something they do not know for sure, but could take a close guess. • Progress to asking something they probably do not know but could come close to answering (e.g., how many steps from their chair to the door). - Reinforce willingness to take a guess • Sometimes allow the learner to check to see if their guess is accurate, sometimes do not allow this to occur.

Phase 4	Best Guess When You Do Not Remember, but Should Know	• Ask the learner to recall information that they were told and should know (e.g., what did I have for lunch). - Reinforce willingness to take a guess • Do this in a wide variety of ways (e.g., mock classroom, conversation, reading books).
Generalization		• Fade the use of priming. • Fade supplemental reinforcers. • Fade taking turns. • Make the teaching more natural (e.g., does not look like a program).

Chapter Twenty-Four
Social Learning Skills

Jonathan Rafuse, Jeremy A. Leaf & Justin B. Leaf

Social Learning skills are those taught to help the learner learn through their environment. In this chapter, we provide five basic and four intermediate social skills programs that fall under the Social Learning Domain.

Nobody's Perfect

Overall Goal	Some of our learners can struggle with not being the best. They may display emotions beyond what is socially accepted when they do not win, are not first, or do not get everything correct. This can be disruptive on many levels, including their ability to access new learning, being stigmatized, or learning from feedback.
Example Objective	When exposed to not winning or not being completely correct, the learner will demonstrate emotional responding commensurate with age in 80% of opportunities.
Social Taxonomy Domain	Social Learning and Social Interaction
Teaching Methodologies	Teaching Interaction Procedure and the Cool versus Not Cool™ procedure
Data Collection	Task Analysis or Estimation
Prerequisite Skills	Frustration Tolerance, Stress Management, Beginning Social Skills, Emotions

Pre-teach Concepts	Learner Learns to Discriminate Cool Responses and Responses Negatively Impacting Social Standing	• Teach the learner to discriminate "keeping it cool" versus not. • Present opportunities to practice this discrimination that are relevant to the learner, scenarios either from the learner's individual experience, or typical of the age and culture the learner is involved. • Developing a stress hierarchy may be necessary and would facilitate more systematic skill development.
Identify/ Describe the Skill	Define the Behavior the Learner will use in the Generalized Environment	• The skill developed and practiced in this Teaching Interaction Procedure is being okay not be the best at something, to produce things that are not perfect, or to make mistakes.

Develop Rationale(s)	The Learner Participates in Developing Meaningful, Personalized Rationales for Participating in the Teaching Interaction Procedure and Subsequent Skill Display	• In collaboration with the learner, explore meaningful rationales for why you should not expect things to be perfect and that it is okay to make mistakes or not be the best. The rationales should be individualized to the learner. • Some examples may include: - If you get something wrong, it is an opportunity to learn what to do instead. When that situation occurs later, you will have new information and will likely be more successful - Learning from mistakes allows you to build more knowledge and skill - Everyone has strengths and weaknesses, nobody is perfect, so holding yourself to that standard is not fair to yourself and is an unrealistic expectation - If you are open to making mistakes or not knowing something, you are able to improve your problem-solving skills and creativity - If you are open to learning from those that have different skill sets than you, you can also learn to share your skillsets with others
Breakdown Skill		• Provide examples of what constitutes perfectionism. - What does a person say/think to themselves? - What does a person say out loud? - How does the person act? • Provide examples of alternatives to perfectionism. - Stay calm - Take pride in effort - Play the game for fun - Focus on what you learned • Provide strategies for counteracting perfectionism. - Set goals that are achievable - Realistic self-appraisal - Focus on strengths as source of self-esteem
Practice Skill	Role-play with Discrimination of the Cool versus Not Cool™ Procedure	• Conduct Role-play demonstration of a variety of situations that commonly occur for the learner including examples of being a perfectionist (i.e., Not Cool) as well as examples of better way of handling these situations (i.e., Cool). • Have the learner rate the behavior of the actor as Cool or Not Cool. - Following Not Cool examples, have the learner join the role-play and demonstrate a better way to handle that situation. • Present opportunities to practice this discrimination that are relevant to the learner, scenarios either from the learner's individual experience, or typical of the age and culture the learner is involved.

Feedback		• Objectively describe parts of the skill performed well (reinforcement) and parts of the skill requiring more practice (corrective feedback). • Repeat role-plays as needed to provide an opportunity to incorporate suggestions and refine performance. • Provide supplemental reinforcement as needed for making improvement and for maintaining self-control during the Teaching Interaction Procedure. This can include token economies, bonus points, behavior contracts, or other reinforcement systems which provide access to preferred items, activities or privileges.
Optional: Supplemental Consequence	The Learner Receives Extra Reinforcement for Maintaining Appropriate Behavior During Teaching	• This can include token economies, bonus reinforcement, behavior contracts, point systems, or other extrinsic consequence increasing the likelihood for further participation in the Teaching Interaction Procedure.
Steps Toward Generalization		• Fade supplemental reinforcers. • Fade use of priming (including specificity and timing). • Fade interventionist presence. • Practice with helpers/cohorts. • Increase the variety of activities and levels of distraction. • Move to more natural environments.

Get Your Head In The Game

Overall Goal	The learner will remain focused on the activity (e.g., work, conversation, play) without getting distracted.
	
	• Head in the game – sustained concentration on the target activity, with all attention (e.g., visual, auditory, cognitive/thinking) focused on the target activity.
	  - Non-verbal behavior: oriented to the target activity, following along, decisive in responding, high levels of attending
	  - Verbal behavior: all questions, comments, statements relate to the target activity
	  - Permeant product: work is accurate, complete, and neat
	• Head out of the game – attending to extraneous stimuli (e.g., materials, people, environmental events) that do not pertain to the target activity.
	  - Non-verbal behavior: orienting towards extraneous stimuli, failure to notice events occurring in the target activity, slow to physically respond
	  - Verbal behavior: questions and comments are unrelated to the target activity, slow to respond verbally to questions
	  - Permeant product: work is inaccurate, incomplete, sloppy

Example Objective	The learner will attend visually and auditorily, and remain appropriately engaged in a representative activity in 90% of intervals observed for five consecutive sessions.
Social Taxonomy Domain	Social Learning
Teaching Methodologies	The Cool versus Not Cool™ procedure, Discrete Trial Teaching, and the Teaching Interaction Procedure
Data Collection	Task Analysis, Estimation Data, or Trial by Trial

Phases

Phase 1	Discrimination Training	• Setup discrimination training between "head in the game" and "head out of the game." • When running role-plays, the interventionist can talk out loud to indicate what they are thinking about.
Phase 2	Self-Reporting	• The objective of this Phase is for the learner to accurately self-report if their head is in the game or not. • During this phase run a variety of target activities (e.g., worksheets, conversations, play). • Periodically ask the learner what they are thinking about/looking at/doing. • Reinforce honest responding by the learner.

Phase 2 (cont.)	Self-Reporting	- If necessary, you can start with a highly engaging activity where the answers are most likely to be accurate and easy to answer (e.g., while playing Pokémon ask what the learner is thinking about, it will most likely be Pokémon)
Phase 3	Isolated Target Activity	• In an environment as distraction-free as possible, begin a target activity. • Reinforce behaviors indicative of the learner having their head in the game. • When the learner's head is out of the game, ask what they are thinking about or looking at, and reinforce honest answers but provide feedback as to what they should be doing instead to keep their head in the game.
Phase 4	Add Distractions to Target Activity	• Create a distraction hierarchy for the learner. • Systematically add distractions starting with low-level distractions and increasing to high-level distractions. • Reinforce behaviors indicative of the learner having their head in the game. • When the learner's head is out of the game, ask what they are thinking about or looking at, and reinforce honest answers but provide feedback as to what they should be doing instead to keep their head in the game.

Considerations		• Meaningful rationales can be helpful to increase motivation. Examples might include:
		  - When your head is in the game, you will finish activities faster
		  - When your head is in the game you are making other people happy; when other people are happy with you, you're more likely to get what you need
		  - When your head is in the game activities are easier
		• Be mindful of competing reinforcement. Possible payoffs for a learner to have their head out of the game might include avoidance of the task and/or access to more desirable experiences.

Steps Toward Generalization		• Practice in a variety of environments. • Make the program more natural. • Fade the timing and specificity of priming. • Use more naturally occurring reinforcers.

Decision Making

Overall Goal	The learner will learn to calmly make potentially tough decisions in the natural environment.
Example Objective	When making a choice the learner will make a decision that is in their best interest in 90% of trials across five consecutive sessions.
Social Taxonomy Domain	Social Learning
Teaching Methodologies	Discrete Trial Teaching
Data Collection	Trial by trial, Ratio, Estimation

Preference Continuum				
Extremely Undesirable	Moderately Undesirable	Neutral	Moderately Desirable	Extremely Desirable

Choice Continuum (Environment)				
Worksheet	Discussion	Clear Practice	Less Clear Practice	Natural Environment

Phases

Overview		• Use Discrete Trial Teaching procedures.
		• Reinforce any choice done in a calm and timely manner (regardless of the choice made).
		• Each phase pairs two choices from the preference continuum.
		• Within each Phase, move from the low end of the Choice Continuum (i.e., Worksheet) to the high end (i.e., Natural Environment)
		  - For the Clear Practice, Less Clear Practice, and Natural Environment the learner must follow through with the choice made
		  - Do not move on to the next level of the Choice Continuum until the learner has demonstrated calm behaviors
		• Do not move on to the next Phase until the learner has demonstrated calm behaviors at the highest end of the Choice Continuum (i.e., Natural Environment).

Phase 1	Extremely Desirable versus Extremely Undesirable	• Present a choice of an Extremely Desirable versus an Extremely Undesirable option. • Reinforce any choice made in a calm and timely manner (regardless of the choice made).
Phase 2	Extremely Desirable versus Moderately Undesirable	• Present a choice of an Extremely Desirable versus a Moderately Undesirable option. • Reinforce any choice made in a calm and timely manner (regardless of the choice made).
Phase 3	Extremely Desirable versus Neutral	• Present a choice of an Extremely Desirable versus a Neutral option. • Reinforce any choice made in a calm and timely manner (regardless of the choice made).
Phase 4	Extremely Desirable versus Moderately Desirable	• Present a choice of an Extremely Desirable versus a Moderately Desirable option. • Reinforce any choice made in a calm and timely manner (regardless of the choice made).
Phase 5	Extremely Desirable versus Extremely Desirable	• Present a choice of an Extremely Desirable versus another Extremely Desirable option. • Reinforce any choice made in a calm and timely manner (regardless of the choice made).
Phase 6	Neutral versus Neutral	• Present a choice of a Neutral versus another Neutral option. • Reinforce any choice made in a calm and timely manner (regardless of the choice made).

Notes:

Notes:

Notes:

Notes: